THE GENIUS OF WRITERS

THE GENIUS OF WRITERS

The Lives of English Writers Compared

JACK HODGES

'He heard . . . about the young man Shelley, who was now quite a famous person, with a carriage of his own, and about some of the other drivers who are in the service of the Company.'

E. M. Forster: THE CELESTIAL OMNIBUS

St. Martin's Press
New York

Library of Congress Cataloging-in-Publication Data

Hodges, Jack.
The genius of writers / Jack Hodges.
p.   cm.
ISBN 0-312-10496-0
1. Authors, English—Anecdotes.   2. Creation (Literary, artistic,
etc.)—Anecdotes.   3. Genius—Anecdotes.   I. Title.
PR106.H63   1994
828'.02—dc20   93-43646
CIP

First published in Great Britain by Sinclair-Stevenson.

First U.S. Edition: April 1994
10 9 8 7 6 5 4 3 2 1

'To dismiss biography as irrelevant to criticism is a new fashion that seems to me downright silly. A novel, a poem or a picture is not merely an object with a shape and texture of its own: it is also a reflection of its creator's personality and experience, which are of natural interest to its admirers, enlarging their comprehension and enjoyment of the work.'

RAYMOND MORTIMER

Contents

Contents

Contents

APPENDICES

Contents

List of Illustrations

Acknowledgements

I am grateful to Oriol Bath for letting me use her drawing of the Omnibus, which I commissioned as a bookplate, on the jacket and the title page.

I also thank the following owners of copyright material who have given me kind permission to quote extracts: Constable & Company Ltd. (James Bridie's *One Way of Living*, David Cecil's *Max: A Biography*, Derek Hudson's *Lewis Carroll: An illustrated biography*), Curtis Brown Ltd., London, on behalf of C. R. Milne (*It's Too Late Now* copyright A. A. Milne 1939), Faber and Faber Ltd. (John Dover Wilson's *Milestones on the Dover Road*), John Farquharson Ltd., on behalf of the Estate of James Hilton (*To You Mr. Chips* published by Hodder & Stoughton Ltd.), Eric Glass Ltd., on behalf of the Estate of Beverley Nichols (*The Unforgiving Minute* published by W. H. Allen & Co. Ltd.), HarperCollins Publishers (C. S. Lewis's *Surprised by Joy: The shape of my early life*, Malcolm Muggeridge's *The Chronicles of Wasted Time*, Harold Nicolson's *Diaries and Letters* ed. Nigel Nicolson), A. M. Heath, on behalf of the Estates of George Orwell and Sonia Brownell Orwell ('Why I Write': *The Collected Essays, Journalism and Letters of George Orwell* published by Martin Secker & Warburg Ltd.), David Higham Associates Ltd. (Graham Greene's *A Sort of Life* published by The Bodley Head, Dylan Thomas's 'Fern Hill' contained in *The Poems* published by J. M. Dent & Sons, Ltd.), Little Brown (Catherine Cookson's *Our Kate*), John Murray (Publishers) Ltd. (John Betjeman's *Summoned by Bells*, Kenneth Clark's *Another Part of the Wood* and *The Other Half*), Peters Fraser & Dunlop Group Ltd. (C. Day Lewis's *The Buried Day* published by Chatto & Windus, Constance Babington Smith's *John Masefield: A Life* published by Oxford University Press, Stephen Spender's *World Within World* published by Hamish Hamilton Ltd., Evelyn Waugh's *A Little Learning: The First Volume of Autobiography* published by Chapman & Hall), Laurence Pollinger Ltd., on behalf of the Estate of H. E. Bates (his Autobiography published by Michael Joseph: *The Vanished World, The Blossoming World, The World in Ripeness*), R.I.B. Library: Reed Book Services

Acknowledgements

(Bernard Crick's *George Orwell: A Life* published by Martin Secker & Warburg Ltd., Michael Holroyd's *Lytton Strachey: A Critical Biography* published by William Heinemann Ltd., W. Somerset Maugham's *The Summing Up* published by William Heinemann Ltd., Christopher Milne's *The Enchanted Places* published by Methuen London, H. V. Morton's *In Search of England, In Scotland Again,* and *In the Steps of the Master* published by Methuen London), Random Century Group (Sybille Bedford's *Aldous Huxley: A Biography* published by Chatto & Windus; on behalf of the Estate of Roald Dahl: *Boy* published by Jonathan Cape Ltd.; Laurie Lee's *Cider With Rosie* published by The Hogarth Press, Ethel Mannin's *Confessions and Impressions* published by Harcourt Brace & Company (Leonard Woolf's Autobiography: *Sowing, Beginning Again*), Mrs. Reichmann (Max Beerbohm's *More, And Even Now, Mainly On The Air,* published by William Heinemann Ltd.), Rogers, Coleridge & White Ltd. (Cyril Connolly's *Enemies of Promise* published by George Routledge & Sons, Ltd.), George Sassoon (Siegfried Sassoon's *Old Century* and *Siegfried's Journey,* published by Faber and Faber Ltd.), The Society of Authors on behalf of the Estate of St. John Ervine (*Shaw obituary*) and of the Bernard Shaw Estate (Shaw's letters to Sister Laurentia, and *Saint Joan*), *The Sunday Times* (Review by Raymond Mortimer: March 17, 1974), Virgin Publishing Ltd. (Robin Maugham's *Conversations with Willie*), A. P. Watt Ltd. (on behalf of the Trustees of the Robert Graves Copyright Trust: *Goodbye To All That* published by Cassell; on behalf of the Literary Executors of the Estate of H. G. Wells: *Experiment in Autobiography* published by Victor Gollancz Ltd.), George Weidenfeld & Nicolson Ltd. (Lord Birkenhead's *Rudyard Kipling,* Frances Donaldson's *Evelyn Waugh: Portrait of a Country Neighbour*).

The excerpts from Vera Britain's books *Testament of Youth* and *Testament of Friendship* are included with the permission of Paul Berry, her literary executor, and Victor Gollancz Ltd. and the Virago Press, and those from *On Becoming A Writer* and *Radclyffe Hall: A Case of Obscenity?* as well as the excerpts from her unpublished letters, with the permission of Paul Berry, the copyright holder.

For any accidental omission or where, after every effort, I have been unable to contact the copyright holder, I ask the indulgence of those concerned. Any inadvertent omissions can be corrected in any future editions.

Preface

The seeds were sown in 1937–9 when Dr Jory confided to his English class (he never spoke harshly) snippets of poets' lives. Certainly at the beginning of the war I chained my bicycle outside Hatchards in Piccadilly. In those days an antiquarian department was their show-piece on the first floor. Dowden's *Life of Shelley*, examined during a lunch-hour, was handed from a towering glass case – two volumes in sumptuous inlaid morocco by Riviere – and after a ransom of six guineas (more than my month's salary) I laid them in the saddle-bag with a sense of awe, I remember, mingled with guilt.

*

Some fifteen years ago I compiled a catalogue to my library, with biographical information on the left-hand pages. It formed, with blank interleaves to allow for expansion, seven small-folio volumes, and a teaching colleague who saw it made the well-intentioned remark that I 'ought to do something' with the material. The longhand offered renewal sufficient of itself. To what other use could unconnected information be put – save a literary encyclopaedia, and how could I vie with standard ones doing a magnificent job already? But I knew that the ample days of my catalogue were over.

Still unclear what 'ought' to be done, I set a practical boundary. I decided to limit myself to English authors, either indigenous or those who had spent their working lives in England. Then I pondered the enigma of a tiny island, often called philistine, yet so fertile in literature. Others could properly boast writers of stature; it was in the profusion her characteristic contribution lay. Reel off Chaucer, Shakespeare and Dickens, you still had Spenser–Bacon–Ben Jonson, Milton–Bunyan–Defoe, Swift–Pope–Congreve, Johnson–Gibbon–Sterne.... The heavyweights pounded in successive waves: Scott–Austen–Wordsworth, Coleridge–Shelley–Keats, Tennyson–Browning–Thackeray, the Brontës–Trollope–George Eliot, Hardy–Wilde–Shaw, Conrad–Kipling–Stevenson, Bennett–Wells–Maugham, Forster–Eliot–Lawrence.... Other weights wrote of angling, or a school bully; another immortalized a valley in Somerset, and a woman did the same with a hamlet in North Oxfordshire. They were the makers of Alice, Sherlock Holmes and Peter Pan; of Toad, Pooh and Aslan; of Squirrel Nutkin and Jemima Puddle-Duck. They had been translated into European and oriental languages; a little black Alice spoke Swahili. They were *virtuosos* who sounded the Latin chords, and struck the notes of Anglo-Saxon for simplicity and strength. While post-war years continued to see specialist lives and ever more monumental editions of their letters, no one – as far as I was aware – had looked at the collective phenomenon. There were no comparative studies of their lives, although plenty on their works.

Mine would be first. I would go back to Chaucer and up to the present day. Since my brief was the English writer, no firm line could be drawn between major names of the literary establishment (who would all be present) and so-called 'popular' writers from whom a selection would be made. Categories other than literature would overlap for, as Holbrook Jackson allowed:

... it is not possible to eliminate the writer from even the most objective writings. . . .

Inevitably names were missing from my catalogue, and suddenly the enormity of hard choices burst. Even that definition of 'English', so straightforward at the time, was not simple at all. What about Burns who had never set foot in England? Was I to ignore Joyce who had never spent his working life in England? (For that matter, he had not spent it in Ireland.) I co-opted both, committing the first of my illogicalities.

In an early draft I restricted myself to a sample of two hundred, giving percentages for every aspect of their lives, with view to a composite portrait at the end. Then this sample chafed. More seriously, I became ashamed of forcing grey areas and 'not knowns' into a fraudulent generalization. Eventually five broad themes were chosen as being the most relevant to creativity. Within them there may be similarities (or dissimilarities) of interest, and that is all I have tried to show. I hope I shall be forgiven for appropriating the Omnibus in Forster's wonderful parable, when he makes Dante the driver at the end. Finally, if my book is a celebration of the English writer, it is no less a celebration of literary biography without which it would not have been possible. It now remains to invite seasoned travellers, as well as those who may not have done very much travelling, aboard.

Southfields, London
September, 1991

PART ONE
MOTIVATION

Samuel Johnson

CHAPTER ONE

Greed or Pride?

I

As usual pithy and feet on the ground, JOHNSON gave his immortal riposte:

No man but a blockhead ever wrote, except for money.[1]

Long years in a Grub Street so savage that when he climbed he still bore the scars and fears, explain why he was so forthright, also why he frowned on GRAY who never had to write for a living.

DE QUINCEY tells how his own *Confessions of an English Opium-Eater* came to be written:

I went up to London avowedly for the purpose of exercising my pen, as the one source then open to me for extricating myself from a special embarrassment (failing which case of dire necessity, I believe that I should never have written a line for the press). . . .[2]

Owing to the meanness of his patron at Eversley, the Rev. CHARLES KINGSLEY offered to furnish *Fraser's Magazine* with 'poetry of almost any pattern at a very moderate sum per yard'.

TROLLOPE's mother, FRANCES, took up writing when her family were reduced to poverty – she wrote thirty-three novels and seven works of non-fiction all after the age of fifty. Mrs OLIPHANT was widowed at thirty-one, with £200 insurance money to pay £1,000 of debt, and 'my faculties such as they are'. Those 'faculties' supported her son, daughter and posthumous son, and within five years she received into her home her widowed brother and three children, for whose maintenance and education she made herself entirely respon-

1 Apl. 5, 1776.
2 *The Collected Writings of Thomas De Quincey* ed. David Masson (1889–90), iii, p. 127.

sible. FRANCES BURNETT, an unpublished author of eighteen, said plainly in a letter to a magazine:

My object is remuneration.[1]

She too, had cause. When she was four, her father died, leaving her mother – with five children – to run the business. They emigrated to the States when she was sixteen. Expecting another child, EDITH NESBIT, when her husband fell ill of smallpox and his business partner absconded, provided for the family by writing verses and stories, and painting cards. ALISON UTTLEY 'decided to write in earnest'[2] after her husband's suicide and with a sixteen-year-old son at Public School.

Others, less pressurized, have been equally frank on a subject no other profession finds inhibiting. I possess two autograph letters by GEORGE MOORE to John C. Squire, editor of *The London Mercury*:

Dear Mr Squire
Your letter contains two grave faults, the first is forgetfulness to enclose the cheque you mention and the second is to write that contributors articles *are invariable paid by the inch*. Think for a moment. was 'invariable' the right word?
    However short my articles they cost at least 25£, when I want more I'll mention the price to you and you will be able to consider the value *of the copy* without the trouble of searching for the tape.
                                        Truly yours
                                        George Moore[3]

The second, written when Moore was about seventy, begins:

Dear Mr Squire,
I hope you will not think the questions I am about to put to you indiscretions. First, how much do you propose to pay for the story you selected to   keep?. . . .[4]

In my collection is an equally tart autograph letter from SIDNEY WEBB to the Editor of (ironically) *Great Thoughts*. It bears the blind crest of the House of Commons:

1 Ann Thwaite: *Waiting for the Party: The Life of Frances Hodgson Burnett* (1974), p. 33.
2 Alison Uttley: *Something for Nothing* (1960), p. 87.
3 Dated August: unpublished.
4 Dated 'Sunday': unpublished.

Dear Sir
I return the enclosed letter & cheque for £2.2.0. When I have time to write an article, Editors give me £25 for it, or more; and then I never sell the copyright, but only specific serial rights.

Yours truly
Sidney Webb
The Editor
Great Thoughts[1]

In his autobiography, LEWIS HIND ascribed his success with editors 'to an innate knowledge of the difference between marketable and unmarketable stuff'.[2] The subtitle reads:

Being Influences and Adventures while earning a living by writing.

Dudley Barker entitled his biography of ARNOLD BENNETT: *Writer by Trade*. BETJEMAN, when he was nearly sixty-eight, declared:

I've had to prostitute myself to live comfortably but I see no point in money except to buy off anxiety. I don't want to be rich. I want to be unanxious.[3]

As a boy at Marlborough and chosen for a walk over the Wiltshire Downs with William Temple, BEVERLEY NICHOLS expressed the thought he would be a writer. 'In which case, Nichols,' the Archbishop said, 'you must never forget that Shakespeare wrote for money.'[4]

II

But the sweat of the artist is also there. WILLIAM MORRIS worked at *The Lovers of Gudrun* from 4.0 a.m.–4.0 p.m., and when he rose from the table he had produced 750 lines. Borys CONRAD wrote of his father:

During the early years of my life he would often remain at his desk writing till far into the night and sometimes he would rise in the small hours of the morning ... and return to his labours. I learned of this because I slept in the dressing-room which opened from my parents' bedroom. ...[5]

Conrad would bend over the little boy's bed and, if he stirred, shake an admonitory finger over his head. W. W. JACOBS told J. K. Jerome

---

1 Dated '18.7.23': unpublished.
2 C. Lewis Hind: *Naphtali* (1926), pp. 41–42.
3 Interview with Graham Lord: *The Sunday Express*, Aug. 18, 1974.
4 *The Unforgiving Minute* (1978), p. 178.
5 *My Father: Joseph Conrad* (1970), p. 22.

that often he would 'spend' an entire morning constructing a single sentence.

Maisie Ward describes a visit she paid to Beaconsfield when CHESTERTON was writing one of his major books. He worked in his study from 10.0 a.m.–1.0 p.m., 2.30–4.30 p.m., and about 5.30–7.30 p.m., the intervals for meals.

His wife and I went to bed about 10.30 leaving him preparing his material for the next day. Towards 1 a.m. a ponderous tread as he passed my door ... woke me to a general impression of an earthquake.[1]

VIRGINIA and LEONARD WOOLF chose to work every morning for seven days a week for about eleven months a year, but Leonard reckoned that out of the sixteen hours of her waking day Virginia 'worked' fifteen, for her book or article she was writing would be 'in the front or the back of her mind' when she was walking of an afternoon or even sitting by the fire.

... and I should guess that she dreamed about it most of the time when she was asleep.[2]

It was this intense absorption which made writing so exhausting mentally for her. He used to say he could tell by 'the depth of the flush on her face' whether she had been writing fiction or criticism.[3] BENNETT worked every morning of the year and sometimes afternoon as well. Even his honeymoon was not allowed to disorganise his working time. He did not take 'a real holiday for over thirty years'.[4]

Douglas Cleverdon has contrasted the way in which DYLAN THOMAS squandered immediately any cash that came into his hands yet 'would spend months on the perfecting of a poem for which some literary journal might ultimately pay him a couple of pounds'.[5]

---

1 *Gilbert Keith Chesterton* (1944), p. 328.
2 *Downhill All the Way* (1967), p. 149.
3 *Ibid.*, p. 54 note.
4 Mrs Arnold Bennett: *Arnold Bennett* (1925), p. 48.
5 *Under Milk Wood* ed. Douglas Cleverdon (Folio Society, 1972), Introduction, p. 6.

III

Next to money, EDMUND GOSSE put fame – 'these are the two chief spurs which drive the author on'.[1] Yet if a writer's drive is to inflate the ego, how do we explain that not a single portrait of the Rev. GILBERT WHITE exists? He debated publishing his correspondence with Thomas Pennant and the Hon. Daines Barrington twelve years before *The Natural History of Selborne* appeared. To avoid a preface, he invented nine letters – as though his modesty 'shrank from even the bare appearance of deliberate authorship'.[2] When THOMAS GRAY heard that his own portrait was being engraved for a collected edition of his poems, he told Horace Walpole:

... if you suffer my head to be printed, you will infallibly put me out of mine.[3]

Sir THOMAS BROWNE said that *Religio Medici* was 'composed at leisurable hours for his private exercise and satisfaction'. Only when it had appeared without his sanction did he issue 'a full and intended copy'. The poetry of GERARD MANLEY HOPKINS was published nearly twenty years after his death; less than six people knew he wrote poetry.

More considerably, why did so many at one time or another choose to be anonymous? – Browning, Carlyle, Kenneth Grahame, Hardy, Andrew Lang (he never signed his literary leaders in *The Daily News*), Lear, Marryat, Scott, Smollett, C. T. Stoneham, Swinburne, Izaak Walton, Watts-Dunton. . . . Some had first or early works unsigned when their ego might be thought most to the fore – *Sketches by Boz*, *Modern Painters*, Barrie's *Better Dead*. *Tom Cringle's Log* appeared anonymously in *Blackwood's* and proved very successful, but to the end of his life MICHAEL SCOTT concealed he had written it.

Why did Barrie and others hide behind *noms de plume*? – Matthew Arnold ('A'), Barrie ('Anon', 'Gavin Ogilvy'), Frances Hodgson ('The Second'), Chatterton ('D.B.', 'Asaphides'), Mary Mackay ('Marie Corelli'), C. Day Lewis ('Nicholas Blake' for his crime stories), De la Mare ('Walter Ramal'), De Quincey ('X.Y.Z.'), Galsworthy ('John

1 *Questions at Issue* (1893), p. 117.
2 *The Natural History of Selborne* ed. Grant Allen (1900), Introduction, p. xxx.
3 Jan., 1753.

Sinjohn'), Desmond MacCarthy ('Affable Hawk'), Hector Munro ('Saki'), Thomas Moore ('Thomas Little', 'Thomas Brown the younger'), R. H. Mottram ('J. Marjoram'), F. W. Rolfe ('Baron Corvo'), Sarah Smith ('Hesba Stretton'), Shaw ('Corno di Bassetto' as Music Critic for *The Star*), Steele ('Isaac Bickerstaff'), Leslie Stephen ('A Cynic'), Stevenson ('L. S. Stoneven', 'Captain George North'), J. I. M. Stewart ('Michael Innes'), Thackeray ('Michael Angelo Tit-marsh', 'Yellowplush', and thirty-eight besides), William Hale White ('Mark Rutherford'), John Wilson ('Christopher North'). . . . LEIGH HUNT signed his papers to *The Traveller*: 'Mr Town, *Junior*, Critic and Censor-general'; his articles in *The Examiner* had a hand pointing; his contributions to *The New Monthly Magazine* went under 'Harry Honeycomb'.

Marie Louise de la Ramée used the pseudonym OUIDA, a childish mispronunciation of 'Louise'. Mary Ann Evans gave herself GEORGE because it belonged to Lewes, and ELIOT because she liked its sound. It did not fool Dickens, who sitting to Frith for his portrait tapped a set of *Adam Bede*:

That's a very good book . . . but unless I am mistaken George Eliot is a woman.

C. S. LEWIS signed his first two books of poetry 'Clive Hamilton': his own first name and his mother's maiden name; later poems he signed 'N.W.' or 'Nat Whilk' – Anglo-Saxon for 'I know not who'. F. ANSTEY was the pseudonym of Thomas Anstey Guthrie, while ANTHONY HOPE, RICHMAL CROMPTON, PETER TERSON, JOHN WYNDHAM, and ANTHONY BURGESS are all extractions from their full names. JOHN OXENHAM was really William Arthur Dunkerley; JAMES BRIDIE, Osborne Henry Mavor; ANNA WICKHAM, Edith Harper; and E. M. DELAFIELD, Edmée Elizabeth Monica de la Pasture. (Even popular thriller writers, SAX ROHMER, SAPPER, LESLIE CHARTERIS, and JOHN LE CARRÉ share this same desire for concealment.) HAROLD PINTER'S estranged wife said: 'His name's David Baron. I don't know where he got Harold Pinter from!'

Among imperishable things given to the world unclaimed were: *Religio Medici* (the authorized as well as the unauthorized edition), *The Compleat Angler*, *Essay on Criticism*, *Robinson Crusoe*, *Gulliver's Travels*, *Elegy in a Country Churchyard*, *The Vicar of Wakefield*, *Lyrical Ballads* (containing *The Rime of the Ancient Mariner*),[1] *Essays of Elia, Oliver Twist, Jane Eyre, Wuthering Heights, In Memoriam, Tom Brown's School-days, The Rubáiyát of Omar Khayyám: Rendered into English verse, Alice's Adventures in Wonderland, Treasure Island.* So lightly did SHAKESPEARE father his brain-children, a learned society was formed to rob him of paternity. GEORGE ELIOT, LEWIS CARROLL, GEORGE ORWELL are more real than their actual names, although it is now fashionable to speak of DODGSON.

Of course, not all concealments were permanent and we can rationalize some. When women writers were scarcely respectable, FANNY BURNEY and JANE AUSTEN hid their identities under 'A Lady'. The BRONTË sisters 'veiled' their names under Currer, Ellis and Acton Bell, cleverly preserving their own initials:

... the ambiguous choice being dictated by a sort of conscientious scruple at assuming Christian names positively masculine, while we did not like to declare ourselves women, because ... we had a vague impression that authoresses are liable to be looked on with prejudice. . . .[2]

ANNE MOBERLY and ELEANOR JOURDAIN, in charge of young women at St Hugh's, probably considered fictitious names more discreet for *An Adventure*[3] claiming to be supernatural. KATHERINE MANSFIELD took her 'writing name' at twenty-one. It symbolized her love-hate relationship with her father: she rejected 'Beauchamp' for the maiden name of her Grandmother who had loved her in early years. DISRAELI might have judged novel writing suspect for a rising politician. VYVYAN HOLLAND could be known as Wilde's son only in more compassionate times. ORWELL knew his parents were aware of his tramping activities but because they might have found *Down and Out in Paris and London* upsetting, he wrote to Gollancz that he would prefer it published 'pseudonymously', and told his agent:

I rather favour George Orwell.

We still have to explain PEPYS locking up his literary fame in his own shorthand. Again, no part of EVELYN's *Diary* – by which he is now remembered – was written for publication. Like Pepys's, it appeared posthumously after more than a hundred years. The tradition runs at

---

1 For the 2nd edition, Coleridge allowed Wordsworth's name to appear but not his own.
2 E. C. Gaskell: *The Life of Charlotte Brontë* (1857), i, p. 335.
3 1911. Its Preface is signed Elizabeth Morison and Frances Lamont.

Magdalene that when Evelyn's *Diary* was published, an MS volume of Pepys was shown to Lord Grenville who took it to bed and at breakfast flourished the key. KILVERT's *Diary* waited a mere sixty years. When NICOLSON's sons asked their father if he didn't write his three-million-word *Diary* for publication, he replied: 'No, that never entered my head.'[1]

DODGSON wrote to his sister-in-law:

It is strange to me that people will not understand that, when an author uses a '*nom-de-plume*', his object is to *avoid* that personal publicity which they are always trying to thrust upon him.

In the same year, at fifty-eight, he took the obsessional step of having a circular printed as an answer to all applications for his autograph:

Mr Dodgson ... neither claims nor acknowledges any connection with any pseudonym, or with any book that is not published under his own name....[2]

JOHNSON, discussing *Junius*, said 'a man ... questioned, as to an anonymous publication, may think he has a right to deny it.'[3] When Thackeray addressed CHARLOTTE BRONTË as Currer Bell, 'she tossed her head and said "she believed there were books being published by a person named Currer Bell ... but the person he was talking to was Miss Brontë – and she saw no connection between the two."'[4] ORWELL had no such objection. To some friends he was known only as George Orwell while others called him by his real name, Eric Blair.

SASSOON wrote:

This instinct for anonymity has been with me all my life. Success was, of course, my objective; but ... I somehow preferred my poems to be more successful than myself. It was also a bit embarrassing to think of my poetry being read by the non-literary people I knew.[5]

In his trilogy of memoirs he used the persona George Sherston.

Against all dissimulation we might contrast MILTON's signature to *The Tenure of Kings and Magistrates*, which at the Restoration nearly cost him his life.

---

1 *Diaries & Letters (1930–1939)* ed. Nigel Nicolson (1966), p. 13.
2 Derek Hudson: *Lewis Carroll: An illustrated biography* (1976), pp. 233–4.
3 1779.
4 Charles & Frances Brookfield: *Mrs Brookfield & Her Circle* (1905), ii, p. 305.
5 *The Weald of Youth* (1942), pp. 13–14.

A strain of exhibitionism has to be admitted. STERNE wrote 'not to be fed but to be famous'. When the young Max Beerbohm called at The Pines to be ushered into a back room, WATTS-DUNTON could always be heard booming mysteriously through folding doors.

... a few moments later its owner appeared. He had been dictating, he explained. 'A great deal of work on hand just now – a great deal of work.'

Beerbohm rumbled him subsequently – 'I used to wonder what work it was, for he published little enough' – yet did not take it hard. '. . . it was a part of the dear little old man.'[1] When I drew STEPHEN POTTER's attention to the above, he wrote:

... the whole set-up ... deserves a new word, Number Two the Pinesmanship. . . . I will put it before the Council that you be named Number One Southfields.[2]

Sassoon records his meeting with JOHN DRINKWATER the night after the Armistice, 1918, in Sir Edward Marsh's flat. Sassoon and Marsh were very tired but Drinkwater 'very soon opened an important-looking leather portfolio which contained manuscripts of his latest poems', and somehow took it for granted to seat himself at a table, reading them aloud by the light of a shielded lamp. The poems were numerous and the unhurrying voice went on past one o'clock. Sassoon adds:

Now I come to think of it, at our subsequent meetings I almost always heard him read his works aloud.[3]

BEVERLEY NICHOLS threatened a mythical wife, should she have nagged, with the sight of the shelves of his published works.

Certain authors signed limited editions, a fashion reaching its peak in the twenties and thirties. GALSWORTHY must have signed his name in that way several thousand times, and MASEFIELD may have exceeded him. I am grateful for these handmade-paper productions, touched by hands that gave them life, but what was Masefield thinking – of whom Nichols said, 'Humility was echoed in everything he did or said'[4] –

1 *And Even Now* (1920), p. 63.
2 Unpublished letter headed The Red House, Aldeburgh, Apl. 1, 1954. The Pines is No. 2 Putney Hill.
3 *Siegfried's Journey* (1945), p. 99.
4 Beverley Nichols: *Twenty-Five* (1926), pp. 38–39.

when he carried out this chore? In his barrack-hut at the beginning of World War II, MALCOLM MUGGERIDGE, Arch-Deflator, autographed 'the requested number of title-pages in an edition of *The Thirties* on special paper'.[1]

V

A few supplied the answer themselves. DISRAELI said that when he wanted to read a novel, he wrote one. *Erewhon* BUTLER said he wrote books to have something to read in his old age. KILVERT asked himself why he kept 'this voluminous journal':

I can hardly tell. Partly because life appears to me such a curious and wonderful thing that it almost seems a pity that even such a humble and uneventful life as mine should pass altogether away without some such record . . . and partly too because I think the record may amuse and interest some who come after me.[2]

LEWIS HIND analysed his early motives as follows:

50% Ambition, and Escape from Environment. 25% Vanity. 20% Earning a Living. 5% Something to Say.

At sixty-three, the figures were different:

50% Earning a Living. 25% Vanity. 25% Something to Say.[3]

NICOLSON told his son he wrote his *Diary* 'because I thought that one day it might amuse you and Ben. . . .' It became a habit –

'Like brushing your teeth?'
'Exactly.'[4]

In an essay devoted to this question, ORWELL gave four reasons which 'exist in various degrees in every writer', and put 'sheer egoism' first. Then came 'aesthetic enthusiasm' (for 'beauty in the external world' and 'the firmness of good prose'), followed by 'historical impulse' (storing up facts 'for the use of posterity'). He interpreted his fourth, 'political purpose', in the fullest sense. For him it meant (after

---

1 *The Chronicles of Wasted Time* (1972–3), ii, p. 84.
2 *Diary*, entry for Nov. 3, 1874.
3 *From My Books* (1925), pp. 11–12.
4 *Diaries & Letters* (1930–1939) ed. Nigel Nicolson (1966), p. 14.

his experience in Spain) writing *against* totalitarianism and *for* democratic socialism.

What I have most wanted to do . . . is to make political writing into an art.[1]

Asked on his eightieth birthday what had prompted him to go on the stage and write his own plays, EMLYN WILLIAMS replied:

I was in love with the English language.[2]

---

1 'Why I Write': *Gangrel* (No. 4, Summer) 1946.
2 Interview with Terry Wogan: BBC1, Nov., 1985.

CHAPTER TWO

Self-Motivation

I

There is evidence of a sense of vocation existing in early years. Lettice Cooper gives as the chief reason why STEVENSON, 'a very clever boy', did not do well at school was that he knew before his teens he wanted most of all to write.

He was convinced that he could teach himself in his own way better than anyone else could teach him.[1]

A contemporary at Mr Thomson's school in Frederick Street, Edinburgh, recalled:

For even then (at 14–15) he had a fixed idea that literature was his calling, and a marvellously mature conception of the course of self-education through which he required to put himself in order to succeed.[2]

At thirteen and again at sixteen, MASEFIELD told his guardian aunt that he wanted to be a writer, and twice she drove him back to sea. SASSOON wrote:

As a child I had believed in my poetic vocation. . . .[3]

ELIOT clearly remembered reading, about fourteen, FitzGerald's translation of *The Rubáiyát of Omar Khayyám* and writing imitative quatrains. He said it was like an experience of conversion.

VICTORIA SACKVILLE-WEST was 'initiated . . . to the possibilities of literature!'[4] when she was twelve, by *Cyrano de Bergerac*. It was thought

1 *Robert Louis Stevenson* (1969), p. 24.
2 Graham Balfour: *The Life of Robert Louis Stevenson* (1901), i, p. 54.
3 *The Old Century and seven more years* (1938), p. 218.
4 Nigel Nicolson: *Portrait of a Marriage* (1973), p. 25.

in the family that her cousin's *Elizabeth and her German Garden* made ten-year-old KATHERINE MANSFIELD decide she too, would write. VERA BRITTAIN first read Shelley's *Adonais* during preparation at St Monica's, and it made her 'finally determine to become the writer that I had dreamed of being ever since I was seven years old'.[1] All her 'early life', ALISON UTTLEY 'wanted to write'.[2] ETHEL MANNIN used to assert that when she grew up she wanted to be 'what I then called "an authoress"':

... it was a flame that burned in me ... always this preoccupation with the written word, since I was seven years old.[3]

ORWELL claimed that perhaps from the age of five or six, he knew that when he grew up he should be a writer. By his seventh birthday the same had become fixed in TERENCE RATTIGAN's mind. BETJEMAN was writing 'weak stanzas' at eight:

I knew as soon as I could read and write
That I must be a poet. . . .
My urge was to encase in rhythm and rhyme
The things I saw and felt (I could not *think*). . . .
The gap between my feelings and my skill
Was so immense, I wonder I went on. . . .[4]

PRIESTLEY, on his ninetieth birthday, said that at sixteen or seventeen he knew he 'was going to be a writer whatever happened', even though he went straight from school into the wool industry.

No one encouraged me ... although my father, who was headmaster of an elementary school, did not oppose me when he saw me begin to write.[5]

BENNETT seems unusual in his declaration that he began to write novels and, later, plays only because people told him he could.

II

Some, equally young, had their vocation recognized or were seen to be set apart. THOMAS MORE, between twelve to fourteen in the household

1 *Testament of Youth* (1933), p. 40.
2 *The Button Box & Other Essays* (1968), p. 10.
3 *Confessions & Impressions* (1930), p. 51.
4 *Summoned by Bells* (1960), p. 17.
5 His son Tom's documentary: *Time & the Priestleys*, ITV, Sept. 2, 1984.

of Cardinal Morton, would at Christmas 'suddenly sometimes step in among the players, and never studying for the matter, make a part of his own . . . which made the lookers-on more sport than all the players beside'.

In whose wit and towardness the Cardinal much delighting, would often say of him unto the nobles that divers times dined with him, 'This child here waiting at the table, whosoever shall live to see it, will prove a marvellous man.'[1]

JOHNSON's infirmities brought the gawky boy of Lichfield his quota of taunts, but William Butt told his children: 'You call him the great boy, but take my word for it, he will one day prove a great man.' In his school at Halifax, STERNE climbed the workmen's ladder to write with a brush on the newly whitewashed ceiling: 'LAU. STERNE'. His usher severely whipped him but, according to Sterne, the master declared 'that name should never be effaced, for (the lad) was a boy of genius and sure to come to preferment'.

Henry Forde, who coached LYTTON STRACHEY for Public School Entrance, told Lady Strachey shortly after her son was twelve:

It would not at all surprise me, if he were to become literary. I do not mean merely fond of letters – that he is sure to be – but a contributor to them, a writer.[2]

A second cousin of ALDOUS HUXLEY told Sybille Bedford that '*everybody knew* when he was five or six *that Aldous was different*'.[3] RATTIGAN, at eleven, already 'a confirmed and resolute playgoer', was regarded at his prep school as the resident theatre expert.[4]

III

It is reasonable to suppose that all those indulging in childhood compositions, not set as a task, had this early sense of vocation. MILTON is said by Aubrey to have been a poet from the age of ten, 'but the products of his vernal fertility,' wrote Johnson, 'have been surpassed by many, and particularly by his contemporary COWLEY'.[5]

1 William Roper: *A Life of Sir Thomas More* (c.1557).
2 Michael Holroyd: *Lytton Strachey: The Unknown Years 1880–1910* (1968), p. 48.
3 *Aldous Huxley* (1973–4), i, p. 3.
4 M. Darlow & G. Hodson: *Terence Rattigan: The Man & his Work* (1979), pp. 28–29.
5 *The Lives of the English Poets* (Dublin ed. 1779–81), i, p. 139.

DRYDEN, on his own testimony, was a boy poet. POPE 'lisp'd in numbers'[1] (a reference to metrical feet) – he claimed to have written *Ode on Solitude* when he was twelve. According to David Low, GIBBON, by thirteen, 'had already covered the main fields of his subsequent masterpiece, applying his mind as well to difficult problems of chronology'.[2]

CHATTERTON was ten when he had a poem *On the Last Epiphany; or Christ's coming to Judgment* published in *Felix Farley's Bristol Journal*. By the date he put, when he transcribed from a pocket book his poem *Apostate Will*, he was eleven years and almost five months. He is the prodigy who knew no one who could help or correct him. He was only fifteen when he wrote some of the Rowley poems.

It was said that BLAKE became an artist at ten, and a poet at twelve. His *Song* – 'How sweet I roam'd from field to field' – was written before fourteen. BURNS was writing constantly by twelve. Before she was sixteen, JANE AUSTEN parodied popular novels of her day.

LEIGH HUNT's father obtained subscribers from his old congregation for his son's first book, *Juvenilia; or a Collection of Poems written between 12–16*. From the age of fourteen, BYRON was pouring out verses – on his beautiful cousin who had died, to Newstead Abbey, to his friends among the boys at Harrow, to the headmaster who had succeeded Dr Drury – and when he left, at seventeen, he wrote his own epitaph:

> My epitaph shall be my name alone:
> If *that* with honour fail to crown my clay,
> Oh! may no other fame my deeds repay!
> *That*, only *that*, shall single out the spot
> By that remember'd, or with that forgot.

KEATS, at sixteen, finished a translation of *The Aeneid* which he had begun at school.

ELIZABETH BARRETT BROWNING described *The Battle of Marathon* as 'her great epic of 11 or 12 years old, in four books'. TENNYSON, the same age, wrote *The Devil and the Lady* like a piece of Elizabethan blank verse. Before he was eight, MACAULAY had written a *Compendium of Universal History*, and a poem *The Battle of Cheviot* in the style of Scott. RUSKIN composed six poems and wrote them 'in imitation of book-print, in my seventh year'.[3]

1 *Epistle to Dr Arbuthnot* (1735), l.128.
2 E.B. (1969 ed.).
3 *Praeterita* (1886–8), i, pp. 76–77.

Probably the most famous childhood compositions are those of the BRONTËS. In microscopic handwriting they invented and peopled the Kingdom of Angria. Later, Emily and Anne founded their own Kingdom of Gondal. By thirteen, Charlotte had written more in quantity than the published work of her maturity. Next year, she catalogued twenty-two of her miniature volumes, each containing 60–100 pages, all written in about fifteen months. Up in the attic at Little Lea, Belfast, C. S. LEWIS and his brother as children, during inclement weather, compiled their own illustrated books. They peopled Animal-Land and India, and as they went on they united the two kingdoms into the state of Boxen.

CHARLES KINGSLEY wrote a hymn at the age of five, which his mother preserved:

> In Heaven we must abide
> Time passes quickly
> He flies on wings as light as silk. . . .

WALTER PATER was described by his biographer, Thomas Wright, as 'one of the most prolific schoolboy authors who ever lived'.[1]

Beginning at thirteen with *Useful and Instructive Poetry*, DODGSON wrote and illustrated several MS magazines for his brothers and sisters, while A. E. HOUSMAN, two years older, got his own to contribute to a magazine that he wrote out and circulated among friends and relations – but he was writing verse 'at eight or earlier'. STEVENSON, at his last school and at home, was the author of many illustrated MS magazines, and one of his stories in *The Schoolboys' Magazine*, when he was thirteen, was entitled 'The Wreckers'. Ten-year-old ELIOT, at prep school, brought out eight issues of his own magazine *The Fireside*.

STEVENSON's first Covenanting novel was attempted on 'reams of paper' at fourteen. Next year, his father had a hundred copies printed of *The Pentland Rising: A Page of History*, and the proud boy's little paper-backed books sold for fourpence each at a missionary sale his mother held in their drawing-room. When WINIFRED HOLTBY was thirteen, her mother had five hundred copies of her daughter's *My Garden and Other Poems* printed in an art cover tied with ribbon, intending to present her with a copy for Christmas. The St Margaret's schoolgirl, out one day with the matron, was startled to see a display in a shop-window and bought her copy for sixpence.

1 *The Life of Walter Pater* (1907), i, p. 98.

MASEFIELD wrote two poems before he was ten, but before then he had composed verses in his head. LYTTON STRACHEY wrote his first recorded quatrain at five, and a long piece *Songs of Animals, Fishes and Birds* at seven. When nine or ten, he wrote the following verse to his sister, who ironically was to die in infancy:

> To me Life is a burden
> But to thee
> The joyous pleasures of the world
> Are all a gaiety.
> But if thou did'st perceive my thoughts
> Then thou would'st sigh and mourn,
> Olivia, like me.[1]

P. G. WODEHOUSE said, in a TV interview with Malcolm Muggeridge:

They tell me I was writing when I was five, but it seems rather extraordinary, doesn't it?[2]

Yet ALISON UTTLEY claimed to have written her first story, of six words, at two. At nine, JAMES JOYCE attacked in verse an enemy of Parnell, Joyce's father being one of Parnell's sympathizers.

Seven-year-old VERA BRITTAIN wrote a three-thousand-word novel, 'copiously and dramatically illustrated', with each short chapter preceded by a quotation – the one above its first chapter was from her own long religious poem. By eleven, she had written five 'novels'. She disputed the view 'often maintained that all children write or tell stories ... of those I have known, this seems to be patently untrue'.

As a child I wrote because it was as natural to me to write as to breathe, and before I could write I invented stories.[3]

So did C. S. LEWIS, and his father wrote them down as Cummie did for STEVENSON. ORWELL's mother took down her son's first poem at the age of four or five. C. S. LEWIS also wrote verse at a very early age, and completed a political novel at twelve. DYLAN THOMAS started to write – always poems – about the age of eight or nine.

CYRIL CONNOLLY, in the year he died, wrote that he had loved poetry 'and occasionally written it since I was six'. When he was with

---

1 Michael Holroyd: *Lytton Strachey: The Unknown Years 1880–1910* (1968), i, p. 41.
2 BBC 1: May 30, 1965.
3 *On Becoming a Writer* (1947), pp. 172–3.

ORWELL at St Wulfric's prep school, they were both writing poetry between the ages of ten to thirteen:

At sunset, or late at night, in the dark, I would be visited by the Muse. In an ecstasy of flushing and shivering, the tears welling up as I wrote, I would put down some lines to the Night Wind. . . . I would compare them with Orwell's being critical of his, while he was polite about mine. . . .[1]

Before he went to school at the age of eight, C. DAY LEWIS was 'quite prolific' in prose, 'writing short stories and sermons with a fine impartiality'. One of his earliest stories, inspired by the yarn of a sea-captain who came to tea, had an opening sentence 'which I have never since equalled, or attempted to equal – "Breakers ahead!" cried the Captain, "backwards! backwards!"'[2] CHRISTOPHER FRY wrote his first play at fourteen – unacted and unpublished, but characteristically verse drama. HAROLD PINTER produced hundreds of poems as a teenager.

When he read of 'Miss Sylvia Marchpane' writing 'half-a-dozen novels, mostly in exercise-books, before she left school' or 'Mr John Merryweather . . . turned to the stage by the present of a toy-theatre on his fourth birthday', A. A. MILNE had to admit 'that whatever other sort of writer I am, I am not (alas!) a "born writer"'.

It is comforting, but not conclusively so, to remember that probably Shakespeare wasn't either.[3]

1 *Enemies of Promise* (1938), p. 212.
2 *The Buried Day* (1960), p. 66.
3 *Autobiography* (US ed. of *It's Too Late Now*, 1939), p. 135.

CHAPTER THREE

Genes or Environment?

I

Some have taken their literary baptism back to the ultimate point. 'From my birth,' declared DE QUINCEY, 'I was made an intellectual creature.'[1] LEONARD WOOLF wrote:

... from the first moment of my existence, perhaps even before I left my mother's womb, I must have been 'a born intellectual'.[2]

Again: 'I was born an introspective individual.'[3] FLORA THOMPSON could not remember the time when she did not mean and wish to write. 'From the very beginning' of his life, MALCOLM MUGGERIDGE never doubted that words were his 'métier'. There was nothing else he ever wanted to do except use them.[4]

Others have had similar statements made on their behalf. Bonamy Dobrée spoke of KIPLING as 'a born writer: his headmaster was aware of it. . . .'[5] W. T. Kirkpatrick, who tutored C. S. LEWIS from 15–17, wrote to Lewis's father:

He was born with the literary temperament.[6]

Caitlin says that DYLAN THOMAS 'had that gift of *knowing*':

it was something that was there from the very beginning; something he was born with, part of his whole substance as a man.

When he performed in pubs, people only saw that side of him.

1 *Confessions of an English Opium-Eater* (1821), Preface.
2 *Sowing* (1960), p. 87.
3 *Beginning Again* (1964), p. 16.
4 *The Chronicles of Wasted Time* (1972–3), i, p. 12.
5 *Writers & Their Work: No. 19: Rudyard Kipling* (revised 1965), p. 18. Published for the British Council & the National Book League.
6 Jan., 1915. R. L. Green & W. Hooper: *C. S. Lewis: A Biography* (1974), p. 45.

He was very aware himself . . . that he had been given some gift that is denied to most, and yet he seemed to go out of his way to hide it. . . .[1]

A. A. MILNE, who did not see himself as a 'born writer', still made an argument for genes:

We may 'carve out' careers for ourselves, but our parentage gave us the implements with which to do it.[2]

II

Certainly a proportion of writers are interrelated, perhaps the most famous example being that Dryden, Swift, and Pope were cousins. Mary Shelley's parents were both revolutionary authors. Lady Anne Ritchie was Thackeray's eldest daughter. Frances Trollope was as celebrated a novelist as her son became, and when Anthony began he turned to her for help in finding a publisher. Kenneth Grahame and Anthony Hope ('When I mention it to his admirers it is always received with a certain incredulity') were cousins. Frances Cornford was the grand-daughter of Darwin; Dame Rose Macaulay's family on her father's side was that of Lord Macaulay. Evelyn Waugh was related on his father's side to Edmund Gosse.

Readers sometimes confused the brothers A. E. and LAURENCE HOUSMAN. Alfred told Laurence that he had met a Greek professor who was interested to learn he was talking to 'the brother of Laurence Housman'. The professor thought *Green Arras* 'the best volume by him that I have seen: the *Shropshire Lad* had a pretty cover'. Alfred signed his letter:

Your affectionate brother (what a thing is fraternal affection, that it will stand these tests!)[3]

Other brothers include George and Lord Herbert of Cherbury, the Wartons, Landors, and Kingsleys; the Vaughan twins and, more recently, the Shaffer twins. The brothers George and Weedon Grossmith collaborated in *The Diary of a Nobody*.

J. W. Mackail married the daughter of Burne-Jones, which made

1 Caitlin Thomas w. George Tremlett: *Caitlin: A Warring Absence* (1968), p. 114.
2 *Autobiography* (U.S. ed. of *It's Too Late Now*, 1939), p. 28.
3 Dec., 1896. Quoted by Richard Perceval Graves: *A. E. Housman: The Scholar-Poet* (1979), p. 130.

Kipling great-uncle of Denis, their novelist son. H. Montgomery Hyde was a cousin of Henry James. Katherine Mansfield and the author of *Elizabeth and her German Garden* were second cousins. Robin Maugham is Maugham's nephew; Richard Perceval Graves, the nephew of Robert Graves. Mary Moorman was G. M. Trevelyan's daughter; Lady Chitty is the daughter of Antonia White. Kingsley and Martin Amis are father and son.

Among more distant affinities, Cowper's mother traced her pedigree to John Donne; Shelley's mother descended from Sir Philip Sidney. Robert Sherard was Wordsworth's great-grandson. J. K. Jerome's father 'could claim relationship with Leigh Hunt'.[1] Monica Dickens's father was the barrister grandson of Charles Dickens. The Sitwells were descended collaterally from the Herberts. C. Day Lewis liked to imagine 'that through my Butler grandmother I may have been distantly related to William Butler Yeats'. His other grandmother, 'a Goldsmith, was directly descended from Oliver Goldsmith's uncle'.[2]

III

Some had famous relatives outside literature. HORACE WALPOLE was the son of Sir Robert; BERTRAND RUSSELL, the grandson of Lord John Russell. CHURCHILL was directly descended through his father from the first Duke of Marlborough. WILLIAM DOUGLAS-HOME's elder brother succeeded Macmillan as Prime Minister.

HENRY JAMES's elder brother, William, was the psychologist and pragmatist. Sir LESLIE STEPHEN's elder brother, Sir James, is bracketed with Blackstone on English Criminal Law. EDMUND GOSSE's father was among the 'experienced naturalists' briefed 'by Hooker, and . . . Darwin after meetings of the Royal Society',[3] before *The Origin of Species* was published. STEVENSON's father perfected the revolving lamp in lighthouses, and invented 'the azimuthal condensing system'. He was elected President of the Royal Society of Edinburgh. The father of JAMES BRIDIE 'made the first electric lighting plant in the country in Queen Street Station',[4] Glasgow.

1 Jerome K. Jerome: *My Life and Times* (1925), p. 26.
2 *The Buried Day* (1960), p. 17.
3 Edmund Gosse: *Father & Son: A Study of Two Temperaments* (1907), p. 118.
4 James Bridie: *One Way of Living* (1939), p. 14.

OSCAR WILDE's father, Sir William, was honorary Surgeon Oculist in Ordinary to the Queen. He had operated for cataract successfully on King Oscar I of Sweden, who became Oscar's godfather and gave him his name. Oscar's mother, an ardent Irish nationalist, was better known at her marriage than her husband. An article under her pen-name 'Speranza' had led to the suppression of *The Nation*.

CONAN DOYLE's grandfather, John Doyle, was the caricaturist 'H.B.', his friends Wordsworth, Scott, Coleridge, Disraeli, Charles Lever, Thackeray, and Rossetti visiting him at Cambridge Terrace. Conan Doyle's uncle, Richard, illustrated Thackeray's *The Newcomes*. KIPLING and Stanley Baldwin were cousins. FORD MADOX FORD's maternal grandfather was Ford Madox Brown. MAUGHAM's brother became Lord Chancellor; GRAHAM GREENE's brother was Director General of the BBC.

S. R. GARDINER took pride in his descent from Bridget, daughter of Oliver Cromwell and wife to Henry Ireton. KENNETH GRAHAME could claim double descent from Robert the Bruce. SHAW was supposed (by the family) to be descended from Macduff. ANNE MOBERLY claimed descent from Peter the Great. The SITWELLS, via their mother, went back to John of Gaunt.

IV

Where exceptional talent is *multiplied* within a family, it is difficult to circumnavigate genes. LESLIE STEPHEN's father and grandfather were writers, and VIRGINIA WOOLF, his child by second marriage, followed a 150-year tradition. LYTTON STRACHEY's forbears had associations with Shakespeare, Locke, and many other writers.[1] His grandfather was appointed to the Examiner's Office of India House – the other assistants being Thomas Love Peacock and James Mill. Lytton's father was made Knight Grand Commander of the Star of India, for an administrative career of 'very great power and importance'.

ALDOUS HUXLEY was grandson of Thomas Henry Huxley, while his mother was grand-daughter to Dr Arnold, niece to MATTHEW ARNOLD, and sister of Mrs HUMPHRY WARD. His brother, Sir Julian, distinguished himself in his grandfather's discipline. G. M. TREVELYAN

1 See Michael Holroyd: *Lytton Strachey: The Unknown Years 1880–1910* (1968), pp. 3–4.

could boast MACAULAY as a great-uncle. His father, Sir GEORGE OTTO TREVELYAN, was a member of Gladstone's Cabinet, and the biographer of Macaulay and Charles Fox.

SIEGFRIED SASSOON's mother, a successful artist, was the daughter of Thomas and Mary Thornycroft. Mary Thornycroft had executed marble portraits of all Queen Victoria's children when they were infants. Uncle Sir William Hamo Thornycroft, RA, sculpted Cromwell's statue which stands outside the House of Commons.

Could I carry on that tradition with my pen? I wondered, and should I ever write as good a poem as my mother's picture of The Hours. . . . ?[1]

On his father's side, Aunt Rachel was editor of *The Sunday Times*.

DAPHNE DU MAURIER was daughter of the actor-manager, Sir Gerald, and grand-daughter of GEORGE DU MAURIER. The BRONTËS represent four precocious siblings, the ROSSETTIS three, the POWYSES seven, the SITWELLS three, the KNOX brothers four. ALEC and EVELYN WAUGH were brothers; AUBERON is Evelyn's son.

V

How far were these literary children motivated by their homes? The great majority of their fathers belonged to the professions, which is usually taken to imply a bookish environment. C. S. LEWIS's father, a solicitor, 'bought all the books he read and never got rid of any of them'. In the 'New House' that his father built when Lewis was seven, they were in every room – even piled in the cistern attic.[2] MASEFIELD from the age of eight lived in the old home of his grandfather, who had been an attorney and Clerk to the Magistrates. In several rooms were many hundreds of books which had belonged to his grandfather's library, but at that stage the boy fell eagerly upon piles of magazines filled with serial stories. ROBERT GRAVES 'read more books than most children do':

There must have been four or five thousand books in the house altogether.[3]

His father wrote poetry and was an inspector of schools. HENRY JAMES,

1 *The Old Century and seven more years* (1938), p. 286.
2 *Surprised by Joy: The shape of my early life* (1955), p. 17.
3 *Goodbye To All That* (1929), p. 52.

whose father wrote books on Swedenborgian theology, is described in his childhood as playing 'with books rather than boys'.[1]

WORDSWORTH's father, an attorney and business agent to Sir James Lowther, required his son to learn by heart large portions of Spenser, Shakespeare and Milton.

WATTS-DUNTON's father, a solicitor, was one of the earliest Fellows of the Geographical Society, and one of the Founders of the Anthropological Society. He took *The Athenaeum* regularly, which led to the boy correcting John P. Collier on a point of Shakespearian scholarship. The correction was noted under 'Literary Gossip' and soon after, his father objected that one of his books had been marked.

'Why, somebody has been writing about this very passage to the Athenaeum.'
'Yes, father, it was me.'
'You!' cried his astonished father, 'you!'[2]

In 'that lovely understanding voice', A. A. MILNE's father (who ran his own school) read *Uncle Remus* to his small sons, a chapter a night. When forty years later Milne wrote *Winnie-the-Pooh*, he 'remembered all that *Reynard the Fox* and *Uncle Remus* and the animal stories in *Aunt Judy's Magazine* had meant to us'. Their father also read *The Pilgrim's Progress* (he had somehow got it into his head that it was 'a religious book').

We didn't tell him the truth. We listened, rapt, and hoped that he would never find out. For it was the only excitement of Sunday. . . .[3]

Nine-year-old STEPHEN SPENDER was implanted by 'the seed of poetry' on a summer holiday in the Lake District, when his father (a lecturer and author) read to him Wordsworth's *We are Seven, A Lesson to Fathers, The Lesser Celandine*:

The words . . . dropped into my mind like cool pebbles . . . and . . . brought . . . a sense of the sacred cloaked vocation of the poet.

While he lay in bed he heard 'the murmuring of my father's voice as he read the Longer Poems of Wordsworth to my mother'.[4] At home, 'he read to us in the evenings from Dickens, Thackeray or Tennyson'.[5]

1 F. L. Pattee: *A History of American Literature Since 1870* (1915), p. 192.
2 James Douglas: *Theodore Watts-Dunton* (1904), p. 56.
3 *Autobiography* (U.S. ed. of *It's Too Late Now*, 1939), pp. 44–45.
4 *World Within World: The Autobiography of Stephen Spender* (1951), pp. 86–87.
5 *Ibid.*, p. 89.

RUSKIN's father, a successful wine merchant, 'read to my mother' after tea:

Thus I heard all the Shakespeare comedies and historical plays again and again, – all Scott, and all Don Quixote, a favourite book of my father's, and at which I could then laugh to ecstasy. . . . My father was an absolutely beautiful reader of the *best* poetry and prose; – of Shakespeare, Pope, Spenser, Byron, and Scott; as of Goldsmith, Addison, and Johnson.[1]

ALEC and EVELYN WAUGH's father at an unusually early age became chairman and managing director of Chapman and Hall; for some eight years of Evelyn's life 'for some three or four evenings a week when we were at home', their father read to them and 'whatever friends might be in the house, for an hour or more' – most of Shakespeare, Dickens and Tennyson, and much of Browning, Trollope, Swinburne, Matthew Arnold. Sometimes he read *The Importance of Being Earnest*, or another play of his youth, and would move about the room in his portraying of the characters. Evelyn wrote that 'the precision of tone, authority and variety . . . I have heard excelled only by Sir John Gielgud':

In these recitations of English prose and verse the incomparable variety of English vocabulary, the cadences and rhythms of the language, saturated my young mind. . . .[2]

At four or five, JAMES BRIDIE was spellbound by his father's reading aloud of Shakespeare:

Except Mr Gielgud and Mr Quartermaine, I have never heard anyone speak Shakespeare's verse with so fine a sense of its values as my father had.[3]

His father, an engineer after circumstances had forced him to abandon medical studies, read aloud to the boys Carlyle, Emerson, the Authorized Version of the Bible, Stevenson, Tennyson, Browning, Coleridge, Ruskin, Darwin, and the *Arabian Nights*.

In some of these works I delighted. Others were agony. . . . I remember that in my first five years, I heard *The Cloister and the Hearth* and Isaiah with pleasure.[4]

DYLAN THOMAS's father, an English teacher, read Shakespeare to him – like an actor – from the time Dylan was only four.

1 *Praeterita* (1886–8), i, pp. 92–93.
2 *A Little Learning: The First Volume of an Autobiography* (1964), pp. 71–72.
3 *One Way of Living* (1939), p. 13.
4 *Ibid.*, p. 28.

MALCOLM MUGGERIDGE's father, secretary to a firm of shirt manu-
facturers in the City, would read aloud 'bits' of Dickens – Dickens was
'a great bond' between them.[1] On Sunday evenings he 'read aloud to
us from the plays of Shakespeare':

> My father read all the parts . . . modifying his voice for the clowns and
> minor characters, and giving everything he'd got to Othello, Lady Macbeth or
> Hamlet. I doubt if he was a particularly good reader . . . though in a way I
> enjoyed (the readings) . . . because of the enormous zest my father put into
> them.

Malcolm was given his second name Thomas after Carlyle, whose
five-volumed works stood in a case with the rest of his father's books
– Rousseau's *Confessions*, Whitman's *Leaves of Grass*, Shaw, Ibsen, *Unto
This Last*, *News from Nowhere*, the Webb's *History of Trade Unionism*,
Tresselli's *The Ragged Trousered Philanthropists*, and other 'socialist
classics'.

> I . . . saw them as the bricks out of which he had constructed his Heavenly
> City. . . .[2]

VI

Some fathers had considerable scholarship and were writers themselves. FANNY BURNEY's father was 'the great Dr Burney', author of *A
General History of Music*. She acted as his amanuensis when he was
writing it, as she had done for his *Tours* of Italy and Germany. DIS-
RAELI's father pioneered literary research, and PALGRAVE's the critical
study of mediaeval history. J. S. MILL's father combined historian,
economist and philosopher. ROSSETTI's was Professor of Italian Literature at King's College, London; ARTHUR RANSOME's, Professor of
History at Leeds; DENIS MACKAIL's, Professor of Poetry at Oxford.
KIPLING's was curator of Lahore Museum. WILDE's father compiled a
three-volume catalogue of the archaeological treasures of the Royal
Irish Academy. CONRAD's father translated Shakespeare into Polish.

Fellow of the Royal Society and twice President of the Royal Geographical Society, LYTTON STRACHEY's father was awarded the
Symons Medal by the Royal Meteorological Society. VIRGINIA

---

1 *The Chronicles of Wasted Time* (1972–3), i, p. 26.
2 *Ibid.*, i, pp. 59–60.

WOOLF's father wrote *History of English Thought in the Eighteenth Century*, and edited the *Dictionary of National Biography*. VYVYAN HOLLAND and STEPHEN SPENDER had fathers with a double first at Oxford: Wilde's knowledge of Greek was profound, and Harold Spender was author of eighteen books, an FRGS, and held an honorary doctorate from the University of Athens. Dr Burnett, father of IVY COMPTON-BURNETT, was described as 'a man of wide culture and experience', whose medical books were renowned for their originality.

EDMUND GOSSE, at nine, gained mention in one of his father's books. In *Actinologia Britannica*,[1] Philip Gosse expressed his debt to the 'keen and well-practised eye of my little son'.[2] Edmund accompanied his father in collecting marine creatures from the 'living flower-beds' then to be found in rock-pools off the Devon coast, and assisted in examining them afterwards in a shallow pan. Neither directed nor approved by his father, the boy spent 'an enormous quantity of time' in a little spare room at the back of the house, preparing little monographs on seaside creatures.

I wrote them out upon sheets of paper of the same size as his printed page, and I adorned them with water-colour plates, meant to emulate his precise and exquisite illustrations.[3]

The man wrote in retrospect:

My labours failed to make me a zoologist. . . . Yet for almost any intellectual employment in later life, it seems to me that this discipline was valuable.[4]

DISRAELI, at fifteen, was sent home from Higham Hall because, against school rules, he had produced and acted in plays enthusiastically received by the other boarders. He decided to spend a year reconstructing his education, and every day the bemused author of *Curiosities of Literature* watched his tall, slippered son coming out of the paternal library with armfuls of books and taking them to various parts of the house.

The last present WILDE gave his younger son Vyvyan was *The Jungle Book*.

. . . he had already given me *Treasure Island* and Jules Verne's *Five Weeks in*

1 (1860), p. 137.
2 Quoted by Edmund Gosse, *Father & Son: A Study of Two Temperaments* (1907), p. 160.
3 *Ibid.*, p. 192.
4 *Ibid.*, pp. 195–6.

a Balloon. . . . He told us all his own written fairy stories suitably adapted for our young minds, and a great many others as well.

When Cyril, the elder boy, asked his father why he had tears in his eyes when he told them the story of *The Selfish Giant*, he replied that 'really beautiful things always made him cry'.[1]

There are less exalted examples where the father was a published author. Before he became Rector of Haworth, the Rev. Patrick Brontë had published two books of verse and two of prose: his first book *Cottage Poems* when he was thirty-four, and his last, *The Maid of Killarney*, at forty-one. JOHN DRINKWATER's father published a book *Plays and Poems*, which reached a second edition the following year.[2] H. V. MORTON's parents were both writers. EVELYN WAUGH's father wrote *One Man's Road*.[3]

I am not, of course, the first to notice the number of writers born in Anglican parsonages: Dryden, Addison, Goldsmith, Cowper, Coleridge, Jane Austen, Tennyson, the Brontës, J. A. Froude, the Kingsleys, R. D. Blackmore, Dodgson, *Erewhon* Butler, Kilvert, W. R. Inge, Newbolt, the Powyses, Hugh Walpole, Ronald Knox, Dorothy L. Sayers, Richmal Crompton Lamburn, C. Day Lewis, Louis MacNeice. MAUGHAM from the age of ten was brought up by his uncle, the Vicar of Whitstable. ERIC GILL's father was curate at a chapel of the Countess of Huntingdon's Connection, but entered the Church of England when Gill was fifteen, and had a curacy at Chichester. Gill declared:

Those children are blessed and fortunate who find themselves born into a family whose professional concern is not . . . 'success', is not 'getting on'. . . .[4]

CHRISTOPHER FRY's father, an Anglican lay-preacher, abandoned his profession of architecture to found his parish in the Bristol slums, and died a premature death. Another group of fathers were either ordained headmasters or nonconformist ministers.

VII

There are many high-ranking appointments: Chaucer's father, Deputy Butler to the King; Sir Thomas More's, a judge; Bacon's, the Lord

1 Vyvyan Holland: *Son of Oscar Wilde* (1954), pp. 53–54.
2 John Drinkwater: *Inheritance: Being the First Book of an Autobiography* (1931), p. 141.
3 Published 1931.
4 *Autobiography* (1940), p. 47.

Keeper and head of the legal profession; Boswell's, a judge both of Supreme Civil Court in Scotland and of Supreme Criminal Court, as well as hereditary Laird; Marryat's, Chairman of Lloyds; Macaulay's, Governor of Sierra Leone; Matthew Arnold's, headmaster of Rugby; Swinburne's, an admiral; Sir Harold Nicolson's, Chargé d'Affaires of the British Legation in Tehran; Ronald Knox's, elevated to Bishop of Coventry and Archdeacon of Birmingham when the boy was six; Graham Greene's, headmaster of Berkhamsted School. Anne Moberley's father was headmaster of Winchester – and Bishop of Salisbury when she was twenty-three. Hugh Walpole's father was Bishop of Edinburgh; P. G. Wodehouse's, a judge in Hong Kong.

Some had inherited wealth. John Evelyn's father was a cultivated landowner. Henry James's father shared one of the largest fortunes in the States: amassed by his own father, an Irish emigrant. OSBERT described the splendour of the SITWELLS' upbringing, their father 4th Baronet:

... the powdered footmen ... stables full of haughty and glossy gods ... orchids in their fragile glass cases ... and in their seasons, ripe peaches and grapes and nectarines and melons within their crystal orchards....[1]

CHURCHILL, son of Lord Randolph, was born and brought up in Blenheim Palace. Lord David Cecil's father was the 4th Marquess, and the Hon. William Douglas-Home's the 13th Earl.

Others also were extremely wealthy. The father of Samuel Rogers was a radical banker with money derived from a glass factory. William Morris's was a discount broker which carried the status of private banker. BEATRICE WEBB's father, Richard Potter, was an industrial magnate in Tadcaster: Chairman of the Great Western Railway of England and, during her girlhood, President of the Grand Trunk Railway of Canada. It did not prevent him from being a devout student of Dante in the original, and of Shakespeare and Plato – nor curb his originality. When Beatrice, at thirteen, asked if he advised her to read *Tom Jones*, he replied: '. . . a nice-minded girl can read anything.' She later decided he was 'the only man I ever knew who genuinely believed that women were superior to men'.[2]

Galsworthy's father was a solicitor and director of companies. G. K. Chesterton's was the head of a firm of house-agents and surveyors

1 *Left Hand, Right Hand!* (1945), p. 124.
2 *My Apprenticeship* (1926), pp. 10–11.

which, when Chesterton was a child, had already been established three generations in Kensington. Radclyffe Hall's bequeathed to her a substantial income.

Some were in what might be termed the higher flights of trade. The generous allowance that Ruskin received from his father enabled him to begin collecting Turners at twenty. T. S. Eliot's father was a wealthy President of the Hydraulic-Press Brick Company in St Louis, Missouri; Lord Kenneth Clark's, the founder of a thread-manufacturing firm; A. J. P. Taylor's, a cotton mill owner. The wealth of Beatrix Potter's parents, on both sides, came from the Lancashire cotton trade.

New-Zealand born KATHERINE MANSFIELD was brought up in the luxury of parlour maids, gardeners, visiting washerwomen and sewing maids. She lived in a house which had a billiard room and a tennis court. Her father had quickly become head of the old importing firm he joined as a youth, as well as director of several companies also in Wellington. Soon after her return from finishing her schooling in England, he was elected chairman of the board of the Bank of New Zealand. Their new house, in which Chaddie hated to feel his sister 'so unhappy', had 'a lovely ballroom' and a croquet lawn.

KENNETH GRAHAME was brought into the world by Dr James Simpson, the Queen's physician of chloroform fame. When three-year-old LEONARD WOOLF was thought to be dying, Sir William Jenner, the Queen's doctor, was called: a descendant of the Jenner who invented inoculation.

All this gives a formidable picture of privilege. I do not think we can escape this fact that most of our writers have not come from the semi-skilled or unskilled. Nigel Cross wrote of the nineteenth century:

In practice, the writing, production and reading of books was a middle-class monopoly . . . the prerequisites for literary success are education, social status, and monied leisure.[1]

As a boy, I heard Canon T. P. Stevens maintain in the pulpit that cranks found a rational explanation for Shakespeare by saying Bacon with his educational advantages must have written the plays – they forgot the Holy Spirit is no respecter of persons. I agree with the theology but observe that writers, like gardens, need the additive of worldly help.

---

1 *The Common Writer: Life in 19th-Century Grub Street* (1985), pp. 2, 5.

VIII

Having said this, among writers from lowlier or less academic origins are names of highest stature: Shakespeare, Ben Jonson, Bunyan, Samuel Johnson, Keats, Dickens, Hardy, Shaw, Wells. Certain qualifications, however, still need to be made. SHAKESPEARE's father, a burgess of Stratford, was an honoured citizen of some status and not until Shakespeare was thirteen did the fortunes of his family begin to decline.

JOHNSON's father, as Sheriff of Lichfield, had something of the civic status of Shakespeare's father in his home town. He was 'a pretty good Latin scholar', and his business of bookseller familiarized his son with unlikely reading from an early age. During the two years that Johnson spent at home after his unfortunate period as usher in the Grammar school at Stourbridge, what he read, he told Boswell, was 'all literature, Sir, all ancient writers, all manly':

... in this irregular manner I had looked into a great many books, which were not commonly known at the Universities, where they seldom read any books but what are put into their hands by their tutors; so that when I came to Oxford, Dr Adams ... told me, I was the best qualified for the University that he had ever known come there.

Dr Adams, who had been present on the night of Johnson's arrival at Oxford, described to Boswell how 'his figure and manner appeared strange to them ... he ... sat silent, till upon something which occurred in the course of conversation, he suddenly struck in and quoted Macrobius. . . .'[1]

BUNYAN had been taught to read at the local school, perhaps a grammar school, before he left early to learn the family trade of travelling tinker. Now the Bible and Foxe's *Book of Martyrs* would lie open to him – twin pillars of his art.

Even DICKENS's father, a clerk in the Navy Pay Office, may be regarded as a minor civil servant. Although there were money difficulties, these did not affect Dickens adversely until he was eleven. SHAW's, too, was a minor civil servant before he took to being an unsuccessful wholesale merchant.

Some parents made important compensation. BURNS was taught for a time by his father, when the itinerant dominie he and his neighbours had engaged for their children left after two very successful years. Like

1 *The Life of Samuel Johnson, LL.D.* (1791). Aetat.19: 1728.

Dickens, Burns was fired by his father's small collection of books, among which he chose first the lives of Hannibal and Wallace. DICKENS's father had some eighteenth-century fiction, together with *The Arabian Nights* and *Don Quixote*. Of a summer evening at Chatham, 'the boys at play in the churchyard', one particular little boy was sitting on his bed 'reading as if for life'.[1]

J. R. GREEN's father was a registrar and maker of silk gowns for the Fellows of Oxford University. His limited education did not always permit him to answer a question put by his family, but his approach and tenderness were exemplary: 'I don't know, but I will try to find out.'[2] From his father, a master mason, HARDY derived his love of music; his mother imparted a love of reading.

FLORA THOMPSON had no romantic illusions about poverty, although she capitalized her own in *Lark Rise to Candleford*. She wrote in old age:

To be born in poverty is a terrible handicap to a writer. I often say to myself that it has taken one lifetime for me to prepare to make a start.

In spite of being poor, her father, a stonemason and bricklayer, taught her to read before she went to school; her mother passed on to her a special gift for story-telling.

H. E. BATES's father, a shoemaker, subscribed to *The Harmsworth*, *The Strand*, *The Windsor*, *Young England*, and he would have these magazines bound up in fat, half-leather volumes. At an early age the boy had access to the stories of Doyle, Kipling and Barrie appearing in their pages. Winter and summer, and not more than five, he was taken for long walks in the Bedfordshire countryside, 'my father striding out athletically, I desperately struggling to keep up'.

I can still smell the bluebells, the honeysuckle, the meadow-sweet, the dog roses and the sheer concentrated fragrance of summer leaf and sap. If I have nothing else to thank my father for – and I have a very great deal – this in itself would be enough.[3]

HAROLD PINTER was brought up in the East End of London yet his Jewish home had a respect for books, and his mother and father cared very much for 'civilised behaviour'.

The absence of parental culture makes KEATS and WELLS more

1 *The Personal History of David Copperfield* (1850), p. 42.
2 *The Letters of John Richard Green* ed. Leslie Stephen (1901), p. 2.
3 *The Vanished World: An Autobiography* (1969), p. 30.

remarkable. Keats's father kept a livery stable in Finsbury, *The Swan and Hoop*. Wells saw light of day over his father's small china shop in Bromley High Street, Kent, where he grew up under the continual threat of poverty. In both cases they were motivated by schools. When Keats went to school at Enfield, Charles Cowden Clarke, son of the headmaster, introduced him to the glories of English verse:

> . . . Ah! had I never seen,
> Or known your kindness, what might I have been?
> What my enjoyments in my youthful years,
> Bereft of all that now my life endears?[1]

Clarke, soon after publication of the first part of *The Earthly Paradise*, wrote to William Morris:

> . . . I am sure that you would not have had a more devoted admirer . . . than in my beloved friend and schoolfellow, John Keats, whom I all but taught his letters.[2]

For Wells, it all began when he was a pupil teacher at Midhurst Grammar and the headmaster had him sit for examinations in elementary science to win grants for the school. The Education Office of the day awarded him a scholarship at the Normal School of Science, South Kensington, where T. H. Huxley was one of the teachers. To that headmaster we owe much, but the *History of Mr Polly – The Door in the Wall* part of Wells is left unexplained. For that I go back to Canon T. P. Stevens.

IX

Apparently straightforward evidence becomes more complicated beneath the surface. It would be easy to imagine SHERIDAN, for example, advantaged with an author-father noted for a *Pronouncing Dictionary*, but in fact the father was indifferent to his talented and loving boy.

BEVERLEY NICHOLS's father, a retired solicitor, meant that the family was surrounded by middle-class appurtenances and values. But Nichols pointed out:

---

1 'Epistle to Charles Cowden Clarke', *Poems* (1817).
2 J. W. Mackail: *The Life of William Morris* (1899), i, p. 200.

There were no books of poetry in our home, and our scanty library was a load of trash.[1]

A more important consideration lay in the fact that the father, an alcoholic, ridiculed the boy's aspirations, in particular his talent as a musical composer recognized at school by Sir George Dyson. It could well be argued that these two professional homes were less advantageous than many of those above, where the father's employment would be designated by employment bureaux as Craft.

It is surprisingly sad that MATTHEW ARNOLD did not have confidence to show his early poems to his father. When the flag went up on the turret over his study at Rugby, Dr Arnold wanted every boy to feel he could have access if he desired, yet it seems, in this particular, his own boy felt the flag was not for him. C. DAY LEWIS – like Goldsmith, born in a parsonage in the Church of Ireland – revealed that his own father, though he loyally 'tried to like my own verse, had little feeling for poetry and less understanding of the creative temper'.[2]

EDMUND GOSSE described his own state as 'almost unique among the children of cultivated parents'. Never once did he have a story read or told at bedtime. It was not neglect – 'They desired to make me truthful'.[3] Among his father's hundreds of books, there was no work of fiction save *Tom Cringle's Log*. When Gosse was eleven, his father permitted Dickens on the ground that 'he exposes the passion of love in a ridiculous light'.[4] He was now attending a day-school, and one day met Sheridan Knowles who recommended he should ask the schoolmaster to read some Shakespeare with them. These lessons were stopped by the father, who prided himself on never having read a page of Shakespeare nor visited a theatre save once. When Gosse was thirteen, he saw an engraving of a statue for the first time and asked his father to tell him about those 'old Greek gods'. His father replied:

There is nothing in the legends of these gods, or rather devils, that it is not better for a Christian not to know.[5]

1 *The Unforgiving Minute* (1978), p. 2.
2 *The Buried Day* (1960), p. 57.
3 *Father & Son: A Study of Two Temperaments* (1907), pp. 26–27.
4 *Ibid.*, p. 267.
5 *Ibid.*, p. 291.

Some had the support of mothers intellectually superior to fathers. SHAW's mother stimulated his cultural interests and directly influenced his musical appreciation. She abandoned her husband to follow her singing teacher to London and four years later, Shaw, at twenty, joined her and his elder sister. He and his mother lived in the same house another twenty-two years until he married, but during that time pursued their own lives.

BARRIE's mother had attended only briefly at a Dame's school but she was a great reader and, when serious housework was done, allowed herself to take out a story by George Eliot or Mrs Oliphant – her greatest delight being a book by or on Carlyle. Barrie's father, a weaver, deeply respected the learning he had little of, and was determined to provide it for his sons.

T. S. ELIOT's mother was a frustrated poet, sending her poems to friends and newspapers. By nurturing her son, she sublimated her sense of what had eluded her, and as an ex-teacher made sure he was introduced to the books she valued – for example, Macaulay's *History of England*. As he grew older, he shared with her the books that meant much to him, and long after coming to England he arranged the publication of her extended poem *Savonarola*. C. J. CORNISH was deeply influenced by his mother's intellectual gifts. D. H. LAWRENCE's mother had been a teacher and had written some poetry. E. M. DELAFIELD's mother was a novelist and dramatist. The mother of WILFRED OWEN championed him when the father, who worked for the railway, lost patience with his bookishness.

IAN MACKAY's father was 'the engine driver who once sneezed his false teeth straight from the footplate into Lough Shin, and died of a strange encounter with a haystack'.[1] The mother brought up three sons by her own efforts. All her spare pence from domestic work went on best literature for their edification. Ian contributed humping coal for the neighbours before school, and by a two to three hour paper round at night. In 1927, when she moved from her cottage, this library numbered over three thousand volumes.

The mothers of Beverley Nichols and Malcolm Muggeridge contributed at a later point in their sons' development. BEVERLEY NICHOLS

1 *The Real Mackay* ed. Stanley Baron (1953): *Profile* by R. J. Cruikshank, p. vii.

was on his way to a performance of *The Importance of Being Earnest* and
called on his mother. She told him that Wilde had stayed at her home
when lecturing in Leeds:

'Your grandmother invited him.'
'But why didn't you tell me this before?'
'I did not think that it was the sort of thing that one cared to mention.'

At breakfast Wilde had 'plaintively inquired if he might perhaps have
a few raspberries. . . .'

– pale yellow raspberries. A request which, in snow-bound Yorkshire, a week
before Christmas, she was unable to satisfy.[1]

MALCOLM MUGGERIDGE records that when his mother was seriously
ill in a nursing home near Bournemouth, she told him that someone
he was very interested in 'had in the past once occupied that house . . .
but she couldn't quite manage the name'.

Then she managed it – Tolstoy. . . . It was only afterwards that I remembered
how touching it was of her to have stored up for me this particular piece of
information which she knew I should cherish.[2]

XI

My headmaster,[3] when I was a boy and later taught in my old school,
held a distinguished reputation. Always impressive taking Assembly,
he held out a vision and this created the illusion he was somewhat
remote – which was why at one staff meeting he rather surprised us
by a down-to-earth reply. He said dogged determination – what he
called 'stickability' – gave a surer guide to future achievement than any
other quality however more compelling. His remark floated across the
years when I was wondering what fire could have sustained achievement so formidable as the following.

Sir JAMES MURRAY spent the latter half of his life in taking the
Oxford English Dictionary[4] to letter T. A clothier's son from Hawick,
he received an elementary education and then the Minto School gave

1 *Father Figure* (1972), pp. 184–5.
2 *The Chronicles of Wasted Time* (1972–3), i, p. 34.
3 H. Raymond King, CBE, DCM, MM, C.de G., MA (Cantab.): pioneer of the Tutorial/
Diligence system.
4 i.e. *A New English Dictionary on Historic Principles* (1884–1928).

him Latin, French and Greek. He was known as the boy who 'always has a book in his pocket'.[1] After he left, he acquired languages as voraciously as Borrow and wrote on local antiquities. He was thirty-six when he graduated at London University – a few years later the selectors choosing him, it seems with misgiving, to edit the enormous project. His philological skills were almost entirely self-taught.

ALFRED RUSSEL WALLACE left school at fourteen, fond of reading and (like Dodgson) of making toys and mechanical things. While still a young lad, he gained an interest in botany. At thirty-five, on his second botanical and zoological expedition, this time alone to the Malay Archipelago, he submitted his concept of Natural Selection to Darwin who – by one of those coincidences in the world of ideas – was writing on parallel lines. The joint paper that the effacing scholars produced for the Linnaean Society has become history. Its significance, from our point of view, is that Wallace had drawn level with an established scholar fifteen years his senior, ex-Edinburgh and Cambridge, and the son of illustrious family.

At thirteen, ROBERT WATT was a ploughboy and afterwards a navvy. At eighteen, he obtained an hour's daily tuition in the classical languages in order to enter Glasgow University – very much as Livingstone, when a cotton-spinner, studied Latin in evening class. After becoming a highly successful GP, Watt was elected founder President of the Glasgow Medical Society and at forty, three years from death, President of the Faculty of Physicians and Surgeons. For thirty years of his short life, he had worked on his *Bibliotheca Britannica, or a general Index to British and Foreign Literature.*[2]

And I shall never forget my surprise when I discovered that the erudite author of *The Anatomy of Bibliomania*[3] was a business man who had left school at fifteen. We are thrown back on a genetic characteristic (his father always had patience – do you remember how his grandfather never gave up?). But the ability to connect facts never previously brought together, as Wallace and Darwin showed, and which someone gave as a definition of genius, is left as insoluble as ever. We are teased by factor X.

1 *D.N.B.*.
2 Published 1824.
3 Holbrook Jackson: his work in 2 vols. (1930–1).

XII

Probably the most dramatic examples where what is known of their origin and shaping yields so little an explanation of creative genius, are Shakespeare and Chatterton. Of SHAKESPEARE – described by De Quincey as 'the protagonist on the great arena of modern poetry, and the glory of the human intellect'[1] – we read that his maternal relatives, the Ardens, were 'of some distinction', that he obtained 'a sound education' in the local grammar school, and that later he was 'on cordial terms with his fellow-actors and dramatists'. A selective book-list following his article in the *Encyclopaedia Britannica*[2] is larger than the bibliographies of Newton, Einstein, Michelangelo, Rembrandt, Bach, Beethoven, Wordsworth and Dickens all combined.

Of CHATTERTON, 'the poor posthumous child of a dissipated Bristol choir-singer', we read that he left Colston's Charity-school when he was fourteen, having received 'a plain education as might fit him for an ordinary mercantile or mechanical occupation'. As a child, he had the freedom of St Mary Redcliffe Church where his family had been sextons for a hundred and fifty years. As an apprentice bound to an attorney in Bristol, the boy poet had a 'little public of heterogeneous individuals – clergymen, surgeons, tradesmen, vintners, and young apprentices like himself'.[3] After he was first articled, he noticed on visiting his mother a thread-paper she had converted from a parchment, and this led to his ransacking the house for other abandoned parchments which his father had retrieved from 'the muniment-room' over St Mary's north porch. He told his mother 'that he had found a treasure, and was so glad nothing could be like it'.[4] Next year we find the metrical innovator, the tragedian of *Aella* at fifteen, who 'in the element of the antique ... rules like a master'.[5]

In an age of faith, David Masson faced the question:

> Now, in the case of Chatterton, it appears, we must first of all take for granted an extraordinary natural precocity or prematurity of the faculties. We are aware that there is a prejudice against the use of this hypothesis. But why

---

1 'Shakspeare', 7th ed. of *E.B.* (1838). *Op. cit.*, iv, p. 17.
2 1969 ed.
3 David Masson: *Chatterton: A Story of the Year 1770* (1874), p. 26.
4 *The Works of Thomas Chatterton* ed. Robert Southey (1803), *His Life*, by G. Gregory, i, p. xxvii.
5 Masson, *op. cit.*, p. 50.

should it be so? How otherwise can we represent to ourselves the cause of that diversity which we see in men than by going deeper than all that we know of pedigree, and conceiving the birth of every new soul to be, as it were, a distinct creative act of the unseen Spirit? That now, in some Warwickshire village, the birth should be a Shakespeare, and that, again, in ... Bristol ... the tiny body should be shaken by the surcharge of soul within it, are not miracles in themselves, but only variations in the great standing miracle that there should be birth at all.[1]

An age which puts men on an inhospitable moon does not put that sort of question, but then we get in the way of thinking that the mystery no longer exists.

Sydney Cockerell said that FRANCIS THOMPSON was 'the greatest enigma' he had ever met.

It seemed utterly impossible that so feeble a manikin could produce titanic poetry like The Hound of Heaven.[2]

The Oxford professor, John Carey, uses the word 'mysterious' in speaking of the intricate metaphors and 'enormous' vocabulary of the severely handicapped CHRISTOPHER NOLAN:[3]

It is mysterious where he gets his vocabulary from.[4]

---

1 *Ibid.*, p. 39.
2 *Friends of a Lifetime: Letters to Sydney Carlyle Cockerell* ed. Viola Meynell (1940), p. 61.
3 See page 357.
4 'The Wogan Programme': BBC 1: Jan. 20, 1988.

CHAPTER FOUR
Motivation by Outsiders

I

Sometimes outsiders are influential that a literary career begins at a certain time or takes a particular path. CHARLOTTE BRONTË wrote that W. S. Williams, the reader to Smith, Elder, & Company, 'first gave me encouragement to persevere as an author'.[1] When A. E. HOUSMAN sent a copy of *Last Poems* to Moses Jackson, his 'greatest friend', he said in his letter:

... you are largely responsible for my writing poetry and you ought to take the consequences.[2]

The turning-point for A. R. WALLACE came in his early twenties when he met the naturalist, Henry Walter Bates, who introduced him to the science of entomology. They went together to the Amazon when Wallace was twenty-five, the expedition being described in his *Travels on the Amazon and Rio Negro*.[3] GALSWORTHY was twenty-seven when Ada, his future wife, said: 'Why don't you write? You're just the person.'[4] His first book, *From the Four Winds*, came out two years later. But six months before that remark, he had written to Monica Sanderson:

I do wish I had the gift of writing, I really think that is the nicest way of making money going. . . .[5]

E. M. FORSTER was very explicit that his tutor Wedd suggested he might write:

He did it in a very informal way. He said in a sort of drawling voice, 'I don't see why you shouldn't write,' and I, being very diffident, was delighted . . .

1 Dec., 1847.
2 George L. Watson: *A Divided Life* (1957), p. 211.
3 1853.
4 H. V. Marrot: *The Life & Letters of John Galsworthy* (1935), p. 101.
5 *Ibid.*, p. 97.

and thought, after all why shouldn't I write?. . . . It is really owing to Wedd and to that start at Cambridge that I have written.[1]

Elsewhere, Forster says: 'Travelling inclined me to write' – and his Aunt Marianne's legacy made that possible. ORWELL, on coming out of the Burma Police, travelled up to Cambridge to see Andrew Gow, his old Eton tutor now a Fellow of Trinity, and seek his advice about taking up a literary career. Gow recalled:

I seem to remember that as he seemed fairly determined . . . I said in a rather noncommittal way that he might as well have a try.[2]

He spent the night in College and Gow put him next to A. E. Housman at High Table, who asked him about Burma.

If RADCLYFFE HALL had not met Mrs Batten (Ladye), her eight novels might never have been written. Radclyffe was thirty when Ladye showed her short stories to William Heinemann, who wrote that one of them, *The Career of Mark Anthony Brakes*, was the best short story ever submitted for his approval. But he told Radclyffe:

I am not going to present you to the public as the writer of a few short stories . . . write me a novel . . . and . . . I shall publish it.

Eight years later, on a brief holiday with Una Troubridge at Lynton Cottage Hotel, Radclyffe watched an elderly woman caring for a domineering mother. Back in Sterling Street, she suddenly said:

I shall write Heinemann's book for him, and I shall call it *Octopi!*[3]

It appeared two years later as *The Unlit Lamp*.

BEATRIX POTTER was encouraged in her drawing by one of her governesses, Miss Hammond, who also introduced her to the study of Natural History. H. E. BATES dated his whole literary career from the moment a young ex-infantry officer, Edmund Kirby, walked into the fourth-year classroom at Kettering Grammar School and said: 'Write me an essay on Shakespeare. I mean from your point of view. Don't tell me he was born in Stratford-upon-Avon . . . I already know that. Don't tell me . . . he wrote *Macbeth* or *The Merchant of Venice*. I already know that too.' Bates declared:

I do not think I am putting it either too highly or fancifully to say that in that

---

1 *Monitor: An Anthology* ed. Huw Wheldon (1962), p. 114.
2 Bernard Crick: *George Orwell: A Life* (1980), p. 105.
3 Vera Brittain: *Radclyffe Hall: A Case of Obscenity?* (1968), pp. 71–72.

one morning in the autumn of 1919 I not only grew up; I grew up into what I was to be.[1]

II

Fellow craftsmen also played their part. An apothecary near the poverty line, in despair of ever marrying the woman he loved, GEORGE CRABBE, at twenty-five, left Aldeburgh for London with the hope of publishing poems such as *The Candidate*, only to find the conditions Chatterton had experienced ten years before. In desperation he too, appealed to a great one – in his case EDMUND BURKE. He delivered a letter containing some of his poetry, and spent the night walking up and down Westminster Bridge. The politician gave some immediate money, and encouraged him to speak of his plans. He helped him publish *The Library*. At Burke's house in Beaconsfield, Crabbe met Fox and Reynolds and through them came to know Johnson. On account of the young man's wide reading and piety, Burke thought him suitable for the Church and commended him to the Bishop of Norwich. Through Burke, Crabbe entered a new profession enabling him to marry, and when he was twenty-eight he published *The Village* – his finest poem – revised by Burke and Johnson.

Under MATTHEW ARNOLD's influence at Westminster Training College, J. H. YOXALL developed lifelong interests in the arts. In curiously parallel lives, both men engaged in Liberal politics[2] and served education – Arnold as school inspector, and Yoxall was a schoolmaster who became President and General Secretary of the NUT.[3] They also sat on Royal Commissions.[4] Both wrote in time left over from official duties. DARWIN and A. R. WALLACE were influenced by THOMAS MALTHUS, whose essay *On Population*[5] was foundation reading for their theory of Natural Selection.

WILDE was at Oxford and writing poetry when WALTER PATER said to him: 'Why do you not write prose? Prose is so much more difficult.'[6]

1 *The Vanished World: An Autobiography* (1969), p. 103.
2 Arnold, for 4 yrs., p.s. to Lord Lansdowne, President of the Council; Yoxall, MP for Nottingham Boro' West (1895–1918).
3 1892–1924.
4 Arnold: Foreign Asst. Commissioner under the D. of Newcastle (1859); Asst. Commissioner on the Taunton Enquiry (1865). Yoxall: Bryce Commission (1894–5).
5 *An Essay on the Principle of Population* (1798).
6 *The Works of Oscar Wilde* ed. Robert Ross (1908), xiii, p. 538.

F. J. FURNIVALL advised KENNETH GRAHAME to give up his poetry and concentrate on prose. In 1914 ROBERT FROST suggested to EDWARD THOMAS, who had written nothing but prose, that he might try poetry. J. K. JEROME had been writing stories, plays, essays, for years 'before anything came of it'. He wrote to LONGFELLOW and received a sympathetic reply. Then it came to him, when he read the last two lines of *The Building of the Ship* –

> That is best which lieth nearest;
> Shape from that thy work of art,

– that he 'would tell the world the story of a hero called Jerome who had run away and gone upon the stage. . . .'[1] The humorous dramatic sketches became his first published book.

Twenty-year-old KIPLING, late one night in the Club at Lahore, felt he 'had come to the edge of all endurance'. He happened to pick up WALTER BESANT's *All in a Garden Fair*. Already the published author of *Departmental Ditties*, Kipling decided to emulate the hero (also a young writer) and write full time.

I could go away and measure myself against the doorsills of London as soon as I had money.

At the end of his life he looked back on that book as 'my salvation', 'a revelation, a hope and strength', and ascribed the 'dream of the future' that he built up in his head to sustain him, 'singly and solely' to Walter Besant.[2]

CHAUCER's *The Parlement of Foules* had such an effect on eighteen-year-old MASEFIELD, working in a carpet factory in Yonkers, that he wrote the date September 6, 1896 in the margin and taking out his watch noted 'the very minute'.[3] JAMES AGATE was around eighteen when the articles of theatrical criticism, in *The Saturday Review*, signed 'G.B.S. . . . made me determine that one day I would be a dramatic critic'.

At seventeen, receiving private cramming at Great Bookham, C. S. LEWIS purchased GEORGE MACDONALD's *Phantastes* on a station book-stall and a few hours later knew that he had crossed 'a great frontier':

1 *My Life and Times* (1925), p. 67.
2 *Something of Myself: For my Friends Known and Unknown* (1937), pp. 65–66.
3 *In the Mill* (1941), p. 96.

45

What it actually did to me was to convert, even to baptize ... my imagination.[1]

At the same age, H. E. BATES discovered STEPHEN CRANE to whom 'I really owe my first conscious hunger to begin writing stories'.[2]

A. A. MILNE's thirty-year friendship with E. V. LUCAS began when Milne was Assistant Editor of *Punch* and Lucas came as acting Editor:

I was encouraged by him to think that I was a good writer. Anybody who likes may differ from him ... but I know that I am a better writer for his appreciation than I should have been without it.

'E.V.''s praise and reassurance enabled him to convey in print a lightness of touch and an 'air of doing it all easily', so necessary in 'writing of that sort'.[3]

YEATS's father introduced his son to EDWARD DOWDEN, who encouraged his earliest poetry to be published. R. H. MOTTRAM, at twenty-one, formed a friendship with GALSWORTHY, who was thirty-seven and encouraged him to write. SASSOON persuaded WILFRED OWEN at Craiglockhart, the shell-shock hospital, to write no more on Beauty and Happiness, but to refute the popular poetaster Jemima and describe the reality of the Front:

... we vowed our confederacy to unmask the ugly face of Mars and – in the words of Thomas Hardy – 'war's apology wholly stultify'.[4]

When her first novel *The Dark Tide* had been rejected a second time, VERA BRITTAIN poured out her 'tale of disappointment' to ROSE MACAULAY who gave her advice with an invitation to tea. The MS was sent to almost every publisher in London.

Her periodic letters were the lamps which lighted that unprofitable year of 1922, so black in its continual discouragement.... But for Rose Macaulay I might well have given up....[5]

Fourteen years later, while Vera was writing *Testament of Youth* – 'in every sense of the word ... a personal Rubicon'[6] – she was 'again and again, convinced that the reading public would never be interested in the story of an obscure free-lance writer', but periodically WINIFRED

1 *George Macdonald: An Anthology* (1946), Introduction.
2 *The Vanished World: An Autobiography* (1969), p. 146.
3 *Autobiography* (U.S. ed. of *It's Too Late Now*, 1939), pp. 239–40.
4 Sassoon: *Siegfried's Journey* (1945), p. 64.
5 *Testament of Youth* (1933), pp. 595–6.
6 *On Becoming a Writer* (1947), p. 187.

HOLTBY read what she had written and urged her to continue.

So I laboured on. Many times I did so only because she insisted.[1]

She wrote of its acceptance, when Gollancz had sent his telegram – 'I shall be very proud to publish it':

This change of fortune was her doing, her achievement; it was she who had made me go on again and again when despair had prevailed.[2]

One of the mysteries of literature is that JANE AUSTEN numbered not a single literary friend among her numerous acquaintance.

III

At an early point in their careers, WORDSWORTH and COLERIDGE interacted. They had first met late midsummer 1795, at Bristol, in the house of Mr Pinney – a man with a similar claim to immortality as Mr Davies, who in his back parlour introduced Boswell to Johnson. Wordsworth was twenty-five, Coleridge twenty-two. It was the year the paper was made, bearing here and there a dated watermark, on which three years later *Lyrical Ballads* would be printed.

In midsummer 1797, Coleridge visited Wordsworth and his sister Dorothy at Racedown. Not 'broad and full' then, as De Quincey would know him, Coleridge 'did not keep to the high road' but, as the house came in sight, 'leaped over a gate and bounded down a pathless field'. That is what their poems would do – and why the first edition of five hundred copies stayed largely on Cottle's shelves.

In a few months, Coleridge settled at Nether Stowey and persuaded the Wordsworths to live at Alfoxden, three miles of Somerset country away. At this time, Coleridge wrote to Cottle:

... I feel myself *a little man by his side*, and yet do not think myself the less man than I formerly thought myself.[3]

He wrote to Southey:

Wordsworth is a very great man, the only man to whom *at all times* and *in all modes of excellence* I feel myself inferior. . . .[4]

1 *Testament of Friendship* (1940), p. 336.
2 *Ibid.*, p. 352.
3 June, 1797.
4 July, 1797.

47

Between the summers of 1797 and 1798, those three – for there was Dorothy, twenty-five, she

... who hath been long
Thy Treasure also, thy true friend and mine. ....[1]

– shared a comradeship and creative partnership of such intensity and joy that few can have experienced anything like it. 'We are three people,' said Coleridge, 'but only one soul.' After this *annus mirabilis*, it was never recaptured quite the same, and Coleridge had to make do with that happiness for the rest of his life.

Their endless meeting, rambling, talking and jotting down caused 'a titled Dogberry of our neighbourhood' to sound an alarm, for the Pitt administration was uneasy not only of invasion but a revolution from within. Coleridge tells how 'a SPY was actually sent down ... *pour surveillance* of myself and friend. ....'

He had repeatedly hid himself, he said, for hours together behind a bank ... and overheard our conversation ... he often heard me talk of one *Spy Nozy*,[2] which he was inclined to interpret of himself, and of a remarkable feature belonging to him; but he was speedily convinced that it was the name of a man who had made a book and lived long ago. Our talk ran most upon books, and we were perpetually desiring each other to look at *this*, and to listen to *that*; but he could not catch a word about politics. ....[3]

Unfortunately, local rumour had done its work. The St Albyn family served notice that the Wordsworths leave as soon as their year's lease ran out. Wordsworth addressed his friend, probably two years later:

... and Thou art one,
The most intense of Nature's worshippers
In many things my Brother, chiefly here
In this my deep devotion.[4]

Wordsworth went on to finish *The Prelude* and do so many more comparable things – *Michael*, *The Immortality Ode*, *Sonnet on West-minster Bridge*. .... But with the departure of those 'beloved faces', Coleridge's fugitive and magical career as a poet virtually came to an end.

... and manhood come in vain,

1 *The Prelude* (1805–6 version), Bk. VI: ll.214–5.
2 Spinoza.
3 *Biographia Literaria* (1817), i, pp. 185–6.
4 *Op. cit.*, Bk. II: ll.476–9.

> And genius given, and knowledge won in vain;
> And all which I had culled in wood-walks wild,
> And all which patient toil had reared, and all,
> Commune with thee had opened out – but flowers
> Strewed on my corse. . . .[1]

Like Arnold, the critic was born when the poet in him died.

Even after their estrangement, his *Biographia Literaria*, which offers a criticism of Wordsworth's poetry, repeatedly declares 'how small the proportion of the defects are to the beauties'. Wordsworth, who continued to refer to him as 'the only wonderful man I ever knew', is called 'my friend', and he still goes back to the beginning of that glorious time:

I was in my twenty-fourth year, when I had the happiness of knowing Mr Wordsworth personally, and while memory lasts, I shall hardly forget the sudden effect produced on my mind, by his recitation of a manuscript poem which still remains unpublished. . . .[2]

IV

BURNS, at twenty-four, wrote in a commonplace book he began at that time:

I never had the least thought or inclination of turning Poet till I once got heartily in love, and then rhyme and song were, in a manner, the spontaneous language of my heart.

Others shared a similar experience. Twelve-year-old BYRON fell in love with his cousin Margaret Parker who, according to what he wrote later, inspired his 'first dash into poetry'.[3]

Herbert Spencer suggested to GEORGE ELIOT she might try her hand at fiction. He also introduced her to G. H. Lewes. As Lettice Cooper wrote:

From the fulfilment of her nature came the release of her pen.[4]

Dudley Barker has noted that BENNETT's 'somewhat restricted

---

1 *To William Wordsworth: Composed on the Night after his Recitation of a Poem &c.*
2 Biographia Literaria (1817), i, pp. 82–83.
3 Ravenna *Journal*, 'Detached Thoughts' (1821–2).
4 *Writers & Their Work: No. 15: George Eliot* (revised 1970), p. 10. Published for the British Council.

periods during which he felt . . . the emotion of sexual love . . . urged him to his finest works of literature'.[1] He fell in love for the first time at thirty-nine, with eighteen-year-old Eleanor Green (a disparity in age not unlike Ruskin's infatuation for Rose La Touche). He believed they were engaged when she did not even read his love letters. It ended swiftly in humiliation and pain, yet during those seven weeks he wrote *Whom God Hath Joined*, his most significant novel up to that time. In the first year of marriage, he wrote his masterpiece, *The Old Wives' Tale*, also *Cupid and Commonsense*, the only one of his eight plays to be produced. When he fell in love with Dorothy Cheston at fifty-five, he wrote *Riceyman Steps*, his only major novel not set in the Five Towns.

Yet until he was twenty-four, and Hill, an art master at Blackheath who was a friend of his father, befriended him and introduced him to the Marriots, Bennett had shown no desire to write. He moved from his lodgings to be their paying guest at 5 Victoria Grove, Chelsea (now Netherton Grove), and they and their artistic friends encouraged him to believe in his creative ability which in his case, they said, must be literary. Dudley Barker observes:

The flaring of genius may be far more accidental than is commonly supposed.[2]

The literary agent, J. B. Pinker, also deserves mention in Bennett's career – and that of many others[3] – for without the agreement he entered into when Bennett was thirty-three, of paying him £50 a month and renewing it year after year even when debts accumulated and his investment seemed uncertain, Bennett would not have had peace of mind to write his major novels.

---

1 *Writer by Trade: A View of Arnold Bennett* (1966), pp. 119–20.
2 *Ibid.*, p. 51.
3 e.g. Conrad, Lawrence, Wells, Katherine Mansfield.

CHAPTER FIVE

Motivation by Gatherings

I

In every period writers come together, which makes their popular image of introvert largely false. When the wandering Erasmus reached Oxford, he felt his search for learning was over:

When I listen to my friend COLET it seems like listening to Plato himself. Who does not wonder at the wide range of GROCYN's knowledge? What can be more ... deep, and refined, than the judgment of LINACRE? When did Nature mould a temper more gentle, endearing, and happy than the temper of THOMAS MORE?[1]

According to Gifford, The Friday Street Club, started by Sir WALTER RALEGH, met at The Mermaid Tavern in Bread Street. This club 'contained more talent and genius than ever met together before or since....' BEN JONSON –

was a member, and here for many years he regularly repaired, with Shakespeare, Beaumont, Fletcher, Selden, Cotton, Carew, Martin, Donne, and many others, whose names, even at this distant period, call up a mingled feeling of reverence and respect.[2]

Gifford wrote long after The Mermaid had been burnt down in the Fire, and all that is certain is that BEAUMONT met Jonson there. Shakespeare may have been present. But if the rest be myth, it presents like all myths a truth in pictorial form.

In the last year of Queen Anne, SWIFT founded The Scriblerus Club to which Pope, Bolingbroke, John Gay and Dr John Arbuthnot all belonged. Thackeray spoke with envy of POPE's friends:

There never has been a society of men more friendly, as there never was one more illustrious.... Pope reverenced his equals. He speaks of Swift with respect and admiration always. His admiration for Bolingbroke was so great

1 Letter to Robert Fisher, Dec. 5, 1499: trans. J. R. Green.
2 *The Works of Ben Jonson* ed. William Gifford (1816).

that when some one said of his friend, 'There is something in that great man which looks as if he was placed here by mistake,' 'Yes,' Pope answered, 'and when the comet appeared to us a month or two ago, I had sometimes an imagination that it might possibly be come to carry him home, as a coach comes to one's door for visitors.' So these great spirits spoke of one another ... St John, the statesman; Gay, the kindliest laugher; Garth, the accomplished and benevolent ... Arbuthnot, one of the wisest, wittiest, gentlest of mankind; the generous Oxford; the magnificent Peterborough: these were the fast and faithful friends of Pope, the most brilliant company of friends ... that the world has ever seen.[1]

BOSWELL waited 'in a state of anxiety' for news of his election to The Literary Club. When 'the agreeable intelligence' came, he 'hastened to the place ... and was introduced to such a society as can seldom be found'.[2] Reynolds, Johnson, Burke, Goldsmith, were among founder members meeting then at The Turk's Head in Gerrard Street – one evening weekly at seven, for dinner and talking till a late hour. Garrick and Charles Fox followed shortly in succession, with himself, and gradually the membership was increased to thirty-five.

At Trinity, Cambridge, TENNYSON with his friend Arthur Hallam joined The Apostles, an exclusive club of undergraduate intellectuals. When he was twenty-nine, Tennyson joined the Sterling Club founded by the Apostles in London.

II

After the taverns came the salons. Mrs Elizabeth Vesey has the credit of being the first Blue Stocking to invite literary and fashionable society. She shared with Mrs Montague and Mrs Boscawen – according to Hannah More – 'the triple crown' among Blue Stocking hostesses.

Lady Blessington and Lady Holland were not on speaking terms. The former had conversed with Byron in Italy; and Wellington, Disraeli, Marryat, and Bulwer-Lytton were of her circle. She and her stepson, Count d'Orsay, invited Dickens at twenty-four to meet Landor, and Talfourd escorted him past liveried footmen at Gore House. When Hans Andersen was there on a visit to England, Dickens brought him signed copies of all his books. In Lady Holland's circle

1 *The English Humourists of the 18th Century* (1853), pp. 193–4, 190–1, 204–7.
2 Apl. 30, 1773. James Boswell: *The Life of Samuel Johnson LL.D.* (1791).

at Holland House sat Sydney Smith, Carlyle, Macaulay, Rogers. Once, tired of MACAULAY's eloquence, she switched the topic to the Christian Fathers only to find that there too, he was in fine flow. She tried again to trip him: 'Pray, Macaulay, what was the origin of the doll?' He veered, and related to the company all about the Roman doll.[1] DICKENS, young and gauche, captivated even her severity.

Mrs Humphry Ward remembered the last three years of J. R. GREEN's life from the age of forty-two, not long after his marriage, when 'the pretty house' at 14 Kensington Square 'was the centre of a small society such as England produces much more rarely than France':

Mr Lecky came – Sir Henry Maine, Mr Freeman, Mr Bryce, Bishop Stubbs sometimes, Mr Stopford Brooke, and many more. It was the talk of equals, ranging the widest horizons, started and sustained by the energy, the undauntedness of a dying man. There in the corner of the sofa sat the thin wasted form, life flashing from the eyes . . . the eternal protesting life of the intelligence. . . .[2]

Constance Wilde held her At-homes in the first-floor drawing-room at Tite Street. All the Pre-Raphaelite Brotherhood came, and Sargent, Irving, Ellen Terry, Sarah Bernhardt, Beerbohm Tree, Swinburne, Ruskin, Browning, Mark Twain, John Bright, Balfour. Lady Cunard assembled ambassadors, cabinet ministers and artists around her beloved Sir Thomas Beecham and 'immortal' GEORGE MOORE. When the young BEVERLEY NICHOLS was invited, he used to spend ten minutes walking round Grosvenor Square, 'summoning up . . . courage' to ring at Number Four. Maugham was another 'pre-luncheon square-walker'.[3]

Lady Ottoline Morrell wrote of her aims at Garsington:

Gather here – all who have passion and who desire to create new conditions of life – new visions of art and literature and new magic worlds of poetry and music. . . .

The composition of her house parties, against a backcloth of a lovely garden, swimming pool, peacocks and permissiveness, reads like the roll-call of twentieth-century Eng. Lit.: Lord David Cecil, Bertrand Russell, Robert Bridges, L. A. G. Strong, Maurice Bowra, G. Lowes Dickinson, Lytton Strachey, Virginia Woolf, Desmond MacCarthy,

1 *The Greville Memoirs* (1874), i, pp. 367–8.
2 *The Associate*: Oct., 1898.
3 Beverley Nichols: *The Sweet & Twenties* (1958), pp. 92–93.

D. H. Lawrence, Middleton Murry, Robert Graves – assorted with Lord Balniel, Asquith, Lady Oxford, and 'a beautiful and brainless deb'. ELIOT on his first visit met Katherine Mansfield and Aldous Huxley. Lady Ottoline belongs to this country's marvellous gallery of eccentrics. LEONARD WOOLF described her 'not unlike one of her own peacocks, drifting about the house and terraces in strange, brightly-coloured shawls and other floating garments, her unskilfully dyed red hair . . . and her odd nasal voice and neighing laugh'.[1] SASSOON was introduced by Robert Ross, and for twenty years was 'indebted to her for innumerable acts of generosity and affection' – only at first did her 'voluminous pale-pink Turkish trousers . . . the paint and powder and purple hair' make him nervous.[2] Of Garsington, ALDOUS HUXLEY paid tribute late in life:

I had the extraordinary fortune to meet a great many of the ablest people of my time. There were the Bloomsbury people . . . Russell I met there, and Roger Fry . . . and then Clive Bell . . . from them I learnt a great deal about art which I really didn't know anything about at all before. . . . The meeting of all these people was of capital importance to me.[3]

III

J. S. MILL at sixteen formed the Utilitarian Society, which for three years met to read essays and discuss them. During the next three years, he gathered 'a dozen or more' companions who met at Grote's house in Threadneedle Street twice weekly from 8.30–10.0 a.m., 'at which hour most of us were called off to our daily occupations'. Their object was to examine such works as Ricardo's *Principles of Political Economy and Taxation*, Du Trieu's *Manuductio ad Logicam*, Hartley's *Observations on Man*, and James Mill's *Analysis of the Human Mind*.

Our rule was to discuss thoroughly every point raised . . . prolonging the discussion until all who took part were satisfied with the conclusion they had individually arrived at. . . .

He made the claim:

1 *Beginning Again* (1964), p. 198.
2 *Siegfried's Journey* (1945), p. 9.
3 The recorded interview with John Chandos, Summer 1961: quoted by Sybille Bedford: *Aldous Huxley: A Biography* (1973–4), i, pp. 69–70.

I have always dated from these conversations my own real inauguration as an original and independent thinker.[1]

Six years after the naming of the Pre-Raphaelite Brotherhood, WIL-LIAM MORRIS and a small circle of close friends at Oxford began calling themselves the Brotherhood. When Morris had sat matriculation in the hall of Exeter College, he found himself next to a boy a year older, who would become his most intimate and lifelong friend, Edward Burne-Jones. They seldom spoke to beyond three or four in their college, but at Pembroke there was a little Birmingham colony where they consorted when they wanted more company. Together with William Fulford, Cormell Price (to be Kipling's headmaster), Dixon, Wilfred Heeley (at Trinity), and Charles Faulkner, they were increasingly inspired by Ruskin.

It was Dixon who suggested to Morris the starting of *The Oxford and Cambridge Magazine*. 'The bond,' wrote Canon Dixon later, 'was poetry and indefinite artistic and literary aspiration: but not of a selfish character, or rather, not of a self-seeking character'.

We all had the notion of doing great things for man . . . according to our own will and bent.[2]

Before the second number, Morris transferred the editorship to Fulford, but he himself contributed poems or prose, sometimes both, to practically every number. A year or so later, he and Burne-Jones worked with other artists, under Rossetti, in painting the murals of *Morte d'Arthur* in the Union Library. When Morris executed the greater part of the roof decoration, Faulkner, Crom (Cormell Price), and Dixon joined him.

The magazine and the ceiling remained the only joint venture of the Oxford Brotherhood, but individual members continued to play an important part in Morris's life. The following year, Dixon, now curate of St Mary's, Lambeth, officiated at his marriage, and Faulkner was best man. Two years later, when the firm of Morris and Company was set up, Burne-Jones and Faulkner were among the seven partners. Faulkner accompanied Morris twice to Iceland, and joined the Socialist League of which Morris was treasurer and editor of its journal. Crom joined Morris and his family when they rowed from Kelmscott House, Hammersmith, to disembark in their Oxfordshire meadow of

1 *Autobiography* (1873).
2 J. W. Mackail: *The Life of William Morris* (1899), i, p. 43.

Kelmscott Manor. Burne-Jones was with him to the end; only in Morris's socialism could he neither follow nor share.

On Monday evenings over the publisher's office in the Strand, Professor Minto, editor of *The Examiner*, entertained his contributors: Dr Garnett, Swinburne, Gosse, Watts-Dunton. Every Friday in their offices in Arundel Street off the Strand, Jerome, John Oxenham and Robert Barr held '*Idler* At Home' tea-parties, which 'became a rendezvous for literary London'; Wells, Doyle, Barrie, frequently came. At No. 18 Woburn Buildings on Monday evenings from 8.0 p.m. till 2.0 or 3.0 a.m., YEATS was at home to friends and aspiring writers:

I always encourage everybody; always.[1]

There the young Masefield met Synge, Lady Gregory, George Moore, Laurence Binyon. Yeats wrote to the young Joyce:

The chief use I can be . . . will be by introducing you to some other writers . . . one always learns one's business from one's fellow-workers. . . .[2]

Once a fortnight, about a dozen including Swinburne, Jerome, Barrie, used to congregate in Paganini's first-floor front in Great Portland Street and, when Paganini turned them out at midnight, the blind poet Philip Bourke Marston would invite them round to the Euston Road where he lived with his father, the dramatist Dr Westland Marston. 'A remnant of us',[3] after Philip's death, formed the Old Vagabond Club which developed into The Playgoers Club, meeting in a coffee-house in Holywell Street, of dubious fame.

WELLS was invited to join the Coefficients who, in 1902 on Beatrice Webb's suggestion, had started to meet monthly to discuss over dinner the affairs of Empire. Newbolt, Russell, and Sidney Webb were among their number.

Seventy-two years after Tennyson, LEONARD WOOLF found at Trinity The Apostles still thrived. Woolf was elected along with Lytton Strachey and Saxon Sydney Turner. He paid tribute to 'the immense importance it had for us, its influence upon our minds, our friendships, our lives'.[4] Among the Fellows of Trinity were four philosophers, all

1 John Masefield: *Some memoirs of W. B. Yeats* (1940), p. 29.
2 Richard Ellmann: *James Joyce* (1959), p. 108.
3 J. K. Jerome: *My Life and Times* (1925), p. 1.
4 *Sowing* (1960), p. 129.

Apostles: J. E. McTaggart, A. N. Whitehead, Bertrand Russell, and G. E. Moore. Maynard Keynes was elected in 1903. G. E. Moore, seven years Woolf's senior, 'was the only great man' whom he had 'ever met and known in the world of ordinary, real life'.[1] Before knocking at his door, Woolf often stood and took a deep breath.

Bloomsbury consisted of a number of intimate friends who had been at Trinity and King's and were now working in London, most of them living in that area. With characteristic care, Woolf differentiates between Old and New Bloomsbury. When he was thirty-one, only three weeks after resigning from the Ceylon Civil Service, he went and dined with Vanessa and one of his Cambridge friends, Clive Bell, in Gordon Square. Afterwards, Virginia, Duncan Grant and Walter Lamb came in.

This was, I suppose, so far as I was concerned, the beginning of what came to be called Bloomsbury.[2]

Old Bloomsbury consisted of the above, together with Adrian Stephen, Lytton Strachey, Maynard Keynes, Forster, Saxon Sydney Turner, Roger Fry, Desmond MacCarthy and his wife, Molly. Five were Apostles. The newer Bloomsbury, beginning nine years later and belonging to the 1920–30s, lost through death Strachey and Fry, and added three more Bells – Julian, Quentin and Angelica, – also David Garnett.

JAMES MURRAY, before he was chosen to edit the N.E.D., joined the Philological Society, where he sought out Skeat, Sweet and Furnivall, scholars who shared his interest in etymology.

The Inklings, a group of kindred spirits, met weekly in c. s. LEWIS's rooms at Magdalen –

theoretically to talk about literature. . . . Is any pleasure on earth as great as a circle of Christian friends by a good fire?

Lewis's brother, Warren, recorded a vintage year 1946,[3] when at most of the meetings TOLKIEN read a chapter from his 'new Hobbit' as they called it. JOHN WAIN won a bet by reading a chapter of *Irene Iddesleigh* without a smile, and DAVID CECIL read a chapter of his forthcoming book on Thomas Gray.[4] Every Tuesday for an hour or so before

1 *Ibid.*, p. 131.
2 *Beginning Again* (1964), p. 21.
3 *Letters of C. S. Lewis* ed. with *Memoir* by W. H. Lewis (1966), p. 14.
4 i.e. *Two Quiet Lives* (1948).

lunch, the same company reverted to the practice of Shakespeare and
Samuel Johnson and met at a pub, The Eagle and Child in St Giles',
better known as The Bird and Baby.

CHAPTER SIX

Motivation by Their Time

I

There is a larger sense in which writers do not work in a vacuum. G. M. Trevelyan wrote of SHAKESPEARE's 'luck' to live in late Elizabethan and early Jacobean times:

He could not have written as he did, if the men and women among whom his days were passed had been other than they were . . . or if the London theatres . . . had not reached a certain stage of development. . . .[1]

Indeed, MILTON doubted whether he himself had not been born 'an age too late'. Dr J. Bronowski said that BLAKE 'was such a poet as no age before his could have made, and no age since has made'.[2] Hazlitt saw WORDSWORTH's genius as 'a pure emanation of the Spirit of the Age. . . .'

He would not have been heard of at any other period.[3]

Sir Frederick Wedmore wrote:

It may be questioned whether men of the widest genius in Art and Literature do not receive an influence from their own time as great as any which they exercise upon it.[4]

Peter Ackroyd decides the same:

The great and the good writers are rarely isolated phenomena: they belong to a larger sphere of publishers, editors, critics and, most importantly, other writers.[5]

The 1890s are often singled out as a time when artists in all walks were contributing to and profiting from the stimulating atmosphere.

1 *English Social History: A Survey of Six Centuries: Chaucer to Queen Victoria* (1944), pp. 201–2.
2 *A Man Without a Mask* (1944), p. 127.
3 *The Spirit of the Age* (1825), p. 231.
4 *Studies in English Art* (1876), p. 167.
5 Review of *The Common Writer* (Nigel Cross), *The Sunday Times*, Jan. 19, 1986.

If they are extended to include the 1880s, George Moore, Wilde, Shaw, Conrad, Doyle, were all doing their best work, reinforced by younger writers: Barrie, Kipling, Wells, Bennett.

As regards literature, I find the 1850s even more remarkable for Thackeray, Dickens, Browning, Trollope, Charlotte Brontë, George Eliot, Ruskin, were at the height of their powers and although time has had greater opportunity to sift and reject, their reputations – with the possible exception of Browning – remain virtually unscathed. As Athens in the fifth century BC, came to fruition after the defeat of the Persians, and Elizabethan England flowered after the débâcle of the Armada, so they – all born during the 1810s – had seen Napoleon put down. They inherited and grew up with the Luddite Riots, the coming of the railway, and the Reform Bill. They saw a young girl come to the throne, Demands for a People's Charter and, in the prime of their lives, the blood and incompetence of the Crimean War. Such events were fused in their imaginative crucibles, together with personal experience and the result of their association with each other.

II

I like to adapt the idea of vintage years. 1859 tempts the connoisseur, for not only did *Origin of Species* appear but *A Tale of Two Cities, Adam Bede, The Ordeal of Richard Feverell*, Mill's essay *On Liberty*, and FitzGerald's translation of *The Rubáiyát of Omar Khayyám*; in addition, these authors were born: Doyle, Grahame, A. E. Housman, Jerome, J. W. Mackail, and Francis Thompson. You may prefer 1809 when Darwin and Tennyson were born, or 1819, another good year – George Eliot, Kingsley, and Ruskin. 1922 is full-bodied: *Ulysses, The Waste Land*, and the first collected edition of *The Forsyte Saga*.

Yet my own choice is 1911, which saw two collections of short stories: *The Country of the Blind* and *The Celestial Omnibus*. WELLS's collection contains *The Door in the Wall* which appeared in *The Daily Chronicle*, July 14, 1906. E. M. FORSTER's story, *The Celestial Omnibus*, appeared in *The Albany Review* for January 1908.

Instead of a door, Forster gave us a bus; instead of a garden, a mountain; instead of a railway extension near East Kensington Station, Bermondsey Gas-Works. There is the same ecstatic acceptance of the vision by a child, and the same imperfect grasp of it by a man. Both little boys are caned. Both stories end in violent death. They are poignantly profound.

I find it impossible that Forster had not been influenced by Wells – if not, what intriguing support to the idea of empathy! But Wilde would have approved, for here was a case of seeing 'a monstrous tulip with four wonderful petals in someone else's garden'[1] and being impelled to grow one with *five* not *three*.

---

1 *Salome* translated from the French of Oscar Wilde (1912), 'A Note' by Robert Ross, p. xviii.

PART TWO
CHILDHOOD

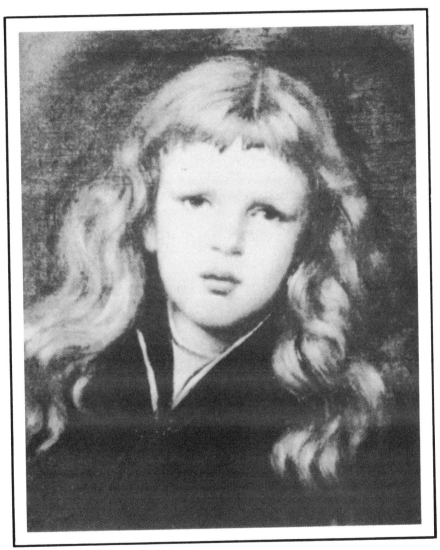

CHESTERTON AT THE AGE OF SIX
from an oil painting by Baccani, 1881

CHAPTER ONE

Golden Time

Contrary to a widely held belief, many writers were very happy in their earliest years. J. B. PRIESTLEY, referring to his own childhood which was not unhappy, jumped to the conclusion that this was exceptional:

I was outside the fashionable literary movement before I even began.[1]

At Kibworth Rectory the KNOX children were so happy that in later years when they could not sleep, they imagined they were there. MASEFIELD wrote at seventy-three or four, '. . . as a little child, I was living in Paradise. . . .'[2] 'Paradisal' was used by EVELYN WAUGH to describe 'an even glow of pure happiness' that remained for him his 'first age . . . lived in joyous conformity to the law of two adored deities, my nurse and my mother'.[3] As he travelled down the Trent from Lincoln when he was thirty, MATTHEW ARNOLD saw 'in the bright morning' his mother's village of Fledborough, and he wrote in a letter:

My recollections of it are the only approach I have to the memory of a golden age.[4]

SHELLEY knew a happy childhood in the grounds and eighteenth-century mansion of Field Place, as well as in the surrounding countryside. At nine, he was the idolized leader of four younger sisters in play – Swinburne held exactly the same position. Helen told how Shelley loved to go into the nursery and sing for them, or when they came to the dining-room for dessert he would entertain one upon his knee with an endless repertoire of fascinating stories. There are accounts that he laughed as a child – which he is supposed not to have done as a man – and played harmless pranks on people living round about.

1 *Margin Released* (1962), p. 10.
2 *So Long to Learn* (1952), p. 13.
3 *A Little Learning: The First Volume of an Autobiography* (1964), pp. 28–29.
4 Nov. 25, 1852.

It can easily be forgotten that DICKENS's early childhood between five and ten coincided with the family's most fortunate time, living at Chatham. Between ten and eleven, he attended an Academy run by William Giles, an accomplished scholar, situated in a largish house on the corner of Rhode Street and Best Street beside Clover Lane.

RUSKIN wrote *Praeterita* towards the end of his life as 'a dutiful offering at the grave of parents who trained my childhood to all the good it could attain'.[1] He put as the first of its blessings the 'quite priceless gift of Peace'.

I had never heard a servant scolded; nor even suddenly, passionately, or in any severe manner, blamed. I had never seen a moment's trouble or disorder in any household matter.[2]

His 'daily dress' at three and a half, was a white frock with a broad light-blue sash and blue shoes. From the age of four, he had his tea in the drawing-room, 'in a little recess, with a table in front of it, wholly sacred to me; and in which I remained in the evening as an Idol in a niche, while my mother knitted, and my father read to her...'[3] On account of his mother's evangelical strictness, his only toys were a bunch of keys, a cart, a ball, and when he was five or six, 'two boxes of well-cut wooden bricks'.

With these modest, but, I still think entirely sufficient possessions, and being always summarily whipped if I cried, did not do as I was bid, or tumbled on the stairs, I soon attained serene and secure methods of life and motion....[4]

He spent contented days observing the squares and colours of the carpet, the patterns in bed covers, dresses, or wallpapers; after the move from Bloomsbury to 28 Herne Hill, when he was four, the garden took the place of the carpet.

The accepted view of him as an over-protected child may be exaggerated for, as Lord Clark pointed out, Ruskin's young letters suggest a boy given every encouragement to think highly of himself.

Seven-year-old WILLIAM MORRIS, in his little suit of armour, rode his pony in the park of Woodford Hall. Always he could look back on this halcyon childhood, and 'when I was a little chap' meant all that

1 *Praeterita* (1886–8), i, Preface, p. vii.
2 *Ibid.*, p. 59.
3 *Ibid.*, p. 51.
4 *Ibid.*, p. 16.

was good.[1] He was a delicate boy whose father's circumstances accorded him calves'-feet jelly and beef tea. WINIFRED HOLTBY's pony rides with her father's old shepherd, the child distinguished by her 'shining gold head and . . . long fair pigtail',[2] recall Morris's content.

Until he was nine, A. E. HOUSMAN lived in a well-organised household of loving parents, younger brothers and sisters, and servants. If the children were upstairs and heard their father going down, they would rush from their rooms and put their legs – 'three or four pairs of them' – through the banisters to have their toes pulled as he descended.[3] His brother LAURENCE gives another delightful picture of Alfred taking him and Basil on to the lawn and teaching them in play. Laurence was the sun and stayed where he was, rotating on his axis; Basil, the earth, went round Laurence, rotating as he went; Alfred, the moon, skipped round Basil without rotating. On his sixty-third birthday, Laurence looked back:

. . . the 'Shropshire Lad' . . . after my father, was the first God we really worshipped.[4]

These wonderfully happy days came to an end when their mother was found to have cancer in both breasts and the dependent father, unable to compensate his children, took to drink.

Two years afterwards, the father confided in his elder boy that he was marrying again, and Alfred wrote to his future stepmother that he would help her look after his brothers and sisters. From then on, as neither child nor adult, he took his responsibilities seriously, encouraging their artistic and literary activities when his own schoolwork was done. He even shared his own particular interests in botany and Gothic architecture, making them all 'great fun' and 'amusing',[5] but it was no longer a normal childhood for him.

MAX BEERBOHM, the youngest of a large family, was especially loved. His own favourite was Dora next to him in age, and even much later in life people noticed that when they met 'they both changed. . . .

---

1 J. W. Mackail: *The Life of William Morris* (1899), i, pp. 8–9.
2 Vera Brittain: *Testament of Friendship* (1940), pp. 19, 21.
3 *The Unexpected Years* (1937), p. 22.
4 *What Can We Believe? Letters exchanged between Dick Sheppard & Laurence Housman* (1939), p. 115.
5 Kate Housman, quoted by Richard Perceval Graves: *A. E. Housman: The Scholar-Poet* (1979), p. 24.

Their eyes danced. . . .'[1] His unusually happy childhood lasted until he went to Marlborough. Lord David Cecil wrote:

Thirteen years of happiness had given him a basic faith in life which was to be like a sort of spiritual bank balance on which he could always draw for reassurance when things went wrong.[2]

EVELYN WAUGH, until he went to Lancing, 'had met only people who seemed disposed to like me':

I am still mildly surprised by rebuffs, such is the confidence which a happy childhood founds.[3]

LEONARD WOOLF tells how his mother adored her children and made life 'very interesting' for them when they were small.[4] ALISON UTTLEY's mother used to read two hours to the children every night in a huge antique-filled kitchen by a blazing fire. VYVYAN HOLLAND records:

Throughout my early years there was one person who always made me happy, and that was my mother, whom I adored.[5]

HAROLD NICOLSON wrote that his mother's adoration 'was a sort of compass-rock in my life'.[6] One of the reasons for EVELYN WAUGH not being sent to a prep boarding school was 'my evident happiness at Heath Mount (a local day school) and my mother's pleasure in my company'.[7] He described his life in the house Underhill at Hampstead from the age of four, where he remained at home till close on thirteen, as one of blissful happiness,[8] and so did his brother ALEC who went away to school.

H. V. MORTON, at forty-one, often watched children in the early teens and wondered if the world to them was as 'exquisite' as it had been to him, and if they could claim as many 'lovely dreams' as those which had once been his:

. . . the only completely magic age in life is between the ages of ten and

1 David Cecil: *Max* (1964), p. 25.
2 *Ibid.*, p. 28.
3 *A Little Learning: The First Volume of an Autobiography* (1964), p. 107.
4 *Sowing* (1960), p. 31.
5 *Son of Oscar Wilde* (1954), p. 35.
6 *Diaries & Letters 1930–39* ed. Nigel Nicolson (1966), p. 347.
7 *Op. cit.*, p. 87.
8 Twice, in the *Face to Face* interview with John Freeman (June 1960), he used the word 'idyllic'.

fourteen, a time when the senses are vividly aware of beauty yet unawakened to evil.[1]

It is Wordsworth; but Morton's upper limit seems sadly high today. He hints at it often, out of his experience:

There is a state of mind for which there is, as far as I know, no name. . . . The only words I can think of are . . . 'well-being' and . . . 'love'. Everyone can, I hope, remember a time in childhood when this state of mind lasted not for seconds but for days and weeks on end.[2]

When DYLAN THOMAS wrote of his childhood, it was always to him a state of innocence and grace.

Even a surfeit of happiness may be noted. LAMB's family were poor and overcrowded, but as youngest of seven he enjoyed virtually *three* mothers: his own, his Aunt Hetty – 'She often used to say that I was the only thing . . . she loved'[3] – and his elder sister Mary. T. S. ELIOT enjoyed, in addition to his mother, the loving protection of his four elder sisters, particularly Ada whose role towards him was almost maternal. He told Ezra Pound there had been only two happy periods in his life: during childhood and from the time of his second marriage.

A surfeit has pitfalls. DODGSON reverted constantly to his happy childhood spent with ten brothers and sisters. His mother's death the year he went to Christ Church, has been thought to have arrested him emotionally so that he looked back to that time.

1 *In Scotland Again* (1933), p. 143.
2 *In the Steps of the Master* (1934), p. 205.
3 'My Relations', *Elia* (1823), p. 160.

CHAPTER TWO

Orphans who were Compensated

I

Our age of psychology puts a premium on children being secure and loved. A significant proportion of writers were orphaned,[1] but it did not always mean deprivation. Though GEORGE HERBERT's father died when the boy was three, we are told he had 'sweet content under the eye and care of his prudent mother'.[2]

GIBBON's mother died when he was ten, but she had neglected him and after her death he was almost entirely in the care of her sister Catherine Porten, 'the mother of his mind'.[3] CECIL DAY LEWIS was four when his mother died, but her sister 'Knos' devoted herself to him – another case of literature being in the debt of a maternal aunt.

From the age of four, EDWARD LEAR, a twentieth child, was brought up by his eldest sister Ann. The family had split up on account of his father's imprisonment for fraud and debt, but even when it came together again and Lear lived in the same house as his mother, she had nothing more to do with him. Ann loved him deeply.

Ever all she was to me was good: – & what I should have been unless she had been my mother I dare not think.[4]

Between the ages of seven and eleven, EDMUND GOSSE led a pressurized life with his widowed father, who was not only the eminent naturalist but also an extreme Calvinist, a 'Brethren'. Fifty years on, he wrote:

I do not doubt that he felt his responsibility to fill as far as might be the gap which the death of my Mother had made in my existence.[5]

1 See Appendix C.
2 Izaak Walton: *The Life of Mr George Herbert* (1670), p. 17.
3 Letter to Lord Shenfield on her death, 1786.
4 Diary, Jan. 17, 1865. Vivien Noakes: *Edward Lear: The Life of a Wanderer* (1968), p. 184.
5 *Father & Son: A Study of Two Temperaments* (1907), p. 92.

He describes his father, prevented by twilight from peering with advantage into his microscope, beckoning him silently and folding him in his arms. So they would stay, 'without a word or movement, until the darkness filled the room'.

And then, with my little hand in his, we would walk sedately downstairs to the parlour, where we would find that the lamp was lighted. I do not think that at any part of our lives my Father and I were drawn so close to one another as we were in that summer of 1857.[1]

Of summer evenings, after he had taken the initiative by 'stamping in playful impatience' and fetching his father's hat and stick, 'we used to sally forth . . . together, hand in hand' among the squares and terraces, or by the Regent's Canal.

These were happy hours . . . when my Father forgot the Apocalypse . . . and our bass and treble voices used to ring out together over some foolish little jest. . . .[2]

When Edmund was eight, they moved from 'the motherless Islington house' to a 'villa' on the South Devon coast, but their walks were not the same. His father 'would stalk on, without a word, buried in angry reverie'. At this time of ferment over the challenge to the Biblical account of creation by the doctrine of natural selection, the fundamentalist 'after long reflection, prepared (in *Omphalos*) a theory of his own . . . that when the catastrophic act of creation took place, the world presented, instantly, the structural appearance of a planet on which life had long existed'.[3] But he who had been 'the spoiled darling of the public' saw his effort of reconciliation rejected. That painful winter father and son had long cosy talks together over the fire:

Our favourite subject was murders. . . . We tried other secular subjects, but we were sure to come round at last to 'what do you suppose they really did with the body?'[4]

His father had now become the self-elected minister of a 'little community of "Saints" in the village' and, when Edmund was ten, proclaimed the keeping of a solemn fast one weekday. There had been frequent 'backslidings' and the gentle congregation was reminded of 'the

1 *Ibid.*, p. 95.
2 *Ibid.*, pp. 96–97.
3 *Ibid.*, p. 120.
4 *Ibid.*, p. 127.

appalling fate of the church of Laodicea'. The father was strict in applying the fast to his own household, and the boy – thin as he was – had slices of dry bread and water three times in the day. He was taken in the dark to a prayer meeting before 'breakfast' and again at night.

During the morning . . . we sat, in a state of depression . . . in the breakfast-room, reading books of a devotional character. . . .[1]

When Edmund was eleven, his father called him over from his little bed in the corner to 'the ancestral four-poster'. He told him 'a new mamma was coming' and said, 'you must guess who she is'. When Edmund suggested the married woman who kept a sweet-shop, his father cut in: 'It is Miss Brightwen' – adding, 'she has been brought up . . . in the so-called Church of England'. It was the boy's turn to sit up 'in the coverlid' and shake a finger at him: 'Papa, don't tell me that she's a pedobaptist?' (a word he had lately acquired).[2] When the stepmother arrived, she became a great ally of the boy.

The separatist nature of the father's religion came to the fore when a local family of Baptists invited his son to 'tea and games', and 'my Father's conscience was so painfully perplexed that he desired . . . we might "lay the matter before the Lord"'. Side by side, father and son knelt before the horsehair sofa.

My Father prayed aloud, with great fervour. . . . It would have been more scrupulous, I thought, to give no sort of hint of the kind of answer he desired and expected.

Confident and beaming ('already, I believe, planning some little treat to make up to me for the material deprivation') he asked him what the Lord had 'vouchsafed'.

. . . my answer came, in the high-piping accents of despair: 'The Lord says I may go to the Browns.' My Father gazed at me in speechless horror . . . there was no road open for him but just sheer retreat. Yet surely it was an error in tactics to slam the door.[3]

II

SASSOON's father left them when Siegfried was five, and died when the boy was nine. *The Old Century* tells of an uninhibited childhood around

1 *Ibid.*, p. 225.
2 *Ibid.*, pp. 249–51.
3 *Ibid.*, pp. 282–3.

an intelligent and artistic mother. There were three sons, Siegfried in the middle, but 'we all behaved as if we were the same age'.[1] He describes the kindly people brought in 'to control the clamour'. There was 'Moony', a retired elementary schoolmaster, 'patient, methodical and unhurrying . . . just the sort of tutor we wanted'.[2] Above all, there was the young groom who took him to his first point-to-point. Later, a German governess came, and an ex-Hussar once a week to instruct in PE.

LEONARD WOOLF was eleven when his father died. He joined his brother at Arlington House, for the headmaster greatly reduced the fees and later did the same for the four younger brothers. Woolf was 'not unhappy' at his private school, but before then he and his elder brother had been tutored at home by Mr Floyd, 'a very humane and civilized man . . . one of those very rare people who never mind looking ridiculous'. Woolf's pet canary used to settle on Mr Floyd's head as he walked up and down teaching them. 'I am afraid, Sir, Chickabiddy has made a mess,' – and Mr Floyd very politely would wipe off the mess with blotting-paper. 'Thank you, my boy.'[3]

C. S. LEWIS lost his mother at nine.

I am a product of long corridors, empty sunlit rooms . . . attics explored in solitude, distant noises of gurgling cisterns and pipes.[4]

Their home at that time was the 'New House' that his father had built two years before. The motherless MASEFIELD had a similar experience when he was eight and the family moved to the Priory in Ledbury after his grandfather's death:

Often I thank God for letting me grow up in such a place . . . a very, very, old house, full of passages, corridors, strange rooms, strange noises. . . .[5]

LEWIS acknowledged the inestimable benefit of a childhood passed often alone in a house full of books. His other blessing was his elder brother Warren, when he came home on holiday from boarding school.

. . . we were allies, not to say confederates, from the first.[6]

1 *The Old Century and seven more years* (1938), p. 15.
2 *Ibid.*, p. 58.
3 *Sowing* (1960), pp. 63–64.
4 *Surprised by Joy: The shape of my early life* (1955), p. 17.
5 Constance Babington Smith: *John Masefield: A Life* (1978), p. 10.
6 *Op. cit.*, p. 13.

After his mother's death, three-year-old RONALD KNOX was sent with an older brother Wilfred to Uncle Lindsey, the vicar of Edmundthorpe. Penelope Fitzgerald compared her great uncle with Mr Dick in having definite ideas how to treat a small boy: 'Amuse it; wash it; feed it.' The two brothers spent four happy years, and their sister Winifred believed the experience led to their growing up 'in absolute dependence on each other'.[1] E. M. FORSTER was only an infant when he lost his father. He was brought up by his mother in 'a haze' of six elderly ladies, all relations, who coddled him for they feared erroneously he had inherited his father's consumption. Two aunts, both religious, were important in the upbringing of CHRISTOPHER FRY who lost his father at three. One of them read Bunyan to him and inspired a love of literature.

STEPHEN SPENDER was twelve on his mother's death, and five years later when his father died his grandmother decided the children should have a companion apart from their devoted maids, and wrote to Caroline Alington.

She was perhaps the first person we had known who treated us as reasonable human beings and who did not act towards us in order to carry out the supposed wishes of my father, or my mother, or my grandmother. . . . My sister and I simply fell in love with her.[2]

1 Penelope Fitzgerald: *The Knox Brothers* (1977), pp. 38–40.
2 *World Within World* (1951), p. 27.

CHAPTER THREE
Orphans who Suffered

I

There is plenty of the suffering we would expect. JOHN MASE-FIELD's mother died when he was six and a half, and his father when he was twelve. He called his Aunt Kate, who together with her husband became guardians of the six children, 'a repulsive hag'. She intended to toughen him at thirteen by sending him to train on an old wooden hulk, the *Conway*. At fifteen he sailed as an apprentice on a four-master, the *Gilcruix*, and rounded the Horn having just celebrated his sixteenth birthday. For thirty-two days the seas were forty feet high and everywhere ice. After four months from sailing, he was discharged at Iquique suffering from a nervous breakdown, only to be taunted by his aunt that he had 'failed to stick it'.[1] She insisted he went back.

VYVYAN HOLLAND was eleven when his Spiritual Father at the Jesuit school in Monaco broke the news of the death of his mother. He was told by the Rector of Stonyhurst, shortly after his fourteenth birthday, about the death of his father who 'wrote beautiful stories'.[2] He speaks of seeing his guardian who was allocated to him and his brother when they returned to England, 'three times during the six years that he had charge of me, and he never visited me once'.[3] At the end of a year at the prep school attached to Stonyhurst, he won three prizes and informed his guardian but received no reply.

... I knew how proud my mother and how pleased my father would have been.[4]

1 Constance Babington Smith: *John Masefield: A Life* (1978), p. 31.
2 *Son of Oscar Wilde* (1964), p. 151.
3 *Ibid.*, p. 163.
4 *Ibid.*, pp. 149–50.

Seven-year-old EDMUND GOSSE was his mother's 'sole and ceaseless companion'[1] for nearly three months during her terminal illness, while his father supported them by his books and lectures. Nine-year-old ALFRED EDWARD HOUSMAN for nearly three years breathed the same 'atmosphere of pain'. As his mother's condition deteriorated she became more reluctant to let Alfred leave her side – but that was where he wanted to be: writing letters on her behalf and praying together for her recovery. She seemed to see him more mature than he actually was, and she opened her heart (like the bereaved Margaret Ogilvy to Barrie) of girlhood memories. At last he was sent away to the home of his godmother, and on his twelfth birthday a letter came from his father telling him his mother was dead. The boy was unable to reconcile that she had died in spite of his prayers, and at the age of thirteen he gave up Christianity although not a belief in God. He began to preserve every written record concerning her. His sister Kate wrote that from this time 'he was sensitive and easily wounded, but wounds he bore in silence'.[2]

KENNETH GRAHAME lost his mother when he was five, and the coocooned father, like Housman's, drank more heavily, unable to cope. The four children were sent to their maternal grandmother who treated them as in *The Golden Age*, 'with kindness enough as to the needs of the flesh, but after that with indifference'.[3] They lived at The Mount in Cooke Dene, Berkshire, where compensation lay in its several acres:

... the orchard (a place elf-haunted, wonderful!) ... fir-wood ... hazel-copse. ... The mysterious sources ... that fed the duck-pond ... the meadow beyond the orchard. ...[4]

After two years there was a move to Fernhill Cottage, Cranbourne, and shortly after that some unsatisfactory months with their father, before he went abroad for twenty years. There was then no more communication between him and the children.

MAUGHAM lost his mother when he was eight – 'a wound that fifty years have not entirely healed'.[5] Shortly before she died of TB, she had herself dressed in an evening gown of white satin and went to the

---

1 Edmund Gosse: *Father & Son: A Study of Two Temperaments* (1907), p. 65.
2 Richard Percival Graves: *A. E. Housman: The Scholar-Poet* (1979), p. 17.
3 *The Golden Age* (1895), p. 1.
4 *Ibid.*, p. 3.
5 *The Summing Up* (1938), p. 316.

photographer – 'so that people would know what she was like'.[1] He kept the photo by his bed all his life. When his father died also, ten-year-old William was brought to England by a French maid who was promptly shipped back to France by his uncle, severing the only link with the life he knew. He admitted it must have been a great nuisance for a childless cleric of fifty to have had a small boy thrust upon him, but he called his uncle 'incredibly idle' and 'a selfish man who cared for nothing but his own comfort'.[2]

ALDOUS HUXLEY's mother had founded Prior's Field School for girls, and forty of the older ones were at her funeral. Her husband and three boys were there, fourteen-year-old Aldous shaking with sobs, for according to Julian, he had loved her even more 'passionately' than his brothers. Sybille Bedford writes:

> Her early influence went very deep; as did her loss; both are keys to his character and development. He very rarely brought himself to speak of her.[3]

VIRGINIA WOOLF was thirteen when her mother died. She suffered a major breakdown during which she heard 'voices' and her pulse raced.

II

SWIFT's father died suddenly, leaving wife, baby daughter and unborn son to the care of his brothers. Although Jonathan's education was not neglected, he did not know the security of a settled home. FIELDING's mother died when he was ten, and a stepmother came on the scene two years later. A result of their disturbed household was Henry being sent to Eton.

J. K. JEROME was twelve when he lost his father. He left school at fourteen to become a railway clerk at Euston, and at sixteen was alone in the house when his mother died. The following two or three years were lonely.

> In the day time I could forget it, but when twilight came it would creep up behind me. . . .[4]

1 *Ibid.*, p. 18.
2 *Ibid.*, p. 252.
3 *Aldous Huxley: A Biography* (1973–4), i, p. 7.
4 *My Life and Times* (1925), p. 45.

Poverty increased his shyness at accepting invitations. He spent one Christmas travelling to Liverpool on one of his free passes, and taking a slow train that did not arrive back till past ten. He dined in a coffee shop near the Docks, and at the only other table occupied a man and woman talked in whispers. Next day he read of a murder in Yorkshire and the arrest of a man and woman in Liverpool.

THOMAS ROHAN's mother died when he was an infant, and his father neglected him. There was 'a dreadful era' when he fetched beer for 'very coarse and brutal men' in an engineering works under railway arches in London.[1] One day on his way fishing, he inquired about an old English drinking-glass behind the dusty window of a marine store dealer in Deptford.

'What the hell do you want a glass for?.... The price is a bob but because you've got such a damned cheek, you shall have it for a tanner.'[2]

It was the first item in his collection and a good one.

J. B. PRIESTLEY never knew his own mother who died just after he was born. It always seemed that someone very important was missing. A little later in his childhood, he had a 'kind and gentle stepmother', but the man was left a legacy of apprehension as a result of that first experience. In his eighties, he admitted his public image had been false and that secretly he was unsure of himself.

... I am always surprised when I am told that somebody likes me.[3]

STEVENSON's parents were wrapped in one another, and in a letter to Mrs Sitwell he made the interesting observation: 'The children of lovers are orphans.' Louis's experience was less detrimental than that of another delicate boy, THOMAS GRAY, anxiety-wracked from his father's violence to his mother.

1 *Confessions of a Dealer* (1924), p. 9.
2 *Ibid.*, pp. 11–12.
3 *Instead of the Trees: A Final Chapter of Autobiography* (1977), p. 87.

CHAPTER FOUR
Fathers who were Positive

I

In spite of the love between GALSWORTHY and his mother, they were 'never really close' and if they talked 'a kind of irritation would begin in me . . . at the closed door I perceived in her mind'. Her many duties, with a large indoor and outdoor staff, circumscribed her. In a Note four years after her death, which he did not publish, he wrote:

My father really predominated in me from the start. . . . I was so truly and deeply fond of him that I seemed not to have a fair share of love left to give my mother.[1]

Twice he mentions his mother's lack of 'speculation' – very different from Old Jolyon for whom his father was the prototype, and who was nearly fifty when his eldest son was born. JOHN MORTIMER speaks of 'the umbilical cord with my father', severed in mature life when he ceased to practise law in the chambers where his father had worked, and where they had worked side-by-side.

COLERIDGE described his father as 'a perfect Parson Adams', who used to set the little boy on his knee and hold long conversations. His death when Coleridge was seven was traumatic. DICKENS's father set his small son on a table to sing or recite. On one of their long country walks when the father used to entertain the boy with stories, Charles told him he would like to own the mansion on Gad's Hill. Long after he discovered that the larger-than-life figure was flawed, Dickens put some of him in Mr Micawber and perhaps Mr Dorrit, both sympathetic characters, while some of his mother seems to have gone into the totally unsympathetic Mrs Nickleby.

CHESTERTON's father seemed the Man with the Golden Key:

1 H. V. Marrot: *The Life & Letters of John Galsworthy* (1935), p. 58.

79

His den or study was piled high with the stratified layers of about ten or twelve creative amusements; water-colour painting and modelling and photography and stained glass and fretwork and magic lanterns and mediaeval illumination ... and there was no incongruity in calling his lantern a magic-lantern.[1]

He 'knew all his English literature backwards'.[2] He made a toy theatre for the children, which he scene-painted and scene-shifted, and for which he wrote and made characters. WILLIAM GOLDING spoke of his father who taught at Marlborough Grammar School:

I have never met anybody who could do so much, was interested in so much, and who knew so much.

DARWIN, who lost his mother at eight, was inordinately fond of his father and spoke of him as 'the wisest man I knew'. MICHAEL SADLEIR, who wrote his father's biography, called him 'my best and wisest friend'.

As a child, A. A. MILNE gave his heart to his father:

If he were there, all was well; if he were away, I asked Mama when he was coming back.... He was the best man I have ever known: by which I mean the most truly good....[3]

After the approach of puberty when (like Dickens) he saw his father as unwittingly fallible, from that time his mother seemed more comfortable to be with.

But still, you had me until I was twelve, Papa, and if there was anything which you ever liked in me or of which you came to be proud, it was yours.[4]

MALCOLM MUGGERIDGE remembers with tenderness that his father 'never had an engagement important enough to stop him from being with me on any special occasion'.[5] At weekends and on Bank holidays the father took his sons bicycling or for country walks. Every weekday the young Malcolm would be at the front gate to accompany him to Croydon East, and in the evening be at the station as his father came up the ramp – 'a small bearded man striding along vigorously':

In those days he was everything to me; the centre of my universe.[6]

1 *Autobiography* (1936), p. 41.
2 *Ibid.*, p. 15.
3 *Autobiography* (US ed. of *It's Too Late Now*, 1939), pp. 38, 40.
4 *Ibid.*, p. 107.
5 *The Chronicles of Wasted Time* (1972–3), i, p. 92.
6 'A Socialist Childhood', BBC 1, Oct. 13, 1966, directed by Kevin Billington.

For some years his father was the only Labour councillor sitting in Croydon Town Hall (in his sixties he was member for Romford). On a Saturday evening, ten-year-old Malcolm would stand before his father's rickety platform at the top of Surrey Street, anticipate his jokes, and join in 'The Red Flag'.

We licked down envelopes almost in our prams; *Vote for Muggeridge* were almost the first three words we learnt. . . . We wore red rosettes. . . . Elections were for us like saints' days or festivals.[1]

STEPHEN SPENDER's father canvassed unsuccessfully as the Liberal candidate for Bath. He sent his sons, fourteen and thirteen, round the streets in a donkey cart, the donkey with a placard in front *Vote for Daddy*. But theirs was no total involvement; they had come up from London – their father at the railway station exclaiming to those around: 'I have brought up my reserves!'[2]

A. J. P. TAYLOR's father was 'a romancer who couldn't make the simplest journey without extraordinary things happening to him, none of them true'.[3] He bathed his small son every night that he could get home in time. When skin formed on the little boy's cocoa, his father scooped it off between finger and thumb and swallowed it. When the little boy shouted 'Worms, Daddy!' over the banisters, he was the one who dealt with them, scraping them out with his finger-nail. The mother was indifferent to the boy, isolated by his intellect even when small. Like Swift and A. A. Milne, A. J. P. Taylor could read at three. Once, when his mother threatened to spank him, his father stood between them and said: 'If you lay hands on that child I'll never speak to you again.'[4]

H. E. BATES's father, together with his grandfather, were the 'great formative influence' on his life.

To the first I owe my literacy and love of music. . . .[5]

His mother – 'excellent mother though she was, exerted no such influence on me'.[6]

During his son's childhood STEVENSON's father was dominant

1 *The Chronicles of Wasted Time* (1972–3), i, pp. 51–52.
2 *World Within World* (1951), p. 7.
3 Interviewed by David Gillard: *The Daily Mail*, Jan. 15, 1977.
4 *A Personal History* (1983), p. 8.
5 *The Vanished World: An Autobiography* i (1969), p. 27.
6 *The Blossoming World: An Autobiography* ii (1971), p. 93.

because at that time of her life the mother was often ill. The father tolerated his son's truancies from school. Their serious differences began in student days over religion and future profession, the bohemian clothes, the black shirt – and Velvet Coat, 'the name I went by'. Not until Stevenson was in California could he write:

Since I have gone away, I have found out for the first time how I love that man; he is dearer to me than all, except Fanny.

Balfour records of the later Bournemouth days:

As the old man's powers began to fail, he would speak to Louis as though he were still a child. When they went to the theatre together, and Louis stood up in his place, the father put his arm round him, saying: 'Take care, my dearie, you might fall.' At night, as he kissed his son, he would say reassuringly: 'You'll see me in the morning, dearie.'[1]

II

Where the father takes over education, the dominance is assured. At Wem in Shropshire, his father in charge of a small Unitarian community, nine-year-old HAZLITT became his pupil and increasingly, his intellectual companion.

From a tiny child J. S. MILL spent much time in his father's study, and was taken with him before breakfast on his walks.

To the best of my remembrance, this was a voluntary rather than a prescribed exercise.[2]

Along the then country lanes when they lived at Newington Green, John, between the ages of four and seven, would tell his father what he had read in Gibbon, Robertson, Hume or his favourite books, Watson's *Philip II* and *Philip III*. From the age of seven he was set to teach the younger children in the family, and he was only eight when Francis Place, staying at Ford Abbey, observed they were kept at their lessons from 6.0–9.0 a.m., and again from 10.0 a.m.–1.0 p.m. Once, because the sisters had made a single mistake not picked up by John, their dinner hour was postponed from midday until evening.

At the age of eight he began both Latin and Greek, and during the

1 Graham Balfour: *The Life of Robert Louis Stevenson* (1901), ii, p. 17.
2 *Autobiography* (1873), p. 7.

next four years read all the classical authors commonly studied in schools and universities. About twelve years old he got down to Logic, studying Aristotle's *Organon*, as well as the *Computatio sive Logica* of Hobbes. At thirteen, he was taken through a complete course of political economy. His father now made him summarize the points handed down during their walks, and these notes were used in the father's own writing of *Elements &c*. At this point, 'what can properly be called my lessons ended'. At about fourteen he went to France, studying chemistry and botany, tackling advanced mathematical problems, making notes on the country and mastering the language. His childhood could not be described as unhappy, although he calls his father 'a stern and impatient teacher'.

The father of the KNOX brothers, a strongly evangelical clergyman, expected his sons to memorise a chapter of the Bible every day. There is an echo of J. S. Mill, for RONALD was reading Virgil at six, which is two years earlier. Until she reached sixteen DOROTHY L. SAYERS was coached by her father, a classical scholar and fine musician. When she also was six, he came into the study carrying Dr William Smith's *Principia*: 'I think, my dear, that you are now old enough to learn Latin.'[1]

TENNYSON's father removed him from the brutal grammar school at Louth when he was twelve. After a short period in a village school, there followed a long period of instruction from his father, a Hebrew and Syriac scholar who perfected himself in Greek in order to teach his sons. Harold Nicolson wrote:

... it was undoubtedly his father's scholarship, his father's library, which gave to Alfred that wide general culture ... which would not have come to him with the same breadth through the more precise curriculum of a private or public school.[2]

When BROWNING was small, his father used to pile up chairs in the drawing-room and call them the city of Troy. Chesterton argued that Browning came out of his home crammed with knowledge yet ignorant of one thing – that to be so learned was exceptional:

He had no reason to suppose that every one did not join in so admirable a game.[3]

1 Janet Hitchman: *Such a Strange Lady: An Introduction to Dorothy L. Sayers (1893–1957)* (1975), p. 24.
2 *Tennyson: Aspects of his Life, Character & Poetry* (1923), p. 39.
3 *Robert Browning* (1903), p. 13.

Rather surprisingly, GOSSE's father showed originality in teaching geography. Starting from the age of three, Edmund 'was to climb upon a chair, while, standing at my side, with a pencil and a sheet of paper, he was to draw a chart of the markings on the carpet':

> Then, when I understood the system, another chart on a similar scale of the furniture in the room, then of a floor of the house, then of the back-garden, then of a section of the street.[1]

A. A. MILNE's father ran his own school, Henley House at Kilburn (to which a young Wells came as their first science master), and later Streete Court, Westgate-on-Sea.

> If I disliked French, and thought mathematics grand, it was because he, who could teach, taught me mathematics, and did not teach me French.[2]

Before going to Rugby, R. G. COLLINGWOOD was educated by his father who had been Ruskin's secretary. VIRGINIA WOOLF was taught by her illustrious father.

According to his brother, C. S. LEWIS at fifteen was inhibited from returning the hospitality of his friend, Arthur Greeves, because their father would have monopolized two frustrated youths by reading to them at length from Macaulay and Burke. The widowed father seemed unable to give the affection that Lewis later found in a surrogate mother Mrs Moore, the mother of 'Paddy', his room-mate at Keble who was killed. Yet he responded imaginatively when he took the desperately unhappy boy away from Marlborough. For over six years he supported Lewis at Oxford, enabling him 'to hang on' till his election to a Fellowship at Magdalen, for which Lewis thanked him 'from the bottom of my heart'.

1 *Father & Son: A Study of Two Temperaments* (1907), p. 22-23.
2 *Autobiography* (U.S. ed. of *It's Too Late Now*, 1939), p. 60.

CHAPTER FIVE

Mothers who Played a Leading Role

I

RUSKIN's father yielded 'to my mother in large things . . . taking his own way in little ones. . . .'[1] The boy was taught by his mother until, at fourteen, he was 'sent as a day scholar to the private school kept by the Rev. Thomas Dale in Grove Lane'.[2] His father 'never ventured to help, much less to cross her, in the conduct of my education'.[3]

My mother never gave me more to learn than she knew I could easily get learnt, if I set myself honestly to work, by twelve o'clock. She never allowed anything to disturb me when my task was set; if it was not said rightly by twelve o'clock, I was kept in till I knew it, and in general, even when Latin Grammar came to supplement the Psalms, I was my own master for at least an hour before half-past one dinner, and for the rest of the afternoon.[4]

He attributed his literary style to 'a course of Bible work' his mother began with him as soon as he could read with fluency, and which continued until he went to Oxford:

She read alternate verses with me, watching, at first, every intonation of my voice, and correcting the false ones, till she made me understand the verse.[5]

ANNA SEWELL was taught by her mother until the age of twelve, when she attended a day school in Stoke Newington. Lady Chitty speaks of Mary Sewell establishing 'a massive ascendancy over her daughter in the schoolroom'. This excessive attachment lasted for life, and her 'Jewel' or 'Darling' seems to have become the substitute for an emotional lack in the mother's marriage.[6] EVELYN WAUGH spoke

1 *Praeterita* (1886–8), i, p. 23.
2 *Ibid.*, i, p. 131.
3 *Ibid.*, i, p. 46.
4 *Ibid.*, i, p. 45.
5 *Ibid.*, i, p. 53.
6 *The Woman Who Wrote 'Black Beauty': A Life of Anna Sewell* (1971), p. 113.

of his mother teaching him very well until he went to prep school.

BARRIE's mother cared for her ten children while his father supported them at his loom and employed a few weavers in the cottage next door. She had an obsessive love for David, her second son, and when, on the eve of his fourteenth birthday, he died from an accident at skating, she was overwhelmed. An elder sister told her six-year-old brother to remind their mother she had another son. In the dark he heard a listless voice: 'Is that you?'

I said in a little lonely voice, 'No, it's no him, it's just me.' Then I heard a cry, and . . . I knew that she was holding out her arms.[1]

After that he tried to play physician by getting her to laugh.

I kept a record of her laughs on a piece of paper, a stroke for each, and it was my custom to show this . . . to the doctor. . . . There were five strokes the first time I slipped it into his hand, and when their meaning was explained . . . he laughed so boisterously that I cried, 'I wish that was one of hers!'[2]

The doctor suggested that if he showed her the paper he might win another laugh. One terrible day he put on David's clothes, went into his mother's room, and gave a rendering of his brother's special whistle which he had learnt from the dead boy's friends. Gradually the mother found some relief by telling him stories about her own childhood, when she had 'played about the Auld Licht manse', and which one day he would use. They read many books together when he was a boy, *Robinson Crusoe* being the first. *The Arabian Nights* they got from the library (a penny for three days), 'but on discovering . . . they were nights when we had paid for knights we sent that volume packing. . . .'[3]

Barrie wrote *Margaret Ogilvy* when she died, and 'sat weeping as he wrote it'. 'It is the story,' wrote Denis Mackail, 'of how a mark was set on a child's soul, as well as of the beginning of twenty-eight years of incessant and unalterable devotion.'[4] At the end he 'had not made her forget'; David 'was not removed one day farther from her'.[5] Andrew Birkin suggests that David, the boy who in dying 'would remain a boy

1 *Margaret Ogilvy by Her Son* (1896), pp. 12–13.
2 *Ibid.*, p. 14.
3 *Ibid.*, p. 46.
4 *The Story of J.M.B.: a biography* (1941), p. 23.
5 *Margaret Ogilvy*, p. 18.

for ever', was the prototype for Barrie's masterpiece – long before 'the spark' he got from the Llewelyn Davies boys.[1]

When LYTTON STRACHEY was an infant, his mother was still in her early forties while his father approached seventy. She encouraged her children to write a lot of poetry, making it fun for them and binding up their best efforts in a family book. She educated them when small, especially by reading aloud. She selected their schools and, in Lytton's case, his university. Although Sir Richard took his ecstatic son, at eleven, to the Royal Naval Exhibition, and to the Crystal Palace, he remained a remote presence. Lady Strachey signed herself 'ever darling, your loving Mama' even when Lytton was a grown man.[2] It seems incredible that married at nineteen, bearing thirteen children and actively participating in their future lives, she could have found time for anything else. Yet she was invited by Lord Bowen to sit beside him in the Court of Appeal and, before Lytton's birth, George Eliot had asked her to be a regular correspondent. Old and blind, sitting one summer evening under a tree in Gordon Square, she recited to the Woolfs the whole of Milton's *Lycidas* 'superbly', without stumbling over a word.[3] LEONARD WOOLF's mother encouraged her children 'from an early age to read "good" books, Scott, Dickens, Thackeray. . . .'[4]

E. M. FORSTER's childhood love-affair with a deeply possessive mother survived, like Barrie's, until the end of her long life. RATTIGAN's mother, in an unhappy marriage, turned to her younger son who sided with her against his father, a diplomat and cricket fanatic. Environmentalists may see in these an explanation of sexual make-up.[5]

D. H. LAWRENCE told Rachel Taylor that his parents' marriage had been 'one carnal, bloody fight'. He had been born hating his father:

. . . I shivered with horror when he touched me. . . . This has been a kind of bond between me and my mother. We have loved each other, almost with a husband and wife love, as well as filial and maternal. . . . It has been rather terrible and has made me, in some respects, abnormal.[6]

WILFRED OWEN was another who adored a possessive mother, for with his father he could share only a love of music.

1 *J. M. Barrie & the Lost Boys* (1979), p. 5.
2 Michael Holroyd: *Lytton Strachey: A Critical Biography* (1967–8), i, p. 17.
3 Leonard Woolf, *Sowing* (1960), p. 189.
4 *Ibid.*, p. 69.
5 Edward Lear and J. A. Symonds were brought up in predominantly female households.
6 Letter, Dec. 3, 1910.

WELLS's parents 'were doubtful of the healthiness of reading', yet his mother was responsible for the first step which led to his writing career. At sixteen, unable to bear its misery any longer, he had run away from his draper's apprenticeship in Southsea, and on no breakfast walked seventeen miles to waylay her as she, then housekeeper at Up Park, came from church. He obtained her consent to be a pupil teacher at Midhurst Grammar School, an offer made by the headmaster, who had coached him in Latin during his earlier employment when he helped in a chemist's shop.

A photo of ELIOT's father shows him seated in a chair, a protective hand pressing to him his ten-year-old son. The pose is a favourite Victorian one but, while in the frontispiece to *Father and Son* a younger Edmund Gosse stands with hands dutifully clasped, Eliot's rest relaxed each upon a paternal knee. In the Eliot story more is known about the relationship of the mother, who recognized the precociousness of their youngest child and nourished it. Perhaps the fact that the father had achieved important success in business, while she was more representative of the arts, brought her closer to him. Although both were in their forties when Eliot was born, his father was becoming deaf, and it is possible she was younger in heart. Her influence was implanted for life.

LAURIE LEE said this about his own. He was three when his father deserted his second wife and eight children from both marriages, sending them 'perhaps just enough, the few pounds'.[1] She brought them up 'out of love and pity . . . unreasoning loyalty and a fixed belief that he would one day return. . . .'[2] In a small Cotswold village, they rented a seventeenth-century cottage for three and sixpence a week ('but we were often six months behind'). It stood in a half-acre of roses at Slad. No mother – and she was 'a country girl, disordered, hysterical, loving . . . muddled and mischievous . . . a buffoon, extravagant and romantic'[3] – received a more wonderful tribute:

Nothing now that I ever see that has the edge of gold around it – the change of a season, a jewelled bird in a bush, the eyes of orchids, water in the evening,

1 *Cider with Rosie* (1959), p. 146.
2 *Ibid.*, p. 71.
3 *Ibid.*, pp. 145, 151.

a thistle, a picture, a poem – but my pleasure pays some brief duty to her . . .
I absorbed from birth, as now I know, the whole earth through her jaunty
spirit.[1]

BLAKE, as a boy, told his parents that coming along Peckham Rye
he had seen a tree filled with angels, their wings bespangling the
boughs like stars. When his father would have beaten him for telling
a lie, his mother's intercession saved him.

1 *Ibid.*, p. 152.

CHAPTER SIX

Unloving Mothers

A mong those who suffered an unhappy childhood, the key figure of mother usually falls short. Johnson, who knew RICHARD SAVAGE, accepted his claim that his mother was the Countess of Macclesfield who, unhappily married and to get a divorce, was prepared to say that Earl Rivers was the father of her child. On being given his custody she abandoned him to the care of a poor woman, and when Earl Rivers on his deathbed wanted to provide for him, she declared he was dead. Johnson comments:

... perhaps the first instance of a lie invented by a mother to deprive her son of a provision (£6,000) ... which she could not expect herself, though he should lose it.[1]

Not long afterwards she apprenticed him to a shoemaker in Holborn.

LAURENCE STERNE disliked his mother and idolized his father. DE QUINCEY was seven when his father died, and a despotic mother made him unhappy. BYRON had to endure the uneven temper of his mother. DICKENS wrote: 'I never afterwards forgot, I never shall forget, I never can forget that my mother was warm for my being sent back' – to Warren's Blacking Factory, at twelve, after he had been withdrawn owing to his father quarrelling with one of the partners. The warehouse was managed by a relative on his mother's side. Dickens told John Forster:

How much I suffered it is utterly beyond my power to tell.

A fortnight after Charles had started there, his father was arrested for £40 debt: the family moving into the Marshalsea, and their eldest boy lodging in Camden Town. On Sundays he called for his elder sister Fanny, a 'pupilage-border' at the Royal College of Music, and took her to spend the day at the prison. He now got his father's consent to

---

1 *The Lives of the English Poets; & a Criticism on Their Works* (Dublin ed. 1779–81), iii, p. 36.

move to Lant Street, and have his breakfast and supper at the Marshalsea. After about six or seven weeks of this arrangement, the paternal grandmother died and the debt was settled out of her savings. The father then provided for two years' tuition at Mr Jones's Classical and Commercial Academy in the Hampstead Road.

His mother's rejection caused LEAR to suffer from periods of depression which he called 'the Morbids'. The earliest of all the 'morbidnesses' he could remember happened when he was about seven, and his father had taken him to a rural circus near Highgate. It was such a fugitive happiness that the little boy cried 'half the night . . . suffering for days at the memory of the past scene'.[1] In middle-age, he wrote:

Considering all I remember to have passed through from 6 years old to 15 – is it not wonderful I am alive? – far more to be able to feel & write.[2]

When BEATRICE WEBB was four, a brother came on the scene, monopolized her mother, and died when Beatrice was seven. The coming of a younger sister a few months afterwards, completed the separation between Beatrice and her mother. 'Beatrice,' wrote her mother, 'is the only one of my children who is below the average in intelligence.'[3]

RADCLYFFE HALL's mother had tried to abort her. The parents were divorced when she was three, but quarrelling continued between mother and stepfather. Her mother's third marriage was to an Italian teacher of singing and, according to Una Troubridge, when Radclyffe was eleven, he gave away her much-loved pet canary to a waiter at a Belgian hotel on the ground that bird and cage were an 'encumbrance'.

Dame EDITH SITWELL described her beautiful young mother's 'wild fire' and her older father's 'queer intellectual coldness'. Neither afforded her any moral support – her father resented his first-born was female and plain. She had a pet peacock and used to walk in the grounds of Renishaw with her arm around its neck. Osbert arrived five years later, and was better accepted, but Sacheverell, the youngest, was favourite. Edith's sense of rejection was heightened in early adolescence by being made to wear her 'Bastille' – an orthopaedic brace and corset to correct curvature of the spine and weak ankles. At night she had to wear a facial brace to straighten her nose. Edith and Osbert were adults when their extravagant mother, her debts disowned by her

1 Vivien Noakes: *Edward Lear: The Life of a Wanderer* (1968), p. 19.
2 *Ibid.* (revised ed. 1979), p. 21.
3 Beatrice Webb: *My Apprenticeship* (1926), p. 11.

husband, landed up in Holloway with a three months' sentence. But seventeen-year-old SACHEVERELL was at Eton where he saw a headline in a newspaper. He was given special leave and journeyed north, utterly stunned. John Pearson comments that the immediate effect was to cement the trio into their 'closed corporation' (a phrase of Osbert's):

For years to come the only people they would trust entirely would be one another.[1]

T. E. LAWRENCE suffered from an evangelical mother who frequently beat him to break his will. Perhaps these earlier, more emotionally involved experiences – and not the Turkish assault disputed by Desmond Stewart – rendered him a masochist.

After a childhood of frequent beatings by an alcoholic mother, errands to 'the pawn' and fetching drink, CATHERINE COOKSON in her mid-twenties left Tyne Dock for the south, bearing the reproach of illegitimacy. Then, for the last three years of her mother's life she brought her home, and for the first time called her 'Mam'. Two days before she died, her mother held her in her arms and said, 'Lass, I've been a wicked woman' –

... and my tears washing away every hurt she had dealt me and the love that I had tried to bring back and supplement for the hate that I had borne her, gave me the power to say, 'You have never done a bad thing in your life.' And ... she really hadn't. ... It was my nervous, sensitive temperament that couldn't stand up against the rough background into which she bore me.[2]

---

1 *Façades: Edith, Osbert, & Sacheverell Sitwell* (1978), p. 97.
2 See *Our Kate* (1969), but the passage appeared in a revised paperback, and was not reprinted in later editions.

CHAPTER SEVEN

Importance of Other Relatives

I

Apart from coming to the rescue of orphaned nephews, nieces and grandchildren, other relatives are important in providing new scenes and experiences and even motivating, sometimes, future writers. SCOTT's imagination was quickened by stories of his Border ancestors, told him by his grandmother when he stayed at Sandy-Knowe after his grandfather's death. An uncle, who had witnessed the execution of 'one or two of our own distant relations', told him of the cruelties after Culloden – 'tales which made so great an impression on me'.

... I remember detesting the name of Cumberland with more than infant hatred.[1]

On leaving Edinburgh High School, Scott spent six months in the romantic village of Kelso with Aunt Jane, who 'was exceedingly attached to me'. After the four hours he was expected to attend the local grammar school, his time was his own and in her large garden stretching down to the Tweed he first read Bishop Percy's *Reliques of Ancient Poetry.*

I remember well the spot ... beneath a huge platanus-tree, in the ruins of ... an old-fashioned arbour. ... The summer day sped onward so fast, that notwithstanding the sharp appetite of thirteen, I forgot the hour of dinner, was sought for with anxiety. ... To read and to remember was in this instance the same thing, and henceforth I overwhelmed my schoolfellows, and all who would hearken to me, with tragical recitations from the ballads of Bishop Percy. ...

To this period he traced 'the love of natural beauty, more especially

---

1 John Lockhart: *Memoirs of the Life of Sir Walter Scott, Bart.* (1837–8), i, p. 18.

when combined with ancient ruins, or remains of our fathers' piety or splendour', which 'became with me an insatiable passion'.[1]

With his library and republican sympathies (he had offered to pay part of Leigh Hunt's fine), SWINBURNE's paternal grandfather, the 6th Baronet, had a powerful influence upon him. His childhood was partly spent on his grandfather's estate in Northumberland where its rocky coast helped to motivate his passion for the sea.

The KEATS children and their mother went to live with the maternal grandmother, Mrs Jennings, following the father's fatal fall from a horse. After six years, when Keats was fifteen, his mother died. His grandmother appointed guardians, and made over a sum of about £8,000 to be held in trust until the three boys came of age. But on her death, owing to legal flaws, these good intentions were 'Jarndyced' by Chancery, and Keats did not receive a penny. E. M. FORSTER was eight when his great aunt, Marianne Thornton, left him £8,000, which he later described as the 'salvation of my life'. It enabled him to go to Cambridge and to travel for two years.

Nine-year-old JOHN DRINKWATER went to live with his grandfather at Oxford – 'I remember my Mother's distress when I went away; it was the last time I saw her, she dying soon afterwards'. He lived with his grandfather five years until he died, 'and I never had a cross word from him'.[2]

I did not tell him of particular troubles, but to be with him was soothing. Also, he liked doing the things that I liked, and he talked to me about serious matters ... always in a way that interested me.[3]

The only deep affection that RADCLYFFE HALL experienced in childhood came from her maternal grandmother. At twenty-one, Radclyffe took her away from a bullying daughter and they shared a house in Kensington for several years. KATHERINE MANSFIELD became her maternal Granny's Kass and from birth was cared for by her, together with the other children, as Mrs Beauchamp 'didn't handle babies'. Katherine slept in beloved Granny Dyer's room. EDITH SITWELL, a difficult child on receipt of unmerited coldness, danced and sang hymns for the Sitwell grandmother who showed affection for 'poor little E.'. VERONICA WEDGWOOD put on record:

1 *Ibid.*, pp. 38–40.
2 *Inheritance: Being the First Book of an Autobiography* (1931), p. 16.
3 *Ibid.*, p. 29.

The love, wisdom and knowledge of my grandfather, Albert Henry Pawson, West Riding of Yorkshire, surrounded my childhood.

H. E. BATES was the son his grandfather had been denied. He described himself growing up in his 'maternal grandfather's pocket, bonded in a great warm mutual affection, neither of us able in the other's eyes to do the slightest wrong'.[1] His grandmother and aunt told his grandfather ' "you'd cut off your head and give it to him if he as much as asked for it" '.[2] To him he owed his 'love of Nature and the countryside' and, to father and grandfather, 'the faculty of thinking through the pores of my skin'.[3]

STEPHEN SPENDER wrote of the time his father died:

When I was fifteen I came under one of the most important influences of my life, that of my maternal grandmother. . . .

She took him to the theatre and 'we used to go to the art galleries and see modern paintings'.[4] She read the latest novels so that she would be able to discuss them.

When I was sixteen my attachment to my grandmother was so great that I count it as the earliest of those friendships through which I have at various times identified my own situation with that of another person. We discussed everything, including art, religion and sex.

Later he realised she may have 'drawn him out' to consult about him with his uncle. Mindful of the poor and generous towards them, she 'lived in some ways less comfortably than the poor'. When his family went to tea, she would pass the cakes saying: 'No, darling, take the one nearest to you. It's the stalest, and was put there on purpose.' Breakfasts and luncheons were punctuated by 'Eat that orange, darling, it's going bad.'[5]

Lady Mason, grandmother of RICHARD SAVAGE, caused him to be placed at a small grammar school near St Alban's. She may also have prevented his mother's scheme to send him into slavery on the American plantations.[6]

1 *The Vanished World: An Autobiography i* (1969), p. 8.
2 *Ibid.*, p. 20.
3 *The Blossoming World: An Autobiography ii* (1971), p. 93.
4 *World Within World* (1951), p. 10.
5 *Ibid.*, pp. 16–17.
6 Stanley V. Makower accepts such an attempt to remove him [*Richard Savage: A Mystery in Biography* (1909), p. 41]. Savage laid the blame on his mother (Preface to his *Miscellaneous Poems*, 2nd ed. 1728). Johnson reports Savage but also raises the possibility of Lady Mason persuading or compelling her to desist (*The Lives of the English Poets* (Dublin ed. 1779–81), iii, p. 37 – sic).

II

When CHARLOTTE BRONTË was six or seven, Miss Branwell, considerably past forty, left her Penzance climate and came to Haworth Parsonage to take charge of her dead sister's family. Aunt Elizabeth was with them twenty-one years until she died. After nine-year-old Charlotte and six-year-old Emily were taken away from the Clergy Daughters' School, she instructed them at regular hours, making her bedchamber into their schoolroom, five-year-old Anne joining them. Ellen Nussey, Charlotte's friend, remembered 'a very small antiquated little lady' who wore very large caps and always dressed in silk.

She amused us by clicking about in pattens whenever she had to go into the kitchen....[1]

When Charlotte was twenty-five and she and Emily were mooting their project of a school, their aunt offered to lend £100[2] – Charlotte had always considered her 'the last person' to do so.[3] Mrs Gaskell doubted if they ever loved her freely.

Through an uncle STEVENSON had a taste of authorship before he could read or write. The children of the family were told there would be an essay competition on the subject of Moses, and Louis dictated his history, probably to Cummie, illustrating the Israelites with pipes in their mouths. The prize went to an older cousin.

When the GRAHAME children were living with Granny Ingles, KENNETH and his elder brother Willie often stayed over Christmas with their uncle John Grahame, at his house in Sussex Gardens. He took them with his own children to the pantomime at Drury Lane, and gave his head clerk afternoons off to escort them to the Zoo and the Tower. Kenneth's elder sister Helen said that another uncle, the Rev. David Ingles, who had been appointed to the parish of Cookham Dene, 'made a good deal of us, taking us on the river and to see his friends at Bisham and elsewhere'.[4] Uncle David was probably the prototype for the Curate in *The Golden Age*. GALSWORTHY's sister Lilian received a shock

1 *The Shakespeare Head Brontë: Their Lives, Friendships & Correspondence* (1932), i, p. 111.
2 Charlotte's letter to Elizabeth Branwell, Sept. 29, 1841.
3 Charlotte's letter to Ellen Nussey, July 19, 1841.
4 Peter Green: *Kenneth Grahame: A Study of his Life, Work & Times* (1959), p. 23.

when she was shown the finished manuscript of *The Man of Property*, for she recognised 'a whole portrait-gallery of relatives'.[1]

THEODORE WATTS-DUNTON was influenced more by his Uncle James than by his own scientific father. James Orlando Watts was a profound student of drama – Greek, English, Spanish, German – and a very great admirer of Shelley. According to Dr Hake, Uncle James was the prototype of the hero's father in *Aylwin*.

Going back to his childhood days at Lorne Lodge, KIPLING always felt grateful to his uncle, Burne-Jones, and 'Auntie Georgie' for the month he spent each Christmas at The Grange, North End Road – the house in which Samuel Richardson wrote *Clarissa Harlowe*, *Pamela*, and *Sir Charles Grandison*. On arriving he 'would reach up to the open-work iron bell-pull on the wonderful gate that led me into all felicity'.

When I had a house of my own . . . I begged for, and was given that bell-pull for my entrance, in the hope that other children might also feel happy when they rang it.[2]

There was a garden of three-quarters of an acre, with fruit trees, leading into fields. At first he was escorted, but then he came by himself. His cousin Margaret remembered that he came in a reefer-coat with brass buttons, and carried a bursting carpet-bag. Auntie Georgie recorded that her children 'had with them their young cousin Rudyard Kipling, now beginning the Anglo-Indian child's experience of separation from his home'. William Morris ('Uncle Topsy') often appeared, discussing picture-frames or stained glass with Burne-Jones. One day, Margaret and Rudyard were 'in the nursery eating pork-dripping on brown bread' when Uncle Topsy surprised them, and climbed creakingly on a rocking-horse to tell a story – the *Saga of Burnt Njal*.

The enjoyment that Kipling and Burne-Jones had in each other's company was kept up in letters when Kipling as a young man returned to India. They used to try and fool each other by elaborately faking old drawings, manuscripts or curios.

STEPHEN POTTER remembered his Uncle Jim and other relatives with the childlike distortion which J. B. Priestley gave as the clue to understanding Dickens's treatment of important characters. Uncle Jim

1 H. V. Marrot, *The Life & Letters of John Galsworthy* (1935), p. 181.
2 *Something of Myself* (1937), p. 11.

lived with them 'permanently temporary' in the second floor back at 36 Nightingale Lane, Clapham Common.

... (for some reason I had always called him Jim, and for a joke they let me continue). ...[1]

Stephen identified him completely with the 'peculiar man' of the song that Jim used to whistle between his teeth when he was cheerful. The boy never saw him as a real person as his sister Muriel did, who had known a lively and different Jim before the tragic death of his wife. Another uncle, Josh, did not live in the house.

'Is Uncle Josh coming to dinner tonight, Mother?' How can I explain the thrill of pleasure if the answer was yes?[2]

There was the manliness of his nickname for Stephen: Step. Uncle Josh had been connected with the stage, and if he were with them at mealtime 'it was as if the foot-lights were turned on. ... It was an occasion.' Uncle Josh's admonitions were better received than loving parental advice.

'Look, Step, never have nails looking like that.' It all fitted in with the manliness, the general stage management, of Uncle Josh.[3]

On the North Carmarthenshire farm of his Aunt Ann Jones, DYLAN THOMAS spent his happy childhood holidays recorded in *Fern Hill*.

> In the sun that is young once only,
> Time let me play. ...
> All the sun long it was running, it was lovely ...
> ... and happy as the heart was long,
> In the sun born over and over,
> I ran my heedless ways. ...

---

1 *Steps to Immaturity* (1959), p. 70.
2 *Ibid.*, p. 93.
3 *Ibid.*, pp. 95, 98.

CHAPTER EIGHT

Nannies

Often the personal governess or nanny showed a deep and remarkable attachment – what Churchill called 'perhaps ... the only disinterested affection in the world',[1] – and then she was rewarded with a very special love. SWIFT's nurse was so fond of him she took the baby with her when she had to return to her family in Whitehaven. She taught him so well, at three he could read any part of the Bible. Then he was sent back to Dublin where Uncle Godwin took charge of the posthumous child.

It is said that STEVENSON's nurse, Alison Cunningham ('Cummie'), refused an offer of marriage so she might not have to leave him. She arrived when he was eighteen months old.

My recollection of the long nights when I was kept awake by coughing are only relieved by the thought of the tenderness of my nurse and second mother (for my first will not be jealous). . . . She was more patient than I can suppose of any angel; hours together she would help and console me. . . .[2]

'She stored his hospitable mind,' wrote Lord Guthrie, with Bible stories and Bunyan, tales of the Covenanters, 'and legends, in prose and verse, of pirates and smugglers, witches and fairies'.[3] BURNS 'owed much to an old Maid of my Mother's', who had, 'I suppose, the largest collection in the county of tales and songs concerning devils, ghosts, fairies, brownies, witches, warlocks, spunkies, kelpies, elf-candles, dead-lights, wraiths, apparitions, cantraips, giants, inchanted towers, dragons and other trumpery'. He declared:

This cultivated the latent seeds of Poesy. . . .[4]

When STEVENSON was thirty-five, he dedicated *A Child's Garden of Verses*: 'To Alison Cunningham, From Her Boy.'

1 *Savrola* (1900), p. 44.
2 Graham Balfour: *The Life of Robert Louis Stevenson* (1901), i, p. 35.
3 *Robert Louis Stevenson: Some Personal Recollections* (1924), p. 27.
4 Autobiographical Letter to Dr John Moore: Aug. 2, 1787.

Cummie, like Byron's May Gray and Betjeman's Maud, was a Calvinist with the difference that she loved him. His parents liked to play whist, and he remembered praying fervently with his nurse that it might not be visited on them. She described the last time she ever saw him, when he said to her before a room full of people:

'It's *you* that gave me a passion for the drama, Cummie.'
'Me, Master Lou,' I said; 'I never put foot inside a playhouse in my life.'
'Ay, woman,' said he; 'but it was the grand dramatic way ye had of reciting the hymns.'[1]

EVELYN WAUGH's 'adored deity' was 'quite young and, in my eyes, very beautiful'.

I think Lucy fully returned my love. She was never cross or neglectful.

A 'regular bible-reader', it grieved her too, that his mother played bridge and his father drank wine. When he was 'taken to the theatre during her régime ... she was markedly unresponsive to my excited descriptions of the event'.[2] ELIOT was 'greatly attached' to his own nurse Annie Dunne, a devout Catholic, who discussed with him when he was six the reasons for believing in God.

Mrs Everest ('Woomany' or 'poor old Woom') had the care of CHURCHILL from the time he was a few months old.

My mother ... shone for me like the Evening Star. I loved her dearly – but at a distance. My nurse was my confidante. ... It was to her I poured out my many troubles. ...[3]

The young subaltern was present as she lay dying – 'and I think my company made her die happy. ...' His jacket was wet, and when she felt it she was 'greatly alarmed' lest he should catch cold. It 'had to be taken off and thoroughly dried before she was calm again'.[4] He told his mother:

I shall never know such a friend again. ... I feel very low.[5]

He arranged her funeral, paid for her headstone, and for many years paid for the upkeep of her grave.

C. S. LEWIS wrote of his brother and Lizzie Endicott as 'two bless-

1 Graham Balfour: *The Life of Robert Louis Stevenson* (1901), i, pp. 36–37.
2 *A Little Learning: The First Volume of an Autobiography* (1964), pp. 29–30.
3 *My Early Life* (1930), p. 19.
4 *Ibid.*, p. 86.
5 Letter to Lady Randolph: July 3, 1895.

ings'. 'Even the exacting memory of childhood' could discover no flaw in Lizzie, their nurse – 'nothing but kindness, gaiety, and good sense'.[1] KENNETH CLARK regarded Lam, his new governess, 'as the first of several pieces of human good fortune which have befallen me in my life'. She came when he was seven, after his mother had heard a German predecessor yelling at him 'You horrid boy, you wicked boy!' while he was weeping.

At last I had someone whom I could love and depend on, and who seemed to share my own interests, even in trees and guinea-pigs.[2]

When his own children needed a governess, he invited her to return, and she remained at Saltwood about fifty years after she had first entered his life at Sudbourne. EDITH SITWELL, at sixteen, found a confidante for her poetry in Helen Rootham, the new governess who was a brilliant pianist. Osbert wrote of her:

She was the first person we had ever met who had an *artist's* respect for the arts. . . .[3]

CHRISTOPHER MILNE presumed he'd had nannies before he was eighteen months old, but the one who came then was 'the one I had been waiting for'.[4] He was the same age as Stevenson when Cummie came.

I was all hers and remained all hers until the age of nine. Other people hovered around the edges, but they meant little. My total loyalty was to her. . . . She was . . . a very good and very loving person; and when that has been said, no more need be added.[5]

They were so much together 'that Nanny became almost a part of me'. Even when his father bowled him a tennis ball in what they called the orchard, she stood at deep cover, and when he had his tonsils out in hospital, she accompanied him. She left when he went to boarding school, and 'Alfred' who had waited many years proved luckier than Cummie's suitor. But Christopher sensed a rival – 'Nanny, don't marry Alfred. Marry me.'[6]

Sir JOHN BETJEMAN's experience was less fortunate:

1 *Surprised by Joy: The shape of my early life* (1955), p. 13.
2 *Another Part of the Wood: A Self-Portrait* (1974), pp. 13–14.
3 *The Scarlet Tree* (1946), p. 145.
4 *The Enchanted Places* (1974), p. 20.
5 *Ibid.*, p. 31.
6 *Ibid.*, p. 33.

Maud was my hateful nurse who smelt of soap. . . .
She rubbed my face in messes I had made
And was the first to tell me about Hell,
Admitting she was going there herself.[1]

He described her to an interviewer as 'a real old tartar' and added:
'One of the worst things you can do to a child is to give him guilt. I
was given the guilt all right.'

BYRON's experience may have led to his subsequent sexual confusion.
He was nine when his nurse Agnes was replaced by her younger sister
May Gray, who 'used to come to bed to him and play tricks with his
person'. According to Hanson, whose 'honourable little companion'
had been unable to retain his feelings, 'she was perpetually beating
him, and that his bones sometimes ached from it'. Hanson went on to
tell Mrs Byron that 'she brought all sorts of Company of the very
lowest Description into his apartments'.[2]

---

1 *Summoned by Bells* (1960), p. 6.
2 *Letters & Journals of Lord Byron* ed. R. E. Prothero (1898–1901), i, p. 10 note.

CHAPTER NINE

Importance of Servants

I

Servants, like relatives, often came up trumps. BEATRICE WEBB
wrote:

I spent my childhood in a quite special way among domestic servants,
to whom as a class I have an undying gratitude.[1]

At the splendid Renishaw Hall the SITWELL parents often drove their
children for understanding and affection to servants. Dame EDITH
recalled her 'dear old nurse (Davis) and the butler'.

From the age of thirteen or fourteen, WELLS was 'allowed to take
refuge' at Up Park, Sussex, where his mother was housekeeper. He ran
a daily newspaper *The Up Park Alarmist* for staff and worked a miniature theatre in his mother's room. He acknowledged 'the place had a
great effect on me' and contrasted the 'vitality' downstairs with 'the
insignificant ebbing trickle of upstairs life'.[2]

RUSKIN singled out in his memories Anne, his father's maid and his
own:

. . . the one I practically and truly miss most next to father and mother . . .
from her girlhood to her old age, the entire ability of her life was given to
serving us.

She was in her element in a sick room. From the ages of fifteen
to seventy-two, she was occupied 'in doing other people's wills
instead of her own, and seeking other people's good instead of her
own'.[3]

When CHARLOTTE BRONTË was nine, Tabitha Aykroyd ('Tabby')
came to live as servant. Mrs Gaskell wrote:

1 *My Apprenticeship* (1926), p. 58.
2 *Experiment in Autobiography* (1934), i, p. 137.
3 *Praeterita* (1886–8), i, pp. 34–36.

Her words were far from flattery; but she would spare no deeds in the cause of those whom she kindly regarded. She ruled the children pretty sharply; and yet never grudged a little extra trouble to provide them with such small treats as came within her power.[1]

It was a tribute to what Tabby had done for them that when she was old and ailing, and the Aunt proposed she should leave the Parsonage and be nursed by her sister (with the Rev. Patrick Brontë supplying any necessary additions), there was silent rebellion among the girls:

Tabby had tended them in their childhood; they, and none other, should tend her in her infirmity and age.[2]

SASSOON described the role of Emily Eyles, nominally parlourmaid. When the three brothers, eight, nine and eleven, 'felt like sitting still in the evening, she used to read to us from our favourite books. . . .'

I remember with gratitude how hard she worked for us and how gaily she did it. Mending torn clothes, tying up cut fingers, cleaning out the parrot's cage, and helping to find the cricket ball when it was lost in the sweet-briar hedge – these were only a few of Emily's extra duties.[3]

Two maids who were sisters, Bertha and Ella, called 'compositely' Berthella, were with the SPENDERS for about fifteen years.

They were so completely part of the family that they did not care for holidays. To them we were 'home' and they made 'home' for us.

When Stephen had decided to be a painter, Ella was prepared to be his model for hours on end. Bertha, the dominating sister, was an intellectual woman who read Dickens, Hardy, Galsworthy, Wells and Bennett from his father's library, and listened to Beethoven's symphonies on the 'wireless'. They accompanied the children everywhere, and 'at a later time when we went out alone, they would sit up all night waiting for us. . . .'[4]

II

ANNA SEWELL's mother, like the Edgeworths whose books she bought, did not approve of servants in the nursery.

1 *The Life of Charlotte Brontë* (1857), i, p. 81.
2 *Ibid.*, i, p. 182.
3 *The Old Century and seven more years* (1938), pp. 61–62.
4 *World Within World* (1951), p. 23.

If children pass one hour in a day with servants, it will be in vain to attempt their education.[1]

Lord CLARK generalized on his own unhappy experience as an only child, when he would be left entirely with the servants and was given, in silence, uneatable food, 'although they themselves lived off the fat of the land'.

. . . the inhuman treatment of servants in England had created a hostility . . . a kind of formalised estrangement, that made any natural act of kindness impossible. The servants felt, in a confused way, that by taking it out on me they were getting back at their employers.

He remembered being given cheese 'so full of weevils that small pieces jumped about the plate'.[2]

Yet HALLAM TENNYSON recorded that the severest punishment his father ever gave him, 'though that was, it must be confessed, slight, was for some want of respect to one of our servants'.[3] The only time Frances remembered CHESTERTON punishing a child was when a small visitor spoke rudely to the maid. Told to apologise, she had retorted, 'What does it matter? She's only a servant.'

And Gilbert, rising in his rare wrath, sent her up to her bedroom. . . .[4]

BETJEMAN's 'sunlit weeks . . . were full of maids'.

Sarah, with orange wig and horsy teeth,
Was so bad-tempered that she scarcely spoke. . . .[5]

1 Richard & Maria Edgeworth: *Practical Education* (1798).
2 *Another Part of the Wood: A Self-Portrait* (1974), p. 12.
3 *Alfred Lord Tennyson: A Memoir by his Son* (1897), i, p. 370.
4 Maisie Ward: *Return to Chesterton* (1952), p. 98.
5 *Summoned by Bells* (1960), p. 6.

CHAPTER TEN

Victorian Cruelty or Insensibility

Privileged and educated Victorians could behave to children in a way which is difficult to understand. SAMUEL *Erewhon* BUTLER placarded his father in the largely autobiographical *The Way of All Flesh*:[1]

... as regards his father ... Ernest could remember no feeling but fear and shrinking. When Ernest was in his second year, Theobald ... began to teach him to read. He began to whip him two days after he had begun to teach him. 'It was painful,' as he said to Christina, but it was the only thing to do....

When Ernest is four, he is unable 'to sound a hard "c" or "k", and, instead of saying "Come," he said "Tum...."'

'I do say tum,' replied Ernest, meaning that he had said 'come'.
    Theobald was ... in a bad temper ... clergymen are seldom at their best on Sunday evening.... 'Now, Ernest, I will give you one more chance, and if you don't say "come", I shall know that you are self-willed and naughty.'
    The child saw well what was coming now, was frightened, and, of course, said 'tum' once more.
    'Very well, Ernest ... I have done my best to save you ...' and he lugged the little wretch, crying by anticipation, out of the room.

After the screams and the beating, Theobald returns to the drawing-room and rings to have the servants in to prayers, 'red-handed as he was'.

THACKERAY, having lost his father at four when in India, was brought to England at five, while his mother and stepfather stayed on for three more years. During his life he enjoyed sympathetic relations with them, yet the scars went deep. At thirty-eight he wrote, in a letter to Lady Eddisbury:

Indeed you do me no more than justice in saying that I have a kind heart

---

1 Published posthumously, 1903.

towards Mothers & children: I was so unhappy myself as a child that I don't think I have said a rough word to one twice in my life. . . .[1]

KIPLING was sent away from his parents at the same tender age. From five until eleven, together with his sister two years younger, he was in a foster-home, Lorne Lodge, in a suburb of Southsea. Mr and Mrs Holloway (Aunt Rosa and Uncle Harry) took in children whose parents were in India. For a shorter period, P. G. WODEHOUSE's mother placed her two boys and a girl in charge of a perfect stranger, a Miss Roper of Bath, and returned to Hong Kong. Another victim of Empire was SAKI, the son of a police officer in Burma (like Orwell), and brought up by maiden aunts in Devon.[2]

Lord Birkenhead[3] conjectures that KIPLING's mother preferred to answer an advertisement and entrust her children to strangers, rather than risk the danger of their growing too intimate with other relatives during the long absence. A surprising feature of the Kiplings' childhood is that not one of their aunts saw fit to visit them at Southsea; their grandmother did visit more than once when Rudyard was six. When he stayed with the Burne-Joneses each Christmas he seemed to them happy and well, and with that undeserved loyalty of children never confided his misery.

Also, badly-treated children have a clear notion of what they are likely to get if they betray the secrets of a prison-house before they are clear of it.[4]

In what he subsequently called the House of Desolation, the little boy was systematically beaten and humiliated to the point that he began to be blind and have delusions. Although his sister Trix did not receive the same treatment, neither of them cared to speak of the Southsea days – 'They hurt too much.'[5] Forty-three years later, when he inspected submarines at Southsea, his wife noted in her diary:

Rud takes me to see Lorne Lodge . . . where he was so misused and forlorn and desperately unhappy as a child, and talks of it all with horror.

He had been a late reader but at seven began to enjoy books, and loss of 'reading-time' became another punishment. When he was eleven, he

1 Aug. 18, 1849. *The Letters & Private Papers of William Makepeace Thackeray* ed. Gordon N. Ray (1945–6), ii, p. 574.
2 See 'The Lumber-Room': *The Complete Short Stories* (1930).
3 *Rudyard Kipling* (1978), p. 13.
4 *Something of Myself* (1937), p. 15.
5 Birkenhead, *op. cit.*, p. 27.

was shut away from Trix for two days because he was a 'moral leper'. She had been told to practise on the piano in the drawing-room for forty-five minutes and not move. She heard 'Aunty' storming at him in the little hall; looking out of the window she saw him going down the little garden to go to school – walking like an old man. A placard, made of strong cardboard and neatly printed by Harry, covered the whole of his back:

KIPLING
THE
LIAR

It is *David Copperfield* made flesh. She ran after him and tried to tear the placard but it was so thick she couldn't bend it and it was sewn with strong twine to his blue overcoat. She took Ruddy's knife and cut and unpicked each stitch, while he said dispiritedly: 'Don't, don't, dear. Leave it alone – it's no good – she'll only beat you too.' At last she wrenched it clear and jumped up and down on it. He crept on to school (to be beaten again) while Trix ran back to face a 'scarlet-faced virago' brandishing the cane.

The little girl screamed: 'You are a wicked woman. . . . How dare you sew that wicked placard on poor Ruddy?' Long after, Trix told Lord Birkenhead:

She threatened me with the cane, and I said: 'That's right; thrash me as if I was Ruddy – you know how I bruise and when I'm black I'll go to the police and show them and have you punished. . . .' I was fighting for Ruddy as well as myself – it was the end of my childhood. He was too broken by fasting and beating to have any kick left in him.[1]

It is baffling that cultivated parents with whom, like Thackeray, he was on the best of terms later in life – Kipling's father illustrated *Kim* – could have been so undiscerning and insensitive to have committed him and his sister to such a place for so long. When eventually the mother came on a visit, appalled at his condition she took both children away.

She told me afterwards that when she first came up to my room to kiss me good-night, I flung up an arm to guard off the cuff that I had been trained to expect.[2]

1 *Rudyard Kipling* (1978), p. 26.
2 *Something of Myself* (1937), p. 17.

In *Baa, Baa, Black Sheep* it is this instinctive reaction by Punch that motivates the mother to act.

Yet nothing of childhood is sadder than the early morning of April 6, 1895, when a young French governess strange to them, hurried away two little boys eight and nearly ten down the steps of a house in Tite Street. Ahead lay exile in foreign schools, the death of both parents before five more years, unfeeling guardians, and always silence surrounding their father. The elder boy would be killed in World War I. Now, within eighteen days there would be a sale of effects in their old home, and unknown to them Lot 237 – described as 'A large quantity of toys' – would be sold for thirty shillings.

It probably contained the 'toy milk-cart drawn by a horse with real hair on it' that their father had brought home and, when he discovered the churns could be removed and opened, had immediately gone downstairs and come back with a jug of milk to fill them. Or the wooden fort that WILDE had spent most of one afternoon repairing and when he had finished, 'insisted upon everyone in the house coming to see how well he had done it and to give him a little praise'.[1]

---

1 Vyvyan Holland: *Son of Oscar Wilde* (1954), p. 53.

PART THREE
EDUCATION

BALLIOL COLLEGE.

CHAPTER ONE

Shadow of Prep School

I

The English tradition of better-off parents sending young children to boarding school affected a fair proportion of writers.

O the cruelty of separating a poor lad from his early homestead![1]

During all the time ROALD DAHL was at St Peter's School, Weston-super-Mare, he slept facing his family. A move to another bed or dormitory meant a fresh calculation, 'but the Bristol Channel was always my guide and I was able to draw an imaginary line from my bed to our house over in Wales'.[2]

The experience divided STEPHEN SPENDER's life 'at the age of nine from all before and after'. When he arrived at the Old School House Preparatory School, Holt, he was 'like an animal or peasant, deprived of his familiar surroundings'.

I often asked myself whether I would experience anything worse than school; and subsequently, during the worst situation I have been in, I have always been able to console myself by thinking: 'This isn't nearly as bad as the beginning of term at The O.S.H..'[3]

OSBERT SITWELL was grateful to the parental acquaintance who, in advance, corrected the popular adage about schooldays and told him the truth.

My boy . . . the next few years . . . will be perfectly horrible and a dreadful waste of time. You must never expect to know a moment's happiness until you grow up.

Sitwell comments:

. . . had I really, when at school, believed that it *was* the best that existence

1 Charles Lamb: 'Christ's Hospital Five and Thirty Years Ago', *Elia* (1823), p. 30.
2 *Boy: Tales of Childhood* (1984), p. 84.
3 *World Within World* (1951), pp. 327–9.

could offer, the blackness of despair which engulfed me would have been even darker.[1]

CYRIL CONNOLLY was eight when he went to St Wulfric's. At first he was miserable there and 'cried night after night'.[2] On the eve of his seventh birthday, LEWIS HIND was sent to school at Guildford and half a century afterwards he remembered having cried himself to sleep. 'Three months short of ten', he was taken by his father to Christ's Hospital Preparatory School at Hertford, and before he had time 'to distinguish one of his boisterous companions from another he was marched into the hall to supper'. Through 'the mist of controlled tears', he saw 'from his seat at the end of the long table . . . far away on the dais, sitting with the supper master, his father, the one familiar figure. . . .'

That comforted him; but before supper was over his father came towards him, patted him on the shoulder, told him the holidays would soon come, and disappeared. . . .

The one comfort of his first term was to begin at the top of the playground and walk slowly down to the gates – 'persuading himself that he was walking in the footsteps that his father had taken'.

. . . soon he realised that his short legs could never take the long strides that his father took. . . . I see him now, his little legs wide apart, trying to balance himself. . . . And I am glad that he is no longer a child.[3]

RONALD KNOX, at seven, joined his older brother Dillwyn at Summer Field. He used in middle age 'to recall deliberately what it was like to be beaten for having an untidy locker, to remind himself "how much better it is to be forty than eight"'.[4]

At St George's, Ascot, which WINSTON CHURCHILL entered four weeks before his eighth birthday, along with MAURICE BARING, the boys sometimes received Punishment by Electricity. They were forced to join hands in a ring and it was a point of honour that no boy broke the circuit when the electric shock was administered. One of ROGER FRY's duties as head boy at that school was to hold down the boys when they were being birched.

At Old School House, STEPHEN SPENDER described a kind word given him by his music master as slipping 'like a banned letter into the

1 *Pound Wise* (1963), p. 72.
2 *Enemies of Promise* (1938), p. 206.
3 'The Child', *Life's Little Things* (1902).
4 Penelope Fitzgerald: *The Knox Brothers* (1977), p. 46.

concentration camp of my childhood'.[1] OSBERT SITWELL used similar phrases of 'dreary internment' and 'labour camps' when he contrasted the life of 'happy plenty' before the age of nine or ten, with the conditions prevailing after it.[2] Wynyard, Watford, where C. S. LEWIS boarded from nine until eleven, with his brother, he called 'Belsen'. Seven years previously, a father had brought a High Court action for brutality. The Lewises left when the school 'collapsed', and shortly afterwards the headmaster was certified insane.[3]

II

Cyril Connolly called the English private school 'one of the few tortures confined to the ruling classes and from which the workers are free'. He saw it as an 'incubator of persecution mania' on the grounds that small boys were 'subjected to brutal partings and long separations which undermine their love for their parents, before the natural period of conflict'.[4] According to Lord Clark:

This curious, and, to my mind, objectionable feature of English education was maintained solely in order that parents could get their children out of the house.[5]

The fatherless SWIFT when he was six, was sent away by his uncles to the grammar school at Kilkenny, the Eton of Ireland. COWPER's father followed the practice when the child was six and just bereaved of an exceptionally loving mother. In his unfamiliar environment of Market Street, the lonely little boy had to contend with a bully of fifteen. Too terrified to look up in his face, he knew him by the buckles on his shoes. The constant terror caused nervous inflammation of his eyes. Eventually the bully got expelled, but Cowper's nerves were impaired for life.

At eight, GIBBON was sent to the school of Dr Wooddeson at Kingston-on-Thames, where Leslie Stephen describes the delicate boy 'bullied as a Jacobite by his fellows, and birched into Latin grammar by his master'.[6]

1 *World Within World* (1951), p. 334.
2 *Pound Wise* (1963), pp. 75–76.
3 *Letters of C. S. Lewis* ed. with *Memoir* by W. H. Lewis (1966), p. 3.
4 *Enemies of Promise* (1938), p. 206.
5 *Another Part of the Wood: A Self-Portrait* (1974), p. 33.
6 *D.N.B.*

The ten-year-old SHELLEY did not take kindly to Sion House Academy, Brentford. Thomas Medwin, a fellow-pupil and older cousin, said:

... he ... turned his back on his new associates, and when he was alone found relief in tears.[1]

The other boys soon found out that the new arrival broke the unforgivable commandment: he *reacted* passionately to their baiting – and so they made it a sport. W. C. Gellibrand, another schoolfellow, described him 'as like a girl in boy's clothes, fighting with open hands. . . .'[2] The dedicatory verses of *The Revolt of Islam* refer to a moment of almost mystical resolve:

> ... A fresh May-dawn it was,
> When I walked forth upon the glittering grass,
> And wept, I knew not why: until there rose
> From the near school-room, voices, that, alas!
> Were but one echo from a world of woes –
> The harsh and grating strife of tyrants and of foes.
>
> And then I clasped my hands and looked around;
> But none was near to mock my streaming eyes. . . .
> So, without shame, I spake: 'I will be wise,
> And just and free, and mild, if in me lies
> Such power; for I grow weary to behold
> The selfish and the strong still tyrannize
> Without reproach or check . . .

Dowden pointed out that the grass near the schoolroom suggests Sion House, for it could not have been Eton. Shelley recalled one particular friendship he had made. The boy may have been Tredcroft, who also came from Sussex.

I imagine it must have been at the age of eleven or twelve. . . . There was a delicacy and a simplicity in his manners inexpressibly attractive. . . . I recollect thinking my friend exquisitely beautiful. Every night when we parted to go to bed we kissed each other like children, as we still were.[3]

TENNYSON, at six, was sent with two brothers to Louth Grammar – 'How I did hate that school!'[4] He hated it so much that when in

1 *The Life of Percy Bysshe Shelley* (1847), i, p. 18.
2 Edward Dowden: *The Life of Percy Bysshe Shelley* (1886), i, p. 16 note.
3 *Ibid.*, pp. 19–20.
4 *Alfred Lord Tennyson: A Memoir by his Son* (1897), i, p. 7.

later life he found himself at Louth, he would not go down the lane where it stood. The Rev. J. Waite used to have boys up one at a time to sit on a form to read their lesson, and then slam and bang them over the head with a book. The Rev. H. W. Sneyd-Kynnersley, CHUR-CHILL's prep-school headmaster, used to inflict on small boys ten or fifteen strokes of the birch at a time, nor did much blood – and on one occasion even diarrhoea – deter him.

III

Three years after his wife's death, the Rev. Patrick Brontë placed Maria, who was ten, Elizabeth, nine, CHARLOTTE, eight, and EMILY, six, at the Clergy Daughters' School, Cowan Bridge. Parents paid for their children's board and lodging, their education being met by subscriptions, but budgeting at the school had to be close.

On the occasions that the Rev. Patrick Brontë brought his daughters, he sat at their table, saw the routine and presumably must have approved. Unfortunately, visitors can never know the life that matters of any institution. Food, which might have been adequate, was too often rendered unfit by the incompetent cook. A fellow-pupil sub-sequently told Mrs Gaskell of a distressing incident concerning Maria, which roused the indignation of those who witnessed it. Already ailing, she had had a blister applied to her side, the sore not perfectly healed. Heroically she was struggling to dress when Miss Andrews, the proto-type of Miss Scatcherd in *Jane Eyre*, took her by the affected arm and whirled her out into the middle of the floor, abusing her for untidy ways.

Miss Evans, the superintendent or principal teacher, set an example of humanity. She recalled in a letter to Mrs Gaskell her memory of Emily – 'a darling child . . . and quite the pet nursling of the school'.[1] But her influence was undermined by the Rev. William Carus Wilson.

This wealthy clergyman, who was one of twelve trustees, besides being treasurer and secretary, assumed most responsibility for running the school. He was an Evangelical devoid of child psychology in its most basic form. Three years after the Brontë children had left, he published *Youthful Memoirs* in which little children on their deathbeds

---

1 E. C. Gaskell: *The Life of Charlotte Brontë* (1857), i, pp. 78–79.

speak in an improbable way. One boy, three and a half, and asked to choose between death or life, replies: 'Death for me? I am fonder of death.' Wilson published his *First Tales*, monosyllabic stories for infants, two years after *Jane Eyre* had appeared. On the first page is a picture of a man being hanged, and the book begins: 'Look there! Do you see a man hung by the neck?' One of his anecdotes seems to refer to a pupil at Cowan Bridge:

> A poor little girl who had been taken into a school was whipped. She asked, 'If they love us, why do they whip us?'
> A little girl of six replied, 'It is because they love us, and it is to make us remember what a sad thing sin is. God would be angry with them if they did not whip us.'[1]

After eight months a shocked father was called to take Maria home where she died, aged eleven, a consumptive like her mother. Three more months and ten-year-old Elizabeth was sent home, also to die from the same condition. Charlotte always believed the school to have been largely responsible for the deaths of her two elder sisters. About the time of Maria's death, typhus broke out affecting forty of the girls but not the Brontës. Charlotte and Emily were removed shortly after Elizabeth. None of the four children had attended a whole year.

IV

MATTHEW ARNOLD, at eight, and his younger brother Tom, were sent to a 'strict' school run by their uncle, the Rev. John Buckland at Laleham. As an HMI of forty, Arnold was to tell his mother that its 'confinement' had made it 'a really bad and injurious school in my time'.

> We never left that detestable little gravel playground except on Sundays.[2]

On Fridays he was regularly given an inferior dinner set apart for those boys who had performed poorly during the week. The uncle pronounced his nephew backward, and after two years the brothers came home, their father admitting to Matthew's godfather (and answering Cyril Connolly's charge): 'I think of keeping him at home

1 *The Brontës: Their Lives, Friendships & Correspondence* (The Shakespeare Head Press, 1932), i, pp. 70–72.
2 Park Honan: *Matthew Arnold: A Life* (1981), p. 19.

to familiarize him with home feelings.'[1] Until they went to Winchester, they were taught by a private tutor, Herbert Hill, a cousin of Southey.

Though not prosperous, J. R. GREEN's father sent him, a little over eight, to Magdalen College School.

I was set to learn Latin grammar from a grammar in Latin! and a flogging every week did little to help me. I was simply stupefied, – for my father had never struck me, and at first the cane hurt me like a blow, – but the *stupid stage* soon came, and I used to fling away my grammar into old churchyards, and go up for my *spinning* as doggedly as the rest.[2]

KENNETH GRAHAME was sent to St Edward's School when he was nine. He had not been there more than a day or so, when the headmaster came into the junior form where he was occupying, as he thought very naturally, the position at the bottom, and catching sight of him asked the master in charge: 'What's that thing doing down there?' He continued that if the boy did not find himself up there – and he pointed to the head of the form – or near it, before the close of work, he was to be severely caned.

Following their father's arrest, VYVYAN HOLLAND and Cyril spent a year largely with their mother in Switzerland and Italy, and now, at nine and ten, were placed in an English school, Neuenheim College in a suburb of Heidelberg. They had changed their names and their clothes were re-marked, but when they went to change for cricket these things had been overlooked and still bore the tabs *Cyril Wilde* and *Vyvyan Wilde*.

... I can see my brother now, in the comparative seclusion of the washing-place, frantically hacking away at the tapes with his pocket-knife.[3]

Vyvyan, the youngest in the school, was 'very unhappy' there. Once, his tormentors shut him in an empty locker just large enough to hold him in a crouching position, and ran away. When a master let him out, he was in a state of hysteria.

I have suffered from claustrophobia ever since. ... The so-called schoolboy code of honour is an amazing thing. It is really a set of unwritten principles laid down by the older boys ... to enable them to do exactly what they like to the smaller boys.[4]

1 *Ibid.*, p. 20.
2 *Letters of John Richard Green* ed. Leslie Stephen (1901), p. 7.
3 Vyvyan Holland: *Son of Oscar Wilde* (1954), p. 94.
4 *Ibid.*, pp. 91–92.

There was an occasion when the whole school was caned because of noise in one of the dormitories and the master on duty could not determine the culprits. Vyvyan felt the injustice as his own dormitory had been very well-behaved – he was actually woken up out of deep sleep to take his beating. One teacher made them write lines holding the paper against the wall at eye-level, which meant rubbing the hands with pumice-stone to remove the inkstains for next lesson, else their knuckles were caned by the same teacher – 'whose eyes would light up with pleasure'.[1] Sometimes Vyvyan made his hands bleed in a desperate effort to get them clean. Until there was a complaint to the headmaster, the smaller boys were taken on cold afternoons for what a master called 'scrum practice', slashing at their buttocks with a cane 'to make them push harder'.[2]

ALDOUS HUXLEY, when he was nine, joined his elder cousin Gervas at the prep school Hillside. They tried to rag and bully him, but Gervas said his cousin 'put on his cloak of invisibility and simply disappeared'. When Gervas was made head boy and sent to Coventry for being over-zealous, Aldous, alone of the fifty boys, stayed loyal.

After lights went out . . . Aldous's shout of 'You swine and curs' silenced the abuse against me. . . . Next day, on the school outing, Aldous walked with me while the rest of the school kept a hostile distance.[3]

V

While allowing that St Wulfric's on the Sussex coast was 'well run and vigorous', CYRIL CONNOLLY said it revolved around the headmistress 'Flip' rather than the headmaster 'Sambo', – '. . . we learnt with her as fast as fear could teach us.'[4]

When angry Flip would slap our faces, in front of the school, or pull the hair behind our ears, till we cried. She would make satirical remarks at meals that pierced like a rapier. . . .

After three years, at eleven, he kept a 'favour chart' which week by week graphed his 'position at her court'. Old boys who came down would ask: 'What sort of favour are you in?'

1 *Ibid.*, p. 93.
2 *Ibid.*, p. 104.
3 Sybille Bedford: *Aldous Huxley: A Biography* (1973–4), i, p. 16.
4 *Enemies of Promise* (1938), p. 207.

Connolly wrote of ORWELL there:

... he alone among the boys was an intellectual, and not a parrot, for he thought for himself, read Shaw and Samuel Butler.... He saw through St Wulfric's, despised Sambo and hated Flip, but was valuable to them as scholarship fodder.[1]

They often walked together over the Downs in their green jerseys and corduroy breeches. Connolly said that from Orwell he learnt about literature, from Cecil Beaton also a boy there, he learnt about art. Connolly and Orwell both won, in consecutive years, the 'Harrow History Prize', similarly the prize for having the 'best list' of books taken out of the library during the term. Bernard Crick believes there is no reason to doubt that the headmaster beat Orwell for bed-wetting.

During STEPHEN SPENDER's first term at The Old School House, he and five or six of the smaller boys were 'particularly hungry' one morning and took more than the quarter slice of bread allocated to them at 11.0 a.m., with the result that when the older boys arrived there was not enough to go round. In an assembly that was called, some admitted their guilt, and the housemaster (related to many bishops) said they were beyond the pale for his own punishment but publicly 'gave the other boys leave to do whatever they liked with us'.

We were outlawed for that afternoon.

Several boys pounced on nine-year-old Stephen, tied some rope round his hands and feet and pulled in different directions. They then flung him down the Kipper Hole at the back of the platform of the school dining-room where heads of kippers were customarily thrown. What worried him chiefly was being late for the music lesson he loved, and when he finally managed to escape and get on his bicycle he arrived 'in a sad state' at the house of his music master.[2]

TERENCE RATTIGAN, at nine, was sent to Sandroyd, near Cobham, and after he had accepted a part in the school play his work deteriorated. The headmaster offered him a choice – a beating or to give up his part. Rattigan chose to carry on with the play.

ROALD DAHL and the other hundred and forty-nine boys of St Peter's School, Weston-super-Mare, walked 'all day long in perpetual fear of the long yellow cane that lay on top of the corner cupboard in the

1 *Ibid.*, pp. 210–12.
2 *World Within World* (1951), pp. 332–3.

headmaster's study'.[1] The Matron 'disliked small boys very much indeed. She never smiled at us or said anything nice. . . .' Even eleven and twelve-year-olds were terrified of her. The source of her power was the headmaster in his study.

At any time she liked, the Matron could send you down in your pyjamas and dressing-gown to report to this merciless giant, and whenever this happened, you got caned on the spot. . . . And the Matron, as we all knew, would follow after the boy and stand at the top of the stairs listening. . . .[2]

One of the masters, Captain Hardcastle, 'had it in for me from my very first day. . . . Perhaps it was because already, at the age of nine, I was very nearly as tall as he was.'[3] During Prep Dahl had the misfortune to break his nib and because he whispered to the boy next to him if he could lend one, Captain Hardcastle accused him of cheating and gave him a 'stripe' – a terrible piece of green-blue paper which had to be handed in to the headmaster 'as soon as prayers were over', and that automatically meant a thrashing. When he tried to explain he was asked, 'Are you calling Captain Hardcastle a liar? For talking in Prep, for trying to cheat and for lying, I am going to give you six strokes of the cane.' Dahl adds:

I was frightened of that cane. . . . It caused severe and scarlet bruising that took three weeks to disappear, and all the time during those three weeks, you could feel your heart beating along the wounds.[4]

From the age of nine until twelve, as tall as most men, CHESTERTON was a day-boy at Bewsher's, Colet Court. Intensely miserable and lonely he went about the place in a dream. He had learnt to read only the year before he began there and his exercise books, when he remembered to bring them, were dirty and scribbled upon with drawings. One master exploded to him in class: 'If we could open your head we should not find any brain but only a lump of white fat!'[5]

The future writer contrasted childhood as a time when one 'wants to know nearly everything' with 'the period . . . called education . . . being instructed by somebody I did not know about something I did not want to know'.[6]

1 *Boy: Tales of Childhood* (1984), p. 92.
2 *Ibid.*, p. 80.
3 *Ibid.*, p. 100.
4 *Ibid.*, pp. 107–10.
5 Dudley Barker: *G. K. Chesterton: A Biography* (1973), p. 27.
6 *Autobiography* (1936), p. 58.

CHAPTER TWO
A Happier Side

I

Obviously it could not all have been woe. GALSWORTHY always remembered the independence he had enjoyed at Saugeen, Bournemouth. A boy could spend his leisure as he liked provided he did not get into mischief. Galsworthy was in the 1st Cricket XI in spite of short sight, but he was a more successful runner. At eleven and a half he beat thirteen-year-olds over short distances, and at twelve was the second best runner in the school.

JOYCE, according to his brother, was happy at Clengowes Wood College as soon as he had settled. Younger even than Lamb or Lewis Hind when they first went away to school, he announced his age on arrival as 'Half past six'.[1] At first he lived in the infirmary instead of a dormitory, so that a nurse could look after him. He rose to head of his class, and like Galsworthy proved himself an athlete – in his case winning cups for hurdling and walking. He began his fascination for cricket. In *A Portrait of the Artist as a Young Man* he remembered when he was pandied, early on, by Father Daly, who insisted that the little boy had broken his glasses himself in order to shirk; but, as is also portrayed, he was encouraged by the rector, Father Conmee, to whom he courageously appealed. Probably, like most small boys, Joyce experienced a mixture of light and shadow. Although the *Portrait* is unsympathetic towards Clengowes, long into his life the man who rejected 'Christianity . . . and religious doctrines' praised to friends his Jesuit masters. Father Conmee moved on to prefect of studies at Belvedere College, and was instrumental in getting Joyce and his brothers there without fees.

SIEGFRIED SASSOON was fourteen when he went, with his slightly younger brother Hamo, to The New Beacon, Sevenoaks. Up to then they had been taught at home. He recalled just arriving:

1 Richard Ellmann: *James Joyce* (1959), p. 26.

123

I stood alone on the edge of the playground feeling newer than I'd ever done in my life as I watched some other boys. . . . I was much larger than most of them, which made me seem, for the moment, acutely inexperienced and help-less. Then a bell began ringing, and while they were crowding in for tea Mr Jackson, the chief assistant master, came to my relief with an encouraging smile. 'Cut along now and get yourself some grub. Feeling a bit hollow inside, aren't you?' he exclaimed in his pleasant voice, and made me seem not quite so new. From that moment I liked Mr Jackson very much.[1]

There was an initial problem about shirts. His mother had provided them with starched 'dickeys' to their Eton collars and nothing else. In the middle of the following morning there was half an hour's break for cricket practice, and Siegfried was eager to show Mr Jackson that 'I could play quite decently, but it wasn't possible . . . to bat in my shirt-sleeves'.

When it came to bowling, the weather being rather warm, he asked why I didn't take my coat off. My embarrassment enabled him to discover what was amiss, and he led me and Hamo off to the matron, who supplied shirts from somewhere.[2]

Mr Jackson took a party of them on the Norfolk Broads during the holidays – 'What a ripping time' they had. After the first term Mr Norman, the headmaster, called him 'Dook Sig.' because his deport-ment had become so dignified. On a Saturday evening, roast-chestnut time, he sat in the big schoolroom while Mr Norman read to them 'from *Moonfleet*, I think . . . he did it splendidly'.

I was now turned fifteen, and Mr Norman had taken to treating me as a person to be relied on. It was nice to be treated like that. . . . Next term I should be at Marlborough, where I should have to begin all over again and not be relied on at all.[3]

When VYVYAN HOLLAND was ten, his mother took him away from Neuenheim College and on the suggestion of Princess Alice of Monaco, Wilde's friend, entrusted him to the Jesuits at the Collegio della Visitazione, where Vyvyan found 'the gentlest, kindest and most sympathetic body of men that I had so far met in my short life, outside my own family circle'.[4] In the cause of modesty a bathing costume

1 *The Old Century and seven more years* (1938), pp. 183–4.
2 *Ibid.*, pp. 185–6.
3 *Ibid.*, pp. 187–9.
4 *Son of Oscar Wilde* (1954), p. 118.

was always provided when one took an infrequent bath (there was only
one bath in the school), and Vyvyan's spiritual adviser was horror
stricken ('Peccato mortale!')[1] when he told him that English boys at
school usually bathed together naked, the masters sometimes joining
them. On his mother's death, he came back to England and, nearly
twelve, entered Hodder Place, the preparatory school attached to
Stonyhurst.

II

Between the ages of seven and nine, KENNETH CLARK was happy at
Wixenford, 'but the almost total lack of instruction was a drawback
that has troubled me all my life'.[2] ERIC GILL was a day-boy at Arnold
House, one of the smallest prep schools in Brighton, numbering thirty
boys.

I was fairly happy at school – not uproariously so, but happy enough.[3]

The headmaster had special genius as a trainer of football.

. . . we beat every other school in the town and neighbourhood, including the
Junior school of Brighton College. We didn't merely beat them; we just ran
over them.[4]

When Gill sat for a scholarship at Bradfield College, 'the Latin floored
me completely',[5] and he went on to Chichester Technical and Art
School at fifteen.

CECIL DAY LEWIS's overall memory of Wilkie's, a day-school in
St Petersburg Place, was of a 'time . . . steeped in happiness'.[6] He
called it 'a humane and lively school'.[7] There was almost no bullying
– 'Nor do I remember a boy ever being caned, though this may have
happened.' To some extent the school was unorthodox. There was no
games-worship (in spite of the headmaster's private passion for cricket)
and it was made clear they were at school to work, yet scholastic success

1 *Ibid.*, p. 127.
2 *Another Part of the Wood: A Self-Portrait* (1974), pp. 33–34.
3 *Autobiography* (1940), p. 30.
4 *Ibid.*, p. 31.
5 *Ibid.*, p. 33n.
6 *The Buried Day* (1960), p. 67.
7 *Ibid.*, pp. 69–70.

was attained 'without resort to the cramming and forcing which often burn out clever small boys'.

The headmaster, Herbert Wilkinson, a first-rate classical scholar, possessed a tender regard for the stomachs of small boys. At lunch there was a choice of two meats and three delectable puddings of the cherry-currant-treacle kind. A 'touch of the grotesque which brings a schoolmaster humanly alive to his boys' was the way he brought lunch to a close – he blew his nose like a ship's steam-whistle, and this would be followed by excavating with his tongue fragments from his teeth.[1] At midday break all went out to play in Kensington Gardens.

A boy of great charm and natural leadership, who joined Wilkie's the same term as Cecil Day Lewis, was Nicholas Llewellyn Davies, the youngest of Barrie's five 'adopted' boys.

On one occasion he took me back to his guardian's house in Campden Hill Square, and introduced me to him. I remember a large, dark room, and a small dark man sitting in it; he was not smoking a pipe, nor did he receive us little boys with any perceptible enthusiasm. . . . After this negative encounter, we went up to an attic and fired with an air-gun at pedestrians in the Square.[2]

When Cecil was ten he was allowed to cycle to and from school, the traffic in 1914 being so light and still largely horse-drawn.

MAX BEERBOHM was at Wilkie's thirty years before, when it had only fifteen to twenty boys. Wilkie had a large blond moustache then – it 'fluttered in the wind when he played touch-last with the little boys at the end of afternoon school'.[3] EDMUND GOSSE's son attended a few years afterwards.

1 *The Buried Day* (1960), pp. 69–70.
2 *Ibid.*, p. 74.
3 David Cecil: *Max: A Biography* (1964), p. 26.

CHAPTER THREE
Public School: Pre-Arnold

I

Roughly as many attended Public School as those who did not. Eton has been the most popular, then a drop to Winchester, Westminster, St Paul's, Charterhouse, Rugby, Harrow, and so on.[1] Among the big names who went to Public School are Spenser, Jonson, Milton, Dryden, Swift, Fielding, Gibbon, Coleridge, Shelley, Thackeray, E. M. Forster, Joyce. Chaucer's training as a page may be taken as the equivalent, so also Sir Thomas More's residence from the age of twelve in the household of Cardinal Morton.

The Public School does not come out well. We should in fairness remember that these critics were exceptionally sensitive and articulate. But it does not come out well.

GIBBON wrote of Westminster: 'At the cost of many tears and some blood I purchased a knowledge of the Latin Syntax.'[2] CHARLES LAMB, 'of tender years, barely turned of seven', on his first day at Christ's Hospital saw 'a boy in fetters'! Elia comments:

I was a hypochondriac lad; and the sight . . . was not exactly fitted to assuage the natural terrors of initiation. . . . I was told he had *run away*. This was the punishment for the first offence. – As a novice I was soon after taken to see the dungeons.

The boy would be locked all day in a little, square 'Bedlam' cell, 'with a peep of light, let in askance, from a prison-orifice at top, barely enough to read by'. He saw only the porter who brought his bread and water – 'who *might not speak to him*' – and the beadle who called twice weekly to thrash him. This was for the second offence. The third time meant expulsion. The runaway was arrayed in the most shameful clothes.

1 See Appendix D.
2 *Memoirs of My Life & Writings* ed. Lord Sheffield (1796).

... he was brought into the hall where awaited him the whole number of his school-fellows ... the awful presence of the steward to be seen for the last time; of the executioner beadle, clad in his state robe. ...

Two governors officiated at these 'Ultima Supplicia', and on one occasion they fortified the beadle 'turning rather pale' with a glass of brandy.

The scourging was after the old Roman fashion, long and stately. The lictor accompanied the criminal quite round the hall.[1]

He wrote of being called out of bed on cold winter nights:

– and this not once, but night after night – in my shirt, to receive the discipline of a leathern thong, with eleven other sufferers, because it pleased my callow overseer, when there has been any talking heard after we were gone to bed, to make the six last beds in the dormitory, where the youngest children of us slept, answerable for an offence they neither dared to commit, nor had the power to hinder.[2]

He mentioned the Rev. James Boyer, the Upper Master, doubling 'his knotty fist at a poor trembling child (the maternal milk hardly dry upon his lips) with a "Sirrah, do you presume to set your wits at me?"'[3]

LEIGH HUNT went to the same school, and the thrashing system then in operation horrified the 'ultra-sympathising and timid boy'. ROBERT SOUTHEY, at eighteen, was expelled from Westminster for attacking corporal punishment in *The Flagellant*, a school magazine he and his friends had founded.

II

Twelve-year-old SHELLEY, slight, almost girlish, arrived at Eton and was put in the Upper Fourth. Dr Keate, on his way to flogging 'half the ministers, secretaries, bishops, generals, and dukes' of that century, ruled Lower School, and by the time Shelley reached the Sixth Form had become headmaster.

As soon as he arrived, Shelley refused to fag for Henry Matthews, declaring such a system tyrannical. He had cut himself off from the possibility of protection by any older boy – boys like Milman, Sumner,

1 'Christ's Hospital Five and Thirty Years Ago', *Elia* (1823), pp. 37–39.
2 *Ibid.*, p. 32.
3 *Ibid.*, p. 44.

Nassau Senior and Coleridge's nephew, Sir John Taylor Coleridge (who would one day review favourably *Laon and Cythna*). 'He stood apart from the whole school,' wrote a contemporary, 'a being never to be forgotten.'[1]

The story of Sion House repeated itself, only this time there were five hundred boys instead of sixty. If a group came across him wandering afield, they gave chase. On dark evenings they assembled by custom, under cloisters before going to Upper School. They 'nailed' Mad Shelley (forty-five years later, there would be Mad Swinburne), who never wore a hat, with a slimy ball of mud; or first one, then another and another would chant his name until the roof echoed with their full force; or those near pushed his books from under his arm. They watched his collapse. 'His eyes,' declared a witness, would 'flash like a tiger's, his cheeks grow pale as death, his limbs quiver,' and another said, 'I seem to hear ringing in my ears the cry which Shelley was wont to utter in his paroxysm of revengeful anger.'[2]

Yet he had much affection to give, and won it from certain among them – the matter-of-fact Packe; Amos, with whom he used to compose and act plays before the audience of one other boy; Robert Leslie and Charles Ball, in his House; Price, considered one of their best scholars. His strongest attachment was to the gentle, younger Halliday brother who accompanied him on his walks:

I loved Shelley for his kindliness and affectionate ways; he was not made to endure the rough and boisterous pastime at Eton....[3]

Books were his other friends. In his leisure he translated much of Pliny's *Natural History*. He asked for some book on chemistry from Uncle Medwin's library, but it was found by his tutor who sent it home. Sir Timothy Shelley returned it to its owner 'as it is a forbidden thing at Eton'. 'I was twice expelled,' he told Godwin, 'but recalled by the interference of my father.'[4]

When he was in Italy, he put into verse a schoolboy feast enjoyed before lock-up with one of his friends, near the Thames in summer. Overall, the bullying was too dreadful for him to relive memories of Eton as a man. His friend, Halliday, continued:

1 Edward Dowden: *The Life of Percy Bysshe Shelley* (1886), i, p. 23.
2 *Ibid.*, pp. 24–25.
3 *Ibid.*, p. 27.
4 *Ibid.*, p. 35.

He certainly was not happy at Eton, for his was a disposition that needed especial personal superintendence, to watch and cherish and direct all his noble aspirations, and the remarkable tenderness of his heart.[1]

A year after leaving Charterhouse, THACKERAY wrote to his mother from Cambridge:

I can not think that school to be a good one, when as a child, I was lulled into indolence & when I grew older and could think for myself was abus(ed) into sulkiness and bullied into despair....[2]

Many years later he expressed himself:

I think the chief good I got out of Charterhouse was to learn to hate bullying and tyranny and to love kind hearted simple children. And I hope my own get the benefit of that sad experience I had there, and so escape rough words & brutal treatment....[3]

TROLLOPE returned to Harrow a second time, after trying Winchester. He felt a miserable outcast at both. MATTHEW ARNOLD at thirteen, with his younger brother Tom, were despatched to Winchester, but did not stay long. Matthew made himself dangerously unpopular by telling Dr Moberly, the headmaster, that his class assignments were 'light and easy'. In the role of father, Dr Arnold confessed: 'I am a coward about schools,' and after a year decided that his own was best. Matthew was enrolled in 'The Twenty' of the Upper Fifth, sleeping in the adult portion of School House. Towards the end of the first year, his father recorded: 'Examined the Twenty. Matt floored.'[4] He was promoted at fifteen as a 'guardian of morality' in the Sixth Form, and to the astonishment of his father won an Open Balliol scholarship.

1 Ibid., p. 27.
2 April 16, 1829. The Letters & Private Papers of W. M. Thackeray ed. G. N. Ray (1945–6), i, p. 59.
3 Letter to G. W. Nickisson, Mch. 1, 1847. Ibid., ii, p. 284.
4 Park Honan: Matthew Arnold: A Life (1981), p. 34.

CHAPTER FOUR

The Mixture as Before

I

Edward Hawkins wrote that if Thomas Arnold were elected to the headmastership of Rugby, 'he would change the face of education all through the public schools of England'. The writers who follow come after Arnold. What happened to them, and what they say, are very similar to what has been put already.

Only four years after Arnold and ironically at *his* school, the sensitive DODGSON, work- rather than games-orientated, still had his life made a misery by persistent bullying. Not long after leaving, he visited Radley where the cubicle system in the dormitory, even for younger boys, won his approval.

From my own experience of school life at Rugby I can say that if I could have been secure from annoyance at night, the hardships of the daily life would have been comparative trifles to bear.[1]

LORD CLARK regretted Winchester being 'one of the few English boarding schools which does not allow boys rooms of their own'.

We all sat in the same large enclosure, round the walls of which were small partitions (known as toyes), like uncomfortable polling booths, with just enough room for two shelves, one to serve as a seat and the other as a desk. For the first year one was not allowed any form of cushion, and as one's bottom was already sore from frequent beating it was extremely uncomfortable.[2]

TERENCE RATTIGAN was more fortunate. When he entered Harrow in 1925, the juniors had rooms which they shared with one boy, while more senior boys had rooms of their own.

At Neuenheim College VYVYAN HOLLAND had his only experience of 'the prefect system', which was Arnold's pride and came to be

---

1 Stuart Dodgson Collingwood: *The Life & Letters of Lewis Carroll* (1898), pp. 30–31.
2 *Another Part of the Wood: A Self-Portrait* (1974), pp. 74–75.

Education

adopted in so many English schools. To Holland it was a system 'where an unpopular boy may well be driven to suicide by the brutality of his fellows, while the masters adopt the callous attitude that it is of no concern of theirs'.[1] C. DAY LEWIS recalled a boy in his house at Sherborne – 'a slow-witted, oafish-looking creature' who was 'kicked around, jeered at or ostracised, day in day out for several years'.

The dull misery on this boy's face must surely have been noticed by the authorities, yet I do not recollect any attempt being made to relieve it. . . .

As head of his house and school prefect, C. Day Lewis 'was not among his persecutors', but admitted 'nor, I'm afraid, did I try hard to discourage them. . . .'[2]

On the eve of World War II, *seventeen* years after leaving Eton, CYRIL CONNOLLY said:

To this day I cannot bear to be sent for, or hear of anyone wanting to see me without an acute nervous dread.[3]

He had come in 1916, 'to be a fag in Chamber 1 . . . the lowest ranks of serfdom'. He describes a society where only boys could cane. The Sixth Form, who in theory ruled the school, could cane boys in College (the scholarship winners); 'Pop', which constituted two dozen self-elected boys who in effect governed the school, could cane boys from any house.

The beatings were torture. We were first conscious of impending doom at Prayers, when the eyes of sixth form would linger on us.

A special fag, 'Senior', sent to fetch the 'wanted' man, at last reached the other fags 'who were shivering with terror – for this was always an agonising quarter of an hour for them – in their stalls'.

Those who were sitting in their tin baths paused with the sponge in the air . . . 'Connolly, you're "wanted".' 'Who by?' 'Wrangham.' 'That's all right. He can't beat me, only tick me off. He's my fag-master.' 'He's going to beat someone. He's got the chair out.'[4]

He describes 'mass executions' when it was not uncommon for all the fags to be beaten. They knelt in turn on the chair, gripping the

1 *Son of Oscar Wilde* (1954), p. 91.
2 *The Buried Day* (1960), p. 116.
3 *Enemies of Promise* (1938), p. 238.
4 *Ibid.*, p. 236.

lower bar. Looking round under the chair they saw 'a monster' rushing towards them with a cane, his face distorted. They were 'beaten for "generality", which meant no specific charge except that of being "generally uppish"'. Connolly confessed that, combined with chamber beatings and bullyings, the result was 'to ruin my nerve'. Fags lived in Chamber and even the little boy who was 'Captain of Chamber' could beat them, not with a cane but a piece of rubber tubing; also a 'Chamber Pop' could beat them in a body. Connolly's work declined, then he got tickets to present his tutor. According to the year in which they had won their scholarship, boys were divided into elections.

My own election were broken under the strain of beatings at night, and bullying by day; all we could hope for was to achieve peace with seniority and then start beating in our turn.[1]

So the system corrupted *them*.

ORWELL, like himself, had won a scholarship to Eton and, according to Connolly, when Orwell was eighteen, just outside Sixth Form, he was beaten by boys in his senior election – 'for being late at prayers', as if he was a fag.

C. DAY LEWIS, during his second term in the Lower Sixth at Sherborne, was dealt with for hubris. He was informed *ten weeks* beforehand.

From then on, I never had a moment's peace of mind. It was not the prospect of the ordeal to come that sapped my nerve so much as the ever-present sense of being marked down for a victim. . . .

Sunday by Sunday, in the afternoon, he waited in his study. When the knock on his door eventually came, he was first forced to swallow 'a concoction of ink and bad cheese'. He was then pushed under a row of desks and brown paper lit. Dragged out choking, not burnt, he was subjected to a series of running-the-gauntlet. Finally he was taken upstairs and flung, still in his Sunday clothes, into a cold bath.

I had managed not to be sick, or to weep or utter a sound throughout. . . . I did not for some years entirely shake off its effects. . . .[2]

1 *Ibid.*, pp. 237–8.
2 *The Buried Day* (1960), pp. 119–20.

Education

Sir JOHN BETJEMAN described how at Marlborough boys humiliated one not of a kind by debagging, pouring ink and treacle over his head, and hauling him up to the ceiling in a waste-paper basket.

> . . . And as he soared I only saw his eyes
> Look through the slats at us who watched below.[1]

The victim would leave the end of term. In his last year it was rumoured Betjeman would be done.

II

In a Preface to the sixth edition of *Tom Brown's School Days*, Thomas Hughes, himself one of Arnold's Praepostors, unashamedly preached. He quoted a letter raising these points:

> Gradually training a timid child to do bold acts would be most desirable; but *frightening* him and ill-treating him will not make him courageous. . . . A groom who tried to cure a shying horse by roughness and violence, would be discharged as a brute and a fool. . . .
> The fact is, that the condition of a small boy at a large school is one of peculiar hardship and suffering . . . and he is deprived of the protection which the weak have in civilized society: for he may not complain; if he does, he is an outlaw. . . .
> What do schoolboys know of those deep questions of moral and physical philosophy, of the anatomy of mind and body, by which the treatment of a child should be regulated?
> Why should the laws of civilization be suspended for schools? . . . .

Fifty years later as BEVERLEY NICHOLS, a new boy at Marlborough, was shown his bed in the dormitory, the prefect pointed to a pair of steel rings hanging from the ceiling: 'You've got six weeks to get your muscles up,'[2] and if when the time came he was unable to do a series of complicated manoeuvres, he was bent over a bed in his pyjamas and a prefect administered ten strokes. If a boy cried, the strokes came harder. Nichols suggested that for the prefects the flogging was 'keenly pleasurable'. Often they came up to the dormitory before lights out, to watch the clumsy practices of frightened boys. Sometimes they would swing a cane down on a pillow as if in anticipation.

He was sent there in 1912 – 'a tall, shy boy, and, according to some

1 *Summoned by Bells* (1960), p. 71.
2 Beverley Nichols: *The Unforgiving Minute* (1978), p. 21.

134

of my contemporaries, I had a habit of constantly glancing over my shoulder, as though I was being followed'. He recalled 'a setting of everlasting winter'.[1] All through the year the windows of their dormitories were open wide and sometimes they woke to find on their beds 'a coverlet of snow'.

After the cold, the accent was on cruelty.[2]

Apart from the cane fully used, there was a punishment Turfing down Basement, 'which could only have originated in the mind of a sadist'. It meant running up and down stone stairs while grinning prefects kept count. A hundred 'turfings' were not unusual.

We were still living in the shadows of *Tom Brown's Schooldays*. And that shadow stretched into the grim distances of Dotheboys Hall.[3]

Nichols spoke of his time at Marlborough as 'those desolate years'.

ROALD DAHL was given the choice by his mother of Marlborough or Repton. He decided on Repton because it was easier to say. The story is the same – of prefects having 'power of life and death' over junior boys, except that here they were called Boazers.

In the dormitory after each beating, half a dozen young experts would inspect the damage and give their opinions 'in highly professional language'. Once Dahl was standing in the middle with his pyjama trousers around his knees when the Boazer caught him as he came through the door. He told him to pull his pyjamas up and get into bed, but as he went out 'he craned his head . . . to catch a glimpse of my bare bottom and his own handiwork'. Dahl was certain he detected 'a little glimmer of pride'.[4]

All through my school life I was appalled by the fact that masters and senior boys were allowed literally to wound other boys, and sometimes quite severely. I couldn't get over it. I never have got over it.

At the end of Dahl's third year, in 1933, his headmaster gained preferment in the Church and not many years after, 'the man who used to deliver the most vicious beatings to the boys under his care' became the Archbishop of Canterbury who crowned Queen Elizabeth II. Dahl saw nothing wrong with a naughty boy having 'a few quick

1 *Father Figure* (1972), pp. 121–3.
2 *The Unforgiving Minute*, p. 20.
3 *Ibid.*, p. 22.
4 *Boy: Tales of Childhood* (1984), pp. 128–9.

sharp tickles on the rump', but when this headmaster delivered a flogging 'the victim was told to wash away the blood before pulling up his trousers'.[1]

Because Dahl loved playing games, his life at Repton 'was not totally without pleasure'. But he was 'the only unBoazered Double Captain' – of Fives and Squash-racquets.

... the authorities did not like me.... I would have let down the whole principle of Boazerdom by refusing to beat the Fags.[2]

III

At the Jesuit College of Stonyhurst, ARTHUR CONAN DOYLE remembered the instrument of correction – 'a piece of india-rubber of the size and shape of a thick boot sole'.

One blow ... would cause the palm ... to swell up and change colour ... the usual punishment of the larger boys was nine on each hand, and ... nine on one hand was an absolute minimum ... the sufferer could not, as a rule, turn the handle of the door to get out of the room in which he had suffered. To take twice nine upon a cold day was about the extremity of human endurance. I went out of my way to do really mischievous and outrageous things simply to show that my spirit was unbroken. An appeal to my better nature and not to my fears would have found an answer at once.[3]

The 'ferula' seems to have been as much in practice thirty years later when VYVYAN HOLLAND was there, in 1900, and the maximum was the same – 'twice-nine' at any one time or day. There were no boy prefects who could inflict punishments. You went 'in cold blood' to one of four Jesuit prefects and said: 'I want twelve ferulas for Father So-and-so.'[4]

DOYLE left at sixteen, having amazed everyone by taking honours in the London Matriculation, but we are left marvelling at the master who said on the last day:

Doyle, I have known you now for seven years, and I know you thoroughly. I am going to say something which you will remember in after-life. Doyle, you will never come to any good.[5]

1 Ibid., pp. 131–2.
2 Ibid., p. 148.
3 Memories and Adventures (1924), pp. 16–17.
4 Son of Oscar Wilde (1954), p. 159.
5 Hesketh Pearson: Conan Doyle: His Life & Art (1943), p. 9.

Yet Kenneth Clark and Roald Dahl received coldness from those standing to them in a pastoral role. When DAHL, at Repton, was about to go to London for an interview with the Shell Company (Eastern Staff), his housemaster said it was hopeless in his case to try. In the event, out of one hundred and seven applicants he secured one of seven vacancies, and back at school his housemaster neither congratulated him nor shook his hand, confining himself to muttering: 'All I can say is I'm damned glad I don't own any shares in Shell.'[1] At Winchester, LORD CLARK's housemaster was 'almost indignant' when he won a scholarship to Trinity College, Oxford.[2]

SWINBURNE left Eton only just turned sixteen, and Jean Overton Fuller suggests his 'peculiar attitude to punishment' amongst other things, may have 'embarrassed the authorities' enough to put to his parents it would be better to take him away.[3]

Fifteen-year-old C. S. LEWIS was released from Malvern after one year in a state of collapse. He had implored his father to take him away which rather surprisingly he did. Warren said his brother should never have seen sent to a public school at all. EVELYN WAUGH, in 'black misery' at Lancing, besought his father 'urgently' to remove him, but his father 'counselled endurance'.[4]

When he had dined with the masters at Wellington, Sir HAROLD NICOLSON recorded:

My old sadness that hung like mist among the bracken suddenly settled down on me again. . . . I must have been *very* unhappy there for the mood to return to me after forty years.[5]

OSBERT SITWELL seldom visited Eton – 'too many pitiful ghosts' haunted its lanes and quadrangles, and the mere sight of a master in cap and gown filled him with misery.[6]

Disillusionment followed quickly for Kenneth Clark and Evelyn Waugh. Believing he was 'at the beginning of a new and exciting life', EVELYN WAUGH had parted from his father 'without a pang',[7] to find

---

1 *Boy: Tales of Childhood* (1984), p. 152.
2 *Another Part of the Wood: A Self-Portrait* (1974), p. 85.
3 *Swinburne: A Critical Biography* (1968), p. 27.
4 *A Little Learning: The First Volume of an Autobiography* (1964), p. 115.
5 *Diaries & Letters 1939–1945* ed. Nigel Nicolson (1967), pp. 261–2.
6 *Pound Wise* (1963), pp. 82–83.
7 *Op. cit.*, p. 100.

that for the first three weeks the new boys were treated as untouchables and bullying set in.

Odium was painful and something quite new to me.... I was harrowed. I had lived too softly for my first thirteen years.[1]

There was a particularly unhappy memory of Ascension Day his first term, when after morning chapel the whole school was dispersed. He wandered out alone with his packet of food and sheltered from the rain under some trees called Lancing Ring – 'and, for the first and last time for many years, wept'.

I have brought up my children to make a special intention at the Ascension Mass for all desolate little boys.[2]

KENNETH CLARK, in the train on the way down to Winchester, spoke to a boy who appeared to be only a year or two older than himself, but received no reply. He approached a group without much more success. The first boy turned out to be head of the house, who sent for him in the library.

...he gave me three or four very painful strokes with a stick, known as a ground ash. 'That will teach you to speak to your seniors,' he said.

Lord Clark adds that 'in the twinkling of an eye the jolly boy from Wixenford became a silent, solitary, inward-turning but still imperfect Wykehamist'.[3]

RAYMOND MORTIMER bracketed Malvern with his 'over-large harsh' prep school at Eastbourne, as 'penitentiaries'.[4] Perhaps the strongest indictment lies in Sir LAWRENCE JONES (who was very happy at Eton) putting on record that never once in his years there did anyone tell him to be kind.[5]

IV

After their disastrous blunder in choosing the foster home in Southsea, KIPLING's parents sent him to the United Services College, Westward

1 *A Little Learning: The First Volume of an Autobiography* (1964), pp. 107, 115.
2 *Ibid.*, p. 110.
3 *Another Part of the Wood: A Self-Portrait* (1974), pp. 36–37.
4 *Try Anything Once* (1976), Autobiographical Preface, p.ix.
5 *A Victorian Boyhood* (1955), p. 200.

Ho! – two years established on a shoe-string, and slowly recovering from the anarchy when problem boys had completed the roll. Bullied for being the only boy to wear spectacles, so blind as to be excused games, and practically the only one not going into the Army, the sensitive lad survived. As he grew older he found firm cronies, and they set up a hide-out amongst the furze where they smoked and read good literature. A positive plus was the unlikely headmaster, Cormell Price (William Morris's 'Crom'), a friend of Kipling's uncle, Burne-Jones. He discerned the boy's literary ability, and was the ideal head for him as Dr Drury had been for Byron. Kipling wrote to his son John, who at ten entered St Aubyns (Stanford's) boarding school at Rottingdean:

I know exactly how homesick you feel at first. I can remember how I felt when I first went to school at Westward Ho! But my school was more than two hundred miles from my home – my Father and Mother were in India and I knew that I should not see them for years. The school was more than two hundred boys of all ages from eighteen to twelve. I was nearly the youngest – and the grub was beastly. . . .[1]

It has been suggested that, by coming to terms with the life, Kipling acquired the fascination for cruelty which surfaces from time to time in his writing.

After four years at Parkstone where Henry Forde took in a few boys for private teaching, LYTTON STRACHEY, at thirteen, was sent by his mother to the experimental school Abbotsholme run in the Public School tradition. One aspect of its originality was that the founder-headmaster, Dr Cecil Reddie, had abolished water-closets. Michael Holroyd writes:

He . . . reintroduced what he conceived to be the more natural method employed by the beasts of the field. Some concessions, however, were made to the higher status of the human being. . . . As they sat in a long military row, the boys looked over a neat dismal garden. . . .[2]

(EVELYN WAUGH described the double-row latrines at Lancing as 'inadequate in number', having no doors, and 'built over a deep open drain which was periodically, but not often, sluiced and disinfected'.[3] Two

1 Oct. 12, 1907.
2 *Lytton Strachey: A Critical Biography* (1967–8), i, p. 58.
3 *A Little Learning: The First Volume of an Autobiography* (1964), pp. 107–8.

lavatories served his whole house when KENNETH CLARK was at Winchester.)

Winter and summer Lytton's day began with a cold bath, then the parade ground for military drill and work with dumb-bells. Lessons began in summer at 6.45 a.m. His afternoon was taken up with games and manual work on the estate. In January, clad only in shorts and jersey, Lytton mended fences, felled trees, or mucked out the cowshed. He was also instructed in boot-making, tailoring, or the preparation of butter. Afternoon school lasted from 4.30–6.0, followed by compulsory glee-singing and artistic training. It seems that he desperately wanted to meet the challenge of his incongruous environment. He made a remarkable Hippolyta in the school production of *A Midsummer Night's Dream*, but before the end of his second term he had to be taken away in a state of complete physical breakdown. Later that year, now fourteen, he went to Leamington College where he was called 'Scraggs' and endured savage bullying. He told Leonard Woolf:

At school I used to weep – oh! for very definite things – bitter unkindness and vile brutality.[1]

In reply to his father who had been shown Lytton's correspondence with his mother, the boy wrote:

Your letter cheered me greatly for you see I am not *very* happy. . . .[2]

After his first year things improved and at fifteen he was made head of his house. At sixteen, his health caused him to miss a whole term and the family doctor would allow him to return only after special arrangements had been agreed. 'My luxurious tea,' wrote Lytton, 'is eyed by my fellows with looks of covetousness.' His biographer comments that 'considering the number of classes he missed over the years, his scholastic achievements are impressive'.[3]

Between the ages of nine and twelve, MASEFIELD was in the junior section of Warwick School which modelled itself on the great public schools.

I was wretched at first. I was too young. And they found that I wrote poetry. I tried to kill myself once by eating laurel leaves but only gave myself a

1 Michael Holroyd: *Lytton Strachey: A Critical Biography* (1967–8), i, p. 65.
2 *Ibid.*, i, p. 67.
3 *Ibid.*, i, p. 68.

horrible headache. Once I ran away, and was brought back by a policeman and flogged. . . .'[1]

Puberty for GRAHAM GREENE, as for Matthew Arnold, was complicated by having to contend with father and headmaster in one. He describes his eight terms at Berkhamsted School as '104 weeks of monotony, humiliation and mental pain'. After four attempts at suicide, he left a note under the whisky tantalus on the black oak sideboard, saying that instead of returning to St John's (his boarding house), he had taken to the Common and would remain 'until my parents agreed that never again should I go back to my prison'.[2] His elder sister Molly, acting as go-between, ran into him.

I could have run, of course, but that hardly suited the dignity of my protest, and so I went quietly home with her.[3]

Near to a nervous breakdown, he was put to bed and his father tenderly interrogated him. Graham's elder brother, studying medicine, was consulted and suggested psycho-analysis – 'and my father – an astonishing thing in 1920 – agreed'.[4]

DOROTHY L. SAYERS, arriving at sixteen, described herself as 'a fish out of water' at the Godolphin School, Salisbury. It understated her misery, not least on the hockey field. As day-boy at Tonbridge, E. M. FORSTER was not forced to play games. He looked back on those years as the unhappiest in a fortunate life.

STEPHEN POTTER said that as a day-boy at Westminster his days never deserved a word more grievous than *unpleasant* or *disappointing*, but they 'were on the whole the worst of my life'. From Number thirty-six Nightingale Lane, he used to cycle to Wandsworth Common Station where he had a special arrangement with Mr Crump in the ticket office. Every evening when he got off the train he would leave his top-hat and tail-coat in a cardboard box – to be put on again next morning 'in my lightning swoop through the station'.[5]

He rowed Number Three in the School Four. They won their first race of the season. By the time of their second, his last year's scar had

---

1 Constance Babington Smith: *John Masefield: A Life* (1978), p. 15.
2 *A Sort of Life* (1971), pp. 86–87.
3 *Ibid.*, p. 89.
4 *Ibid.*, p. 91.
5 *Steps to Immaturity* (1959), pp. 112, 116–7.

opened up and he had ragged surfaces between the bottom and the top of the leg.

The edges of the weal were permanently parted slightly, like lips; and I knew it would hurt.

They lost, and he thought he had caught a crab. But *The Daily Telegraph* reported floating debris, adding:

But for the excellent watermanship of No. 3 . . . the boat might well have overturned.[1]

The future Lifemaster achieved another kind of fame by winning the Pancake Race.

V

BEERBOHM in his late twenties wrote an essay on being in a hansom on his way to the theatre, when he noticed a small boy looking at him enviously from a hansom alongside, a trunk and play-box visible.

. . . gradually I became fulfilled with a very great compassion for him. . . . Even now, much of my own complacency comes of having left school. . . . Such an apparition as that boy . . . makes me realise my state more absolutely. . . . I am at a happier point in Nature's cycle.[2]

The two towers of Wellington College above the pines brought to HAROLD NICOLSON in middle-age 'a wave of depression', followed by exhilaration when he realised that his 'old sadness' could never return – 'and my heart sang hymns at heaven's gate'.[3]

DODGSON, a few years after leaving Rugby, wrote in his diary:

I cannot say that I look back upon my life at a Public School with any sensations of pleasure, or that any earthly considerations would induce me to go through my three years again.[4]

---

1 *Ibid.*, pp. 185–7.
2 'Going Back to School', *More* (1899).
3 *Diaries & Letters 1939–1945* ed. Nigel Nicolson (1967), pp. 261–2.
4 Stuart Dodgson Collingwood: *The Life & Letters of Lewis Carroll* (1898), p. 30.

CHAPTER FIVE

The Quality of Education

I

Critic though he may have been of its way of life, LORD CLARK recalled in mature age how Winchester College through its architecture had helped to make him an aesthete. Among its buildings, 'the gothic chantry and its surrounding cloisters were my favourites . . .' Indeed, thirty years after he left, he made an anonymous gift of some of the original glass of the Jesse window that had been taken out in the early nineteenth century for restoration, and which he had seen offered for sale – 'I have never written a cheque with greater emotion.'[1] But what may be surprising is that he, and others in various public schools, did not see their education remotely being the standard of excellence that is assumed of a great Public School, by virtue of wealth and tradition.

Lecturing in America at fifty-two, GALSWORTHY reflected on his time at Harrow:

What an odd life educationally speaking! We lived rather like young Spartans . . . I should say we were crammed, not taught . . . we were debarred from any real interest in philosophy, art, literature and music, or any advancing notions in social life or politics.[2]

SASSOON's last year at Marlborough was spent in the second division of the Lower Fifth, exactly half-way up the school. The final report on the future writer ran: 'Lacks power of concentration . . . seems unlikely to adopt any special career.' He himself, did not put the blame on intermittent illnesses – which he might very well have done. Prepared to confess his semi-idleness, he said something more:

. . . my own explanation is that I have a mind which absorbs information slowly and can only learn easily when its visual imagination is stimulated.

1 *Another Part of the Wood: A Self-Portrait* (1974), pp. 59–60.
2 H. V. Marrot: *The Life & Letters of John Galsworthy* (1935), pp. 42–43.

Public schools haven't time to worry about the artistic temperament or people with latent abilities of which they themselves are unaware.

He decided to wear his Old Marlburian tie as 'a badge of emancipation from an educational experience that I had found moderately pleasant but mentally unprofitable'.[1]

LEONARD WOOLF described St Paul's as 'Spartan in intellectual toughness and severity'. He summarised the aims of his headmaster, F. W. Walker:

The object of a public school was, in his view, to give the boys the severest and most classical of classical educations.[2]

E. H. Shepard was a pupil at this time and remembered the Old Man's habit 'of going the rounds':

He would sail majestically down the corridor, and it was useless for any boy doing penance outside a door to try and hide behind the lockers.[3]

Being quite good at games, Woolf was able to carry off the fact that he was a swot. Allowing he was never bullied nor 'actively miserable at school', he goes on:

But my modus vivendi with masters and boys was attained only by the conceal-ment or repression of a large area of my mental life which had the highest significance for me....[4]

LORD CLARK reckoned that the only times at which he had learnt anything of lasting value at Winchester were the several occasions during his first year when he had been ill in bed.

The reason was that my housemaster's wife used to bring me books. She had a complete set of the *Studio*. . . . She also lent me a book which had a far more lasting effect – *Turner's Golden Visions* by C. Lewis Hind.[5]

He had been fond of running, and having fainted after his weekly run was found to have pneumonia. His parents sent down their doctor, Lord Dawson, 'who said that the rigours of wartime Winchester (1917) had been too much for me and advised . . . a term at home'. His own

1 *The Old Century and seven more years* (1938), pp. 231–2.
2 *Sowing* (1960), p. 73.
3 *Drawn from Life* (1961), pp. 70–71.
4 *Op. cit.*, p. 90.
5 *Another Part of the Wood: A Self-Portrait* (1974), p. 65.

reaction was that 'now at last I had the opportunity of educating myself. We had a large bookcase full of books. . . .'[1]

BEVERLEY NICHOLS had spent his pocket-money on some postcards of the French Impressionists – a whole tray of them 'reduced', in a shop on the Queen's Parade, Torquay.

I loved my postcards so much that I stuck two of them inside my desk. One of them was Manet's picture of spring flowers . . . the second was Cézanne's 'Les Baigneurs'.

His form-master at Marlborough ignored the Manet and 'seized my little Cézanne'. He 'tore it up and threw it into the fire, to the evident delight of my class-mates'.[2]

II

Not only Art went by default but more traditional subjects also – or were criticized for the way in which they were taught. BEERBOHM said that of French, Algebra, even Science, he knew next to nothing when he left Charterhouse. RAYMOND MORTIMER, who went to Malvern, said that his own schools had 'taught him hardly anything about English literature . . . nor was there a single lesson in . . . science except elementary mathematics'. Yet in spite of such heavy specialization in the classics, he could not afterwards read Latin or Greek without a dictionary, 'to his deep regret and shame'.[3] A. A. MILNE 'did no English at Westminster'.

In my seven years there I never wrote so much as one essay for authority.

He took the Mathematical Tripos at Cambridge and wrote:

That I was ruined as a mathematician was Westminster's doing.[4]

More damning things even than these were said. Twenty-seven years after leaving Wellington, HAROLD NICOLSON wrote in his *Diary*:

I have no affection for the school whatsoever and no pride in it. I feel a grievance against it for having retarded my development.[5]

1 *Ibid.*, pp. 67–68.
2 *The Unforgiving Minute*, pp. 4–5.
3 *Try Anything Once* (1976), p. x.
4 *Autobiography* (US ed. of *It's Too Late Now*, 1939), pp. 135, 153.
5 *Diaries & Letters 1930–1939* ed. Nigel Nicolson (1966), p. 113.

RAYMOND MORTIMER described Malvern as 'one of the most philistine and brutal schools of the period (he was there 1909–1913), where unhappiness dulled his ability to learn'.[1]

BEVERLEY NICHOLS described an institution at Marlborough called Early School. Every morning they 'raced across a wind-swept courtyard ... in order to sit in an icy classroom ... making notes about matters of complete unimportance'. When he went to the headmaster to read a prize essay, the headmaster (later to become the Bishop of Bath and Wells) placed him by the fireplace and came to stand by his side.

He then proceeded casually to slid his hand down the back of my trousers and pinch me gently on the behind throughout the entire reading. This struck me as rather peculiar behaviour from the headmaster.

Nichols declared that he 'learned absolutely nothing whatsoever during three cold and wasted years'.[2] The ethos was games.

... nothing else mattered. I learned this within a few hours of my arrival, and the discovery filled me with apprehension, because I was never good at games.[3]

However, he broke the school record for the quarter mile. C. T. STONEHAM said of Brighton College that he had learnt little except to box and play football.

CYRIL CONNOLLY at Eton paralleled the experience of Leonard Woolf at St Paul's, that to be 'highbrow' was to be unpopular.

It was not smart at Eton to work; to be a 'sap' was a disgrace.... Even in College, among the seventy scholars, 'sapping' was discredited.... Intelligence was a deformity ... a public school taught one to conceal it.

Not until he was eighteen was he being initiated into Eton's 'inspired teaching', which 'owing to the intransigence of the boys could only appear at the top, where there were five real teachers'. Then he 'would dine with the Provost and the Headmaster, or Mr Headlam and Mr Marten would come to tea'.[4] J. DOVER WILSON wrote on his life at Lancing where his uncle was headmaster:

It was not until I reached the sixth form that I came across a real teacher, Ernest Crawley.[5]

1 *Op. cit.*, p. ix.
2 *The Unforgiving Minute* (1978), pp. 3–4.
3 *Ibid.*, p. 20.
4 *Enemies of Promise* (1938), pp. 275–7.
5 *Milestones on the Dover Road* (1969), pp. 24–25.

DODGSON complained of spending 'an incalculable time in writing out impositions – this last I consider one of the chief faults of Rugby School'. He conceded:

I made I suppose some progress in learning of various kinds, but none of it was done *con amore*.

His headmaster Dr Tait, who had succeeded Arnold, acknowledged cordially in a leaving letter to Archdeacon Dodgson: 'His mathematical knowledge is great for his age.'[1]

But JOYCE would be an exception. When he won a second exhibition at Belvedere College and was courted by the Dominicans, his father let him choose. Joyce elected to stay 'with the Jesuits'. They gave him a good training in English and equipped him with Latin, French, Italian. (He was to 'speak four or five languages fluently enough'.[2]) In his last year he may have disappointed *them* by insubordination and an indifference to the faith.

---

1 Stuart Dodgson Collingwood: *The Life & Letters of Lewis Carroll* (1898), pp. 29–30.
2 His letter to Harriet Weaver, June 24, 1921: *Selected Letters of James Joyce* ed. Richard Ellmann (1975), p. 281.

CHAPTER SIX

Adapting to their Environment

I

U nlikely temperaments found Public School life even con-
genial. Entered at nine years old to an Eton eighty years
away from Shelley's, THOMAS GRAY spent probably the nine
happiest years of his life. When someone asked in later life what had
first given him a taste for poetry, he replied, 'Reading Virgil at Eton
as a boy of eleven.'

He belonged to a teenage quartet, the Quadruple Alliance, each of
whom had a romantic pet-name from the stories and plays which
they read and acted together – his was *Orozamades*, Horace Walpole's
Celadon, Richard West's *Zephyrus*, and Thomas Ashton's *Almanzor*.
Instead of participating in games, they went to the river with books or
simply sat chatting. Boisterous life must have gone on all around, and
it seems marvellous they were permitted this tolerance to live entirely
with each other. Two centuries on, CECIL DAY LEWIS, whose experience at Sherborne was more mixed, wrote poetry in the day-room
'with twenty or thirty other boys hanging around', which only later
struck him as strange that such an activity was 'never molested or
commented upon unfavourably'.[1]

Lord David Cecil wrote that by the time GRAY and his friends were
eighteen 'no young men can ever have been more exquisitely
civilised'.[2] FIELDING was happy at Eton.

As Gray had collected and catalogued butterfly-orchis and bog
asphodel at Eton, so WILLIAM MORRIS at the Marlborough of 1848–
1851 played neither cricket nor football but collected birds' eggs. The
school was five years established. There was no prefect system and in
hours allotted to games most boys went on country rambles. Morris's

1 *The Buried Day* (1960), p. 108.
2 *Two Quiet Lives* (1948), p. 96.

148

fondness for going off alone and even talking to himself made him rather an eccentric figure, and his schoolfellows afterwards remembered him by his brief outbreaks of violent temper. He was not unhappy there, for being unusually strong saved him much bullying, but the school meant little to him in after life.

The loose discipline of his headmaster, Dr Wilkinson, proved advantageous for Morris. J. W. Mackail wrote:

Under the elaborate machinery and the overpowering social code of the modern public school the type is fostered at the expense of the individual: with a boy like Morris the strain would have been so great that something must have snapped.[1]

Even as a day-boy – which meant leaving home in summer at six, – WALTER PATER would have found life at King's School, Canterbury, totally incompatible but for his friends, René McQueen and Henry Dombrain. Like Gray at Eton, he withdrew into a closed society. 'You are a great deal too much together,' complained the headmaster. 'You are like the Twelve Apostles at Cambridge, and I am sure you would have far more influence for good in the school if only you would mingle with the other boys.'[2] He called them 'The Triumvirate' and said they were like three cherries on a stem. The other boys called them 'The Three Inseparables'.[3] They not only attended at the Cathedral with the school, but stole away from games to attend other services. They were confirmed together. Pater gave McQueen on his eighteenth birthday a copy of Bishop Andrewes's *Manual of Devotion*.

In a very moving way Pater had put his religion into practice the previous year when a number of boys at school set upon him. One of them delivered a 'dreadful' kick, which may have permanently affected his way of walking. The Rev. George Wallace, the headmaster, knew the offender and wanted to expel him, but Pater, lying ill for many weeks, earnestly requested that the boy be forgiven. The Rev. George Wallace was affected to tears, and two years afterwards at Pater's final Speech Day he told him:

I heartily trust that the good deed of yours which I cannot forget may still cast its light and point the way of many of your schoolfellows and show them the beauty of that charity which thinketh no evil and is quick to forget the wrong.[4]

1 *The Life of William Morris* (1899), i, p. 16.
2 Thomas Wright: *The Life of Walter Pater* (1907), i, p. 92.
3 *Ibid.*, i, p. 87.
4 *Ibid.*, i, pp. 140–1.

Education

A. E. HOUSMAN wore a black mortar-board like the other sixty or seventy boys at King Edward's School, Bromsgrove. Elected at eleven years old, he was one of twelve new foundation scholars who were day-boys now admitted on complete educational equality with boarders. Instead of compulsory games or athletics, the day-boys could work in a study room which suited Housman much better. Afternoon school was usually from 4.0–6.0 p.m., and in summer work began at 7.0 a.m., but his home at Perry Hall was almost next door. Even when he was thirteen and the family moved to Fockbury House, it was only one and a half miles away. The following year, Herbert Millington succeeded Dr Blore as headmaster, an important figure for Housman's classical development. As head boy at eighteen, he ended his schooldays brilliantly, winning prizes in English, Latin and Greek verse, drawing and French – also an open scholarship to St John's, Oxford.

Sir MAX BEERBOHM said that he himself 'ought to have been very happy' at Charterhouse.[1] Indeed, so lovingly spoilt at home, he ought to have been very unhappy and was *not*. Thirteen years after its move to Surrey, the school (1885–1890) was untypically tolerant, games not being compulsory – a significant factor in the happiness of all who have been mentioned in this section. The psycho-analyst to whom GRAHAM GREENE was sent at sixteen, 'had made sure that I would be excused all games',[2] and JAMES HILTON was rarely so happy in his life as when, taking a hot bath after a football game at Ley's, he 'reflected that no one would compel me to indulge in such preposterous pseudo-activity for another forty-eight hours'.[3]

BEERBOHM 'greatly disliked being a monitor's fag' at thirteen, but like Aldous Huxley at his prep school he had the capacity of withdrawing himself into his own world. His contemporary, Vaughan Williams, remembered him coming out of the school library enthusiastically reciting Edward Lear. His Eton collar broader and whiter than anybody else's, aloof, liking Latin verse, and not thrilled at making others fag for him, made him different from the other boys yet he was not teased – perhaps because he laughed at himself. From the age of fifteen he contributed to the school magazine two series of cartoons: *Charterhouse Types* and *Exeat Sketches*. 'There was something sarcastic about

1 *Mainly On the Air* (1946), p. 92.
2 *A Sort of Life* (1971), p. 107.
3 'A Chapter of Autobiography', *To You Mr. Chips* (1938), p. 42.

him even as a boy!' grumbled only one of his old schoolfellows.[1] In his last term one of the masters, Alexander Todd, encouraged his first appearance as a parodist, his privately printed fourteen-line poem in Latin elegaics *Carmen Becceriense*, with English notes. The poem poked fun at the recitals given by the music master, Mr Becker, and the notes mocked those in school editions of the classics.

At the end of an undistinguished career – no colours, no prizes, and never made Head Monitor – the headmaster, W. Haig Brown, could still write to Mrs Beerbohm:

I do not like the prospect of parting with your son . . . he has maintained so high a character that his absence will be a loss to the School. His artistic power will be much missed by many whose portraits he has often drawn and among these I may reckon Yours most faithfully. . . .[2]

II

After his devastating experience as a small child at Market Street, COWPER, a natural scholar, enjoyed Westminster. The fact that he could find happiness and friendship at a Public School contradicts what he said in *Tirocinium*:

Great schools suit but the sturdy and the rough.

BYRON liked and respected Dr Drury, his headmaster at Harrow, who had assured him on his first day that he would be privately coached until he could be put in a form with boys of his age. Almost at once the Byron charm worked on him as presently, after the taunting and bullying over his lameness and special boots, it did on the school. The headstrong and fearless boy had a style of his own. Often he limped up the hill with a book, to sit on the tomb of an unknown John Peachey under an elm.

In his first year as a fag at thirteen, he offered to stand in for Robert Peel who was being bastinadoed by a bully. When he had fags of his own, he chose the youngest and most beautiful boys and protected them. These passionate friendships worried Dr Drury who at one time asked him to resign, but this was withdrawn. Eventually in work he was third in the school, if idle during his last term. He was their best

1 David Cecil: *Max: A Biography* (1964), p. 36.
2 May 14, 1890.

swimmer, and one of the Cricket XI who played in their first match against Eton, in 1805. According to one of the boys, he had to have a runner because of his lameness.

In 1929, TERENCE RATTIGAN, another Harrovian, opened the school's innings in the Eton and Harrow match at Lord's, when he was eighteen. Next year, his last, he lost form and was dropped after the final trial. He wrote a telegram to his father who was coming, and his friend heard his sobs.

Rattigan had won a scholarship to Harrow, his parents needing to accept the money with the award. He was remembered as 'a very clever boy who quickly went up to the top of the school'.[1] He himself looked back on those days as among his happiest. Instead of participating in athletics, football or boxing, he compensated by cricket, racquets and squash, and became a hero to the junior boys because of his clemency. Like Byron, he did not conceal his attachment to the most attractive ones entering his House.

During his time there he practised writing plays. He wrote an article to *The Harrovian* on the conflict between 'entertainment' and 'instruction' in drama – anticipating the issues of the Kenneth Tynan onslaught midway in his professional career. He also found time to write to *The Times* complaining of compulsory OTC parades, a letter noticed by Stanley Baldwin, himself a Harrovian, who brought it to the attention of the Commons. With such extraneous activities he still managed to win a scholarship in Modern History to Trinity College, Oxford.

JAMES HILTON was allowed to opt out of 'the almost compulsory Officers' Training Corps' at The Leys School, Cambridge. The paradox 'obsessed' him that on Sundays they heard sermons preaching brotherly love and on Mondays they watched cadets on the games field 'bayoneting sacks with special aim for vital parts of the human body'.[2]

His father had shown originality in letting him, at fourteen, choose his own public school. He toured England on this 'interesting quest', and only a few headmasters were 'elaborately sarcastic and refused to see me'.[3]

Strangely perhaps, since I was not *the type*, I was quite happy at (shall we say?) Brookfield.

1 B. A. Young: *The Rattigan Version* (1986), p. 10.
2 'A Chapter of Autobiography', *To You Mr. Chips* (1938), p. 46.
3 *Ibid.*, p. 33.

He never received corporal punishment; he was never bullied. 'The sexual aberrations that are supposed to thrive at boarding-schools' never came his way. He played the piano 'dashingly rather than accurately' at Speech Day concerts. He enjoyed 'lazy afternoons at the Orchard, Grantchester, with strawberries and cream for tea' and 'liked to attend Evensong at King's College Chapel'.[1] The school 'must have been less rigid than many schools in enforcing conformity to type'[2] for, as Editor of the school magazine, he 'wrote pacifist and revolutionary poetry without being either persecuted or ostracised'.[3]

As a Harrovian during 1881–1886, GALSWORTHY fitted in very well but not as the potential writer. His housemaster wrote to Galsworthy's father:

...if only he was not so weak in composition he might really distinguish himself at Harrow.[4]

At the early age of seventeen, he was made head of his House. A boy remembered 'it was no disagreeable duty to act as his fag'. Another referred to an 'interview on the subject of cutting fagging, which might have been painful but was not'.[5] Galsworthy, who had been a choirboy at his prep school at Bournemouth, now possessed a very attractive light baritone voice, and a contemporary recorded that 'his call for "boy" when he wanted the fag on duty was always recognizable, being pitched on a more musical note than most'.[6] His housemaster wrote to him on leaving:

I shall always look back to you ... as my ideal head, without exaggeration.[7]

Captain of the Football XI, Captain of the School Gymnastic VIII and winner of the Mile, he arrived at New College, Oxford, his heart overstrained.

III

G. K. CHESTERTON, taller at twelve than most men, became a day-boy at St Paul's. The school had moved to Hammersmith three years

1 *Ibid.*, pp. 41–43.
2 *Ibid.*, pp. 38–39.
3 *Ibid.*, p. 48.
4 H. V. Marrot: *The Life & Letters of John Galsworthy* (1935), p. 37.
5 *Ibid.*, p. 41.
6 *Ibid.*, p. 43.
7 *Ibid.*, p. 48.

previously, less than a mile from his home in Warwick Gardens.

Because of failure to keep up, he sat in a class of boys two years younger and this continued more or less throughout the whole of his time. Edward Fordham said, 'We thought him the most curious thing that ever was.' The lanky boy would stride along 'apparently muttering poetry, breaking into inane laughter'. His form reports ran: 'Too much for me. . . .' – 'Wildly inaccurate . . . never thinks' – 'A very fair stock of general knowledge' – 'A great blunderer with much intelligence' – 'Can get up any work but originates nothing' – 'He has a decided literary aptitude' – 'Not on the same plane with the rest: composition quite futile . . . Not a quick brain. . . .'[1] When found wandering round the playground during school hours he said he thought it was Saturday. Masters found themselves accepting his excuse that he had forgotten to do his homework. When physical exercises became compulsory boys queued to watch his bizarre attempts on the trapeze or parallel bars.

Suddenly, when Chesterton was fifteen or sixteen, Edmund Bentley, two years his junior and a popular boy, recognized in this outcast the range and depth of his reading – his 'other' education that had been going on at home. There is supposed to have been a boyish scrap, but it ended in the inventor of clerihews making him his best friend. About a dozen boys gathered, all a year or so younger than Chesterton – most to gain brilliant scholarships to Oxford – and the Junior Debating Club began.

The idea had originated with Lucian Oldershaw, but there was never any argument about putting the oldest boy in the Chair. They met weekly in each other's homes, for one of them to read a paper on a literary topic followed by discussion, and there was always a substantial tea provided by the host's mother. Nothing ever again was taken more seriously by Chesterton than the JDC. At one meeting he expressed his belief in 'the good effect such a literary institution might have as a protest against the lower and unworthy phases of school life'. On another occasion at Oldershaw's house, 'the Chairman spoke seriously to Mr F.' (Fordham) about being too 'exuberant'.[2] He idealized their friendships. After a year Oldershaw had another idea – their own magazine *The Debater*, to every number of which Chesterton contributed verse and prose. Examples of his titles are: *Royal Death Scenes, On*

---

1 Maisie Ward: *Gilbert Keith Chesterton* (1944), p. 28.
2 *Ibid.*, p. 39.

Shakespeare's Method of Opening his Plays, The Happiness of Genius.
Masters and boys were nonplussed at such pieces by the boy who, according to one of his reports, did 'not trouble himself enough about work at school'.

A copy of *The Debater* was laid on the table of the High Master. Later, in Kensington High Street he buttonholed Chesterton, and with a characteristic bellow – he may have been the prototype of Sunday – informed him that he had a literary gift which might come to some account one day. Now in his last term, Chesterton at eighteen, in 6B, the highest form he reached, won the Milton Prize for a poem on St Francis Xavier – a competition always previously won by boys in the Eighth Form, St Paul's equivalent for Sixth. A notice appeared on the board shortly after:

G. K. Chesterton to rank with the Eighth.
– F. W. Walker, High Master.

When Chesterton's mother visited the school for advice on his career, Walker told her: 'Six foot of genius. Cherish him, Mrs Chesterton, cherish him.'[1]

In his last year at St Paul's, LEONARD WOOLF was 'both surprised and flattered' to be elected to this debating society by the founder members, who had now left but still 'met in rotation in the houses of the members' on Saturday afternoons.[2] He spoke of his contact with Chesterton and the other members bringing 'a new breath of intellectual fresh air into my school life'.[3]

IV

Rupert Brook at Rugby, and Ronald Knox at Eton, had different experiences from Dodgson and Cyril Connolly. Fifty years after Dodgson, RUPERT BROOKE looked back at his five years and almost every hour seemed 'golden and radiant ... always increasing in beauty as I grew more conscious'. The compounding of friendship, games and books, enabled him to say:

1 *Ibid.*, p. 42.
2 *Sowing* (1960), p. 91.
3 *Ibid.*, p. 93.

I could not (and cannot) hope for or even quite imagine such happiness elsewhere.[1]

Sixteen years before Connolly, RONALD KNOX at twelve joined his older brother Dillwyn, and shortly after arrival wrote to his mother:

... I am very happy here. . . .
PS Floreat Etona.

Mr Goodhart, the Master in College, made 'little expeditions into one's room just as one is getting into bed, and remarks on pictures and things'.

He told me the picture of Rembrandt was the sort of thing you could look at for hours. . . .[2]

As Captain of the School, Knox was known as the cleverest boy in living memory.

SASSOON, down with double pneumonia at Marlborough, was prayed for in chapel by 'Tup' – the headmaster Canon Bell 'might not remember who I was, but he had prayed for me by name. . . .' Having sampled the sanitorium beef-tea, Sassoon's mother departed smartly for the Ailesbury Arms, ordered beefsteaks, and surprised everybody by going down in the kitchen where 'with her own hands she concocted some of the strongest beef-tea ever made in Marlborough'. His occasionally choleric housemaster visited him early in convalescence: 'Well, you Siegfried, your mother is a wonderful woman. I am not at all sure that she didn't save your life.'[3]

Good old Gould. . . . Every night after lights out he went round the dormitories with a shaded candle. One heard him approaching with his short shuffling steps, and sometimes as he tilted his glimmer of light on my upturned face he would mutter 'Good night, you Siegfried.'[4]

NEWBOLT described his life at Clifton as 'smooth and prosperous'.[5] His widowed mother bought a house with a view of the Close so that her two sons could be day-boys, entering by a wicket-gate and reporting for Chapel or early-morning baths. The quiet study allotted to them at home 'was a much more favourable place for evening prep-

1 *Memoir*, written by his Mother, Aug. 1915: *Collected Poems* (1918).
2 Penelope Fitzgerald: *The Knox Brothers* (1977), p. 56.
3 *The Old Century and seven more years* (1938), pp. 211–2.
4 *Ibid.*, p. 209.
5 *My World As In My Time: Memoirs of Sir Henry Newbolt* (1932), p. 57.

aration than any that can usually be found in a boarding-house'.[1] He reached the Sixth Form before he was sixteen, and left as Head of the School. When his housemaster retired and he was invited to the last House Supper, he wrote in his Journal at thirty-six:

It's a pure marvel, a School, and the intangible invisible thing we call 'House-feeling' is about the most wonderful thing in it.[2]

At sixty, he became President of the Old Cliftonian Society.

Conditions improved for MASEFIELD after his first year at Warwick School. A Junior House was opened so that the smaller boys 'might be under a milder regime by themselves'.[3] In his last year at Stony-hurst, before he was taken away at sixteen and a half, VYVYAN HOLLAND 'really began to enjoy school life for the first time'.

I took up gymnastics and played lawn tennis reasonably well. . . . I passed the Higher Certificate Examination. . . .[4]

He received the much coveted Primi Ordinis prize – awarded to all boys who gained two-thirds of the maximum marks – every year he was at the school.

When GRAHAM GREENE reached the Sixth Form of Berkhamsted School, life for him was 'transformed'.

There were not many of us and we enjoyed frequent blank periods when we worked alone in the library. . . .[5]

As soon as CECIL DAY LEWIS had 'begun to master the taboos, totems, catchwords, gradations and general mystique of the half-savage tribe we were', he moved through Sherborne School 'with some confidence'.[6] Under his command the PT squad won the Public Schools Physical Training shield two years running. Head of his house, twice winner of the School Prize Poem, and Editor of the school magazine, the day lay ahead when he should 'revolt against public-school tradition as Sherborne then maintained it, with its false heroics, its facile religiosity and distorted values'.[7]

He began to acquire a liking for English poetry when the Rev. Henry

1 *Ibid.*, p. 54.
2 *Ibid.*, p. 204.
3 Constance Babington Smith: *John Masefield: A Life* (1978), p. 15.
4 *Son of Oscar Wilde* (1954), pp. 162–3.
5 *A Sort of Life* (1971), p. 106.
6 *The Buried Day*, (1960) p. 107.
7 *Ibid.*, p. 111.

Robinson King (his future father-in-law) became bored with his pupils and, whipping out a volume of verse, read aloud to himself till the end of the lesson.

A few of us listened.[1]

He also owed a special debt to Sherborne for the stress laid on physical training and gymnastics:

They taught us a lightness on the feet, a correct posture, ease of carriage and economy of movement which ... are considerably responsible, I believe, for my own good health in later life.[2]

VERA BRITTAIN acknowledged that at St Monica's the games and drill made the girls 'lithe and hard', and when she served as a VAD during World War I, she 'had reason to thank them for the powers of endurance of which they laid the foundation'.[3] ALEC WAUGH attended Sherborne, and 'enjoyed every aspect of the life'.[4] So did WODEHOUSE at Dulwich – in his fame, he flew over to England to report matches for the school magazine.

RICHMAL CROMPTON at eleven, went to boarding school – 'a vast, rambling former convent' – and loved everything about it, the 'larks', the games, the work. In the Cambridge Higher she was 'the best candidate of her year in classics', and gained a scholarship to Royal Holloway College, which she loved even more.

Himself a critic, yet BEERBOHM expressed himself in a way which, I imagine, all Public Schools would hope their old boys and girls could say:

The main thing that I had learnt there (Charterhouse) ... was a knack of understanding my fellow-creatures, of living in amity with them and not being rubbed the wrong way by their faults, and not rubbing them the wrong way with mine.[5]

A. A. MILNE allowed 'tolerance ... Westminster's great quality'.[6]

1 *Ibid.*, p. 108.
2 *Ibid.*, p. 126.
3 *Testament of Youth* (1933), p. 35.
4 *The Early Years of Alec Waugh* (1962), p. 28.
5 *Mainly On the Air* (1946), p. 92.
6 *Autobiography* (U.S. ed. of *It's Too Late Now*, 1939), p. 155.

CHAPTER SEVEN

Other Schools

I

A mong the big names who did not go to Public School are Shakespeare, Pope, Johnson, Wordsworth, Scott, Keats, Tennyson, Dickens, Hardy, Shaw, Wells, D. H. Lawrence. Some who attended other schools have been very damning of school.

CARLYLE, at ten, went to Annan Academy where apparently he suffered from bullying. He defined school as a place of torment where youth is confined behind windowless walls and has books flung at it. J. K. JEROME commented:

If only they would fling the right books it would be something.[1]

STEVENSON (who did not learn to read till he was seven) attended Mr Henderson's prep school round the corner from home and, on reaching eleven, he went down the hill to Edinburgh Academy, but his schooling was interrupted by ill-health – as well as truancy later. Like Beerbohm whose 'heart was always out of bounds',[2] he tended to be an outsider, preferring riding and swimming to games. A way of gesticulating, copied from Cummie, set him apart and the boys called him 'the little Frenchman', possibly also because his mother had taken him to the South of France during the winter when *she* was ill. When his mother again went abroad, he joined his two cousins at Spring Grove, near Isleworth, but was so unhappy that he wrote:

My dear Papa ... I do not feel well, and I wish to get home.

After a term his father promised he should not again be sent away. For three years before going to university he attended Mr Thompson's school of twenty pupils in Frederick Street, only a short walk from home.

J. K. JEROME obtained a presentation to the Philological School, later called Marylebone Grammar.

1 *My Life and Times* (1925), p. 30.
2 *Mainly On the Air* (1946), p. 93.

School hours were from nine till three . . . home lessons would take me until ten or eleven o'clock. . . . It was a silly system; and in most schools it still continues.[1]

Forty years later in 1914, JAMES HILTON at his grammar school in North-east London, often did not finish till nearly midnight. It struck him as 'remarkable that an age that restricts the hours of child-employment in industry should permit the much harder routine of schoolwork by day and homework in the evenings'.[2] More than seventy years after Hilton, no one questions the same system – ironical now many adults take early severance.

Jerome approved, as did De Quincey at Manchester Grammar, that corporal punishment was never used, but spoke cuttingly of schools in general:

What a boy learns in six years at school, he could with the aid of an intelligent bookseller, learn at home in six months.[3]

THACKERAY, who attended private schools in Southampton and Chiswick, and then entered Charterhouse, said:

. . . the benefit of ten years schooling was a little Latin & very little Greek – which a year at any other time would have given me. . . .[4]

JOHN DRINKWATER complained of 'no brutalities' at Oxford High (now the City of Oxford School) – only dullness: ready to admit that *he* must have been insufferably dull:

My classes were dull, the school-life in general, apart from the sports, was dull. . . . I do not think that from first to last I sat down to a single lesson with the smallest degree of interest.[5]

JAMES BRIDIE was bullied at Glasgow Academy. His early schooldays came back as a time of 'suffering agonies of tedium mitigated only by apprehension':

If it had been possible, in the circumstances, to interest me, my Masters would have done so. . . . But what a torture the round of school is! It is worse than a convict prison. To adults it would be unbearable. . . .[6]

1 *My Life and Times* (1925), p. 30.
2 'A Chapter of Autobiography', *To You Mr. Chips* (1938), p. 27.
3 *Op. cit.*, p. 30.
4 Letter to his Mother, Dec. 31, 1830: Ray, *op. cit.*, i, p. 138.
5 *Inheritance: Being the 1st Book of an Autobiography* (1931), p. 202.
6 *One Way of Living* (1939), p. 47.

MALCOLM MUGGERIDGE approved of his father, a Socialist, for 'very properly and logically' sending him and his brothers to the local elementary and secondary schools.

Neither type of school was likely to make any very strong impression on the boys who went through them, and I emerged unscathed and largely unlettered.

His secondary school, for which he presumably passed a scholarship, later became Selhurst Grammar School.

... it had just opened and, in the conditions of the 1914–18 war, was largely staffed with a bizarre collection of aged and incompetent teachers. . . .[1]

But his biggest broadside was against Education – 'the great mumbo-jumbo of this age'.[2]

H. E. BATES was granted a 'Free Place' at Kettering Grammar School. He speaks of himself in those early years as 'the victim of extraordinary sensitivity and abysmal shyness', in spite of playing for the 1st Football XI at the age of fourteen, and collecting prizes in both the Open and Under-15 100 yards in one afternoon.

It was simply that a great sensitivity of temperament was there. . . . There was, however, an adult hand in readiness to bruise it. . . . The hand was that of Scott, the headmaster. . . .

One day when he was in the fourth form he was suddenly summoned to Scott's study, 'without being told why, there to be immediately and relentlessly whipped, also without being told why. . . .'

I was stunned and lacerated by a monumental sense of injustice; for some hours I actually lost my power of speech.[3]

It was only some considerable time later that he discovered his 'crime' had been to allow a dull class-room neighbour to crib a single sentence from him at a weekly exam.

Owing to unsatisfactory staffing due to World War I, he became filled with 'a vast apathy'.[4] Before the 'growing squad' of 'erstwhile mistresses' began to drift away and the arrival of a new English master who was to be fundamental to his development as a writer[5] –

1 *Chronicles of Wasted Time* (1972–3), i, pp. 62–63.
2 'Twilight of Empire', directed by Kevin Billington, BBC 1, Nov. 10, 1964.
3 *The Vanished World: An Autobiography i* (1969), pp. 77–79.
4 *Ibid.*, p. 82.
5 See pages 43–4.

I believe I still thought of becoming a professional footballer . . . but I longed most of all to leave the place and never see it again.[1]

VERA BRITTAIN enjoyed a happier experience. At thirteen, she was sent away to the recently founded St Monica's at Kingswood in Surrey, the eldest of her mother's sisters being one of the two Principals. After 1930 it ranked as a public school, but when Vera Brittain attended, before World War I, 'the mildness of the intellectual competition . . . the lovely peace of the rich, undisturbed country, left scope for much reading of Dante and Shakespeare, of Shelley and Browning and Swinburne, and gave the opportunity for dreams. . . .'[2]

II

For nearly seven years THOMAS CHATTERTON was an inmate of Colston's Charity School, situated at St Augustine's Back in Bristol, which he entered at seven years and nine months. Every boy was tonsured, and wore a blue coat and yellow stockings like Christ's Hospital boys. The school hours in summer were from 7.0 a.m. till noon, and from 1.0 p.m. till 5.0 p.m.; in the winter, from 8.0 a.m. till noon, and from 1.0 p.m. till 4.0 p.m. Throughout the year, the boys went to bed at 8.0 p.m.

When Chatterton was indentured to a Bristol attorney, he wrote a very abusive anonymous letter to Mr Warner, the headmaster, which was traced back to the office and was the occasion of Mr Lambert striking him. Masson conjectures that the motives 'for sending it had probably been personal'.[3]

EDWARD LEAR did not go to school until he was eleven, but what happened about his epilepsy is not known. When he was thirty-six, he wrote to Fortescue:

I have had myself to thank for all education. . . .[4]

Seven-year-old ETHEL MANNIN went to a council school near her Clapham home – 'an enormous barracks of a building attended by some six hundred children'.[5]

1 *The Vanished World: An Autobiography* i (1969), p. 102, quoted from *The Old School* ed. Graham Greene (1934).
2 *Testament of Youth* (1933), p. 38.
3 David Masson: *Chatterton: A Story of the Year 1770* (1874), p. 18.
4 Vivien Noakes: *Edward Lear: The Life of a Wanderer* (1968), p. 90.
5 *Confessions & Impressions* (1930), p. 32.

When I got slapped it was for stupidity, never for bad conduct.... The slappings would make one's arm sting and the red marks would stay for a long time.... One could get 'the cane' for very bad conduct in class, talking, laughing, or writing notes, or eating sweets, or for very bad work.... I once in my childhood's simplicity told a teacher that I did not understand the sums I had been set; she shook me and sent me back to my place and told me to stop there until I did understand them. I was dazed beyond speech.[1]

For quoting in a set essay on Patriotism the words of Dr Johnson she had heard her father use at home – 'Patriotism is the last refuge of a scoundrel' – she was lectured on her wickedness and stupidity by the headmistress and made to kneel for a whole morning in the school hall, 'a punishment popular in this school' (1908–1914). On Empire Day she would not salute the Flag:

My Flag was the Red Flag, according to the creed set forth by my father, and the communist teacher who had admired my essay deriding patriotism.... So whilst the rest of the school marched through the playground and saluted the Flag – the girls' salute a ladylike waving of handkerchiefs – I knelt in the hall with my beating heart and my hurting knees and my terrific sense of martyrdom for a splendid cause.[2]

The elementary school which MALCOLM MUGGERIDGE attended before he went on to his secondary school, stood in an asphalt playground and was 'one of those stark bare buildings which successive Education Acts spawned over the country'. When the headmaster offered prayers, 'we had some difficulty with the aspirate in "hallowed be thy name", and were sometimes required to repeat it several times before we said it to his satisfaction'. His first teacher was Miss Corke.

I did not then, of course, know, but she had become friendly with another elementary school teacher in Croydon – D. H. Lawrence.... Some of his poems are addressed to her, and one of his novels – *The Trespasser* – deals with a tragic incident in her life, about which she also wrote a novel, *Neutral Ground*.[3]

BLAKE rejoiced in his escape altogether. When he was ten, he attended the drawing school of Henry Pars in the Strand.

Thank God! I never was sent to school
To be flogg'd into following the style of a fool.

1 *Ibid.*, pp. 36–37.
2 *Ibid.*, pp. 44–45.
3 *Chronicles of Wasted Time* (1972–3), i, pp. 63–64.

CHAPTER EIGHT

In Praise of Individual Teachers

I

If they were scathing in expressing abuses, they had a fine regard for individual teachers. BEN JONSON said he owed Camden, his headmaster at Westminster, 'All that I am in arts, all that I know'. WORDSWORTH went to Hawkshead Grammar School whose young headmaster, the Rev. W. Taylor, 'loved the Poets' and believed the boy was

> ... not destitute
> Of promise....
> ...when I at his command,
> Began to spin, at first, my toilsome Songs.[1]

CHARLES KINGSLEY went to the grammar school at Helston, the Eton of the West, where Coleridge's youngest son, Derwent, opened his own library to the boys and gave them the freedom of the Cornish countryside. Kingsley called him 'the dear old master'.

KIPLING dedicated *Stalky & Co.* to his headmaster, Cormell Price:

> Bless and praise we famous men –
> Men of little showing –
> For their work continueth,
> And their work continueth,
> Broad and deep continueth,
> Great beyond their knowing!

He appointed Kipling at fifteen editor of their *Chronicle*, and gave him 'the run of his brown-bound, tobacco-scented library'.[2]

Many of us loved the Head for what he had done for us, but I owed him more than all of them put together, and I think I loved him even more than they did.[3]

1 *The Prelude* (1805–6 version), Bk. X: ll.511–5.
2 *Stalky & Co.* (1899), p. 217.
3 *Something of Myself* (1937), p. 36.

In the Sixth Form at Bromsgrove School, A. E. HOUSMAN came under the enthusiastic tuition of the headmaster, Herbert Millington, who gave him as a prize when he was seventeen, *Sabrinae Corolla*, a volume of translations into Latin or Greek verse from English, German and Italian. Many years later, in his inaugural lecture at Cambridge, Housman said that this gift 'implanted in me a genuine liking for Greek and Latin'. When Housman was at the Patent Office, Millington published a classical volume of his own, and there was acknowledgement in the foreword of 'the debt I owe to my own pupil and distinguished friend, Mr A. E. Housman, for his valuable criticism of these verses. . . .'[1]

LAURENCE HOUSMAN, who with the other brothers were at the school, recorded with gratitude the name of the Rev. F. W. Parsons, his Form-master, who actively encouraged 'my love of English literature and poetry'.

. . . next to my own family there is nobody, I think, to whom I owe so much for that 'leading out' of my young mind, which is the right literal meaning of education, as I do to him. . . .

He mentioned another of his Form-master's virtues – 'the setting of impositions that required intelligence'.[2]

LEWIS HIND spoke of a book on his shelf, which he had received at Christ's Hospital – Milton's poems, inscribed 'Best Class-Life of John Milton'. It was a private purchase by John Wingfield, 'who loved Milton, who passed his love on to me, and . . . first showed me what noble literature can be. . . .'

If I think to-day that *Lycidas* is the finest elegy in the language, and that *On His Blindness* is one of the finest sonnets, it is, I suppose, because John Wingfield read them to us after school hours, often with a husky, breaking voice, in the class-room of the Upper Fourth. . . . And because the thoughts of youth are long, long thoughts.[3]

Not until LEONARD WOOLF was sixteen and had got into A. M. Cook's form, did any of his teachers at St Paul's ever suggest it was possible to read a work of literature for pleasure. Cook, 'an extremely cultivated man', asked him to walk round the playground with him during morning break, and for the remainder of his time in the form 'we always spent this quarter of an hour together'.

1 Herbert Millington: *Translations into Latin Verse* (1899).
2 *The Unexpected Years* (1937), p. 89.
3 *Naphtali* (1926), p. 15.

I owe an enormous debt to A. M. Cook. He talked to me not as a master to a pupil or as an adult to a boy, but as an equal to an equal. . . . He encouraged me to read very widely. . . .

When Woolf left for a higher form, Cook gave him a copy of Bacon's *Essays*, beautifully bound, and inscribed: 'L. S. Woolf first in written work in L.M.8. St Paul's School 1897: from A.M.C.' He describes the choice of 'the pale blue and gold of the Zaehnsdorf binding' for Bacon's 'curious prose' as characteristic of the man.[1]

BEERBOHM called 'Wilkie', the headmaster of the prep school in Bayswater, 'far the best teacher I ever had':

. . . he gave me my love of Latin and thereby enabled me to write English well.

He also described him 'so very sympathetic with the mind of a small boy'.[2] C. DAY LEWIS used similar words – 'we sensed . . . a warmth towards us, an intuitive understanding of the way small boys' minds work'.[3] Of another prep school head, Mr Norman of The New Beacon, SASSOON, even at fourteen, 'realized that "Corkeye" was a magnificent schoolmaster. . . .'[4]

C. DAY LEWIS called Nowell Smith ('the Chief'), 'the most disinterested man I have ever personally known'. He described him moving towards the pulpit, 'a small, slight figure . . . with the red MA hood slipping off one shoulder'.

. . . when he stood up there his eyes behind the gold pince-nez . . . alert yet aloof, a little worried, tremendously intelligent – and . . . the rare, sweet smile . . . then one could hardly fail to recognise the sincerity that shone through his authority. . . .

Nowell Smith's 'patient efforts to civilise Sherborne' included inviting first-class musicians to play in the Big School. To them Lewis owed his love for instrumental music, 'particularly for Bach . . . and for Chopin's passionate and heart-rending melodies'.[5]

KENNETH CLARK responded to the unconventionality of his headmaster Montague John Rendall, and when later he was able to present some pieces of mediaeval glass to Winchester College that had belonged to the Jesse window he wanted them to be associated with only Rendall's name.

---

1 *Sowing* (1960), pp. 90–91.
2 Letter to Rothenstein, quoted by Cecil, *op. cit.*, p. 26.
3 *The Buried Day* (1960), p. 69.
4 *The Old Century and seven more years* (1938), p. 189.
5 *Op. cit.*, pp. 113–4.

There was an element of absurdity in him, but a far more considerable element of greatness.

Lord Clark recalled the lantern lectures Rendall gave during winter terms on favourite Italian artists.

I can never describe what these lectures meant to me. . . . The very existence of religious art was virtually unknown to me.

The first of the series, on Saint Francis of Assisi, 'was for me like a religious conversion. . . .' His own *Civilisation* series had contained 'a not so distant echo of Monty Rendall'. The headmaster 'enriched' Clark's life at Winchester through the institution of Shrogus – the Shakespeare Reading and Orpheus Glee-Singing Society.[1]

JAMES HILTON wrote that Mr Chips was a composite creation, but that one of his prototypes was 'my father', who did not train aristocrats or plutocrats – 'he employed his wise and sweetening influence just as valuably among the thousands of elementary schoolboys . . . in a London suburb'.[2]

II

On the death of George Wollaston, NEWBOLT described his house-master at Clifton as 'unique' – 'an aristocrat in mind, without being Conservative'.

But I can't tell you what he was to his boys – I judge by what he was to me: just the old saying 'a liberal education'. The rest I think I really might have got from books, or from any kind of teachers: but education he gave me perpetually – at lunch, at tea, at dinner, in the garden and the drawing-room and the Close, books, poetry, languages, pictures, music, travel – every taste that makes life delectable and passionate. . . .

Yet Wollaston had not a single boarder in his House. Newbolt finished this letter to Lady Hylton:

No, I can't tell you how his going empties the world. . . . I had only one mother, and one Wollaston – now I am just a leaderless fellow like the rest.[3]

He was then sixty-three, and had known Wollaston for nearly fifty years.

1 *Another Part of the Wood: A Self-Portrait* (1974), pp. 61–63.
2 *To You Mr. Chips* (1938), p. 63.
3 *The Later Life & Letters of Sir Henry Newbolt* ed. Margaret Newbolt (1942), pp. 61–62.

At Lancing, J. DOVER WILSON felt he had been 'robbed of half my birthright' being crammed for a history scholarship instead of coming under the full charge of Ernest Crawley and reading with him Homer and Aeschylus. Crawley's room was hung with Arundel reproductions of all the ancient gods and goddesses, and on the top of the bookshelves below them were plaster casts.

It was an experience thrilling beyond words for a lad growing up in a very Victorian atmosphere to visit that chamber of beauty once a week, to have his essay looked at.

Crawley did, however, 'look after my essays and my education generally in literature, elementary philosophy and so on'.

He disciplined my feeble attempts at style, and I owe him much, and not only for this. He opened the door of the world to many of the boys who came under his eye.[1]

SASSOON had affectionate memories of Pat O'Regan in the Lower Fifth form-room on Sunday evening, reading poetry aloud and then offering half-a-crown for the boys to write some.

Thank you, Mr O'Regan for those half-crowns (I nearly always won them). You were the only person at Marlborough who ever asked me to write poetry. The first time I won the prize you had my verses framed and hung them in the form-room.[2]

C. S. LEWIS described Harry Wakelyn Smith ('Smewgy') as one of his two greatest teachers, although he knew him at Malvern only a year. Never had he experienced such courtesy in a teacher. Of his two years in Great Bookham under W. T. Kirkpatrick ('Kirk', – 'Great Knock'), a private tutor, Lewis wrote:

I owe him in the intellectual sphere as much as one human being can owe another. That he enabled me to win a Scholarship is the least that he did for me.

Again, in mediaeval language, 'Smewgy taught me Grammar and Rhetoric and Kirk taught me Dialectic.'[3]

C. DAY LEWIS spoke of W. B. Wildman, classics master, as one of Sherborne's finest teachers:

The first man I ever knew who was gifted with that excess of life which of all human qualities I respond to most whole-heartedly.

1 *Milestones on the Dover Road* (1969), p. 25.
2 *The Old Century and seven more years* (1938), pp. 216–7.
3 *Surprised by Joy: The shape of my early life* (1955), p. 141.

Should the Senior Science Master come into their room and leave, 'Wildie would ostentatiously fan the air with his bandana handkerchief, ask someone to open a window wider, and wheeze out, "Poor little man! What a life! Making *smells* all day!"'

... Personality bulged out of him as ebulliently as his body bulged in its clothes. . . .[1]

EVELYN WAUGH made an exception of J. F. Roxburgh at Lancing, a dandy with panache. When he entered the form-room it was 'a moment of exhilaration'.

J.F. appeared always jaunty and fresh as a leading actor on the boards. . . . He never gave the impression of performing a routine task. I think he found the spectacle of us positively stimulating.[2]

Once a week he took the whole Upper Sixth in 'general' subjects, ranging from Greek sculpture to a recent political book that had come under his notice. Waugh remembered an occasion after chapel when he examined the mixed metaphors in one of Cowper's hymns.

CYRIL CONNOLLY singled out at St Wulfric's, a master, Mr Ellis ('Daddy Ellis') who befriended him.

He called me Tim Connolly and built up a personality for me as the Irish rebel, treating me as an intelligent and humorous person.[3]

At Old School House, STEPHEN SPENDER used to stare at Mr Greatorex who conducted their singing, and think the domed bald head belonged to one of the most beautiful people he had ever seen. When because of bullying authorized in an astonishing way by the housemaster,[4] he had nearly arrived late for his piano lesson, 'almost blinded by tears', Greatorex said, 'Tell me what is the matter,' and told him that the time would come when he would be happier than most people.[5] Later in life, Spender wrote and thanked him for having made the remark, confirming it was true.

ROALD DAHL recorded that alone among the teachers at Repton, Corkers, meant to teach maths, was a character and an original:

Corkers was a charmer, a vast ungainly man with drooping bloodhound cheeks and filthy clothes.

1 *The Buried Day* (1960), pp. 109–10.
2 *A Little Learning: The First Volume of an Autobiography* (1964), pp. 158–9.
3 *Enemies of Promise* (1938), p. 209.
4 See page 121.
5 *World Within World* (1951), p. 333.

Once, he doubled a square of tissue paper from his pocket and told them if he went on doubling it fifty times, the thickness would be the distance from the earth to the sun – which he proved on the blackboard. On another occasion he brought in a two-foot grass snake for every boy to handle, in order to cure a fear of snakes.

I cannot remember all the ... thousands of splendid things that old Corkers cooked up to keep his class happy.[1]

III

ERIC GILL expressed the debt he owed to Edward Johnston, when he had attended his class of writing and lettering at the Central School of Arts and Crafts then in Regent Street:

I owe everything to the foundation which he laid.... He profoundly altered the whole course of my life and all my ways of thinking.... I fell in love with him.[2]

After a year or more, when Gill was nineteen, Johnston invited him to share his rooms in Lincoln's Inn.

Of the kind people at the Collegio della Visitazione, VYVYAN HOLLAND remembered three especially 'with deep affection'. There was his own division Prefect, Father Dominico Giusta, 'from whom I never had a harsh word that I did not richly deserve'. Then, Father Alphonso Stradelli was the Spiritual Father – the priest to whom any boy in a Jesuit school has almost immediate access if he is in any distress.

In the course of my eight years of Jesuit schooling I never knew one Spiritual Father who was not a help and a comfort to those in trouble.

The third priest, Father Modesto Cerutti, he remembered best – the chief classical master and 'true friend':

He understood my worries and my sorrows and comforted me; and he provided an inexhaustible supply of stamps for my collection.[3]

VERA BRITTAIN paid tribute to the lessons which Miss Heath James gave in History and Scripture at St Monica's:

From the unimaginative standpoint of pre-war examinations they were quite

1 *Boy: Tales of Childhood* (1984), pp. 136–8.
2 *Autobiography* (1940), pp. 118–20.
3 *Son of Oscar Wilde* (1954), p. 118.

unpractical, but as teaching in the real sense of the word – the creation in immature minds of the power to think . . . to perceive analogies – they could hardly have been surpassed.[1]

HAROLD PINTER, inspired by Joseph Brearley, his English master at Hackney Downs Grammar School, said of him: 'He's a brilliant man.'

EMLYN WILLIAMS, at Holywell County School, was one of Miss Cooke's 'black beetles'. She gave him hot cocoa after his five-mile walk of a morning, and had her family make him a pair of Yorkshire-leather boots. She sent him to France for a working holiday. She sent him to Christ Church, Oxford, for an Open Scholarship in French, and he immortalized her in *The Corn is Green*.

1 *Testament of Youth* (1933), p. 39.

CHAPTER NINE

University – Its Popularity, Abstentions, and Distraction

The majority of our writers have gone to university: Oxford the most popular, with Cambridge well ahead of London, Edinburgh, Dublin, and then the rest. As regards the popularity of individual colleges, Balliol and Trinity (Cambridge) come easily first, with Christ Church a good lead on Trinity, Oxford.[1]

Formidable names are often missing: Chaucer, Shakespeare, Defoe, Pope, Keats, Dickens, Hardy, Shaw. Defoe, a dissenter, and Pope, a Catholic, would have been prohibited, as was Donne at Hart Hall, Oxford, from taking a degree. JAMES MILL was urged in vain to enter his brilliant son at university; he entered India House instead, where at seventeen he was appointed to a junior clerkship in the examiner's office under his father. YEATS, the son of a painter, spent three years at the Metropolitan School of Art in Dublin; G. K. CHESTERTON had no regrets about studying Art for three years at the Slade.

H. E. BATES passed his Oxford and Cambridge Certificate third in honours and his school thought he should go to Cambridge, but when his father said it would take every penny, he 'informed him simply and with no hesitation, I wouldn't go'. Long after, he wrote:

I have never been sorry about that decision. I have never regretted University.[2]

Five months short of his twenty-first birthday, with his first novel accepted by Jonathan Cape, he was dining with his future publishers and enjoying an extended conversation with their reader Edward Garnett.

HOLBROOK JACKSON was almost entirely self-educated, earning his living at fifteen. Others shared the same slender basis of a formal education. V. S. PRITCHETT at fifteen left Alleyn's School, Dulwich, to

---

1 See Appendices E & F.
2 *The Vanished World: An Autobiography* i (1969), p. 126.

work in the leather trade. At fourteen, FREDERICK MARRYAT joined the Royal Navy, CHARLES KNIGHT was taken by his publishing father as an apprentice, and FRANK SWINNERTON started as an office boy at Chatto and Windus. At fourteen, IAN MACKAY left Wick High School – 'with a legendary reputation of scholarship' – and ALAN SILLITOE began to work in a factory (neither his father nor grandfather could read or write). GRANVILLE-BARKER began his stage training at thirteen; WILLIAM ALLINGHAM at that age entered a bank with which his father was connected. Twelve-year-old HOWARD SPRING left school to sell newspapers. LESLIE THOMAS was a Dr Barnardo's boy.

But sometimes the public schoolboy knew financial disadvantage which dogged him to university. PATER, on being awarded the Exhibition (£60) for three years at Oxford, received an additional £30 as a gift from the school, and some friends gave him a present in money. Ironically, at Queen's his slender resources made it impossible for him to decorate his rooms – which earned the name *The Spartan Chambers*. After a year or two his circumstances improved, but a tutor noted that 'decorative features were used with guarded moderation'.[1] J. DOVER WILSON went to Lancing on a scholarship, and reached Caius on a history scholarship:

> The college ... was very good to me from the beginning, for they allowed me to live at home while receiving the full total of the scholarship. My parents were so poor that this was indeed the only way I could have managed.[2]

Among non-public-schoolboys who went to university are Johnson (for one year), Wordsworth, Scott, Tennyson, Wells, D. H. Lawrence. Browning put in half a session at University College, London. Radclyffe Hall's education consisted of occasional attendance at dayschools and a year at King's College, London.[3]

RUSKIN went up to Christ Church with his mother in lodgings nearby, because a frustrated love affair had put his unstable genius under strain:

> She had always been my physician as well as my nurse ... and my day was always happier because I could tell her at tea whatever had pleased or profited me in it.[4]

---

1 Thomas Wright: *The Life of Walter Pater*, i, p. 160.
2 *Milestones on the Dover Road* (1969), p. 28.
3 See Appendices E & F.
4 *Praeterita* (1886–8), i, p. 368.

R. C. SHERRIFF's widowed mother accompanied him when he went up
to New College to read History at thirty-three, for she was dependent
on her bachelor son.

The life caused some to act out of character. MILTON in his first
year at Christ's, Cambridge, was rusticated after a clash with his tutor.
On his return he was assigned to another and graduated in normal
time, leaving with the nickname 'The Lady' – a reference, it seems, to
his physical delicacy and moral purity. WILDE was rusticated for most
of a term, and fined £47.10s. (half the amount of his demyship for the
year), when he overstayed the vacation in Greece and Italy:

I was sent down from Oxford for being the first undergraduate to visit
Olympia.[1]

JOHNSON 'disregarded ... all authority'.[2] WORDSWORTH indulged
in much 'good-natur'd lounging'.[3] CHARLES KINGSLEY suffered guilt
that at Magdalene he had lived for a while as a backslider; his first
physical relations with a woman took place probably at this time with
a prostitute. GISSING got expelled from Owen's College, Manchester,
for stealing, and a month in prison followed.

MATTHEW ARNOLD affected at Balliol a certain dandyism[4] and
struck some of his contemporaries as a trifler. GALSWORTHY at New
College, Oxford, did not find Jurisprudence exciting and had the reputation of 'best-dressed man in College'.[5] At University College,
Oxford, Hogg discovered even SHELLEY, one afternoon, newly
invested by the tailor in a 'blue coat with many glittering buttons ...
splendid in his blue and gold'. The arch-dandy and eccentric must be
BYRON, who took 'super-excellent' rooms at Trinity, Cambridge. He
bought a fine grey horse which he rode every morning in a white hat
and a silver-grey cloak. In his second year he brought a young mistress
from Brompton, the boxer Jackson, and his fencing master Angelo. In
his last year he paraded a pet bear on its hind legs up those noble steps.
He told the authorities he wanted it 'to sit for a fellowship'.

1 H. Montgomery Hyde: *Oscar Wilde: A Biography* (1976), p. 29.
2 James Boswell: *The Life of Samuel Johnson, LL.D.* (1791). Aetat. 20: 1729.
3 *The Prelude* (1805–6), Bk. VI: l.202.
4 See page 319.
5 H. V. Marrot: *The Life & Letters of John Galsworthy* (1935), p. 66.

CHAPTER TEN

Disillusionment

Surprising names did not like what they found. GRAY was unusual in preferring school; he could hardly wait until he should no longer have to endure 'college impertinencies' and 'lectures daily and hourly'. He wrote to West:

Must I plunge into metaphysics? Alas! I cannot see in the dark. . . . Must I pore upon mathematics? Alas! I cannot see in too much light. It is very possible that two and two make four, but I would not give four farthings to demonstrate this ever so clearly. . . .

Oddly for one who later chose to spend most of his life at Cambridge, he compared it to Babylon after the owls had built there.[1] BOSWELL ran away from Glasgow University to submit to the Roman Catholic Church. GIBBON spoke of his fourteen months at Oxford as the 'most idle and unprofitable' of his whole life.

WORDSWORTH disliked the narrowness of the curriculum and the worldly tone. He had

A feeling that I was not for that hour,
Nor for that place. . . .[2]

RUSKIN found 'the change from our front parlour at Herne Hill . . . appalling':

. . . from first to last, I had the clownish feeling of having no business there.[3]

COLERIDGE at Jesus, Cambridge, discovered (like Johnson) his desultory and extensive reading to be far in advance of the other undergraduates'. BYRON worked hard at Cambridge in spite of his dandyism, but complained:

Nobody here seems to look into an Author, ancient or modern, if they can avoid it.

1 Dec. 1736.
2 *The Prelude* (1805–6), Bk. III, ll.80–81.
3 *Praeterita* (1886–8), i, p. 357.

DE QUINCEY repeated what he had done at Manchester Grammar and 'eloped' from Worcester, Oxford.

J. R. GREEN quarrelled with the way history was taught during his time at Jesus, Oxford; he considered the subject degraded by dons setting prescribed fragments of books. A. J. P. TAYLOR, who gained a First at Oriel, writes:

On a more serious level I learnt precisely nothing. I increased my knowledge of history, my understanding of it, not at all. I did not even learn how to write.[1]

A.E HOUSMAN was 'disgusted' by Jowett's 'disregard for the niceties of scholarship'.[2] ROBERT GRAVES, who went to St John's, Oxford, after his war service, was not happy about the insistence on eighteenth-century poets and found it difficult to concentrate on Anglo-Saxon grammar. BETJEMAN did not like the 'booming' voice of his tutor, C. S. Lewis. On account of a blister, Betjeman came to an Old English tutorial wearing exotic carpet slippers, hoping his tutor would not mind; Lewis replied he should mind very much wearing them himself but did not object to his wearing them. MALCOLM MUGGERIDGE echoed Gibbon:

For me, the years at Cambridge were the most futile and dismal of my whole life.[3]

1 *A Personal History* (1938), p. 84.
2 Richard Perceval Graves: *A. E. Housman: The Scholar-Poet* (1979), p. 49.
3 *Chronicles of Wasted Time* (1972–3), i, p. 79.

CHAPTER ELEVEN

No Degree

S ome through religious or ethical principle went down without a degree. DONNE would have found it impossible to take the Oath of Supremacy required at graduation. GIBBON, after a year at Magdalen, Oxford, had read himself into the Roman Catholic Church and, when his father angrily made it known, the university was shut against him. SHELLEY, after five months at University College, Oxford, was expelled for his pamphlet *The Necessity of Atheism* on sale in the town.

There were other honourable reasons. Poverty forced JOHNSON from Oxford after four terms. His feet had begun to appear through his shoes, but when a new pair were set at his door he flung them away. It was poverty which had caused him to lounge at the College gates, keeping a circle of young students from their studies – 'if not spiriting them up ... against the College discipline'. He told Boswell:

Ah, Sir, I was mad and violent. It was bitterness which they mistook for frolick. I was miserably poor, and I thought to fight my way by my literature and my wit. . . .[1]

TENNYSON left Trinity, Cambridge, because his father had died leaving debts. G. A. HENTY left Caius to volunteer for hospital service in the Crimea.

The 'terribly sensitive' ROBERT ROSS, starting at King's, was ducked in the Fountain as an 'aesthete', although he had rowed in the college boat. The experience caused 'a violent brain attack'[2] when he became near suicidal, so that his brother came and took him away. Those who had done it said they were sorry but he did not return. SACHEVERELL SITWELL found Oxford, post-World War I, 'something of a desert'[3]

---

1 James Boswell: *The Life of Samuel Johnson LL.D.* (1791), Aetat.20: 1729.
2 Letter by Oscar Browning, March 1889: quoted by H. Montgomery Hyde, *Oscar Wilde: A Biography* (1976), p. 121.
3 Quoted by John Pearson: *Façades: Edith, Osbert & Sacheverell Sitwell* (1978), p. 132.

and left after a term. His fellow undergraduate at Christ Church, William Walton, who was to be an adopted brother of the Sitwells, commented:

... there was absolutely no point for him in staying. He was so well read that he knew far too much about absolutely everything.[1]

Some had themselves to blame. STEELE threw up cap and gown to ride as a gentleman volunteer in the second troop of Horse Guards under the command of the second Duke of Ormonde. A century later, embarrassed over college debts, COLERIDGE ran away after two years at Jesus, Cambridge, to enlist in the 15th or King's Regiment of Light Dragoons, G. Troop. He masqueraded under Private Silas Tomkyn Comberbacke:

A very indocile equestrian[2] . . . I ride a horse, young, and as undisciplined as myself.

He was thrown three times within a week, 'and run away with . . . almost every day'.[3] When two officers were holding a classical conversation, the private ventured to amend a quotation from Eusebius. On recovery from shock, they elicited his story and communicated with his family so that his brothers bought him out. Another reminiscence which 'fell from Coleridge's mouth' was, that a Latin sentence scribbled on the walls of the stable at Reading caught the attention of Captain Ogle of the regiment, and led to Comberbacke's detection. Coleridge returned to Cambridge after an absence of four months. But his Pantisocratic scheme with Southey dominated the Long Vacation, and there was a broken love affair, so that he went down at the end of the year. When Sir RICHARD BURTON was rusticated from Trinity, Oxford, due to 'eccentric behaviour', he sailed to Bombay and joined the Indian Army.

THACKERAY left Trinity, Cambridge, having lost £1,500 at play. SWINBURNE 'was not formally but informally expelled'[4] from Balliol – according to Edmund Gosse, the landlady had complained to the college of 'late hours and general irregularities'.[5]

1 *Ibid.*, p. 135.
2 To Capt. James Coleridge: Feb. 20, 1794.
3 To the Rev. George Coleridge: End of March, 1794.
4 Swinburne writing on Nov. 25, 1902; quoted by Philip Henderson: *Swinburne: The Portrait of a Poet* (1974), p. 44.
5 *The Life of Algernon Charles Swinburne* (1917), p. 63.

Distracted by literature, FRANCIS THOMPSON failed his medical exams at Manchester three times and went to seek a livelihood in London. BEERBOHM, having achieved a Third in Honours Moderations, got caught up with *The Yellow Book*; he told an interviewer:

I have been too much interested in the moderns to have yet had time for the ancients.[1]

He left Merton, Oxford, before his finals. BETJEMAN was sent down from Magdalen, having 'Failed in Divinity!' Thirty years later, he remembered C. S. Lewis's chilling response:

> I sought my tutor in his arid room,
> Who told me, 'You'd have only got a Third.'[2]

RONALD FIRBANK, during his whole time at Trinity Hall, never sat a single examination.

Sir CHARLES SEDLEY left Oxford without a degree but later, like Johnson, obtained a DCL.

1 Quoted by David Cecil: *Max*, p. 101.
2 *Summoned by Bells* (1960), p. 109.

CHAPTER TWELVE

Without Academic Distinction

A group did not do very well. SWIFT was granted his BA *Speciali gratis*. RUSKIN had his course broken by a haemorrhage, but took pass schools on return with an Honorary Fourth. DESMOND MACCARTHY at Cambridge, and ROSE MACAULAY at Oxford, graduated *aegrotat* in History. HENRY SWEET achieved a Fourth in Literary Humanities, and C. DAY LEWIS a Fourth in Greats. DARWIN, at Christ's, Cambridge, came tenth in the list of graduates not seeking honours; *Erewhon* BUTLER, at St John's, was listed twelfth in the Classical Tripos.

WORDSWORTH, having abandoned the idea of reading mathematics for honours, and with that all chance of a fellowship, settled for a BA without honours. Because maths were 'totally uncongenial'[1] to him, MACAULAY was refused honours at Trinity, Cambridge, and therefore disqualified from competing for the chancellor's medals, but he was allowed to pass in the mathematical tripos of 1822. C. S. LEWIS never did pass the Responsions examination at Oxford, being exempted later on because of his military service. Warren, his brother, believed that 'Jack' could never have passed any examination in elementary mathematics. A love of maths got A. A. MILNE a scholarship to Westminster and an exhibition to Trinity, Cambridge. It got his son CHRISTOPHER scholarships to Stowe and to his father's college. Both achieved Thirds, but Christopher, returning after a six-year break for World War II when he took English, 'could offer the better excuse'.[2]

NEWMAN overworked at Trinity, Cambridge, and sank to a Third. MATTHEW ARNOLD gained a Second and not the First expected of a Balliol scholar. Both men atoned by winning an Oriel fellowship.

J. R. GREEN read 'for fun, that is not for the class list, dread Moloch of Oxford innocents',[3] and ended his time at Jesus 'only just ... escaping of malice prepense the compliment of an "honorary fourth"'.

1 Matthew Arnold told Clough, 'the mathematics were ever foolishness to me' (Sept. 23, 1849). Cf. Gray's letter to Richard West, quoted on page 175.
2 Christopher Milne: *The Enchanted Places* (1974), p. 165.
3 His letter to 'T.O.', 1858.

Leslie Stephen adds: 'His interests . . . lay outside the regular field of university study. . . .'[1] Raymond Mortimer gave the same reason for E. M. FORSTER taking a Second:

> . . . like several of the cleverest men I have known . . . he read so widely outside his examination subjects.[2]

JOYCE took a pass degree at University College, Dublin, having read practically every 'important creative work published in the late nineteenth century'.[3] EVELYN WAUGH, at Hertford, Oxford, gained a Third in the History School – 'not even a good one'[4] – and wrote later to a younger man:

> I hope you are not cast down by your result in Schools. Of my contemporaries, those who achieved any success in after life nearly all got thirds or were sent down.[5]

J. E. FLECKER, HUGH WALPOLE, HAROLD NICOLSON, took only Thirds.

After being an enthusiastic student at Ashburne House, Manchester, ALISON UTTLEY was awarded third-class honours in physics. MALCOLM MUGGERIDGE, at Selwyn, Cambridge, 'did nothing and just managed to get a pass degree' in the Natural Science Tripos.[6] At Glasgow, JAMES BRIDIE read medicine largely to please his father, and took double the normal time to pass his finals.

Lord DAVID CECIL reported on himself: 'Has made progress.' Three times he had failed the entrance to Christ Church because of his hopelessness at maths. As Goldsmith Professor of English Literature from the age of forty-six, his lectures were crowded to the doors. The same might be said of A. E. HOUSMAN – ploughed in Greats, while his friends Alfred Pollard and Moses Jackson gained Firsts. A year later in a retake he failed in Political Economy, but was granted a pass degree. Ten years after that, largely as a result of his articles in *The Journal of Philology*, his application for the Latin Chair at University College, London, was endorsed by fifteen of the foremost scholars of the day. After holding the Chair nineteen years, he was Professor of Latin at Cambridge for another twenty-five.

---

1 *Letters of John Richard Green* ed. Leslie Stephen (1901), pp. 14–15.
2 His review of P. N. Furbank's *E. M. Forster, A Life: The Sunday Times*, July 24, 1977.
3 Ellmann, *James Joyce* (1959), p. 78.
4 Assessment by his tutor, C. R. M. F. Cruttwell.
5 *Evelyn Waugh & his World* ed. David Pryce-Jones (1973), p. 233.
6 Malcolm Muggeridge: *Chronicles of Wasted Time* (1972–3), i, p. 79.

CHAPTER THIRTEEN

Wise in Their Conceits

G EORGE MOORE pointed out the artist's 'unerring and ineffable instinct' which guides him to his proper food.[1]

Perhaps we should see STERNE preparing for his vocation when at Jesus, Cambridge, he 'read a little' and 'laugh'd a great deal'? Or GRAY, who after four years at Peterhouse had succeeded in writing Latin verses of considerable merit? Or WORDSWORTH, who at St John's devoted himself entirely to the poets – none of whom had anything to do with his degree course?

Or SWINBURNE, whose tutor Jowett at Balliol disapproved of his spending so much time on poetry? Or A. E. HOUSMAN, at St John's, Oxford, spending too much time on Propertius instead of studying the Greats syllabus? Or STEVENSON, who at the University of Edinburgh 'set store . . . by certain other odds and ends that he came by in the open street while he was playing truant'?[2]

Or then again, BEERBOHM, who at Merton, Oxford, neglected his studies 'to talk, dream, read modern books, and be himself'? Or A. A. MILNE, withstanding his tutor at Trinity and editing *The Granta* ('The Cambridge *Punch*') when he needed to work harder in maths to justify his Exhibition? Or SASSOON, who at Clare changed Law for the History Tripos mid-stream and then decided a future poet could manage without a BA?

Or SHERRIFF, lured from New College, Oxford, as a freshman of thirty-three to write screen-plays for Hollywood? Or C. DAY LEWIS, who spent too much time 'in desultory reading' at Wadham, and hawking his privately-printed first volume of verse round the Oxford and Nottingham bookshops?[3] Or RATTIGAN, at Trinity, Oxford, having *First Episode*, a collaborative venture with his friend Philip Heimann, put on

1 *Confessions of a Young Man* (1886), p. 156.
2 Quoted by Graham Balfour: *The Life of Robert Louis Stevenson* (1901), i, p. 70.
3 C. Day Lewis: *The Buried Day* (1960), pp. 167–8.

at the Q and then at the Comedy Theatre, and deciding neither to take finals nor the Diplomatic entry exam, but to begin his dramatic career at once?

CHAPTER FOURTEEN

A Liberal Education

I

Some have set as much, or greater, store on a liberal education, which has taken many forms and either substituted or complemented a formal one. GEORGE MOORE, before the formulation of Lifemanship, made capital out of *not* going to either Oxford or Cambridge:

> I went to the 'Nouvelle Athenes' . . . a *café* on the Place Pigalle.[1]

WILDE placed value on belonging to a labourers' gang when he was an undergraduate. A troop of young men, some like himself only nineteen, were going to the river or tennis-court or cricket-field and Ruskin 'going up to lecture in cap and gown' had met them.

> He seemed troubled and prayed us to go back with him to his lecture, which a few of us did, and there he spoke to us not on art this time but on life. . . . He thought, he said, that we should be working at something that would do good to other people, at something by which we might show that in all labour there was something noble. Well, we . . . said we would do anything he wished.

> When they came back in winter he asked them to make a road across a great swamp which lay between two villages, Upper and Lower Hinksey.

> So out we went, day after day, and learned how to lay levels and to break stones, and to wheel barrows along a plank. . . . And Ruskin worked with us in the mist and rain and mud of an Oxford winter, and our friends and our enemies came out and mocked us from the bank.[2]

Wilde worked with Alexander Wedderburn, Lang, and Alfred Milner;

---

1 *Confessions of a Young Man* (1886), pp. 132–3.
2 'Art & the Handicraftsman': *Miscellanies* (xiv, 1st Collected Edition: Ross, 1908), pp. 306–7.

Arnold Toynbee was appointed by Ruskin to be their foreman. Later, Wilde wanted 'to get to the point' when he should be able to say 'that the two great turning-points in my life were when my father sent me to Oxford, and when Society sent me to prison'.[1]

CHARLOTTE BRONTË saw her debt to a younger Ruskin. The first two volumes of *Modern Painters*, which she read at thirty-two, made her feel how 'ignorant' she had previously been:

Hitherto I have only had instinct to guide me in judging of art; I feel more as if I had been walking blindfold – this book seems to give me eyes.[2]

F. D. Maurice's *Kingdom of Christ* was a turning-point in KINGSLEY's life. SHAW told Dame Laurentia:

The saint who called me to the religious life when I was eighteen was Shelley.[3]

CATHERINE COOKSON 'began her education' at twenty, with Lord Chesterfield's *Letters to his Son*. She was a laundry checker in 'Harton Institution' and, finding a reference in Elinor Glyn's *The Career of Catherine Bush*, had followed it up in the library.

With Lord Chesterfield I read my first mythology. I read my first real history and geography. With Lord Chesterfield I went travelling the world.[4]

J. K. JEROME said whatever knowledge he possessed was picked up for himself in later years:

To the British Museum reading-room, with its courteous officials, I remain grateful. . . . To the Young Men's Christian Association I return thanks. . . .[5]

Looking back, J. B. PRIESTLEY could see 'quite clearly' that his most formative period was neither school nor the Cambridge years after World War I:

It was 1911–14, when nobody was trying to educate me nor paying for me to be instructed, when in fact, I was working (though as little as possible) . . . in the wool office.

They sat on high stools, like Dickens characters, and he became 'adroit' at looking as if he were entering up the bag book on his high desk – 'when in fact I was reading the poems of Yeats or Chesterton's last

1 *De Profundis* ('1st complete version', 1949), p. 82.
2 Letter to W. S. Williams, July 31, 1848.
3 Sept. 4, 1944. 'The Nun & the Dramatist', *The Cornhill Magazine* (Summer 1956), p. 454.
4 *Our Kate: An Autobiography* (1969), p. 159.
5 *My Life and Times* (1925), pp. 30–31.

Education

essays, lying inside my open drawer, which could be closed in a flash'.[1]
As a clerk in a boot-and-shoe warehouse, seventeen-year-old H. E.
BATES conducted his own 'voyage of literary discovery'.[2] He was alone
practically all day; after he had done a few orders and answered a few
telephone calls, he read voraciously.

II

JOHNSON looked back on his nine months' stay, at sixteen, with his
cousin Cornelius Ford ('Neely') at Stourbridge, as the most important
event that had happened to him following his birth. The ex-Cambridge
don, now clergyman, had warmed to the boy and extended a visit
intended to be a few days; his cultivated friends – a milieu new to
Johnson – were equally impressed. Ford became his tutor of a rare
kind: urging the importance of general knowledge and the art of conversation, but died a few years later, only thirty-seven. At eighteen, in
his father's bookshop, Johnson met Gilbert Walmesley. A lawyer who
gave him the idea of wanting a legal career, he was an older man than
Cornelius, and one whom Johnson knew well into his maturity. In
spite of their difference in age, 'he never received my notions with
contempt'.

His studies had been so various, that I am not able to name a man of equal
knowledge.[3]

Both men were formative influences in Johnson's life.

Bitterly disappointed at not going up to Oxford because his Uncle
John disapproved, seventeen-year-old KENNETH GRAHAME was dining
in a Soho restaurant when he met Dr F. J. Furnivall. The fifty-year-old
scholar and eccentric, founder of literary societies as well as a social
benefactor in the East End, was extolling certain authors to his party
and invited Grahame to join their table. Next year Grahame became
a member of The New Shakespere Society, meeting Fridays at University College, Gower Street, and Furnivall invited him at twenty-one
to become Honorary Secretary, an office he was to hold for eleven
years. At twenty-five, he was persuaded by Furnivall to undertake vol-

1 *Thoughts in the Wilderness* (1957), pp. 47–48.
2 *The Vanished World: An Autobiography i* (1969), p. 144.
3 Samuel Johnson: *The Lives of the English Poets* (Dublin ed. 1779–81), i, pp. 524–5.

untary work at Toynbee Hall in Stepney. Grahame showed him his prentice writings and received, as we have already seen, valuable advice.[1] Through him Grahame met his fellow-contributors to *The National Observer* and *The Yellow Book*. It was a rich private life continuing all through his extremely successful career at the Bank. It made their consultative physician, Dr Kingdon, complain:

Kenneth should think *less* of books and *more* of being what he has come to be in the city.[2]

Denied Newcastle High School and anything beyond, BENNETT came to London at twenty-one. In his new solicitors' office in Lincoln's Inn Fields, he caught the fascination of antiquarian book-collecting from an older clerk, and began a sideline of postal selling which he continued for some years. Then, when he was nearly twenty-four, he came to live with the Marriotts – the first people he had known whose love of art and intellectual pursuits was entirely disinterested. Among their circle of charming professional people, the Sharpes implanted his love of classical music. He met the architect Edwin Rickards who, he later said, had influenced his view of life more than any other man. Under Mrs Sharpe's influence he read, in the original, Guy de Maupassant, the Goncourts – and Turgenev in French translation. He now found himself reading avidly books he had bought for prestige alone. The society of these people made an impact that Shelley must have experienced when he stayed with the Boinvilles, but Shelley was matching like with like. For Bennett the experience was formative. It even made him attend to smaller matters such as time-keeping and clothes, which later got out of proportion.

RADCLYFFE HALL's real education began when she fell in love with Mrs George Batten ('Ladye'), a cultivated and considerably older woman, and took up her challenge that people who had loved and been loved by her had always used their brains and been persons of significance. KATHERINE MANSFIELD called her editor, A. R. Orage, 'my master'.

. . . you taught me to write, you taught me to think; you showed me what there was to be done and what not to do.[3]

1 See page 45.
2 Patrick Chalmers: *Kenneth Grahame: Life, Letters and Unpublished Work* (1933), pp. 112–3.
3 Feb. 9, 1921.

Through a communist teacher at her elementary school, ETHEL
MANNIN learned 'about George Bernard Shaw, the Fabians . . . and
the Independent Labour Party'.

On Saturday afternoons in summer we used to go out to Richmond. . . . In
the winter she would take me to St Mary's Church, Westminster, where
Goss-Custard gave organ recitals. . . . I wrote her the most passionate of
love-poems . . . she was educating me, though in a way that would have
horrified the Board of Education had it known anything about it.[1]

At fourteen, she left school 'and began getting educated in the real
sense'.[2]

MALCOLM MUGGERIDGE said it was impossible for him to convey
what he owed to Hugh Kingsmill 'for the enormous enhancement of
living I derived from the stimulation of his mind and imagination'.

There is scarcely a book I care about which is not, as I turn over its pages,
evocative of him. . . .[3]

The 'happiest three years' he had known were when the Muggeridges
were living at Whatlington and the Kingsmills at Hastings, just before
World War II. His marriage with Kitty and his close friendship with
Hugh Kingsmill, he describes as 'two of the greatest blessings of my
life'.[4]

MICHAEL FOOT, on arriving to live in London in the mid-1930s,
went to Hyde Park where he heard the Socialist orators, faded by then
'but still magical' – Tillett, Mann, Lansbury, Maxton. He heard the
Rev. Dr Donald Soper who was young, advocating 'Socialism and
pacifism in ever-fluent classical English'. He became 'an addict' of
Bonar Thompson, 'the one-man satirist of the universe, this world and
the next'.

Bonar Thompson's scepticism was, I suppose, the sanest thing in the land. . . .
He knew Shakespeare and Dickens and Yeats and Sean O'Casey and a few
others besides, as well as any man ever knew them.[5]

Meanwhile, STEPHEN SPENDER at twenty-one found 'a sense of
fulfilment' in dining with the Woolfs in Tavistock Square, staying with

1 *Confessions & Impressions* (1930), pp. 45–46.
2 *Ibid.*, p. 34.
3 *Chronicles of Wasted Time* (1972–3), ii, p. 64.
4 *Ibid.*, i, p. 85.
5 *Debts of Honour* (1980), pp. 118–20.

the Nicolsons at Long Barn, and being invited to Garsington. These people gave him what he had failed to obtain from Oxford.

For Bloomsbury was largely a product of King's ... a group of people who were together at Cambridge.

As Huxley had expressed his own debt to Garsington,[1] so Spender writes:

What can I feel but gratitude that I was taken into this great wave of the talent of my time? When I had been bathed in it, I was imperceptibly changed.[2]

III

For nearly six years after university, MILTON studied at home, perhaps first at Hammersmith, and then at Horton near Windsor, for the liberal education Cambridge had denied. He read the Greek and Latin authors. He also read philosophy and all kinds of history. He would surely have read the Hebrew Bible, and continued his boyhood reading in French and Italian literature. Nor, on the evidence of his poetry, did he neglect Jonson or Shakespeare. Sometimes he visited London, either to purchase books or to keep up-to-date in mathematics and music – for he played with his father's skill on viol and organ. J. R. Green points out:

His youth shows how much of the gaiety, the poetic ease, the intellectual culture of the Renascence lingered in a Puritan home.[3]

To this period belong his own compositions *L'Allegro*, *Il Penseroso*, *Comus* (his Masque presented at Ludlow Castle), and *Lycidas*.

In the following century, THOMAS GRAY escaped into a life of 'learned leisure' when Richard West died in his mid-twenties, the closest of their Eton quartet –

... one who has walked hand in hand with you, like the two children in the wood. ...[4]

With only a small patrimony, he did that rare thing of constructing a life in conformity with his temperament. Going back to his old college,

---

1 See page 54.
2 *World Within World* (1951), pp. 166–7.
3 *A Short History of the English People* (illus. ed. 1892–4), iii, p. 945.
4 Letter from West to Gray, Nov. 14, 1735.

in rooms rent free, he assembled his modest collection of books and prints. There was the little harpsichord on which he played Scarlatti and Palestrina, and his *pièce de résistance* – a pair of blue and white Japanese vases.

Always there were flowers.

My gardens are in the windows. . . .[1]

Here he had access to libraries for that reading which occupied the rest of his life.

First he took a belated degree in Law, but did not practise. The next six years he spent on an intensive study of best Greek authors, and then he traced the development of English poetry, going back beyond Provençal poetry to Anglo-Saxon and Norse. Among his antiquarian pursuits he acquired 'a great knowledge of Gothic architecture', and for the last ten years of his life he resumed his love of botany:

He . . . often said that he thought it a singular felicity to have engaged in it; as, besides the constant amusement it gave him in his chamber, it led him more frequently out into the fields; and, by making his life less sedentary, improved . . . his health and spirits.[2]

Each course of study proliferated like a nest of Chinese boxes. The development of English poetry meant learning Icelandic; Gothic architecture led on to heraldry and mediaeval history. He had been 'a considerable botanist at fifteen', and now he turned to Linnaeus and Aristotle, and 'went regularly through the vegetable, animal, and fossile kingdoms'.

His range was inexhaustible – metaphysics, morals, politics, painting, gardening, dress, even cookery. . . . If a friend sought advice how to decorate his home, Gray would research wallpapers and glass, pattern sizes and cost. Every branch of learning (except 'pure mathematics, and . . . studies dependent on that science') had its relative notebook with interminable lists and classifications. When he left Cambridge for three years, it was to research in the newly opened British Museum. Yet all this industry had 'only self-improvement and self-gratification for its object'.[3] There was no *lucrative* motive for his reading whatever. On the mixed reception of his *Pindaric Odes* at forty-one, he laid aside his slender output of poetry almost entirely.

1 Letter to Mr Nicholls, June 24, 1769.
2 *The Poems of Mr. Gray prefixed by Memoirs of Life by W. Mason* (1775), p. 341.
3 *Ibid.*, p. 335.

Reading, he has often told me, was much more agreeable to him than writing. . . .[1]

His friend and posthumous editor said:

. . . there was hardly any part of human Learning, in which he had not acquired a competent skill: in most of them a consummate mastery.[2]

An anonymous obituary spoke of him as 'perhaps the most learned man in Europe'.[3] Professor Tillotson always referred to him as 'our most learned poet'.

At a time of great depression when he lost his religious faith, RUSKIN, whose education was almost entirely informal, deplored his own studies:

I've picked up what education I've got in an irregular way – and it's very little. I suppose that on the whole as little has been got into me and out of me as under any circumstances was probable . . . granting liberty and power of travelling, and working as I chose, I suppose everything I've chosen to have has been about as wrong as wrong could be. . . .[4]

But EDWARD LEAR, less advantaged, was incorrigible. He wrote to his friend Fortescue, at forty-seven:

I am almost thanking God that I was never educated, for it seems to me that 999 of those who are so, expensively and laboriously, have lost all before they arrive at my age . . . whereas, I seem to be on the threshold of knowledge. . . .[5]

When DICKENS's father was asked where his son had been educated, he replied: 'Why, indeed, sir, (ha! ha!) he may be said to have educated himself!' BEVERLEY NICHOLS, ex-Marlborough and Balliol, said: 'I am entirely self-taught.'[6]

---

1 *Ibid.*, p. 171.
2 *Ibid.*, p. 343.
3 Quoted by Mason: *ibid.*, p. 402.
4 Letter to C. E. Norton, Feb. 25, 1861. Quoted by Joan Evans: *John Ruskin* (1954), p. 264.
5 Sept. 2, 1859.
6 *The Unforgiving Minute* (1978), p. 1.

CHAPTER FIFTEEN

Grand Tours

I

A tour in France and Italy as a complement to formal studies was a practice not confined to the eighteenth century. Some writers went on this Grand Tour in the seventeenth, and some continued the tradition in the nineteenth – even in our own.

MILTON, after the finest education any father could provide, set out at twenty-nine with a letter of introduction from his neighbour Sir Henry Wotton, and one servant. During a short stay in Paris, the English ambassador introduced him to Grotius. He visited Leghorn and Pisa, and stayed about two months in Florence. It was the custom in their literary circles, which he now frequented, for everyone to give some proof of his wit and reading, and Milton won a considerable reputation and much affection by reading his Latin poems. He may, however, have offended the English Jesuits when he made a call on Galileo under house arrest.

He continued south through Siena to Rome, where he spent another two months viewing the antiquities. The Keeper of the Vatican Library, who had lived in Oxford, introduced him to Cardinal Barberi who, 'at a musical entertainment, waited for him at the door, and led him by the hand into the assembly'.[1] Milton went on to Naples 'in the company of a hermit',[2] and by him was introduced to John Baptista Manso, Marquis of Villa, who had been the intimate friend and patron of Tasso. This venerable man personally conducted him around the city. On Milton's departure from Naples, Manso, who a few years later was to praise the younger man's morals and bearing, now apologized that he had not been able to do more, because Milton had spoken too freely on matters of religion.

At this stage of his travels came news of Charles attempting his first punitive expedition against the Scots Covenanters, which prompted

---

1 Samuel Johnson: *The Lives of the English Poets* (Dublin ed. 1779–81), i, p. 143.
2 *Ibid.*, i, p. 144. Trans. *Pro Populo Anglicano Defensio Secunda* (1654).

Milton not to proceed to Sicily and Greece. While he was returning to Rome, he heard from some merchants of Jesuit plots against him. Nevertheless, he spent two more months there, making no effort to conceal his Protestant faith. When he arrived back in Florence he was greeted as if he had come home. He stayed another two months, then, after a short visit to Lucca, crossed the Apennines and passed through Bologna and Ferrara to Venice. He spent a month surveying the sights, before shipping the books he had collected in Italy. He proceeded through Verona and Milan, probably by the Simplon Pass, to Geneva. Here he had daily discussions with Giovanni Diodati, the learned professor of Theology, and uncle of a schoolfriend Charles who had died while Milton was in Italy.

Four years later, with 'that bloody difference betweene the King and Parliament broken out',[1] JOHN EVELYN, from the age of twenty-three, spent three years travelling in France and Italy. At the Battle of Braineford (Brentford) he had come in 'wth my horse and armes just at the retreate',[2] but obtained leave of the King to travel since 'his brother's, as well as his own estates, were so near London as to be fully in the power of the Parliament'.[3] Mr Thicknesse, 'a very deare friend of mine', accompanied him.[4] In Venice, Edmund Waller 'newly gotten out of England, after ye Parliament had extremely worried him', was in his company.[5]

His *Diary* highlights the hazards for travellers of that time. He went by horse, 'boate', post, 'barg', mules, a 'filuca', post horses, 'carrion mule (which are in the world the most wretched beasts)',[6] 'asse (instead of stirrups we had ropes tied with a loope to put our feete in)',[7] coach. He made Naples 'the *non ultra* of my travels, sufficiently sated with rolling up and downe'.[8]

Natural hazards were severe enough. A forest towards 'Fontaine Bleau ... abounds with staggs, wolves, boares, & not long after a lynx or ounce was kill'd amongst them, which had devour'd some passengers'. Normandy 'so abounds with wolves that a sheepheard

1 Oct. 3, 1642.
2 Nov. 12, 1642.
3 *Memoirs of John Evelyn, Esq. FRS* ed. William Bray (n.e. 1827), i, p. xv.
4 Nov. 6, 1643.
5 Mar. 23, 1646.
6 Jan. 25, 1645.
7 Mar. 23, 1646.
8 Feb. 8, 1645.

whom we met told us one of his companions was strangled by one of them the day before, & that in the middst of his flock'.[1] 'Fearfull' tracts of the 'Alpes' were 'onely inhabited by beares, wolves, and wild goates'.[2] There was peril of waters. Embarked at 'Canes' for Genoa, and making out into the wind, they 'almost abandon'd to despaire, our pilot himself giving us up for lost'.[3] There were land-thieves and water-thieves. On horse through the Forest of Orleans, 'foure' of the company behind were slain by 'rogues'.[4] At Marseilles they went over-land to 'Canes . . . for fear of the Pickaron Turkes, who made prize of many small vessels about these parts'.[5] He wrote of Genoa as 'unsafe to strangers'.[6] Out of Rome to Naples on 'ye Appian . . . we were faine to hire . . . 30 firelocks to guard us through the cork-woods (much infested wth ye banditti)'.[7] From Naples, they returned overland to Rome 'for fear of Turkish pirates hovering on that coast'.[8]

They had officials to placate – or overcome. At 'Canes', before embarking for Genoa, they 'procur'd a bill of health (without which there is no admission at any towne in Italy)'.[9] At 'approch' of Milan, 'some of our company, in dread of ye Inquisition (severer here than in all Spain), thought of throwing away some Protestant books and papers'. Admiring the pictures in 'ye Governor's Palace' in Milan, he peeped 'into a chamber where the greate man was under the barber's hands' and had to retire with all 'speede', on hearing the Governor tell a negro slave sent to question him, that he was a 'spie'.[10] On mules in the Alps, they were beaten off their saddles, arrested, then fined, because Captain Wray's dog had killed a goat.

He also had valet trouble. On the way, at Tours, 'one Garro, a Spaynard borne in Biscay, having misbehaved, I was forced to discharge him'.

. . . he demanded of me (besides his wages) no less than 100 crownes to carry him to his country; refusing to pay it, as no part of our agreement, he had the

1 Mar. 7, 1644.
2 Mar. 23, 1646.
3 Oct. 11, 1644.
4 Apl. 12, 1644.
5 Oct. 7, 1644.
6 Oct. 17, 1644.
7 Jan. 28, 1645.
8 Feb. 8, 1645.
9 Oct. 11, 1644.
10 Mar. 23, 1646.

impudence to arrest me; the next day I was to appear in court . . . but it was so unreasonable a pretence that the Judge had not patience to heare it out . . . he rose from the Bench, and making a courteous excuse to me, that being a stranger I should be so us'd, he conducted mee through the Court to ye streete-dore.

Even then, 'This varlet afterwards threatened to pistol me'.[1] At the end of the tour, in Paris, his valet Hebert 'robb'd me of cloths and plate to the value of threescore pounds'.

. . . I recover'd most of them, obtaining of the Judge, with no small difficulty, that the processe against the thiefe should not concerne his life, being his first offence.[2]

Sickness too, was never far away. From a 'mischance' in Rome he had 'a sore hand' beginning to fester.[3] In Padua, unused to drinking wine 'cool'd with snow and ice', angina and sore throat almost cost him his life. 'The Cheife professor' applied all the remedies, and then 'old Salvatico (that famous physician) . . . made me be cupp'd and scarified in the back in foure places, which began to give me breath'.[4] At Geneva he had a dangerous attack of smallpox:

Being extreamly weary and complaining of my head . . . I caus'd one of our hostesses daughters to be removed out of her bed and went immediately into it whilst it was yet warme, being so heavy with pain and drowsinesse that I would not stay to have the sheates chang'd. . . . I afterwards concluded she had been newly recover'd of the small pox.

He was bled (which the physician acknowledged he should not have done 'had he suspected ye small pox'), and purged, and leaches applied.[5] Evelyn well satisfied his curiosity among the antiquities – 'stupendi-ous' being a favourite word in his descriptions. In Rome ('resolved to spend no time idly here') he engaged the services of a 'Sights-man'.[6] In Padua he met Earl Arundel, who gave him directions 'what curiosities I should enquire after in my journey'. Like all English travellers at that time, Evelyn 'pack'd up . . . purchases of books, pictures, casts. . . .'[7]

1 *Diary*, Aug. 1, 1644.
2 May 22, 1647.
3 Jan. 25, 1645.
4 Sept. 29, 1645.
5 Mar. 23, 1646.
6 Nov. 4, 1644.
7 Mar. 23, 1646.

But he was curious about *life*. At Marseilles he saw the 'gallys'. The 'Captaine of the Gally Royal' entertained him in his 'cabine'.

The rising forward and falling back at their oare is a miserable spectacle. . . .[1]

In Rome he was 'invited by a Jewe of my acquaintance to see a circumcision'.[2] He also saw 'a gentleman, hang'd in his cloak and hatt for murder'.

They struck the malefactor with a club yt first stunn'd him, and then cut his throat.[3]

In Padua he attended 'the famous anatomie lecture, celebrated here. . . .'[4]

Like Pepys, Evelyn cherished learning and curiosity all his life. He witnessed in Paris when he was twenty-nine, at the hospital of La Charité, an operation of cutting for the stone:

A child of 8 or 9 yeares old underwent ye operation with most extraordinary patience, and expressed greate joy when he saw the stone was drawn.[5]

The following year, he went to the Châtelet or prison, 'where a malefactor was to have the question or torture given to him, he refusing to confess the robbery with which he was charg'd'. He observed the way they bound him, 'lying aslant' from iron rings in the walls, and then 'slid an horse of wood under the rope wch bound his feete. . . .' Sticking 'an horne' into his mouth, they 'poured the quantity of two bouketts of water down his throat, and over him. . . .' Evelyn 'was not able to stay the sight of another malefactor to succeede. . . .'

It represented yet to me, the intollerable sufferings which our Blessed Saviour must needes undergo when his body was hanging with all its weight upon the nailes on the crosse.[6]

II

When JOSEPH ADDISON was a fellow of Magdalen College, Oxford, his poems found favour with the Whigs, and his royal pension was

1 Oct. 7, 1644.
2 Jan. 15, 1645.
3 May 6, 1645.
4 Before Mar. 20, 1646.
5 May 3, 1650.
6 Mar. 11, 1651.

presumably meant for him to acquire French and Italian abroad with view to a diplomatic post. At twenty-seven he left England for four years, much of the time as tutor to Edward Montagu, the son of one of his patrons.

After a short stay in Paris he settled at Blois, and on his return to Paris he conversed with Boileau. Next year he left for Italy. Sailing from Marseilles, his ship was driven by a storm into Savona – perhaps in his mind when he wrote his paper:

As I have made several voyages upon the sea, I have often been tossed in storms, and on that occasion have frequently reflected on the description of them in ancient poets.[1]

He crossed the mountains to Geneva, and travelled through Milan to Venice. He visited San Marino, Rome, Naples, and like Evelyn climbed Vesuvius. He visited Capri, and returned by Ostia to Rome. After spending autumn there, he went to Florence and, crossing Mount Cenis, arrived back in Geneva.

HORACE WALPOLE, at twenty-one, invited GRAY who, very differently circumstanced, could not have dreamt of going on a Grand Tour, to accompany him. They visited Paris, Rheims, and Lyons.

Mr Walpole had a little fat black spaniel, that he was very fond of, which he sometimes used to . . . let it run by the chaise side.

On their way to Geneva, they were 'in a very rough road, not two yards broad at most; on one side was a great wood of pines and on the other a vast precipice'.

. . . it was noon-day . . . when all of a sudden, from the wood-side . . . out rushed a great wolf, came close to the head of the horses, seized the dog by the throat, and rushed up the hill again with him in his mouth. This was done in less than a quarter of a minute; we all saw it, and yet the servants had not time to draw their pistols, or do any thing to save the dog. If he had not been there, and the creature had thought fit to lay hold of one of the horses; chaise, and we, and all must inevitably have tumbled about fifty fathoms perpendicular down the precipice.

When they reached Lanebourg, at the foot of Mount Cenis, there was 'no room for any way but over the very top of it'.

Here the chaise was forced to be pulled to pieces, and the baggage and that to be carried by mules: we ourselves were wrapped up in our furs and seated

---

1 *The Spectator*, No. 489, Sept. 20, 1712.

upon a sort of matted chair without legs, which is carried upon poles in the manner of a bier, and so begun to ascend by the help of eight men. It was six miles to the top. . . . The descent is six miles more, but infinitely more steep than the going up; and how the men perfectly fly down with you, stepping from stone to stone with incredible swiftness. . . . We were but five hours in performing the whole, from which you may judge of the rapidity of the men's motion.[1]

Then they went through Turin, Genoa, Bologna, and in Florence they lived with the English Minister, Sir Horace Mann. After going to Rome and Naples, they returned to the Minister in Florence.

But while Walpole needed this social relaxation, feeling the farther he travelled 'the less I wonder at anything', Gray was insatiable, eager to press on. Shy, dependent, intensely vulnerable, he could not accept that his boyhood friend had a different temperament to his own. Eventually they left intending to go to Venice, and on the way at Reggio parted in anger, Gray going on alone. Lord Cecil is fair to Walpole:

Walpole could not be expected to plan his tour just to suit Gray's tastes.[2]

Later, with another companion Chute, Walpole discovered that Gray was financially embarrassed over how to get home, and he sensitively contrived that a loan should seem to come from Chute. Much later, Walpole blamed his own sense of superiority as a Prime Minister's son – 'though I have since felt my infinite inferiority to him'.

I treated him insolently: he loved me and I did not think he did.[3]

Gray returned through Verona, Milan, Turin, and Lyons. He visited again the Grande Chartreux which had made such an overwhelming impression upon him. It inspired him now to write a Latin ode. He continued to note carefully all that he saw in picture-galleries and churches, making a virtue of recording one's impressions on the spot. Both men were away from England two years.

Only ten weeks after they had first met in Mr Davies's shop, Johnson offered to accompany BOSWELL to Harwich, preliminary to his continental travels.

I could not find words to express what I felt upon this unexpected and very great mark of his affectionate regard.

1 Gray's letter to his Mother, Nov. 7, N.S.1739.
2 David Cecil: *Two Quiet Lives* (1948), p. 123.
3 Quoted by Cecil, *ibid.*

It meant a special four-day journey by a man more than thirty years his senior. They set out early in the morning on Friday, August 5th, 1763, in the Harwich stage-coach.

Johnson advised him when abroad to be as much as possible with 'the Professors in the University, and with the Clergy', for then he might hear 'the best account of every thing in whatever country I should be, with the additional advantage of keeping my learning alive'. When he recommended him to keep a journal, Boswell was able to tell him he had done this for some time. In the church at Harwich, Johnson counselled him to pray: 'Now that you are going to leave your native country, recommend yourself to the protection of your CREATOR and REDEEMER.'

My revered friend walked down with me to the beach, where we embraced and parted with tenderness, and engaged to correspond by letters. I said, 'I hope Sir, you will not forget me in my absence.' JOHNSON. 'Nay, Sir, it is more likely you should forget me, than that I should forget you.' As the vessel put out to sea, I kept my eyes upon him for a considerable time, while he remained rolling his majestic frame in his usual manner; and at last I perceived him walk back into the town, and he disappeared.[1]

Boswell was to be away three years, between the ages of twenty-two and twenty-five. He went to The Hague and Berlin. In Switzerland he interviewed Rousseau and Voltaire. For nine months in Italy he conscientiously studied the sights – in Naples striking up a friendship with John Wilkes. He proposed to three countesses in Turin almost concurrently, and on a tour of Corsica interviewed Paoli, its heroic chieftain.

Embedded impenetrably in the GOLDSMITH legend is that, about twenty-five, after dallying with medicine at Edinburgh and Leiden, Oliver begged his way with a flute through Flanders, France, Switzerland, Italy and the Tyrol.

III

BYRON at twenty-one sailed from Falmouth in the Lisbon packet, accompanied by his Cambridge friend John Hobhouse, the faithful

---

1 James Boswell: *The Life of Samuel Johnson, LL.D.* (1791). Aetat.54:1763.

valet William Fletcher, and two more servants who were sent home at Gibraltar. In Lisbon, Byron got diarrhoea and mosquito bites.

But what of that? Comfort must not be expected by folks that go a pleasuring.

They rode on horseback via Seville down towards the southern tip of Spain, sailing in a frigate from Cadiz to Gibraltar where they boarded the Malta packet. In Malta Byron engaged in a platonic affair with Mrs Spencer Smith, who had been rescued from Napoleon's soldiers by an Italian nobleman. In typical contrast he also received lessons in Arabic from a monk. In relatively unknown Albania, Ali Pacha entertained them and lent not only guides but an escort of warriors. At this stage of his travels, *Childe Harold* was begun. Attempting a sea passage to Greece, they were stranded after a storm, but befriended by the unlikely Suliotes. Full of admiration for these violent men, Byron could not refrain in his letters from digs at Fletcher, who carried an umbrella and suffered 'from cold, heat, and vermin'. With a Suliote escort they reached Missolonghi overland. In Athens Byron watched with anger Lord Elgin's men despoiling the Parthenon. Hobhouse recorded with satisfaction that the Turkish town prefect beat a man who had insulted the two Englishmen, with fifty strokes of a rod. They sailed for Smyrna in a sloop of war and then by frigate to Constantinople, on the way putting in at the Island of Tenedos where Byron swam the Hellespont. Sailing from Constantinople, Hobhouse now returned to England, while Byron and Fletcher, with two Albanians and a Tartar, landed at Zea and returned to Athens. There, wintering in a Capuchin convent, Byron formed a strong attachment to the young Nicolo Giraud who taught him Italian. He made several expeditions to Patras where he contracted a dangerous attack of malaria, which left its legacy.

Eventually after two years abroad Fletcher was sent on ahead, 'having been toasted and roasted, and baked, and grilled, and eaten by all sorts of creeping things . . .', and Byron embarked on a frigate, bringing home two Greek servants.

I have seen everything most remarkable in Turkey, particularly the Troad, Greece, Constantinople and Albania. . . .[1]

DISRAELI, at twenty-five, planned his travels more as Byron did – first to Spain, in his case the home of his ancestors, and so via the

1 Letter to Robert Dallas.

Mediterranean, Greece and Turkey, with the addition that he went on to make his pilgrimage in Jerusalem. He went with a friend, William Meredith, engaged to Disraeli's sister.

On the way out, Disraeli shows himself as one more writer who anticipated and displayed a complete understanding of Lifemanship principles. A rival, James Clay, had appeared at Malta who beat the garrison at rackets, and the future prime-minister wrote:

To govern men you must either excel them in their accomplishments, or despise them. . . . Yesterday at the racket court, sitting in the gallery among strangers, the ball entered, and . . . fell at my feet. I picked it up, and observing a young rifleman excessively stiff, I humbly requested him to forward its passage into the court, as I really had never thrown a ball in my life. This incident has been the subject of conversation at all the messes today.[1]

The officers got tired of 'that damned bumptious Jew boy' with his flamboyant clothes and banned him from their mess, but when he paid his calls on the island half its inhabitants followed him, and the governor laughingly approved. Disraeli left Malta in one of those miniature caravans so dear to Byron – Clay was there, an astonishing capitulation, also Tita, the poet's former gondolier changing his profession to valet, while himself, another echo of the romantic hero, sported the fancy dress of a Greek pirate.

In Jerusalem the dandy was replaced by another Disraeli, who knelt as a Christian Jew in the Holy Sepulchre. It was as if a new mood of seriousness was preparing him for the personal tragedy so near at hand. Meredith had separated temporarily on this stage of the journey and they now rejoined in Egypt. But almost immediately the young friend was smitten fatally with smallpox. The little group has similarities with another two years ahead – Tennyson, his sister, and Hallam.

On the return journey, Disraeli shut himself away in his cabin and wrote *Alroy* and *Contarini Fleming*. His father, which was hardly surprising for one who wrote *Curiosities of Literature*, employed Tita at Bradenham.

During his first long vacation at Oxford, twenty-year-old WILDE accompanied his 'old' tutor Professor Mahaffy and sailed to Leghorn, visiting Florence, Bologna, Venice, Padua, Verona, and Milan. William Goulding, a Cambridge undergraduate, went with them. From Wilde's

1 Letter to his father. Quoted by André Maurois: *Disraeli: A Picture of the Victorian Age* (1927), p. 46.

letters, Venice captivated him even more than Florence, and he described Milan with its 'white stone and gilding' as 'a second Paris'. He did not have enough money to see Rome as he wished, and at Milan had to leave his friends who were going on to Genoa. Feeling 'very lonely' but having had 'a delightful tour', he took the diligence over the Simplon Pass to Lausanne.

Nearly two years later at Easter, he went again with Mahaffy, 'to see Mykenae and Athens'.[1] Besides Goulding there was another young man George Macmillan. The four sailed to Genoa, and via Ravenna went to Brindisi where they embarked for Corfu and then Zante. They got up at 5.30 a.m. to have their first glimpse of the Greek mainland. The country still had a notorious reputation of bad roads and very real danger from brigands and kidnaps. All the party were armed. Disembarking at Katákolona they rode on horses across the Peloponnese, which took them a week for their guide, who owned the horses, objected to speed. At one point the guide seized Wilde's bridle, drawing his knife. When Wilde immediately pointed his revolver at him, the knife was replaced with a theatrical baring of the breast. From Epidaurus they sailed to the Piraeus and reached Athens. This was the holiday that caused Wilde to be fined and rusticated for most of the summer term because he was late back. He had written in vain to his College Dean:

I hope you will not mind if I miss ten days at the beginning: seeing Greece is really a great education for anyone and will I think benefit me greatly, and Mr Mahaffy is such a clever man that it is quite as good as going to lectures to be in his society.[2]

E. M. FORSTER'S imagination at twenty-two and twenty-three was fed by Greece and Italy in the way that India inspired his maturity.

IV

GALSWORTHY'S father sent him to the New World and not the Old. He was in love with 'someone who wouldn't have done at all',[3] and

1 Letter to Reginald Harding, Apl. 2, 1877. Vyvyan Holland: *Son of Oscar Wilde* (1954), p. 239.
2 Quoted by H. Montgomery Hyde: *Oscar Wilde: A Biography* (1976), p. 29.
3 Letter by Galsworthy many years later, 1906. Quoted by H. V. Marrot: *The Life & Letters of John Galsworthy* (1935), p. 70.

Old Jolyon packed him off to investigate the affairs of a coal-mining company in Canada. He was twenty-four and had been called to the Bar a year. After staying at Quebec and at Victoria, he joined his brother who was out there on Vancouver Island. They had a camping trip beyond Mount Banson to the level of the lakes, where they stayed in a log cabin. On arrival before nightfall, Galsworthy went out hunting with their Indian Chief, Louis Goode ('for very little'). They succeeded in losing themselves for some hours, by which time it was pitch dark – 'a gruesome sensation in those immense woods'. Next day they made a raft 'of three logs of cedar split, 20 feet long . . . joined together by pegs and cross beams, and went up the lake fishing from her. . . .'[1]

The following year his father sent him overseas again, to acquire knowledge of navigation and maritime law. He had read for the Chancery Bar, but his father thought he could use this knowledge at the Admiralty Bar. Together with his friend, Ted Sanderson, therefore, he visited Australia. There had been a plan to visit Stevenson in Samoa but, unable to get a boat from Sydney, they boarded a tramp steamer bound for Fiji. On the way at Noumea, a French Convict Settlement, they had their first taste of a South Sea Island. From Suva they went to the little island of Ovalan, then to Levuka. On a neighbouring island, cannibalism broke out not long after they had left. From Levuka they went by native cutter to the Ba river in Viti Levu, where they stayed with Galsworthy's cousin, a sugar-planter. Against advice, they made a long march over the mountains to see 'something of the island life of the natives'. In a native village the Chief gave them 'a fine clean hut' to themselves. On their march Ted went down with dysentery, and Galsworthy managed to get a runner to take a note down to the coast. On his return with drugs eight men carried Ted in a grass hammock – 'they did twenty-eight miles in one day' – supervised 'with infinite care' by Galsworthy.[2]

When they were back at Adelaide after a trip to New Zealand, a sailing-ship *Torrens* took them to Cape Town. They discovered that Conrad was first mate, and on the first night he fought a fire in the hold without any of the seventeen passengers being aware of it at the time. Galsworthy got on 'capitally at "lessons"' with the Captain. Every day they set the chronometer and took sights, if possible, of the sun.

---

1 Galsworthy's letter at the time: Marrot, *ibid.*, p. 71.
2 Ted Sanderson's account: Marrot, *ibid.*, pp. 80–81.

Then we sit down together and work out the longtitude. At twelve o'clock more sights, and then down again and work out the latitude, correct the longtitude, and prick our places on the Chart, of which I have one lent me for the voyage. So that I do the daily work of the Captain.

In the afternoon the Captain gave him a good hour on various branches of the craft – navigation, manoeuvring, &c.

I am awfully glad to have some study to pass away the time. . . .[1]

He also read for two hours either at navigation or at maritime law. Except for two gales, one of which lasted 'about 36 hours' and they had 'to ride it out under one closely-reefed topsail', carrying away seven sails, the voyage was favourable and they kept the long watches with Conrad. Galsworthy wrote:

. . . he . . . has a fund of yarns on which I draw freely. He has been right up the Congo and all around Malacca and Borneo . . . to say nothing of a little smuggling in the days of his youth. . . .[2]

Sanderson said that Galsworthy had missed Stevenson but found Conrad. It was a friendship for life. Galsworthy had scarcely got back home when his father sent him on another mining inspection – to Russia.

v

Travel for RUSKIN was an integral part of his art training. When he was fourteen, his family began a series of tours in Europe – Northern France, Flanders, the Rhine and the Black Forest, Switzerland. His first visit to Italy, taking in Rome, Naples and Venice, was with his family at twenty-one when his university course had been interrupted through suspected TB.

His second visit, the most memorable in his life, came five years later, unaccompanied by his parents. He took the brother of his mother's maid as valet, and on the Swiss border renewed the services of an elderly mountaineer guide. It was a tour of discovery in North Italy. He sketched happily in the churches, at Pisa having a scaffold set up to copy the frescoes. He made drawings of architectural details

1 Apl. 8, 1893. Marrot, *ibid.*, pp. 85–86.
2 Apl. 23, 1893. *Ibid.*, p. 88.

with a new power. The things he saw provided material for his second volume of *Modern Painters*. The following year he pointed them out to his parents, but without his newly experienced freedom this third visit proved an anticlimax.

HENRY JAMES was scarcely one when his father took him and his elder brother William abroad. Five years later, the father contemplated taking his 'four stout boys' to Europe (the younger ones, Garth and Robertson, included) – that they might 'absorb French and German and get such a sensuous education as they cannot get here'. James was twelve before they eventually sailed, visiting Geneva, London, Paris and Boulogne. By then, he later acknowledged that his father had already influenced him towards a cosmopolitan outlook like his own:

The whole perfect Parisianism I seemed to myself always to have possessed mentally – even if I had but just turned twelve.

His first adult visit to Europe on his own was at twenty-six, when he met in England such literary celebrities as Ruskin, Rossetti, Morris, Leslie Stephen, and Darwin. He went on to make a Grand Tour, and Italy – which he had never visited as a boy – made as powerful an impact upon him as it had for Ruskin the second time when he was on his own.

STEVENSON's father believed in 'the educational value of travel', so that when Louis was eleven he went with his parents to Germany. At twelve, he accompanied them to the South of France, Italy, Austria and Germany. A cousin who was with them some of the time, said:

... he began to take Louis to the smoking-room with him; there my uncle was always surrounded by a group of eager and amused listeners – English, American, and Russian – and every subject, political, artistic, and theological, was discussed and argued ... his keen admiration of art and architecture seemed to be shared by Louis; they would go into raptures over a cathedral, or an old archway, or a picture. . . .[1]

1 Mrs Napier to Graham Balfour, & quoted by him: *The Life of Robert Louis Stevenson* (1901), i, p. 60.

CHAPTER SIXTEEN

Academic Success

Among the brilliant successes at university was OSCAR WILDE. At Trinity, Dublin, he was twice placed in the First Class in the university examinations. He was elected to a Foundation scholarship, won the Berkeley Gold Medal for Greek, and a Classical Demyship to Magdalen.

My dear Oscar, you are not clever enough for us in Dublin. You had better run over to Oxford.[1]

There he won the Newdigate Prize for his poem *Ravenna*, and gained a double first in Moderations and Greats. When he took the oral examination in New Testament Greek for 'Mods.', he was given the chapter on Paul's shipwreck, containing tricky nautical terms. He had seen no need for preparation – he had been in bed, having mistaken the day, when he was summoned. He translated impeccably. When they stopped him, he replied:

Please may I go on? I want to see what happened to St Paul.[2]

GERARD MANLEY HOPKINS had won a similar double first – Jowett calling him 'the star of Balliol'.

MAUGHAM spent a year at Heidelberg University before entering St Thomas's Medical School. Concurrent with his medical studies which earned him both MRCS and LRCP by the time he was twenty-three, when he abandoned medicine, he speaks of himself going 'systematically through English, French, Italian, and Latin literature'.[3] On his first journey to Florence, before he entered medical school, he had translated Ibsen's *Ghosts* from a German version – to acquire knowledge of dramatic technique and 'by way of relaxation'.[4]

1 Mahaffy's reported remark, quoted by H. Montgomery Hyde: *Oscar Wilde: A Biography* (1976), p. 14.
2 Vyvyan Holland: *Son of Oscar Wilde* (1954), p. 26.
3 *The Summing Up* (1938), p. 91.
4 *Ibid.*, p. 114.

T. S. ELIOT's education was notable: four years at Harvard, his special interest philosophy, then a year at the Sorbonne reading literature as well; a further three years at Harvard under Josiah Royce, George Santayana and, for a time, Bertrand Russell. Finally he studied in Germany and at Oxford, on a one-year travelling scholarship. At Merton College he compiled his doctoral dissertation on F. H. Bradley, and read Plato and Aristotle under H. H. Joachim.

DOROTHY L. SAYERS, 'one of the most brilliant scholars of her year', attained a first-class honours in French and the examiners published a rare tribute to her French Prose composition. Not until five years later, did Oxford at last decide to grant full degrees to women students and, on October 14th, 1920, Vera Brittain and Winifred Holtby were among the excited undergraduates thronging the Sheldonian Theatre to witness this historic ceremony. Dorothy was among those receiving not only a BA but an MA, which meant a quick change from the basket for the relevant hood.

Although his reading was done through a powerful magnifying glass, or Braille when he could get hold of the books, ALDOUS HUXLEY entered Balliol the same time as his cousin Gervas, of the same age. Raymond Mortimer, who met him there and became his lifelong friend, spoke of him as 'dazzling, *dazzling*. . . .'

The erudition: he had read everything.[1]

He always stood at lectures; he took no notes, and typed his essays. Miss M. Marshall remembered him 'standing near a pillar by the doorway against the window just listening. . . .'[2] He came down with a First in English, and the Stanhope Historical Essay Prize. In a letter to his brother Julian, he believed 'the sheltered, the academic life' for 'a man of high and independent spirit', to be 'the fullest and the best of lives. . . .'

I should like to go on for ever learning. I lust for knowledge. . . .[3]

C. S. LEWIS arrived at University College, Oxford, as a Scholar, and left for a year in Flanders. Wounded at Arras, he returned to Oxford to gain a First in Hon. Mods., a First in Greats, and a First in English. ISRAEL ZANGWILL graduated at London with triple honours.

1 Sybille Bedford: *Aldous Huxley: A Biography* (1973–4), i, p. 44.
2 *Ibid.*, i, p. 52.
3 *Ibid.*, i, p. 64.

CHAPTER SEVENTEEN
The Triumph of University

L ashed by his headmaster's tongue and riding whip at Highgate
School, GERARD MANLEY HOPKINS declared:

> I had no love for my schooldays but for Oxford I was very fond.

During his first term, he wrote to his mother: 'I am almost too happy.'
MAX BEERBOHM said that 'undergraduates owe their happiness chiefly
to the consciousness that they are no longer at school';[1] DOROTHY L.
SAYERS might have said the same. T. E. LAWRENCE, who gained a First
in Modern History, summed up the essential difference:

> ... that working against hazardously-suspended penalty which made my life
> from 8 to 18 miserable, and Oxford, after it, so noble a freedom.

Some stayed or haunted the place for life. THOMAS GRAY, at twenty-
five, put down roots as a fellow-commoner at Peterhouse, Cambridge.
On the fourth floor and obsessively fearful of fire, he had an iron bar
fixed outside his window to take a rope-ladder ordered from London.
At thirty-nine, he 'migrated' across the street to Pembroke Hall, after
some undergraduates on his stairs had placed a tub below his window
and raised the alarm. E. M. FORSTER, at sixty-seven, was made an
honorary fellow of King's, Cambridge, and for his later years his old
college became home. BENJAMIN JOWETT and G. M. TREVELYAN each
became Master of his old college – Jowett of Balliol at fifty-three, and
Trevelyan of Trinity (Cambridge) at sixty-four.

Among dons were Gray (appointed Professor of Modern History
three years before he died, he gave no lectures), Jowett, Ruskin, Kingsley, Matthew Arnold (for ten years he held the Oxford Chair of Poetry,
and was the first professor to lecture in English instead of Latin),
Dodgson, Leslie Stephen, Pater (whose lectures Max Beerbohm found
inaudible – 'a form of self-communion. He whispered them'),[2] Edward

---

1 'Going Back to School', *More* (1890).
2 David Cecil: *Max: A Biography* (1964), p. 48.

Dowden, A. E. Housman, Lowes Dickinson, Quiller-Couch, G. M. Trevelyan, Lytton Strachey, J. R. R. Tolkien, C. S. Lewis, Nevill Coghill, Stephen Potter, Lord David Cecil, Geoffrey Tillotson, A. J. P. Taylor, Dame Iris Murdoch, Kingsley Amis.

CHARLES KINGSLEY, as Regius Professor of Modern History at Cambridge, used to be cheered every time he reached a climax. In vain would he beckon for quiet, and stammer: 'Gentlemen, you must not do it.' He was as popular as Edmund Gosse when Clark Lecturer at Trinity College, but in both cases their published lectures provoked an attack on their scholarship. Gosse, with no academic degree, had been recommended by Browning, Tennyson, and Arnold.

Robert Graves and Malcolm Muggeridge taught English at Cairo University. Peter Quennell was Professor of English Literature and Language at a Japanese government university, the Tokyo Bunrika Daigaku. William Empson was Professor of English Literature in Tokyo and then at Pekin, where he returned for six years as Professor of Western Languages. At twenty-five, JOYCE lectured on 'Ireland, Island of Saints and Sages' at the Universita del Popolo, in Trieste. Five years later, he delivered two lectures on Defoe and Blake. When after a few months he gave a series of twelve Monday night lectures on *Hamlet*, 'Dr' and variously 'Professor' James Joyce was complimented for 'this highly successful experiment of lecturing in English to an Italian audience'.

The widow of Sir HENRY NEWBOLT discovered that what her husband 'had faintly pencilled on a small scrap of paper to read over to himself at night was the Latin Grace of his old College at Oxford – Corpus Christi'.[1]

---

1 *The Later Life & Letters of Sir Henry Newbolt* ed. Margaret Newbolt (1942), p. 404.

PART FOUR
METHOD

Yours faithfully,

T. Carlyle

Thomas Carlyle.
From the drawing by Daniel Maclise, R.A.

Eng by J.S. Waddington Ld

CHAPTER ONE
Non-Sedentary

I

An image of the writer sitting at a desk would not be universally true. If WORDSWORTH sat with a pen, it made him perspire and brought on a pain in his chest. Most of his poetry was composed while he was walking and then dictated to one of his 'Devotees' (the term was Coleridge's). When he was thirty-four, they included his wife, his sister, and his sister-in-law, Sara Hutchinson, who had just come to live with them. His daughter Dora, born at this time, would one day be a fourth. Dorothy wrote of her brother:

In wet weather he takes out an umbrella[1], chuses the most sheltered spot, and there walks backwards and forwards, and though the length of his walk be sometimes a quarter or half a mile, he is as fast bound within the chosen limits as if by prison walls. He generally composes his verses out of doors, and while he is so engaged he seldom knows how the time slips away, or hardly whether it is rain or fair.[2]

Usually of a morning CHARLES KINGSLEY paced his strip of lawn – the Quarterdeck – then rushed indoors to stand at a shelf in his study and set down a paragraph at a time. The procedure was the same for his first novel *Yeast*, prior to his breakdown, except that the conscientious parson worked into the night and composed under the moon. DODGSON, on the authority of his nephew, 'very seldom sat down to write, preferring to stand while thus engaged'.[3] For his 'workroom' in the early days, J. K. JEROME 'often preferred the dark streets to my dismal bed-sitting-room'.

1 The unexpected sight of Borrow's green and bulging umbrella made Watts-Dunton mutter to Gordon Hake: 'Is he a genuine Child of the Open Air?'
2 To Lady Beaumont, May 25 (and c.30), 1804: *The Letters of William and Dorothy Wordsworth* ed. the late Ernest de Selincourt. 2nd ed. Revised Chester L. Shaver, Mary Moorman, Alan G. Hill (1967–79), i, p. 477.
3 Stuart Dodgson Collingwood: *The Life & Letters of Lewis Carroll* (1898), p. 389.

Method

Portland Place was my favourite study. . . . With my note-book and a pencil in my hand, I would pause beneath each lamp-post and jot down the sentence I had just thought out.[1]

HENRY JAMES accommodated himself in various ways. He had a desk by a window at which he could write standing. There was a day bed, with a swivel-desk attached, on which he could write lying. In front of the window was a large knee-hole desk at which he could write sitting.

II

For the larger activity of composition, many more writers have chosen to be walking. Shortly after his arrival in London, JOHNSON took lodgings at Greenwich, intending to finish his tragedy *Irene*. He told Boswell that 'he used to compose, walking in the Park'.[2] During HAZLITT's stay at Nether Stowey, COLERIDGE told him –

that he himself liked to compose in walking over uneven ground, or breaking through the straggling branches of copsewood; whereas Wordsworth always wrote walking up and down a straight gravel-walk, or in the same spot where the continuity of his verse met with no collateral interruption. . . .[3]

When TENNYSON walked with his son Hallam, 'he would often chant a poem that he was composing, and add fresh lines'.[4] He made the lines of *Enoch Arden* as he paced up and down the meadow called Maiden's Croft, near his Isle of Wight home.

In 'the tremendous process' of beginning a new book, DICKENS described himself walking 'up and down the house, smiting my forehead dejectedly; and to be so horribly cross and surly, that the boldest fly at my approach'.[5] Part of his writing process also was to walk incredible distances at night, choosing mean streets. André Maurois comments that 'this was a habit . . . kept from childhood and seemed

1 *My Life and Times* (1925), p. 68.
2 James Boswell: *The Life of Samuel Johnson*, LL.D. (1791). 1737: Aetat.28.
3 'My First Acquaintance with Poets'.
4 *Alfred Lord Tennyson: A Memoir* by his Son (1897), ii, p. 210.
5 To Angela Burdett-Coutts, Nov. 12, 1842: *The Letters of Charles Dickens*: The Pilgrim Edition (1965–81), iii, p. 367.

essential to the flow of his inspiration'.[1] It did not have to be London. When *Dombey* struck a difficult patch in Lausanne, he spent a night or two in Geneva wandering about the streets. He walked before and after writing at his desk. He confided in Miss Coutts:

Between ourselves, Paul is dead. He died on Friday night about 10 o'Clock; and as I had no hope of getting to sleep afterwards, I went out, and walked about Paris until breakfast-time next morning.[2]

J. R. GREEN told a friend that he had three articles to write in thirty-six hours, but had got them into shape that day during his walks in London streets.[3] A. E. HOUSMAN, in his early thirties, sometimes composed as he walked along a footpath from Highgate towards Hampstead Heath. When, at first, *G. K.'s Weekly* was printed in Clerkenwell, CHESTERTON 'descended' each week in a taxi to dictate any gaps. Desmond Gleeson wrote:

... if inspiration flagged, he would take a walk round Clerkenwell. . . . He never returned without the required inspiration.[4]

According to Gosse, far from writing *Songs Before Sunrise* in a mood of exaltation which the verses might suggest, SWINBURNE wrote them when he was attending the brothel in St John's Wood where the young girls whipped 'fearfully severely'.[5] From his rooms in Dorset Square he walked through Regent's Park, composing as he went and, sometimes being early, would sit and write down the verses already formed in his head. During the years of his marriage, BARRIE, before he wrote, walked up and down, up and down. Even in his Adelphi flat the interminable to-and-fro-ings went on, the same silences for his friends. STEPHEN POTTER 'when working, always paced up and down' – his first wife banished him 'to a wood-and-glass hut in the garden'.[6]

After 9.0 p.m. and they had put away their sewing, the BRONTË sisters walked round and round the dining-room table, at first planning their future but in later years discussing the plots of their novels. If Ellen Nussey were there, she and Charlotte walked with arms encircling each other, and behind them came Emily and Anne

1 *Dickens* trans. Hamish Miles (1934), p. 40.
2 Jan. 18, 1847: *The Letters of Charles Dickens*: The Pilgrim Edition (1965–81), v, p. 9.
3 *Letters of John Richard Green* ed. Leslie Stephen (1901), p. 65.
4 Quoted by Maisie Ward: *Return to Chesterton* (1952), p. 218.
5 Jean Overton Fuller: *Swinburne: A Critical Biography* (1968), p. 146.
6 Alan Jenkins: *Stephen Potter: Inventor of Gamesmanship* (n.d.), pp. 85–86.

similarly entwined. Charlotte, who survived her sisters, continued this ritualistic pacing alone.[1]

CARLYLE prepared for his lectures *Heroes and Hero Worship* largely on horseback.

1 E. C. Gaskell: *The Life of Charlotte Brontë* (1857), i, p. 161.

CHAPTER TWO
Pursuit of Peace

I

Those of nervous disposition did not find it easy to insulate themselves from distraction. CARLYLE, at fifty-eight, built his sound-proof room on the third floor of (then) No. 5 Cheyne Row. It cost £169. He declared at first:

. . . all the cocks in nature may crow round it, without my hearing a whisper of them![1]

But when he moved in, disillusionment followed. The workmanship was inferior. From his eyrie he now heard distant railway whistles and bells – 'evils that he knew not of' in the lower rooms. T. E. LAWRENCE sound-proofed the walls of the bungalow that his father built him at the bottom of their garden. After one term in College, he was allowed to live there, and surrounded by mediaeval things – his brass-rubbings on the walls – he wrote his thesis, later published as *Crusader Castles*, researched during his Long Vacation in Syria. PRIESTLEY stuffed twists of cotton wool into his ears.

MAUGHAM bricked up the wall of his writing-room to shut out the Côte d'Azur because 'it distracted me from my work'.[2] At No. 3, The Grove, Highgate – where Coleridge had spent the last eighteen years of his life – PRIESTLEY in his study turned his back on 'a wonderful view uninterrupted by habitation of any kind'.[3] ROALD DAHL closed the curtains of his writing-room which was 'small, tight, dark – a kind of womb'.

Nobody cleans it or dusts.[4]

---

1 Letter to Mrs Aitken: Aug. 11, 1853.
2 Robin Maugham: *Conversations with Willie* (1978), p. 62.
3 Vincent Brome: *J. B. Priestley* (1988), p. 102.
4 BBC TV documentary, 1985.

CHRISTOPHER MILNE believes a lot of sympathy has been wasted on those who write in garrets:

If you are a writer what you want above all else is quiet.

He chose to write *The Enchanted Places* in a room lit by a small skylight with no heating (in November). It had 'never been decorated, never even *cleaned* since we came here twenty-two years ago . . . and it suits me perfectly'.[1] His father's room at Cotchford Farm had been 'very small and damp and dark', which made A. A. MILNE's wife say: 'It really is just like a third class railway carriage in here.'[2]

DICKENS needed the reassurance of familiar things laid out on his desk – his bronzes of two fighting toads, a dog fancier smothered with puppies and dogs, a paper knife, a gilt leaf bearing a rabbit. At Gad's Hill, the first thing he did every morning, before going to work, was to make a complete circuit of the garden, and then go over the whole house to see that everything was in its place. Before ARNOLD BENNETT began writing, he went round his study to ensure that nothing after dusting had been moved so much as an inch. His pretty French wife felt the strain of keeping their dogs from barking. On hearing that Galsworthy liked his wife to play the piano softly in the next room, Bennett asked Marguerite to bring in her sewing – but it was not a success. WILDE wrote on Carlyle's writing-table which he had bought – 'I doubt not . . . with the hope . . . of . . . recalling memories of Titanic labour. . . .'[3] In Paris, before his marriage, he used another fetish against idleness – a white dressing-gown modelled after the monk's cowl of Balzac. He had a study fitted up at the top of the house, but Sherard believed he never wrote there:

. . . what writing he did do in Tite Street, was done . . . in the little room on the right of the entrance passage.[4]

Most of *An Ideal Husband* was written at St James's Place where he took rooms –

it being quite out of the question to secure quiet and mental repose at my own house when my two young sons were at home.[5]

1 *The Enchanted Places* (1974), p. 130.
2 *Ibid.*, p. 131.
3 Robert Harborough Sherard: *Oscar Wilde: The Story of an Unhappy Friendship* (1902), p. 28.
4 *Ibid.*, p. 105.
5 In cross-examination at 2nd Trial.

COLERIDGE told Poole that he needed 'a House with a Garden',

& large enough for me to have a Study out (of) the noise of Women & children – this is absolutely necessary for me.[1]

The eldest daughter of DICKENS wrote that her father 'never could bear the least noise when he was writing, and waged a fierce war against organ-grinders, bands, &c.'

We little ones had to pass the door (of his study) as quietly as possible. . . .[2]

EVELYN WAUGH's daughter, Harriet, said: 'You tiptoed in the hall when he was working in the library.'[3] PRIESTLEY's daughter Rachel said: 'Certainly we had to tiptoe around certain parts of the house in his working hours.' Her sister Sylvia said: 'We all silenced each other if we were forced to invade the forbidden area.'[4]

TENNYSON told Emily Sellwood during their early years of courtship:

I require quiet, and myself to myself, more than any man when I write.[5]

At Berneval, after his imprisonment, WILDE told Ross:

. . . to work I must be isolated.[6]

Callers could be a problem for someone hospitable like JOHNSON. 'Sir,' he said to Boswell, 'I am obliged to any man who visits me.'[7] He had scruples about allowing 'his servant to say he was not at home when he really was', and told Boswell that when he wanted to study he went up to his library without mentioning it beforehand.[8] That was at No. 1 Inner Temple Lane, with his library 'contained in two garrets over his Chambers'. At Ayot St Lawrence, SHAW worked in a revolving summer house at the bottom of his garden and, since it was three minutes' walk

1 Feb. 14, 1800: *Collected Letters of Samuel Taylor Coleridge* ed. Earl Leslie Griggs (1956–71), i, p. 572.
2 'Charles Dickens at Home': *The Cornhill Magazine*, Jan. 1885.
3 Nicholas Shakespeare's 'The Waugh Trilogy': *Arena*, BBC 2, April 1987.
4 Brome's interviews Sept. 10, 1985 and Feb. 6, 1986: Vincent Brome: *J. B. Priestley* (1988), pp. 107–8.
5 1839. *Alfred Lord Tennyson* by his Son, i, p. 173.
6 H. Montgomery Hyde: *Oscar Wilde: A Biography* (1976), p. 329.
7 May 24, 1763.
8 July 18, 1763: James Boswell: *The Life of Samuel Johnson, LL.D.* (1971): Aetat.54.

from the house, his wife was able to inform callers honestly that he was out.

In a little summer house that he had designed and painted in a meadow overlooking Freshwater Bay, TENNYSON wrote down *Enoch Arden* in his MS book. MEREDITH slung a hammock-cot in the Norwegian chalet that he had put up in the garden of Flint Cottage, and there could be heard from the terrace carrying on dialogues with his characters. The real Swiss chalet,[1] that DICKENS received as a Christmas present, was set up on ground he owned opposite Gad's Hill. He built a connecting tunnel under Rochester High Road (*à la* Pope) so that he could work there secretly spring and summer. On Boar's Hill, MASEFIELD wrote in a hut in his garden which was enclosed by tall gorse bushes. H. E. BATES worked in his garden hut at Little Chart, with blankets on a cold day. DAPHNE DU MAURIER at Menabilly worked not in a gracious room but a garden shed.

To get away from Lime Street and Lloyd, his unstable lodger, COLERIDGE went to Ash Farm, Culbone, where sitting downstairs he took two grains of opium and read from *Purchas's Pilgrimage*. Sleeping deeply for three hours during which 'images rose up before him as things', he awoke eagerly to write – but 'a person on business from Porlock' called and detained him more than an hour. Then he found that 'with the exception of some eight or ten scattered lines and images, all the rest had passed away'.[2] *Kubla Khan, a Vision in a Dream*, instead of two to three hundred lines, remained a fragment of fifty.

In September 1893, WILDE took a set of chambers at St James's Place and arrived daily at 11.30. During his first week he completed the first act of *An Ideal Husband*. In the second week, Alfred Douglas drove up at noon.

I had to take you out to luncheon at the Café Royal or the Berkeley. Luncheon with its liqueurs lasted usually till 3.30. For an hour you retired to White's. At tea-time you appeared again. . . . You dined with me either at the Savoy or at Tite Street. We did not separate as a rule till after midnight, as supper at Willis's had to wind up the entrancing day. That was my life for those three months. . . .[3] While you were with me you were the absolute ruin of my art, and in allowing you to stand persistently between Art and myself I give to myself shame and blame in the fullest degree. . . . I should have forbidden you my house and my chambers except when I specially invited you.[4]

1 Now in the grounds of the Dickens Centre, Rochester.
2 Coleridge's Note prefaced to the poem.
3 *De Profundis* ('The Complete Text': 1949), p. 16.
4 *Ibid.*, p. 18.

A year later,[1] Wilde was trying to finish *The Importance of Being Earnest* at Worthing by himself when Douglas suddenly appeared, insisting 'on being taken to the Grand Hotel at Brighton'.[2]

Just before his marriage, MAUGHAM would be working on *Of Human Bondage* when Syrie wanted him to take her to a place like Henley. Barbara Back, his friend of many years, said:

Syrie simply didn't understand how important his writing was to Willie.[3]

She remembered that after one of their parties Maugham had complained that he couldn't stay up night after night and work the next morning, to which Syrie retorted that their parties had made him the best-known author in London. Maugham replied:

But I'd rather be less well known and write better.[4]

In the penultimate year of her young life, WINIFRED HOLTBY rented a small furnished cottage at Withersea on the Yorkshire coast to work on *South Riding*, but too soon everybody found out her address. The following year, she took lodgings in a modest house in Hornsea, in the hope of repeating the progress made the previous spring. To 'achieve real concentration', VERA BRITTAIN bought a gamekeeper's cottage, Allum Green Corner, with her final savings from *Testament of Youth*. She calculated that two miles from Lyndhurst would be 'far enough from town to deter those car-driving visitors who "drop in" unannounced to torpedo a working day'. She set up 'an open south-facing summer house' beyond her small lawn, and here while her children were away at school finished *Testament of Friendship*, the biography of her friend. As she wrote hour after hour, in that early summer of 1939, intrusive young ponies staggered on spindly legs over the green.[5] ORWELL went to Jura, an island in the Inner Hebrides, to write *Nineteen Eighty-Four*.

III

The Romantic poets, like Impressionist painters later in the century, worked outdoors – SHELLEY in the pine-woods, by a deep pool, outside

1 October 1894.
2 *De Profundis* ('The Complete Text': 1949), p. 32.
3 Robin Maugham: *Conversations with Willie* (1978), p. 42.
4 *Ibid.*, p. 44.
5 *Testament of Experience* (1957), pp. 200–2.

Pisa. His 'study' was described by Trelawny when one day he went to find him:

One of the pines, undermined by the water, had fallen into it. Under its lee, and nearly hidden, sat the poet.[1]

To avoid startling him, Trelawny opened the books lying nearby – one was Sophocles, the other Shakespeare. Shelley 'was writing verses on a guitar':[2]

> Ariel to Miranda: – Take
> This slave of music . . .

KEATS took his chair out at breakfast and, under a plum tree in the garden, wrote his *Ode* to a nightingale which had built its nest near Wentworth Place.

GALSWORTHY was at home in the sun. His nephew described him sitting on the lawn of an evening at Wingstone, a blotter on his knee and china inkpot at his feet. As the shadows moved, he edged his chair along the lawn and his spaniel followed him. MASEFIELD told reporters he always wrote out of doors whenever he could –

until the rain makes the ink run, or the frost freezes it on my pen.[3]

1 Edward John Trelawny: *Recollections of the Last Days of Shelley and Byron* (1858), pp. 70–1.
2 *Ibid.*, p. 74.
3 *Westminster Gazette*: May 22, 1930. Quoted by Constance Babington Smith: *John Masefield: A Life* (1978), p. 196.

CHAPTER THREE
An Inner Insulation

THACKERAY heads a group who seem unruffled by external interference. When the Rev. Whitwell Elwin heard him tell his daughter that he was going to Greenwich to write 'a bit of Philip', he exclaimed:

'Write Philip at a tavern at Greenwich!'. . . . 'Yes,' he replied, 'I cannot write comfortably in my own room. I do most of my composition at hotels or at a club. There is an excitement in public places which sets my brain working.'[1]

WILLIAM MORRIS did not object to being interrupted even when composing poetry. Mary De Morgan found him alone one day in the tapestry room of Kelmscott Manor, writing at a side table. 'Where are you going, Mary?' he called as she turned to go.

'I thought you were busy writing poetry.'. . . . 'What the devil has that got to do with it?' he cheerfully replied. 'Sit down and tell me a tale.'[2]

SHAW declared:

I had either to write under all circumstances or not to write at all. . . . A very considerable part of my plays has been written in railway carriages between King's Cross & Hatfield; and it is no worse than what I have written in the Suez and Panama canals.

TROLLOPE also, as Postal surveyor, 'found that I passed in railway-carriages very many hours of my existence'.

I made for myself . . . a little tablet, and found, after a few days' exercise that I could write as quickly in a railway-carriage as I could at my desk. I worked with a pencil, and what I wrote my wife copied afterwards.[3]

KIPLING always worked on the voyages to South Africa, when he and his family went to winter in the house that Cecil Rhodes had presented to them. He worked in a small cabin on the noisy promenade deck, or

1 Elwin: *Some Eighteenth Century Men of Letters* (1902), i, pp. 245–6.
2 J. W. Mackail: *The Life of William Morris* (1899), i, pp. 222–3.
3 *An Autobiography* (1883). i, pp. 136–7.

seated at a high folding table on the deck itself. After a few moments he would walk up and down just as if he were at home in Burwash, completely unaware of the interest he engendered – particularly when he had put on his dressing-gown one evening by mistake.[1]

J. K. Jerome called CONAN DOYLE a 'tremendous worker':

He would sit at a small desk in a corner of his own drawing-room, writing a story, while a dozen people round about him were talking and laughing. He preferred it to being alone in his study. Sometimes, without looking up ... he would make a remark, showing he must have been listening to our conversation; but his pen had never ceased moving.[2]

After playing golf of an afternoon, TERENCE RATTIGAN either joined his friends at the bar or they accompanied him home. If he wished to write, he sat in the window and brought out a notebook, putting his feet on a stool, while his friends played the record player and talked. If they suggested they should leave, he told them cheerfully not to bother.[3]

Their son tells how MARJORIE and C. H. B. QUENNELL prepared 'the Books', the series of *A History of Everyday Things*. They worked in the living-room, in the evening, at twin desks side by side, their three children and two dogs gathered about the hearth.

My father ... did not demand or expect a complete hush, and was apt to keep the radio blaring out ... the sheer volume of sound ... did nothing to impair his extraordinary gift of concentration. He worked steadily, his gold-rimmed spectacles glinting and his long hand swiftly moving.[4]

WILLIAM GOLDING wrote much of *Lord of the Flies* in class when he was a schoolmaster. 2,000 words of it 'were scribbled in the choir stalls of Salisbury Cathedral during a rehearsal for the school Founder's Day concert'.[5]

Leonard Woolf described VIRGINIA as 'extremely sensitive to noise', yet surprisingly when writing she usually seemed 'to acquire a protective skin or integument which insulated her from her surroundings'.[6]

1 Lord Birkenhead: *Rudyard Kipling* (1978), p. 230.
2 *My Life and Times* (1925), p. 164.
3 See Michael Darlow and Gillian Hodson: *Terence Rattigan: The Man and his Work* (1979), p. 211.
4 Peter Quennell: *The Marble Foot* (1976), p. 84.
5 Interview with Victoria Glendinning: *The Sunday Times*, Oct. 19, 1980.
6 *Downhill All the Way* (1967), pp. 52–53.

CHAPTER FOUR

Regulars

I

TROLLOPE's posthumous revelation that he worked to routine – a fixed rate of 1,000 words an hour, mainly before breakfast – shocked his admirers, who had expected to hear more about inspiration. It is unfair to single out Trollope, who was not alone in having a regular procedure. De Quincey marvelled at SOUTHEY, producing 'so many lines . . . by contract, as it were, before breakfast'.[1] HARDY told Robert Graves that he could once sit down and write novels by a timetable.

MILTON's ordered day began at 4.0 a.m. when he had the Hebrew Bible read to him, and he was working before breakfast. Meditation, reading and dictation occupied his morning. His greatest poems were composed in his head, especially at night. Paid amanuenses or his two nephews, his daughter Deborah, or his friends, would take dictation from him, correct copy, and read aloud in Greek, Latin, Italian, or French. (He required that Elwood, who read Latin to him, 'should learn and practise the Italian pronunciation'.)[2] The blind man liked to dictate with a leg flung over one arm of his chair. In the evening there was reading of poetry, and he retired about nine.

With financial ruin staring him in the face, his wife and darling grandson seriously ill, SCOTT still completed his daily task – thirty printed pages of *Woodstock*.

SOUTHEY, according to De Quincey, *never* rose before 8.0 a.m., though he went to bed at 10.30 p.m. From breakfast at 9.0, to dinner about 5.30 or 6.0, was his main period of literary toil. If there were visitors, he sat over his wine after dinner; if not, he retired to his library

---

1 *The Collected Writings of Thomas De Quincey* ed. David Masson (1889–90), ii, p. 319.
2 Samuel Johnson: *The Lives of the English Poets* (Dublin ed. 1779–81), i, p. 175.

;ain from which, about 8.0, he was summoned to tea when he read
.he London papers.

But, generally speaking, he closed his *literary* toils at dinner; the whole of the
hours after that meal being dedicated to his correspondence.[1]

The post reached Keswick about 6.0 or 7.0 p.m., yet all his letters were
answered on the same evening which brought them. There is a parallel
in this last point with LEONARD WOOLF when he was Office Assistant
in Jaffna, and the new Government Agent, F. H. Price, taught him
that ninety-nine out of every hundred letters received, requiring an
answer, should be answered on the day they were received. Woolf
wrote:

Ever since the year 1906 I have practised it in my private life and have
insisted upon it in every government office or business for which I have been
responsible.[2]

TENNYSON's hours were 'quite regular'. His son tells us:

... he breakfasted at 8, lunched at 2, dined at 7.... He worked chiefly in
the morning over his pipe, or in the evening after his pint of port, also over
his pipe.[3]

Eleven-year-old Hallam had to warn Thomas Wilson, staying at Far-
ingford, 'not to trouble him when he was smoking his first morning
pipe, when he used to think that his best inspirations came'.[4]

DICKENS, after rising at seven, breakfasting at eight, always sat down
to his desk at the same time, just before 10 a.m., and did not rise again
until 2.0 p.m. – regardless of output.

I always sit here for that certain time.

His son, Henry, said that his father saw it as 'his business to sit at his
desk during just those particular hours in the day', whether anything
came of it or not. Dickens told Miss Coutts that before starting a new
book –

unless I were to shut myself up obstinately and sullenly in my room for a

1 Masson, *op. cit.*, ii, p. 318.
2 *Growing* (1961), p. 107.
3 *Alfred Lord Tennyson* by his Son, ii, p. 210.
4 *Ibid.*, i, p. 512.

great many days without writing a word, I don't think I should ever ma] beginning.[1]

He told Nathaniel Dodge:

... four hours at his desk and four hours afield – on foot or on horseback ... was the rule of his working life.[2]

Graham Balfour observed when he stayed at Vailima that STEVENSON rose at 6.0 a.m. or perhaps earlier.

From my bed in the cottage I commanded a view of his verandah ... in the midst there would be the one spot of bright light where Tusitala, the only other person awake of all the household, was already at his labours.

About 6.30 a light breakfast was taken to 'the master', who 'continued to work by himself, chiefly making notes', until soon after eight when Mrs Strong (Stevenson's daughter-in-law) joined him as his amanuensis until nearly noon. Everybody then met for 'a substantial meal ... in the large hall'.[3] The afternoon might include a ride or a stroll, or a game of croquet or tennis. Dinner was at six. Balfour thought his cousin did most of his reading after 8.0 p.m. when the members of the household went to their several rooms, but Stevenson was in bed soon after ten, if not before. DOYLE, in South Norwood days, worked from breakfast to lunch, and from 5.0 p.m.–8.0 p.m., averaging 3,000 words a day. Many of his ideas came to him of an afternoon when walking or tricycling, playing cricket or tennis.

BENNETT'S routine was meticulous – early morning tea at seven, reading in bed, bath, breakfast at nine on the dot, reading of newspapers, and then 'a thinking walk'[4] either in the forest or through the town before he began the day's writing. This was when he lived at Valvin near Fontainebleu, but when he had started *The Old Wives' Tale* he rose earlier and took a four-mile walk from 8.30 to 9.30 a.m., even in heavy rain. He knew, before he had written a word, that this would be his masterpiece 200,000 words long. He knew he would start it on October 8th, 1907, and finish on August 30th, 1908. And it all happened just like that.

VIRGINIA WOOLF wrote her novel from 10.0 a.m.–1.0 p.m. She very

1 *The Letters of Charles Dickens* ed. Walter Dexter (1938), i, no. 487.
2 An American scrap-book presented to the Boston branch of the Dickens Fellowship in May 1939: quoted by Una Pope-Hennessy: *Charles Dickens* (1945), p. 300.
3 *The Life of Robert Louis Stevenson* (1901), ii, pp. 119–20.
4 Dudley Barker: *Writer by Trade: A View of Arnold Bennett* (1966), p. 154.

rarely sat at the littered table in her work-room but in a very low disembowelled chair.

> ... on her knees was a large board made of plywood which had an inkstand glued to it, and on the board was a large quarto notebook of plain paper which she had bound up for her and covered herself in (usually) some gaily-coloured paper.[1]

Later, perhaps in the afternoon, she typed out what she had written, all further revisions being made on the typewriter. When LYTTON STRACHEY was writing *Queen Victoria* he worked every morning alone in his library for about three hours, during which time he usually set down some three hundred words in ink. Michael Holroyd adds that 'with all Lytton's major works, the preparatory reading ... took up almost twice as long as the actual writing'.[2]

RATTIGAN, in a silk dressing-gown, wrote from 10.30 a.m.–3.0 p.m., a housekeeper bringing him a light lunch on a tray. After two hours' relaxation, walking or playing golf or tennis, he continued from 5.0–8.0, seldom beyond 9.0 p.m. He wrote in longhand in exercise books, his secretary doing his typing. His background music changed from jazz to Puccini. Lying on a sofa, he rested against his knee a writing board given him, when a young man, by his mother. At Sunningdale a board was specially made to fit an armchair.[3]

With the death of Gerald Haxton causing MAUGHAM to go into a decline, Robin Maugham went out to his uncle in the wilds of Yemassee. 'His discipline was incredible,'[4] the nephew wrote. Each day, Maugham went to the small cottage turned into a writing room and worked on his notebooks, which he published as *A Writer's Notebook* dedicated to Gerald Haxton.

On days when he did not have to go into *Tribune*, ORWELL at the Canonbury Square flat pounded his typewriter from 6.30 a.m. until midday, pausing for a cooked breakfast. After the death of Eileen, Crick speaks of 'a new iron regime'[5] which left only the middle part of day for recreation. He now rose at a quarter to eight, breakfasting half past and working until noon but, after high tea and his little

1 *Downhill All the Way* (1967), p. 52.
2 *Lytton Strachey: A Critical Biography* (1967–8), ii, p. 347.
3 See Michael Darlow and Gillian Hodson: *Terence Rattigan: The Man and his Work* (1979), p. 207.
4 *Conversations with Willie* (1978), p. 85.
5 Bernard Crick: *George Orwell: A Life* (1980), p. 347.

boy Richard had gone to bed, he began again. With Cadbury's cocoa punctiliously at ten, he went on until 3.0 a.m.. Susan Watson (his housekeeper and child's nurse) became so used to his typewriter that she awoke in alarm if it stopped.

CHRISTOPHER MILNE wrote that 'an author today . . . may well envy my father' who, 'with cooks to cook and maids to wash and scrub', was able to write 'from about 10.30 in the morning until just before lunch and from after tea until just before dinner, and . . . could then do just as he pleased for the whole of the rest of the day'.[1] SHAW characteristically inscribed one of his books to his housekeeper and gardener:

To Henry and Clara Higgs, who have had a very important part in my life's work, as without their friendly services I should not have had time to write my books and plays nor had any comfort in my daily life.

II

Among those less organized, BYRON habitually rose not until midday – even late afternoon. A prolonged toilet, exercise and social converse meant it was past 11.0 p.m. when he sat down to work, continuing until 2.0 or 3.0 a.m. T. E. LAWRENCE, 'tinkering at the second draft of *Seven Pillars of Wisdom*' at All Souls, worked by night, going to bed at dawn. That was why Robert Graves never visited his rooms in the morning before eleven o'clock or half past. During World War II at Witham, DOROTHY L. SAYERS, also a late riser, wrote best after her husband had gone to bed.

WILLIAM GOLDING has no 'fetishist thing' about when and how he works, no routine, 'it's not the Trollope thing at all. I write my books when it's possible to.'[2]

CHURCHILL asked Beverley Nichols, while still in Oxford, whether he had worked regularly at his novel *Prelude*. Nichols replied: 'I don't see how you can do work in that manner if it is to have any sort of claim to be emotional.'

'Nonsense. . . . You should go to your room every day at nine o'clock . . . and say to yourself, "I am going to sit here for four hours and write!". . . . If you sit waiting for inspiration, you will sit there till you are an old man.'[3]

---

1 *The Enchanted Places* (1974), pp. 112–3.
2 Interview with Victoria Glendinning: *The Sunday Times*, Oct. 19, 1980.
3 Beverley Nichols: *Twenty-Five: Being a Young Man's Candid Recollections of his Elders and Betters* (1926), p. 64.

The sentiment echoes JOHNSON who maintained that a man could write any time 'if he sits doggedly to it'. WILLIAM MORRIS was equally forthright:

That talk of inspiration is sheer nonsense, I may tell you that flat . . . it is a mere matter of craftsmanship.

Again –

If a chap can't compose an epic poem while he's weaving tapestry, he had better shut up, he'll never do any good at all.[1]

TROLLOPE may have had his watch before him requiring '250 words every quarter of an hour', but routine did not prevent him 'leaving the ground' and identifying with his characters:

I have wandered alone among rocks and woods, crying at their grief, laughing at their absurdities, and thoroughly enjoying their joy. I have been impregnated with my own creations till it has been my only excitement to sit with the pen in my hand, and drive my team before me as at quick a pace as I could make them travel.[2]

When he closed the Barsetshire series he insisted that Barset had been to him 'a real county, and its city a real city'.

. . . the spires and towers have been before my eyes, and the voices of the people are known to my ears, and the pavement of the city ways are familiar to my footsteps.[3]

---

1 J. W. Mackail: *The Life of William Morris* (1899), i, p. 186.
2 *An Autobiography* (1883), i, p. 234.
3 *The Last Chronicle of Barset* (1867), ii, p. 384.

CHAPTER FIVE

What Dickens Said

Side by side with his life as structured as Bennett's, and which had 'no faith in the waiting-for-inspiration theory',[1] DICKENS said:

> I hold my inventive faculty on the stern condition that it must master my whole life, often have complete possession of me ... and sometimes for months together put everything else away from me.[2]

It is an archetypical statement. It suggests that his inspiration (which at other times, according to his son, he seems to have denied) came not from within, that it was a power spasmodic in duration and peremptory in its demands. Other writers have borne this out.

Whistler frightened GEORGE MOORE when he told him: 'You care about nothing except your writing.'[3] ORWELL's wife, Eileen, told Lydia Jackson:

> If we were at opposite ends of the world and I sent him (her brother Lawrence) a telegram saying 'Come at once' he would have come. George would not do that. For him his work comes before anybody.[4]

Mrs Gaskell used *possession* in connection with CHARLOTTE BRONTË, who had told her it was not every day that she could write.

> Then some morning, she would wake up, and the progress of her task lay clear and bright before her, in distinct vision. When this was the case, all her care was to discharge her household and filial duties, so as to obtain leisure to sit down and write out the incident and consequent thoughts, which were, in fact, more present to her mind at such times than her actual life itself. Yet

---

1 Henry Dickens on his father.
2 *The Letters of Charles Dickens* ed. Walter Dexter: Nonesuch Press (1938), i, p. 782. See also, for a slightly variant version: Gladys Storey: *Dickens and Daughter* (1939), p. 92. (e.g. 'faculty' is replaced by 'capacity'.)
3 Desmond MacCarthy: *Portraits* (1931), p. 203.
4 Quoted by Bernard Crick: *George Orwell: A Life* (1980), p. 264.

notwithstanding this 'possession' (as it were) . . . never was the call of another for help, neglected. . . .[1]

At the time of his 'first spring flood of *Dymer*', when his surrogate mother, Mrs Moore, wanted him 'jobbing in the kitchen and doing messages in Headington', c. s. lewis confided to his journal:

Domestic drudgery . . . as an alternative to the work one is longing to do and able to do (at that time and heaven knows when again) it is maddening.[2]

aldous huxley described d. h. lawrence getting the urge to write and then writing 'for eighteen hours a day'.

It was very extraordinary to see him work, it was a sort of *possession*; he would rush on with it, his hand moving at a tremendous rate.[3]

eliot used the phrase 'a kind of demonic possession by one poet'[4] for his scribbling in boyhood of à la FitzGerald-Omar quatrains, and then Byronic stanzas.

kipling's 'Daemon' had been with him 'in the *Jungle Books*, *Kim*, and both Puck books, and good care I took to walk delicately, lest he should withdraw'.

Note here. When your Daemon is in charge, do not try to think consciously. Drift, wait and obey.[5]

Perhaps thackeray, beginning *Denis Duval*, was trying too hard:

. . . for the last ten days I have been almost *non compos mentis*. . . . I sit for hours before my paper, not doing my book, but incapable of doing anything else, and thinking upon that subject always, waking with it, walking about with it, and going to bed with it. Oh, the struggles and bothers – oh, the throbs and pains about this trumpery![6]

virginia woolf's Daemon was so much in charge that when she was finishing *The Waves*, she –

reeled across the last ten pages with some moments of such intensity and intoxication that I seemed only to stumble after my own voice, or almost after

1 *The Life of Charlotte Brontë* (1857), ii, p. 8.
2 Mar. 17–25, 1924. *Letters of C. S. Lewis* ed. with a *Memoir*, by W. H. Lewis (1966), p. 92.
3 London interview with John Chandos, June 1961. Quoted by Sybille Bedford: *Aldous Huxley: A Biography* (1973–4), i, p. 210.
4 *The Use of Poetry and The Use of Criticism* (1933), p. 34.
5 *Something of Myself* (1937), p. 210.
6 To Mrs William Ritchie, May 1863: Lady Ritchie's Biographical Introductions to *The Works of William Makepeace Thackeray* (1910–11), xxi, p. xiv.

some sort of speaker (as when I was mad) I was almost afraid, remembering the voices that used to fly ahead.[1]

Leonard comments:

– here surely is an exact description of the inspiration of genius and madness, showing how terrifyingly thin is the fabric of thought often separating the one from the other. . . .[2]

According to his friend J. T. Smith, BLAKE would work night after night 'when he was under his very fierce inspirations, which were as if they would tear him asunder. . . .'[3]

ORWELL said that, like all writers, he was 'driven on by some demon whom one can neither resist nor understand'. He allowed that the 'demon' may be 'the same instinct that makes a baby squall for attention'.

And yet it is also true that one can write nothing readable unless one constantly struggles to efface one's own personality.[4]

1 *A Writer's Diary* (1953), p. 169: Feb. 7, 1931.
2 *Beginning Again* (1964), p. 31.
3 Alexander Gilchrist: *The Life of William Blake* (1973 R. of 2nd ed. 1880), i, p. 359.
4 'Why I Write': *Gangrel* (No. 4, Summer), 1946.

CHAPTER SIX

Inspiration (Continued)

I

S HAW never wavered that *The Adventures of the Black Girl in Her Search for God* had been written as set down on the fly-leaf of the first proof which he sent, at seventy-six, to his friend Dame Laurentia McLachlan:

> An Inspiration
> which came in response to the prayers of the nuns
> of Stanbrook Abbey
> and
> in particular
> to the prayers of his dear Sister Laurentia
> for
> Bernard Shaw.

She asked him to withdraw the book and renounce its blasphemies. He replied:

... when my wife was ill in Africa, God came to me and said 'These women in Worcester plague me night and day with their prayers for you. What are you good for, anyhow?' So I said I could write a bit. . . . God said then 'Take your pen and write what I shall put in your silly head.' When I had done so, I told you about it, thinking that you would be pleased, as it was the answer to your prayers. But you were not pleased at all. . . . So I went to God and said, 'The Abbess is displeased.' And God said, 'I am God, and I will not be trampled on by any Abbess that ever walked. . . .' So I leave you to settle it with God and his Son as best you can; but you must go on praying for me, however surprising the results may be.[1]

Their friendship had begun nine years previously when Sydney Cockerell succeeded in bringing these of his friends together, and Shaw and his wife Charlotte called on her at Stanbrook Abbey.[2] A few

1 July 24, 1933.
2 Apl. 24, 1924.

months later,[1] she received her copy of *Saint Joan* inscribed 'To Sister Laurentia from Brother Bernard'.

On his visit to the Holy Land with Dean Inge, in 1931, she asked him to bring back a little stone. In a long letter he wrote that 'the appearance of a woman with an infant in her arms takes on the quality of a vision'.

I swam in the lake of Tiberias with a pleasant sense that this, at least, was Christ's lake on which nobody could stake out the track on which he walked. . . . God must feel sick when he looks at Jerusalem. I fancy he consoles himself by turning to Stanbrook. . . .[2]

He forwarded her stone but said it was for the garden and that another, for herself, would follow – 'the explanation' would be 'satisfactory'.[3] The Shaws duly arrived[4] with a piece of silver, crafted by Paul Cooper in the form of a mediaeval reliquary. A foot in height, it featured a piece of rock on four slender columns while above, on the summit, the Holy Child with one hand held the globe and raised the right in blessing. Shortly afterwards, Cockerell suggested that she write to Shaw to put an inscription. He replied:

Why can it not be a secret between us and Our Lady and her little boy? . . . We couldn't put our names on it – could we? It seems to me something perfectly awful. . . .
Dear Sister: our finger prints are on it, and Heaven knows whose footprints may be on the stone. . . .[5]

He tried to prepare her for *The Adventures of the Black Girl*.

The truth is, dear Sister Laurentia, I have finished with all these deities, who seem to me more or less grotesque signboards announcing that the Holy Ghost is lodged within, though It is there only as It is everywhere. . . . Perhaps I should not disturb the peace of Stanbrook with my turbulent spirit. . . .

He told her the story 'is very irreverent and iconoclastic but I don't think you will think it fundamentally irreligious'.[6] In the event she was shattered.

She told him she felt partly responsible because of their friendship

1 Oct. 1, 1924.
2 St Patrick's Day, 1931.
3 June 12, 1931.
4 Sept. 1931.
5 Oct. 25, 1931.
6 Apl. 14, 1932.

– that he seemed quite insensitive to the feelings of those who accepted the Incarnation – that if he had lampooned her parents he could not expect it to be lightly taken without some act of reparation. This was when she appealed to his stature to say publicly he had been wrong.

After his reply – the letter with which we began – Shaw did not dare call at Stanbrook. Then, a little over a year later, on her Archbishop's advice, she sent him her Golden Jubilee card which he mistook as an announcement of her death. He wrote to the 'Ladies of Stanbrook':

> There was a time when I was in such grace with her that she asked you all to pray for me. . . . But we never know exactly how our prayers will be answered; and their effect on me was that . . . I wrote a little book which, to my grief, shocked Dame Laurentia. . . . She has, I am sure, forgiven me now; but I wish she could tell me so. In the outside world from which you have escaped it is necessary to shock people violently to make them think seriously about religion, and my ways were too rough. But that was how I was inspired.[1]

She replied by return of post. Within a few weeks he was taking steps to safeguard her from publicity, by depriving himself of the pleasure of denying rumours in the press about her influence on his work.

On her Diamond Jubilee, when he was eighty-eight, he wrote:

> But you have lived the religious life: I have only talked and written about it. . . . I count my days at Stanbrook among my happiest.[2]

When he was nearly ninety-two he typed a letter to 'Beloved Sister Laurentia', telling her that he had received a visit from 'another very special friend', Gene Tunney, the undefeated heavyweight boxer – 'who is connected in my thoughts with your subject, the efficacy of prayer'. Gene's wife, with ten hours to live, was healed of a very rare complaint because Gene had prayed. A doctor suddenly arrived on their 'pleasure island in the Adriatic', who had the special qualifications for dealing with double appendicitis.

> . . . even one coincidence is improbable, and a bundle of them as in this case hardly credible in a world full of miracles. . . . I do not doubt it; and it goes to confirm the value I instinctively set on your prayers.[3]

At ninety-three, he wrote:

> I get piles of medals of the Blessed Virgin, with instructions that if I say a

1 Oct. 3, 1934.
2 Sept. 4, 1944.
3 Aug. 17, 1948.

novena she will give me any help I ask from her; and I have to reply that we are in this wicked world to help her and not to beg from her.[1]

His last letter, at ninety-four, closed:

God must be tired of all these prayers for this fellow Shaw whom He doesn't half like. He has promised His servant Laurentia that He will do His best for him, and we had better leave it at that. The thought of Stanbrook is a delight to me. It is one of my holy places.[2]

Their friendship and series of letters had extended over twenty-six years. Sydney Cockerell said to a member of the Stanbrook community that he had never seen Shaw 'so abashed by anyone but William Morris'.

With Morris and your dear Abbess he was on his good behaviour and seemed to admit that he was in the presence of a being superior to himself.

This side of Shaw deserves to be better known, and it has seemed useful to place his claim of inspiration in its fuller context. It is a side of him which speaks disconcertingly in his plays when, for example, Joan is interviewed by Robert:

JOAN I hear voices telling me what to do. They come from God.
ROBERT They come from your imagination.
JOAN Of course. That is how the messages of God come to us.[3]

Canon T. P. Stevens, as a young curate, saw this side of him when Shaw was about fifty-four and had 'accepted an invitation to address the theological students at their hostel in Mecklenburgh Square'.

His fee for a lecture at that time was a hundred guineas, but he agreed to speak to us for nothing. When I arrived at the hostel, Shaw was standing on the doorstep. As I approached he said, 'Do you think there is the slightest chance of getting into this house; I've been knocking and ringing for ten minutes!' I happened to know an area bell he had missed. . . . A maid opened the door. . . . He put a book down on the hall table (which was instantly gathered up with plates and dishes), and waited while I went into the dining-room to speak to the Warden. . . . I was told to take him up to the Common Room. . . . I found him a chair and a copy of *The Westminster Gazette* and, feeling he would be bored with me, I withdrew. Some twenty minutes later two professors and forty students sauntered into the room. . . . Shaw . . . began by saying he had been rehearsing a new play all day and that he was

1 Sept. 2, 1949.
2 July 1950.
3 *Saint Joan* (1942), p. 11.

tired and hungry, but he was quite prepared to talk on the most thrilling subject in the world – religion. He talked for over an hour like a being inspired. God to him was the great driving force of the universe, striving, struggling, creating. He compared his own stately theology to the puny notions of a group of students who looked upon the Creator as a peevish, disappointed Being who had to be cajoled and propitiated and Who was very watchful and touchy on Sundays. There were no fireworks, no appeals to the gallery and, so far as I can recall, little humour.

. . . I remember going into Mecklenburg Square, when it was all over, like a man who had suddenly stepped into a bigger world. From that moment, I knew the inner meaning of *conversion*. It was pure benevolence on Shaw's part to address that meeting, and the reception he got would have sent many a smaller man away in a huff.[1]

II

WILLIAM LANGLAND called the first part of his poem: *The Vision concerning Piers Plowman*. MILTON asked for his lips to be touched:

> And chiefly Thou, O Spirit! that dost prefer,
> Before all temples the upright heart and pure,
> Instruct me, for Thou know'st; Thou from the first
> Was present. . . .
> . . . what in me is dark,
> Illumine: what is low, raise and support. . . .[2]

With the Bible more real than Bedford Gaol – '. . . a text leaps out upon him and grapples him as if it were an angel or demon'[3] – BUNYAN wrote *The Pilgrim's Progress . . . Delivered under the Similitude of a DREAM. . . .* 'DREAM' seems to have been very important to him. On the title-page of the first edition he quotes Hosea: 'I have used Similitudes'.[4] 'DREAM' alone is printed in upper case, and is twice as tall as 'Pilgrim's Progress'. The third edition, the following year, has a portrait of him dreaming his tale. Langland identified himself with the imaginary vagrant dreaming among the Malvern Hills, and his poem is a series of dreams. J. R. Green wrote:

1 *Cassock and Surplus: Incidents in Clerical Life mainly in London* (1947), pp. 119–20.
2 *Paradise Lost* (1667): Bk. I, ll.17–23.
3 Edward Dowden: *Fragments from Old Letters* (1914), p. 132.
4 XII, 10.

It is only in a dream that he sees Corruption, 'Lady Mede,' brought to trial, and the world repenting at the preaching of Reason.[1]

To STEVENSON, inspired by dreams, they were 'man's internal theatre':

When the bank begins to send letters and the butcher to linger at the back gate, he sets to belabouring his brains after a story . . . and, behold! at once the little people begin to bestir themselves . . . and labour all night long, and . . . set before him truncheons of tales upon their lighted theatre. . . . Often enough the waking is a disappointment. . . . And yet how often have these sleepless Brownies done him honest service, and given him . . . better tales than he could fashion for himself.[2]

One winter night in 1885, Fanny (like Mrs De Quincey), woken by her husband's nightmare screams, roused him in pity, but Stevenson said: 'Why did you wake me? I was dreaming a fine bogey tale.' He had dreamed, 'in considerable detail', two or three scenes which would go to form *The Strange Story of Dr Jekyll and Mr Hyde* – 'including the circumstance of the transforming powders'. As soon as it was light he began to write 'with intense concentration' and Lloyd Osbourne, passing his door, saw him 'sitting up in bed, filling page after page and never apparently pausing for a moment'.[3] But of *The Beach of Falesá*, Stevenson said:

It just shot through me like a bullet in one of my moments of awe, alone in that tragic jungle.

TENNYSON dreamed long passages of poetry.

A. E. HOUSMAN, in his Leslie Stephen Lecture delivered at seventy-four, said that sometimes during his walks –

there would flow into my mind, with sudden and unaccountable emotion, sometimes a line or two of verse, sometimes a whole stanza at once, accompanied, not preceded, by a vague notion of the poem which they were destined to form part of.

He made it clear that the process did not start in the brain:

. . . there would usually be a lull of an hour or so, then perhaps the spring would bubble up again. I say bubble up, because, so far as I could make out,

---

1 *A Short History of the English People*: Illustrated Edition: ed. Mrs J. R. Green and Miss Kate Norgate (1893–4), ii, p. 497.
2 'A Chapter on Dreams': *Across the Plains* (1892), pp. 240–1.
3 Graham Balfour: *The Life of Robert Louis Stevenson* (1901), ii, pp. 12–13.

the source of the suggestions that preferred to the brain was an abyss which I have already had occasion to mention, the pit of the stomach.[1]

On arriving home he wrote them down, leaving gaps –

and hoping that further inspiration might be forthcoming another day. Sometimes it was, if I took my walks in a receptive and expectant frame of mind; but sometimes the poem had to be taken in hand and completed by the brain ... involving trial and disappointment, and sometimes ending in failure.[2]

When a youthful LEWIS HIND was commissioned to interview Millais, the painter told him:

One day the inspiration comes, and then it goes. It's all stomach.[3]

RICHARD CHURCH, explaining how a novel began, repeated the word 'emotion':

... for my part it begins, not with an idea, but with an emotion.[4]

KIPLING, when he had come back to England, told E. Kay Robinson that he saw his business as 'to get in touch with the common folk here ... and then after the proper time to speak *whatever may be given to me*'[5] (my italics). MASEFIELD, at thirty-two, heard a man's voice within him which he did not know, saying clearly: 'The spring is beginning.' He was walking alone through some woods on a fine day in April 1911. Some weeks later, he was accompanying a friend down a lane in Great Hampden. In the early morning dew a ploughman and his team came up a rise in a field close-by – like an image from Chaucer or Langland. At dusk he went through the beechwoods and beyond a line of old thorn the common had never seemed more beautiful. In a moment of ecstasy he cried out, 'I will write a poem about a blackguard who becomes converted – and settles down honestly at the plough.'[6] He had his notepad, and before he went back had written the beginning of *The Everlasting Mercy* with all the rest clear before him.[7]

1 In the light of this, one wonders whether the Old Testament insistence on heart and bowels as the seat of emotion, has not been too hastily and contemptuously overthrown by our modern substitution of the brain.
2 *The Name and Nature of Poetry* (1933).
3 *Naphtali* (1926), p. 134.
4 *Speaking Aloud* (1968), p. 194.
5 Letter, March 1890. Quoted by Lord Birkenhead: *Rudyard Kipling* (1978), p. 126.
6 John Masefield: *So Long to Learn* (1952), pp. 186–7.
7 See Constance Babington Smith: *John Masefield: A Life* (1978), pp. 105–6.

ALISON UTTLEY would not have approved of routine. A little over a year before she died, she insisted to an interviewer:

My stories come to me and ask to be written. They come without asking at all sorts of strange times. But if I don't write them down they go away.[1]

MAUGHAM used almost identical language:

You don't just *get* a story. . . . You just have to wait for it to come to you. I've never written a story in my life. The story has come to me *and demanded to be written*.[2]

WINIFRED HOLTBY told Phyllis Bentley that the idea for *South Riding* had suddenly come to her 'after a rather depressing evening spent with my-young-man-who-never-will-be-more-than-my-young-man':

. . . quite, quite irrelevant. But it came just like . . . that, when I was getting rather desperately undressed for bed. I've felt like a prince ever since. You know.

Nearly a year afterwards, she told Lady Rhondda that her new novel 'about local government' was 'all bubbling and boiling in my head'.[3]

HARDY told Robert Graves he had been pruning a tree when the best story he had ever conceived suddenly came complete with characters, setting, even some dialogue, but by the time he sat down at his table all was utterly gone. 'Always carry a pencil and paper,' he advised him. Poetry, he prized more highly than fiction, because it always came to him by accident.[4]

SIEGFRIED SASSOON, in April 1919, was on his way to bed when a few words 'floated' into his head 'as though from nowhere'. He picked up a pencil and wrote them down. Still standing, he added a second line.

It was as if I were remembering rather than thinking. . . . In this mindless, recollecting manner I wrote down my poem in a few minutes.

He then read it through 'with no sense of elation'. But in the morning he was so pleased with his lines that he sent them to Masefield, who made 'the generous comment that it was the only adequate peace celebration he had seen'. Sassoon goes on:

1 Interview with Sally Brompton: *The Daily Mail*, Jan. 17, 1975.
2 Robin Maugham: *Conversation with Willie* (1978), p. 136.
3 Vera Brittain: *Testament of Friendship: The Story of Winifred Holtby* (1940), p. 341.
4 Robert Graves: *Goodbye to All That* (1929), p. 377.

What I have been unable to understand is that there was no apparent mental process during its composition.

Unlike his other poems, 'Everyone Sang' was composed without emotion,[1] and needed no alteration afterwards. . . . I wasn't aware of any technical contriving.'[2] Presumably, if he had not been by his writing table at the time, the poem would have gone away. When ELIOT worked at the bank, a colleague noticed that he 'often seemed to be living in a dreamland . . . he would often in the middle of dictating a letter break off suddenly, grasp a sheet of paper and start writing quickly when an idea came to him. . . .'[3]

The same urgency applies even when the origin of an idea can be traced. On Sunday, March 14, 1802, WORDSWORTH and his sister sat at breakfast in Dove Cottage. They were talking about the pleasure they always shared at the sight of a butterfly, and she made a chance remark that, as a child, 'I used to chase them a little but . . . I was afraid of brushing the dust off their wings, and did not catch them. . . .' Dorothy recorded in her Journal:

. . . with his basin of broth before him untouched, and a little plate of bread and butter he wrote the poem to a butterfly! He ate not a morsel, nor put on his stockings but sat with his shirt neck unbuttoned, and his waistcoat open while he did it.'

The poem ends:

> But she, God love her! feared to brush
> The dust from off its wings.

---

1 Cf. part of Wordsworth's definition of poetry: '. . . it takes its origin from emotion recollected in tranquillity. . . .' (Preface to 2nd Edition of Lyrical Ballads, 1801.)
2 Siegfried's Journey (1945), pp. 140–1.
3 Peter Ackroyd: T. S. Eliot (1984), p. 78.

CHAPTER SEVEN

Nescio

With Trollope's clarity and an added objectivity, WILLIAM GOLDING saw the 'people' (not 'characters') of *Rites of Passage*:

> If I have described them clearly it is because I see them clearly, and I hear their speech: I see them and I hear them.[1]

At Tavistock House, DICKENS's eldest daughter Mamey was, for a time, a great invalid and, after a worse attack of illness than usual, he suggested she should be carried to his study and lie on the sofa while he worked – 'an immense privilege'. For some time the only sound was the rapid working of his pen. She recalls what then followed:

> ... suddenly he jumped up, went to the looking-glass, rushed back to his writing-table and jotted down a few words; back to the glass again, this time talking to his own reflection, or rather to the simulated expression he saw there ... then back again to his writing. After a little while he got up again, and stood with his back to the glass, talking softly and rapidly for a long time, then *looking* at his daughter, but certainly never *seeing* her, then once more back to his table.... It was a curious experience, and a wonderful thing to see him throwing himself so entirely *out* of himself and *into* the character he was writing about.[2]

HAROLD PINTER, at forty-seven, in a rare TV interview, reinforced his caginess about the themes of his plays, and extended still further Golding's objectivity about characters. Pinter's characters are 'strangers' to him rather than 'friends', and when he looks at his plays it is with 'some curiosity ... they have an existence of their own'. He wrote *The Room* in four days, all the time acting in *The Birthday Party*. 'It took its own form' – he 'let it happen' – and 'wrote it totally without calculation'. If when he is writing a doorbell rings in his script, he has

---

1 'The South Bank Show': London Weekend TV, Nov. 1980.
2 'Charles Dickens at Home: With especial reference to his relations with Children': *The Cornhill Magazine*, Jan. 1885.

'no idea who will enter the room'. His characters appear 'out of the blue'. Their life in the play, and the lines they deliver, are all that he (and we) know about them. He said that now he has 'gaps' when he can't write. DOROTHY L. SAYERS did not remember inventing Lord Peter Wimsey:

My impression is that I was thinking about writing a detective story, and that he walked in, complete with spats. . . .[1]

Honoured as a master craftsman of the novel, GOLDING renounced such credentials in his Nobel Prize speech:[2]

I fumble. I practise a craft I do not understand and cannot describe.

ORWELL expressed the same failure to understand his literary demon,[3] and THACKERAY said:

When I am in labour with a book I don't quite know what happens.[4]

RICHARD CHURCH told the Royal Society of Literature:

You see that I am really confessing that I do not know or at most only half-know, how a novel begins.[5]

Even WELLS, who had an explanation for most things, could not explain the creative process behind his short stories:

I found that taking almost anything as a starting point and letting my thoughts play about it, there would presently come out of the darkness, in a manner quite inexplicable, some absurd or vivid little incident more or less relevant to that initial nucleus. Little men in canoes . . . would come floating out of nothingness, incubating the eggs of prehistoric monsters unawares; violent conflicts would break out amidst the flower-beds of suburban gardens. . . .[6]

In one of his last appearances on TV, BETJEMAN reverted to the classical solution:

I think there is such a thing as the Muse. . . . I regard myself as not writing

---

1 'How I Came to Invent the Character of Lord Peter': *Harcourt Brace News*, New York, i, July 15, 1936, pp. 1–2.
2 Dec. 1983.
3 See page 233.
4 Letter to Mrs William Ritchie, May 1863.
5 *Speaking Aloud* (1968), p. 194.
6 *The Country of the Blind and Other Stories* (1911), Introduction, p.iv.

my own verse but as a sieve which has to sort things out. . . . You can't force what has to be inspired. . . .

– and, in an aside:

The Muse – what an evocative creature!

Asked, in a recent interview, how he had come to write *Look Back in Anger* and what he now thought of that play, JOHN OSBORNE replied: 'I never quite believe it myself. . . . It is why I believe in God.'[1]

GRAY told Dr Wharton:

I by no means pretend to inspiration; but yet I affirm, that the faculty, in question, is by no means voluntary; it is the result (I suppose) of a certain disposition of mind, which does not depend on one's self. . . .[2]

1 Interviewed by Melvyn Bragg: *The South Bank Show*, ITV, Nov. 10, 1991.
2 Apl. 9, 1758.

CHAPTER EIGHT
Non-Blotters

Basically there are two ways of writing – either with drafts requiring revision, or a spontaneous flow substantially accurate from the first. SHAKESPEARE, an example of the second, had Ben Jonson's disapproval:

I remember, the Players have often mentioned it as an honour to Shakespeare that in his writing (whatsoever he penn'd) hee never blotted out line. My answer hath beene, would he have blotted a thousand. . . .[1]

JOHNSON urged that if a young writer did not achieve spontaneity, the effort of composition would be too irksome in mature life. He said: 'I wrote forty-eight of the printed octavo pages of the Life of Savage at a sitting; but then I sat up all night.'[2] When Sir Joshua Reynolds asked him 'by what means he had attained this extraordinary accuracy and flow of language', he replied that by constant practice from early on, 'and never suffering any careless expression to escape him, or attempting to deliver his thoughts without arranging them in the clearest manner, it became habitual to him'.[3] Boswell tells us that many of the *Idler* essays 'were written as hastily as an ordinary letter'.

Mr Langton remembers Johnson, when on a visit at Oxford, asking him one evening how long it was till the post went out; and on being told about half an hour, he exclaimed, 'then we shall do very well.' He upon this instantly sat down and finished an Idler, which it was necessary should be in London the next day. Mr Langton having signified a wish to read it, 'Sir, (said he) you shall not do more than I have done myself.' He then folded it up, and sent it off.[4]

When post time drew near, SMOLLETT on a visit to George Home at Paxton, Berwickshire, retired for an hour to scribble off the next

---

1 *Timber; or Discoveries Made upon Men and Matter* (1640).
2 James Boswell: *The Life of Samuel Johnson, LL.D.* (1791): 1744. Aetat.35.
3 *Ibid.*: 1750. Aetat.41.
4 *Ibid.*: 1758. Aetat.49.

instalment of *The Adventures of Sir Launcelot Greaves* appearing in *The British Magazine*.

The Lives of the English Poets, Johnson says, he wrote 'in my usual way, dilatorily and hastily, unwilling to work, and working with vigour and haste'.[1] HAZLITT, according to Patmore, never wrote until he was in actual want of money, and then he wrote very rapidly and discharged his engagements punctually.

SCOTT, who came to authorship comparatively late, was also an impromptu writer. His narrative flowed like his fireside talk, with few corrections. From childhood he had been mining a vast quarry of riches, and Leslie Stephen suggested that 'the most striking incidents' were 'modifications of anecdotes which he had rehearsed a hundred times before' to his guests at Abbotsford.[2] He wrote a volume of *Woodstock* in exactly fifteen days. SHELLEY took three days to write *The Witch of Atlas*. BYRON, like Burns, always wrote at white heat.

Hallam pointed out that TENNYSON generally took less time to compose his more imaginative poems. *Guinevere* and *Elaine* were each written in a few weeks, and hardly corrected at all. He took about a fortnight to write *Enoch Arden*.

My father said that he often did not know why some passages were thought specially beautiful, until he had examined them. He added: 'Perfection in art is perhaps more sudden sometimes than we think; but then the long preparation for it, that unseen germination, *that* is what we ignore and forget.'[3]

ARNOLD'S wife told Mrs Clough:

Matt never wrote until the last moment & when his subject had thoroughly been formed in his mind.[4]

Dame IRIS MURDOCH, in a TV interview, said she spent more time 'inventing' than 'writing', and added that it was important to establish 'the deep things right at the beginning'.[5] JOHN MORTIMER, on a similar occasion, said:

I write quickly and never rewrite, but I take a long time to think what to write.

The Entertainer took JOHN OSBORNE, who always writes quickly, eleven days – ('but the misery of what goes on before').

1 Entry for April 13, 1781: *Prayers and Meditations* (1785).
2 *Hours in a Library* (1874), i, pp. 231–3.
3 *Alfred Lord Tennyson* by his Son, i, p. 453 note.
4 Dec. 16, 1893.
5 *Bookmark*, BBC 2, Oct. 4, 1987 (made for Icelandic TV).

DICKENS, in his earlier days, 'never' copied and corrected 'but very little', 2,000 words a day being an average stint. MARRYAT, at forty-four, boasted of turning out 15,000 words in a single day. In a private letter he declared he had written sixty-five pages of *Japhet* in a single day. That same year he wrote *Mr Midshipman Easy* in three weeks. WELLS's incredible pace in his late twenties seemed to accelerate as he grew older. H. E. BATES dispensed with a shorthand typist and reverted to basics. He could produce a novel in longhand within a month or six weeks – and paid for it afterwards with nervous prostration.

According to Meredith, on their meeting in the Isle of Wight, SWINBURNE 'composed before our eyes his poem *Laus Veneris*'.[1] Uncharacteristically, STEVENSON finished the last fourteen chapters of *Treasure Island* in a fortnight.

When KIPLING's prose was going well, he wrote fast. Caroline recorded that he began *The Brushwood Boy* on August 23, 1895, and finished it, complete with verses, on September 19. He composed a poem in his head. Only when he had got it completely right mentally, did he write it down in his clear, small hand.

There is no line of my verse or prose which has not been mouthed till the tongue has made all smooth, and memory, after many recitals, has mechanically slipped the grosser superfluities.[2]

Hind commented: 'His mouth was his pen.'[3] BELLOC, when he dictated his later books, had a whole chapter in his mind. LYTTON STRACHEY told Ralph Partridge that he composed in his head entire paragraphs before committing them to paper.

Lewis Hind, as editor of *The Academy*, had dealings with FRANCIS THOMPSON who kept a commonplace book.

He bought these books at a cheap stationer's for a penny apiece; in them the whole of his poetry was written, in upright, even calligraphy, a boyish handwriting, with hardly an alteration.[4]

In the same capacity, Hind –

never altered a word in an ARNOLD BENNETT proof. And there was rarely an erasure in his copy. His orderly mind said to his obedient hand: 'Write my ... thoughts in copperplate calligraphy, always with the same number of

1 *D.N.B.*
2 *Something of Myself* (1937), pp. 72–73.
3 *Authors and I* (1921), p. 168.
4 *Ibid.*, pp. 274–5.

words upon a page, for though I suspect that I have the artistic temperament I am also a business man ... and it is those qualities that will advance me quickly in the world.[1]

Bennett wrote the last 5,000 words of *Anna of the Five Towns* in seventeen hours, from 9.45 a.m.–2.45 a.m. next morning with breaks only for meals. A story of 5,100 words, contained in *The Loot of Cities*, took him a day – from 9.40 a.m. – 12.40 a.m. allowing four hours for meals and sleep.[2]

CHESTERTON achieved his enormous output by dictating to a secretary – always very slowly – and once he had dictated, he rarely made corrections. If it was an article, she then had to take it on her bicycle to Beaconsfield Railway Station. If it was a book, his wife usually read the proofs. Before she took over the management of their finances, they had an arrangement that she was paid a halfpenny for a comma left out, a penny for any correction of spelling or style, twopence if she made a suggestion which was accepted, and sixpence if it was particularly good.[3]

When STEPHEN SPENDER told Auden, in their younger days, that he turned out four poems a day, AUDEN said that he wrote one poem in three weeks.[4] COWARD wrote *Private Lives* in four days, and claimed not one word was changed. *Blithe Spirit* was written from Sunday to Friday in the one week, four lines only being cut. RATTIGAN reckoned that, barring difficulties when work might have to be dropped even for months, a play including revision took eight weeks, but film scripts quicker than that.

ORWELL (like Dickens, but round the other way) changed his method as he grew older. When T. R. Fyvel told him that John Beavan, the London editor of *The Manchester Guardian*, had praised his typing, he said that in earlier days he had written out pieces by hand up to five times[5] but now he did many of them straight on to the typewriter. He saw it as a deterioration. George Woodcock 'used to be surprised to watch Orwell writing an almost perfect "As I Please" piece straight on

---

1 *Ibid.*, p. 53.
2 See Dudley Barker: *Writer by Trade: A View of Arnold Bennett* (1966), p. 103.
3 See Dudley Barker: *G. K. Chesterton: A Biography* (1973), pp. 192–3.
4 'Profile of Stephen Spender': ITV South Bank Show, Nov. 10, 1985.
5 Orwell told Fyvel that he had typed out the full MS of *Down and Out in Paris and London* (1933) five times.

the typewriter, with no second version', and thought 'this facility . . . lay in the extent to which his writing was tied into his existence'.

I mean . . . he liked to talk out his ideas in long monologues over cups of strong tea and hand-rolled cigarettes of black shag, and not long afterward one would see the evening's talk appearing as an article, and not long after that the third stage would be reached when it was incorporated into a book, as many of his conversations during 1946 and 1947 found their final form in *Nineteen Eighty-Four*.[1]

After Lord Clark and his wife had made friends with MAUGHAM, they were invited every March to stay at the Villa Mauresque. Every morning, Maugham 'retired to a large room at the top of the house and wrote at a table in a firm, clear hand'.

His MSS are almost entirely free from corrections. I can guarantee this as several times he showed them to me to consult me, very flatteringly, about an epithet, or even a critical judgement.[2]

RICHARD CHURCH worked away slowly with 'very little revision and alteration . . . beyond the usual sand-papering to get rid of superfluous adjectives and abstract nouns'.[3] He claimed to have avoided either extreme – Conrad's 'costiveness' of five hundred words on a good day, and Bates's 'diarrhoea' or Trollope's 'prodigious' three thousand (before his other work as a Postal Surveyor):

. . . I have found out . . . that an average output of twelve hundred words a day enables me to sail steadily along without undue strain.[4]

1 'Prose Laureate': *Commentary* (N.Y.1969), p. 75. Quoted by Bernard Crick: *George Orwell: A Life* (1980), p. 306.
2 Kenneth Clark: *The Other Half: A Self-Portrait* (1977), p. 116.
3 *Speaking Aloud* (1968), p. 190.
4 *Ibid.*, pp. 192–3.

CHAPTER NINE
Preliminary Drafters

Probably Pope and George Moore represent, in their working methods, the greatest contrast to Shakespeare and Johnson. Johnson wrote of POPE:

... to make verses was his first labour, and to mend them was his last.[1] ...
He is said to have sent nothing to the press till it had lain two years under his inspection.[2]

GEORGE MOORE told Geraint Goodwin that he would like on his tombstone:

Here lies George Moore, who looked upon corrections as the one morality.

When he was sixty-six, he developed his method of dictating about 1,500 or 2,000 words a day and then later revising the whole book. As a letter to a friend put it, this laborious way of writing made his life pass 'in loneliness and composition'.

Swift complained to Delany that in a poem 'of not two hundred lines', his friend ADDISON had made him 'blot fourscore lines, add fourscore, and alter fourscore'.

GIBBON composed the first and two last chapters of Volume I of his *History* three times – the second and third chapters twice. CARLYLE, working on *The French Revolution*, wrote:

After two weeks of blotching and blaring I have produced two clean pages.

'The events of fifteen years' took MACAULAY 'fifteen years to record'.[3]

WORDSWORTH held that 'absolute success' in the making of verse 'depends on innumerable *minutiae*. . . .' His editor, de Selincourt, went so far as to say: '. . . no poet ever revised his work for press more meticulously than he', and that 'Wordsworth retained his critical acu-

---

1 *The Lives of the English Poets* (Dublin ed. 1779–81), ii, p. 401.
2 *Ibid.*, p. 403.
3 Raymond Mortimer: *Channel Packet* (1942), p. 68.

men far longer than his creative energy.'[1] For thirty-five years he touched and revised *The Prelude*, and his justly famed lines on Roubillac's statue of Newton in Trinity College Chapel were written when he was over sixty:

> The marble index of a mind for ever
> Voyaging through strange seas of Thought, alone.[2]

Shelley wrote:

> Wordsworth informs us he was nineteen years
> Considering and retouching Peter Bell....

– and commented:

> ...Heaven and Earth conspire to foil
> The over-busy gardener's blundering toil.

TENNYSON was unable to revise his work properly until he had seen it set up in type. 'Poetry,' he said, 'looks better, more convincing in print.'[3] Hallam shows that very often the latest edition reinstated the reading in his father's first MS draft. In the first edition of *Maud* appeared the line:

I will bury myself in my books, and the Devil may pipe to his own,

later amended to:

I will bury myself in myself, &c.

The critics praised this improvement, but it was actually his original thought in the first MS.[4] One wonders if Stephen Spender had something similar in mind when he defined writing as 'a process of recovering the first idea'.

A. E. HOUSMAN composed one stanza of *A Shropshire Lad* – the last section beginning 'I hoed and trenched and weeded' – thirteen times:

...and it was more than a twelvemonth before I got it right.[5]

ROBERT GRAVES surprised Hardy when he told him that a poem he had shown him was 'in its sixth draft and will probably be finished in

1 William Wordsworth: *The Prelude, or a Growth of a Poet's Mind* ed. Ernest de Selincourt (1926), Introduction p.xlvi.
2 Bk. III: ll.62–63.
3 Quoted by Theodore Watts-Dunton: *Old Familiar Faces* (1916), p. 144.
4 *Alfred Lord Tennyson* by his Son (1897), i, p. 118.
5 *The Name and Nature of Poetry* (1933).

two more'.[1] DYLAN THOMAS took months, in hundreds of worksheets, to produce a single poem. BETJEMAN, after transferring his first notes, already revised, to foolscap, crossed out and changed again.

Then I start reciting the lines aloud, either driving a car or on solitary walks. . . .

Dickens referred to 'the little pages of manuscript' belonging to the unfinished novel *Denis Duval* that THACKERAY had carried about, often taking 'them out of his pocket here and there, for patient revision and interlineation' before 'Death stopped his hand'.[2] I remember seeing, in the V and A, the last page of the unfinished MS of *Edwin Drood*, found on DICKENS's desk when he died. Crossings out, insertions and loops were a moving witness to the toil that composition exacted – even for one of the most prolific professionals – during his latter life.

The pains STEVENSON took, and the number of times he wrote and rewrote his work, are legendary, although the speed with which he wrote his successive drafts is equally spectacular. He rewrote the fifteenth chapter of *Prince Otto* no less than seven times. There exist four drafts of the beginning of his last and greatest novel *Weir of Hermiston*. He was so pleased with the first draft of *Dr Jekyll and Mr Hyde* that he read it excitedly to his wife. She had to tell him that he had mishandled a wonderful theme, and 'after a while . . . she found him sitting up in bed (the clinical thermometer still in his mouth), pointing with a long denunciatory finger to a pile of ashes'.[3] He then wrote a more wonderful draft in three days, the same time that his first draft had taken which he burnt – over sixty thousand words altogether in six days, – but it was another month or so before he was ready to offer it to Longman's. Afterwards he said that it would not have done to try and rework it. WILLIAM MORRIS thought the same. J. W. Mackail points out that the original MS of the Prologue to *The Earthly Paradise* was written in a four-lined stanza.

Something . . . dissatisfied him, and instead of remodelling the poem he deliberately wrote the whole tale anew in couplets, so as not to be fettered by the earlier version.[4]

1 Robert Graves: *Goodbye to All That* (1929), p. 376.
2 'In Memoriam', his obituary of Thackeray: *The Cornhill Magazine*, Feb. 1864.
3 Graham Balfour: *The Life of Robert Louis Stevenson* (1901), ii, p. 13.
4 *The Life of William Morris* (1899), i, pp. 52–53.

Aldous Huxley said that D. H. LAWRENCE –

never corrected anything; because if he was dissatisfied ... he would start again at the beginning.[1]

WINIFRED HOLTBY found that even by revision she could not make her first draft of *The Crowded Street* what she wanted. Vera Brittain describes her nearly breaking her chair by lifting it and banging it violently on the floor.

Then ... she tore the book in half and crushed it into the waste-paper basket so that no remnant of the original should tempt her to imitation in the task of rewriting.[2]

She wrote her novels quite differently from her journalism. Vera Brittain tells that when her friend 'was writing a novel, no expenditure of time was too long. ...'

She liked to sit in a low armchair with her notes beside her on a table, and a block of cheap paper on her knee. After an hour or two of preliminary torment, she would cover the pages at terrific speed with the large sprawling calligraphy which always suggested that she was too hurried to form her letters. Often she wrote the same paragraph half a dozen times over, discarding sheet after sheet until the floor was covered with crumpled balls of illegible hiero-glyphics.[3]

Winifred told Lady Rhondda:

Every good piece of writing I have done that has given me in retrospect the slightest satisfaction has been done after hours and hours of labour. I must retire into myself and fight and fight to get form and thought hammered hard together.[4]

On the other hand, she seldom made more than one draft of her journalism. Leonard WOOLF said that even with a review, VIRGINIA –

would write it and rewrite it again from end to end five or six times, and she once opened a cupboard and found in it (and burnt) a whole mountain of MSS: it was *The Voyage Out* which she had rewritten (I think) five times from beginning to end.[5]

Lewis Hind saw BEERBOHM composing one of his dramatic articles for *The Saturday Review*:

1 London interview with Chandos, *cit.*: quoted by Sybille Bedford: *Aldous Huxley: A Biography* (1973–4), i, p. 210.
2 *Testament of Friendship* (1940), p. 162.
3 *Ibid.*, p. 139.
4 *Ibid.*, p. 140.
5 *Beginning Again* (1964), p. 81.

He would write, through spacious mornings, on cream laid paper, in large important calligraphy. . . .

He blacked out erasures 'with an artistic blackness' –

Because the artistic heart of Max would not allow even the printer or the printer's reader to guess at the toil that went to a perfect paragraph.[1]

At the end of his life, having developed an elliptical manner of story-telling, KIPLING recommended 'well-ground Indian Ink' and 'a camel-hair brush'. After reading your final draft and considering 'faithfully', black out 'where requisite'. When dry, 're-read and you should find that it will bear a second shortening'. An oral reading may then indicate 'a shade more brushwork'.

The shorter the tale, the longer the brushwork. . . . I have had tales by me for three or five years which shortened themselves almost yearly.

The magic of 'the Higher Editing' lay in the Brush and the Ink.[2] WELLS, uncharacteristically (like Stevenson with *Treasure Island*, but round the other way), wrote and rewrote *The Time Machine* six times in seven years.

P. G. WODEHOUSE was 'always revising'.

I'm always re-reading the stuff and spotting a place where it needs another paragraph or another scene or something.[3]

Even KEATS, in a draft of *Ode to a Nightingale*, had put as his first or earlier reading:

> Charm'd the wide casements, opening on the foam
> Of keelless seas, in fairy lands forlorn.[4]

– which seems to come as a great shock to the fledgling student, usually feminine.

CHARLES KINGSLEY was an exponent of each method. When his wife reminded him of an old promise about 'baby must have his (book)' – *The Heroes* having been written for his older children, – he did not answer. Hastily finishing breakfast, he locked himself in his study and half an hour later returned with the first chapter of *The Water-Babies*

---

1 *Authors and I* (1921), p. 41.
2 *Something of Myself* (1937), pp. 207–8.
3 Interviewed by Malcolm Muggeridge: BBC 1, May 30, 1965.
4 Cf. *Lamia and other Poems* (1820): 'Charm'd magic casements, opening on the foam Of perilous seas, in faery lands forlorn.' (Stanza VII: ll.9–10.)

'written off without a correction'.[1] Yet his intended masterpiece *The Saint's Tragedy* had taken five years: 'I do not like to be hurried or bound to time in St E.'[2]

1 7,000 words in half an hour? Elspeth Huxley queried whether 'Fanny's wifely devotion' had misled her. (*The Kingsleys* (1973), p. 118.)
2 Charles Kingsley: *His Letters and Memories of his Life* ed. by his Wife (1876), ii, p. 137.

CHAPTER TEN

State of Copy

Before the typewriter came into general use, compositors had an appalling task. Randolph Hughes, editing *Lesbia Brandon*, frequently found SWINBURNE's handwriting 'very near to . . . indecipherable'.[1] As late as the 1920–30s, WINIFRED HOLTBY, who hated typing and only occasionally had a secretary, arranged for many of her journals to accept her 'half-formed' handwriting. She placed in *The Saturday Review* an essay 'Eutopias and Paradises' – a title her friend called 'engaging',[2] but 'detatchment' and 'nusance' were more typical of her spelling. WILLIAM MORRIS's was equally precarious. A quite common word in *The Life and Death of Jason* was left uncorrected throughout because a printer's reader had assumed that it must have been intentional. DICKENS had trouble with 'stationary'. BARRIE wrote to Mrs Inge:

I am so glad you spell 'fulfil' wrongly. It has given me a lot of trouble in my time.[3]

ORWELL spelt 'aggression' with one 'g'.

When HENRY JAMES was fifty-four, he engaged a shorthand typist for his letters to relieve a chronic condition of writer's cramp, but soon he was dictating the rest of *What Masie Knew* directly to the typewriter. He became so used to the sound of his machine that if it broke down another would not do. The typewriter affected his style, making it exclusively Mandarin and identifiable as his 'later manner'.

It vexed the unpractical DE QUINCEY that he had never learnt to sharpen properly a quill-pen. DICKENS used goose-quills and blue ink, occasionally black; he wrote on blue-grey paper measuring eight and three quarter inches by seven and a quarter. KIPLING reminisced how

---

1 *Lesbia Brandon: An historical and critical commentary* (1952), Foreword, p. xx.
2 Vera Brittain: *Testament of Friendship* (1940), p. 162.
3 Dec. 20, 1925: unpublished letter: Bell, Book & Radmall Ltd. Catalogue No. 55, Sept. 1991.

in Lahore for his *Plain Tales* he used 'a slim, octagonal-sided, agate penholder with a Waverley nib'. Eventually came 'a silver penholder with a quill-like curve'. In Villiers Street 'I got me an outsize pewter ink-pot'. He then abandoned hand-dipped Waverleys, 'a nib I never changed', for 'the pin-pointed "stylo" and its successor the "fountain"'. He later used 'a slim, smooth, black treasure . . . picked up in Jerusalem'. For ink he demanded the blackest.

All 'blue-blacks' were an abomination to my Daemon.

His 'writing-blocks' were made for him 'to an unchanged pattern of large, off-white, blue sheets, of which I was most wasteful'.[1] GALS-WORTHY's nephew expressed his surprise at the simplicity of his uncle's materials –

typing paper (of a day before typing had become so universal among writers) on to which, later, his writing would be faithfully transcribed by A.G. (his wife) . . . and that 'J' pen to which he remained faithful to the end, for he was always impatient of everything which came between his thought and the written word.[2]

CARLYLE, a lover of order about the house, wrote messily and indecisively from scattered notes. With misgivings he sent copy to the printer, but that only began more revision, recast proofs and then further alterations to those. When BARRIE was fifty-nine, a small lump appeared on his right forefinger, so that he trained himself to write with his left hand. To his surprise, his notorious handwriting improved, and he then fantasized about the right-handed and left-handed author. He told Cynthia Asquith:

Anything curious or uncomfortable about *Mary Rose* and *Shall We Join the Ladies?* came from their being products of my left hand.

Later he wrote with either hand but, significantly, *Farewell, Miss Julie Logan*, towards the end of his life, was with his left.

The Countess Guiccioli told Lord Malmesbury that BYRON wrote all the last cantos of *Don Juan* on playbills –

(some of which I saw myself) or on any old piece of paper at hand, and with repeated glasses of gin-punch by his side. He then used to rush out of his room to read to her what he had written, making many alterations and laughing immoderately.[3]

1 *Something of Myself* (1937), pp. 229–30.
2 Quoted by H. V. Marrot: *The Life and Letters of John Galsworthy* (1935), pp. 403–4.
3 Lord Malmesbury: *Memoirs of an Ex-Minister* (1884).

BARRIE wrote half of *The Professor's Love Story* on the inside of old envelopes and John Hare, who rejected it, growled afterwards: 'How could I guess the fool was a genius?' BETJEMAN wrote down his lines 'on the backs of cigarette packets and old letters, crossing out and changing', but he transferred the whole to foolscap. Because of wartime paper shortage, TOLKIEN wrote much of *The Lord of the Rings* on the back of undergraduates' exam answers.

When VERA BRITTAIN wrote *Testament of Youth*, she had no idea of having the MS bound for her children. In a secondhand copy, I chanced upon her original letters to G. T. Bagguley, a binder from her home town.

I am sorry that my manuscript was in such a disorderly state; another time I must be more careful, but it is perhaps interesting to have an original manuscript which was written quite unselfconsciously, and with no idea of binding or keeping in any special way.[1]

Whatever the state of ORWELL's health, his journalistic copy arrived on time, impeccably typed and to size.

1 I possess four signed, typewritten letters spanning April 19–May 24, 1934, all headed 19 Glebe Place, Chelsea. The above quotation is from the last in the sequence. At first she was 'prepared to pay up to £10' for this 'something of an heirloom for my children', but 'as the book has gone into a 7th edition, which means more royalties', she found 'that I can allow you to go up to £20. . . .' The MS apparently made two volumes foolscap ('I take it you do not intend to cut the pages'), bound in full blue levant morocco with 'a small amount of gilt tooling' and 'a cloth case to hold them'. She particularly wanted 'an inscription inside saying that it was bound by yourself in the town where I was born (Newcastle), or words to that effect'. During the course of the transaction, Mr Bagguley sent her 'two little books on Staffordshire, which will be most valuable for my novel', also the new edition of the local guide – 'All this material is extremely valuable to me.' My copy of *Honourable Estate* is inscribed: To Mr G. T. Bagguley, with best wishes and thanks, from Vera Brittain, November 2nd, 1936.

CHAPTER ELEVEN

Hazards Affecting MSS

I

There are curious cases of the author being careless with MSS. BELLOC's book on Milton, held by some to be one of his best, took ten days of dictating, after which he left it to his secretary to prepare it for publication. In his fame, BARRIE sent Hodder and Stoughton the MS of *Peter Pan* in an untidy brown-paper parcel, without a covering letter to say it was for publication.

Professor Tillotson relished the story of TENNYSON's leaving his 'book of Elegies' – the early MS of *In Memoriam* – in a cupboard when he moved from lodgings in Mornington Place, and asking his friend, Coventry Patmore, to collect it. Tennyson's letter ran:

... you know what I mean, a long, butcher-ledger-like book.[1]

T. E. LAWRENCE lost most of his original draft of *The Seven Pillars of Wisdom* – he reckoned eight of ten books – when changing trains at Reading. It has never come to light.

The most remarkable accidental loss must be when CARLYLE lent the MS of the first volume of *The French Revolution* to his younger friend, John Stuart Mill, who without Carlyle's permission lent it to Mrs Taylor, his future wife. The MS was used by her maid during successive weeks to light the fire. The news was broken by a distraught Mill on March 6, 1835. The first words Carlyle said to his wife when Mill had gone, were: 'Well, Mill, poor fellow, is terribly cut up; we must endeavour to hide from him how very serious this business is to us.'[2] It is a provoking story, for Mill from his cradle had been brought up amongst books and MSS. Carlyle was depending on this work for solvency, having recently moved into Cheyne Row. He had kept no

1 Feb. 28, 1850.
2 Told to Froude by Mrs Carlyle. J. A. Froude: *Thomas Carlyle: A History of his Life in London*, 2nd ed. (1885), i, p. 28.

notes nor marked his passages. The more affluent Mill was immensely relieved when Carlyle accepted his offer to 'repair' the loss of time and labour, but a £200 cheque was immediately returned with firm instructions to be halved. Within six months he 'finished that unutterable burnt MS'.[1] When Tennyson asked him how he had felt at the time, he answered, 'Well, I just felt like a man swimming without water.'[2] Another analogy, repeated in his letters, was 'it is as if my invisible schoolmaster had torn my copybook when I showed it, and said, "No, boy! Thou must write it better." '[3]

TENNYSON lost the earliest MS of *Poems, chiefly Lyrical* 'out of his great-coat pocket one night while returning from a neighbouring market town'. His brother Frederick commented:

This was enough to reduce an ordinary man to despair, but the invisible ink was made to reappear, all the thoughts and fancies in their orderly series and with their entire drapery of words arose and lived again ...

Hallam explains:

My father's poems were generally based on some single phrase like 'Someone had blundered': and were rolled about, so to speak, in his head, before he wrote them down: and hence they did not easily slip from his memory.[4]

WATTS-DUNTON would have had *The Coming of Love* published by Morris at the Kelmscott Press, if certain portions of the MS had not been lent and lost. By the time the complete poem was eventually assembled, Morris had become fatally ill.

I should have been the most favoured man who ever brought out a volume of poems.[5]

BARRIE's rarest printed work, *The Boy Castaways*, mentioned in the Dedication to *Peter Pan*, was limited to two copies, one for Arthur Llewelyn Davies and the other for himself. Such rarity might justify its inclusion as a MS. It told the Terrible Adventures of Three Brothers (the Llewelyn Davies boys: George, eight, Jack, nearly seven, and Peter 'a good bit past four') in the summer of 1901 on Black Lake Island, near the Barries' country home, and Barrie had got it bound up 'handsomely' by Constable, with thirty-five photographs. The boys' father

1 Journal: Sept. 21, 1835.
2 *Alfred Lord Tennyson* by his Son (1897), i, p. 267.
3 Journal: March 7, 1835.
4 *Alfred Lord Tennyson* by his Son, i, pp. 267–8.
5 *The Coming of Love and Other Poems* (1898), Prefatory Note, p. ix.

instantly lost his in a railway carriage. The mature Peter remarked: '... doubtless his own way of commenting on the whole fantastic affair.'[1] In the nursing home, however, separated from his boys and tragically afflicted, he asked for the surviving copy.

Between one and two o'clock on Thursday night, January 28, 1819, in 'the house at Town End',[2] accidental fire destroyed five or six opium dreams or visions that DE QUINCEY had intended to include, with others, in the enlarged edition of his *Confessions*.

The spark of a candle (fell) unobserved amongst a very large pile of papers in a bedroom, when I was alone and reading. ... My attention was first drawn by a sudden light upon my book ... a large Spanish cloak ... thrown over, and then drawn down tightly, by the aid of one sole person, somewhat agitated, but retaining her presence of mind, effectually extinguished the fire.[3]

As editor of *The Westmorland Gazette*, he had been scouring curiosities from other journals, spread on the floor, to fill his own columns for Friday, press day. The paper reported:

Mr De Quincey was sitting up writing; in a single moment a volume of smoke passed between him and his paper ... in half a minute a great fork of flames, extending to a place about four feet distant, sprung out from a crevice on one side of the grate. The rest of the family, who were then asleep, were called up ... in half an hour (water being at hand) the fire was extinguished ... the room being strewed on that evening with newspapers, and the timbers of the house all old, there was little doubt that in ten minutes the fire would have been inextinguishable in a place so remote from fire engines. ...[4]

His rival, *The Westmorland Advertiser and Kendal Chronicle*, congratulated him on rescuing his family. On June 23, 1902, CONRAD's lamp exploded setting his round table ablaze, on which was the whole of the second part of *End of the Tether* ready to go to Blackwood.

The widespread brush fire which burnt down ALDOUS HUXLEY's home in the Hollywood Hills, two and a half years before he died, destroyed his library and all his papers, including the MSS of two unfinished novels, one probably on Catherine of Siena. Fortunately *Island* on which he was working was able to be retrieved.

1 Andrew Birkin: *J. M. Barrie and the Lost Boys* (1979), p. 88.
2 As described by De Quincey in a letter in my possession (Nov. 26, 1825) to his landlady, Mrs Benson of Ambleside. A 17th cent. inn, The Dove and Olive Branch, it became Dove Cottage only after the famous tenancies.
3 *Confessions of an English Opium-Eater*, revised by the Author (1856), Prefatory Notice, p. xiv.
4 *The Westmorland Gazette*, Jan. 30, 1819.

An unexpectedly high number of authors have deliberately destroyed their finished work. LAMB burnt some of his poems after the 'terrible calamities' when his sister on becoming insane had killed their mother. A few days afterwards, he wrote to Coleridge:

... with me the former things are passed away, and I have something more to do than to feel – God almighty have us all in his keeping ... mention nothing of poetry. I have destroyed every vestige of past vanities of that kind.[1]

It was his only irrational act during that time. By the next month he was writing poetry again. GERARD MANLEY HOPKINS burnt all his poems when, at twenty-two, he was received into the Church of Rome and entered the Society of Jesus. He called it 'the slaughter of the Innocents', and for eight years he renounced the poetic for the priestly vocation. Of the destruction by MORRIS of his early poems which he did not choose to be included in *The Defence of Guenevere*, Canon Dixon said:

It was a dreadful mistake.... But he had no notion whatever of correcting a poem and very little power to do so.[2]

SWINBURNE, at twenty-two, tore up *Rosamund* and burnt it. Jowett, his Oxford tutor, had sent him to study quietly under the Rev. William Stubbs near Romford, and Swinburne read the poem to him and his wife. Stubbs criticized his treatment of love and expected that he would modify certain passages, but Swinburne looked at him for a long time without speaking, then screamed and rushed upstairs, refusing to come down for supper. He told them in the morning that, having destroyed the whole of the MS, he had repented and spent the whole of the night writing it out again from memory.[3] CRABBE, after his poem *The Newspaper*, did not publish for twenty-two years and most of what he wrote during that time he burned.

While the composition of *Tristram Shandy* was still going forward, STERNE's friend Croft assembled a select audience at Stillington Hall to hear the author read from his work. Perhaps they had dined too well, for it is said that Sterne, perceiving them to have fallen asleep,

1 Sept. 27, 1796.
2 J. W. Mackail: *The Life of William Morris* (1899), i, p. 52.
3 See Edmund Gosse: *The Life of Algernon Charles Swinburne* (1917), pp. 62–63.

flung his MS angrily into the fire. His host retrieved the scorched pages. On one occasion DESMOND MACCARTHY disbanded a collection of his own writings because it 'fell so far below the standard' of Leslie Stephen in *Hours in a Library.*

In the last year of his life, JOHNSON burnt large masses of his papers including 'two quarto volumes, containing a full, fair, and most particular account of his own life, from his earliest recollection'. Boswell confessed that having accidentally seen them he had read a great deal in them, and apologised to Johnson for the liberty he had taken.

He placidly answered. 'Why, Sir, I do not think you could have helped it.' I said . . . that it had come into my mind to carry off those two volumes, and never see him more. Upon my enquiring how this would have affected him, 'Sir, (said he,) I believe I should have gone mad.'[1]

BYRON'S prose *Memoirs*, which he had written alongside *Don Juan*, ended up one month after his death in Murray's grate at 50 Albemarle Street. They had been originally consigned to Thomas Moore – 'My life and adventures . . . is not a thing that can be published during my lifetime' – and he urged they should be sealed if need be, but largely on Augusta's instigation they were burnt and Hobhouse, jealous for his friend's fame, approved.

W. H. DAVIES had second thoughts about his MS of *Young Emma* – the story of his young wife he had picked up as she got off a bus – and asked Jonathan Cape to return it and to destroy the two typewritten copies.

As she is only 24 years of age and has every prospect of outliving us all I have come to the conclusion that the MS must be destroyed. . . .[2]

Cape, who had reservations also about such a book harming the poet's reputation, returned the MS and told him the two copies would be destroyed the following week – 'in case you might on reflection feel that to destroy everything is a little too drastic'. Davies replied slightly less categorically:

. . . you can destroy the two type-written copies as soon as you like.[3]

They were in fact kept in a safe for fifty-five years, and the book was published posthumously, in 1980, a year after its heroine had died.

1 James Boswell: *The Life of Samuel Johnson, LL.D.* (1791): 1784: Aetat.75.
2 W. H. Davies: *Young Emma,* with a foreword by C. V. Wedgwood (1980), p. 10.
3 *Ibid.*, p. 11.

William Plomer, who had been shown the MS in 1972, reported to Cape that 'if authors of repute wish their unpublished writings to be destroyed, they should destroy them themselves'.[1]

1 *Ibid.*, p. 13.

CHAPTER TWELVE

The Pleasures of Authorship

Of all his long list of pleasures, LEONARD WOOLF at eighty-eight found writing to be one of the 'most reliable and to have remained unaffected by the vampirism of senility'.

It is, oddly enough, a physical as well as a mental satisfaction. I like to feel the process of composition in my brain . . . one of the most unfailing pleasures is to sit down in the morning and write.[1]

THACKERAY mentioned this physical aspect of composition when he wrote to Mary Holmes at the time of finishing *Esmond*:

. . . all my thoughts pretty near are given to my business for wh. time presses & wh. must be done – And when I get to a *hitch* in the narrative, my body gets out of order and I grow nervous & unwell. Hence departure from London. Here (at Brighton) I do very well, and worked all day till 7 o'clock yesterday never stopping to read even a newspaper – I hope to go to Church (the letter is dated Good Friday), and do another good day to-day.[2]

KIPLING used the word 'physical':

Mercifully, the mere act of writing was, and always has been, a physical pleasure to me.[3]

Also, C. DAY LEWIS wrote:

. . . indeed it is only while I am engaged upon a poem that I have a *positive* sense of physical well-being, however exhausting or futile the struggle with words.[4]

ANITA BROOKNER, interviewed in 1985, feels well, even puts on weight when she is writing, and falls ill when her novel is finished.[5] A. E. HOUSMAN, although in his Leslie Stephen lecture saying the opposite

1 *The Journey Not the Arrival Matters* (1969), pp. 183–4.
2 April 9, 1852. *The Letters & Private Papers of W. M. Thackeray* ed. G. N. Ray (1945–6), iii, p. 28.
3 *Something of Myself* (1937), p. 206.
4 *The Buried Day* (1960), p. 24.
5 *Book Four* presented by Hermione Lee: Channel 4, Sept. 8, 1985.

– 'I have seldom written poetry unless I was rather out of health' –
allowed the experience to be 'pleasurable', at the same time 'generally
agitating and exhausting'.[1]

STEVENSON said that writers were so lucky because they were paid
for their pleasures while other men had to pay for theirs – 'What shall
(the writer) have enjoyed more fully than a morning of successful
work?'[2] Two years before his marriage, he wrote from Paris:

What a blessing work is! I don't think I could face life without it; and how
glad I am I took to literature! It helps me so much.[3]

J. B. PRIESTLEY, who said shortly before he died that he was 'more a
writer than a human-being really', enjoyed his long, prolific and varied
writing life and 'always turned to it with eagerness'. In his final chapter
of autobiography, he wrote:

I have been able to write just what I wanted to write and have been handsomely
rewarded for it.[4]

ALDOUS HUXLEY, as a schoolmaster at Eton, wrote:

I never really feel I am performing a wholly *moral* action, except when I am
writing.[5]

Dame IRIS MURDOCH, in a rare TV interview, declared that writing
fiction was 'more fun' than writing philosophy.[6]

For LEWIS HIND until he was fifty, writing 'was a task':

Talking, as a means of self-expression, was easier and pleasanter . . . the kind
of writing I enjoyed doing were the little *Things Seen* . . . which I turned out
with ease, and which, I suspect, was a fairly complete expression of what talent
I possessed.

But after he had passed the 'awkward age of fifty', he made the discovery that he was beginning to enjoy writing.

It became less of a task. I had discovered the proper pen, the proper kind of
paper, and the proper way of sitting at a table, sideways, with the right arm

1 *The Name and Nature of Poetry* (1933).
2 'Letter to a Young Gentleman who Proposed to Embrace the Career of Art': *Across the
Plains* (1892), p. 278.
3 Quoted by Graham Balfour: *The Life of Robert Louis Stevenson* (1901), i, p. 155.
4 *Instead of the Trees: A Final Chapter of Autobiography* (1977), p. 151.
5 Quoted by Sybille Bedford: *Aldous Huxley: A Biography* (1973–4), i, p. 96.
6 *Bookmark*, BBC 2, cit.

resting on a big, blue blotting-pad (blue is the proper colour), and the light falling over the left shoulder, so that one can look out of the window. . . .[1]

He was now too, writing at greater length.

They are illustrative of the *pleasures* of authorship.

1 *From My Books* (1925), Introduction, p. 10.

CHAPTER THIRTEEN
The Pains of Authorship

O other writers, because of their disposition or the circumstances affecting a particular book, cause one to reflect upon the *pains*. Starting his life's work and making uncertain starts, GIBBON was often tempted to throw away the labours of seven years. A photograph of CARLYLE, taken by Robert Tait, shows him seated at his desk and miserably holding his head: the paraphernalia of *Frederick*, the books, papers and references littered about him. GEORGE MOORE died regretting he had been unable to accomplish his last book:[1]

... telling the story of how writing was forced upon me and the persecution I have undergone for forty years and which is just ended, leaving me a wreck.

MAUGHAM, when he was ninety-one, said to his nephew:

I wish I'd never written a single word. It's brought me nothing but misery.... My whole life has been a failure....[2]

When Kingsley had questioned his regard for truth, NEWMAN wrote *Apologia Pro Vita Sua* 'in seven weeks, sometimes working twenty-two hours at a stretch, "constantly in tears, and constantly crying out with distress"'.[3] GEORGE ELIOT said: 'I began *Romola* a young woman; I finished it an old woman.' She was forty-three. CONRAD, at forty-six, said of what many regard as his masterpiece:

Nostromo is finished; a fact upon which my friends may congratulate me as upon a recovery from a dangerous illness.

Two years later, he gave up working regularly 'from sheer impossibility':

The damned stuff comes out only by a sort of mental revulsion, which lasts

---

1 *A Communication to My Friends* (1933).
2 Robin Maugham: *Conversations with Willie* (1978), pp. 16–17.
3 Lytton Strachey: *Eminent Victorians* (1918), p. 85.

for two, three, and more days up to a fortnight, which leaves me limp and not very happy.[1]

At fifty-two, he wrote to Galsworthy:

I sit twelve hours at the table, sleep six, and worry the rest of the time, feeling age creeping on and looking at those I love. For two years I haven't seen a picture, heard a note of music, had a moment of ease in human intercourse – not really.[2]

'Believe me,' said Conrad again, 'no man paid more for his lines than I have,' which was probably true. VIRGINIA WOOLF wrote in her *Diary*: 'I wonder whether anyone has ever suffered so much from a book as I have suffered from *The Years*.'[3]

KENNETH GRAHAME told his friend Constance Smedley he hated writing – it was sheer physical torture. MASEFIELD was only thirty-two when he told Elizabeth Robins:

When I go out at the end of a day's work, I have been dying on the cross for eight hours, that the world may have a fairer soul, or something beautiful, at least, which otherwise it would not have. And I am dead for the day. My life . . . is burned out.[4]

After ELIOT's death, his wife Valerie said: 'He felt he had paid too high a price to be a poet, that he had suffered too much.'[5] WINIFRED HOLTBY told Sarah Millin:

. . . I know that some of the most gay and vital stuff that I have written I wrote in such pain that I used to cry over the paper.[6]

John Mortimer expressed that DYLAN THOMAS's life and letters read like 'a cry of despair. . . .'

About the time that ORWELL began in earnest *Nineteen Eighty-Four*, he used the same word as Conrad's:

Writing a book is a horrible, exhausting struggle, like a long bout of some painful illness.[7]

RICHARD ADAMS has conceded: 'Nothing can make the task of writing

1 1905.
2 Dec. 22, 1909.
3 *A Writer's Diary*.
4 Feb. 1910. Quoted by Constance Babington Smith: *John Masefield: A Life* (1978), p. 101.
5 Interview in *The Observer*: Feb. 20, 1972.
6 Quoted by Vera Brittain: *Testament of Friendship* (1940), p. 345.
7 'Why I Write': *Gangrel* (No. 4, Summer), 1946.

entirely pleasurable.'[1] CHRISTOPHER FRY, interviewed at seventy-nine, said that for forty years he had been hoping to find a plot for a one-act play to make a double bill with *A Phoenix Too Frequent*, but if one came along he did not intend to rush – 'I wish I liked writing better.'[2]

CHATTERTON wrote to Horace Walpole:

Though I am but sixteen years old, I have lived long enough to see that poverty attends literature.

COLERIDGE compared the husbandman putting his seed in the ground and in return for industry 'he shall have bread, and health, and quietness. . . .'

The AUTHOR scatters his seed – with aching head, and wasted health, and all the heart-leapings of anxiety; and the follies, the vices, and the fickleness of man promise him printers' bills and the Debtors' Side of Newgate as full and sufficient payment.[3]

1 *Watership Down* (limited ed. by Paradine, 1976), Foreword.
2 *The Observer* supplement: Nov. 2, 1986.
3 To Poole: Dec. 1796. *Letters of Samuel Taylor Coleridge* ed. Ernest Hartley Coleridge (1895), i, pp. 191–2.

CHAPTER FOURTEEN

Collaboration with Family and Friends

I

There are memorable examples of family collaboration. MARY LAMB was commissioned to retell for children the plays of Shakespeare, but eventually her brother CHARLES took the greater tragedies. *Tales from Shakespear* appeared the same year as *Mrs Leicester's School*, which contained ten tales for young people: seven by Mary and three by Charles.

Poems by Two Brothers was really by Alfred, Charles, and Frederick TENNYSON. The preface states that the ages of the poets were between fifteen and eighteen, but Tennyson in old age made a small correction: 'I was between 15 and 17....'

When they were still unknown, the BRONTË sisters had 'a small selection' of their poems printed privately at a cost of £35.18s.3d. plus £2 for advertising at first, and then a further £10. Charlotte records:

... in the autumn of 1845 (she twenty-nine) I accidentally lighted on a MS volume of verse in my sister Emily's handwriting.... Of course I was not surprised, knowing that she could and did write verse.... To my ear they had ... a peculiar music, wild, melancholy, and elevating ... it took hours to reconcile her to the discovery I had made, and days to persuade her that such poems merited publication.... Meanwhile my younger sister quietly produced some of her own compositions, intimating that since Emily's had given me pleasure I might like to look at hers....[1]

Poems by Currer, Ellis, and Acton Bell, appeared at the end of May 1846. Notices followed in *The Critic*, *The Athenaeum* (singling out Ellis), and *The Dublin University Magazine*, an extract from *The Critic* being then appended to the other advertisements:

---

1 Biographical Notice prefixed to second edition of *Wuthering Heights and Agnes Grey* (1850), ed. by Charlotte Brontë. Quoted by E. C. Gaskell: *The Life of Charlotte Brontë* (1857), i, pp. 334–5.

They in whose hearts are chords strung by Nature to sympathise with the beautiful and the true, will recognise in these compositions the presence of more genius than it was supposed this utilitarian age had devoted to the loftier exercises of the intellect.[1]

A Mr F. Enoch requested their autographs. But after a year only two copies had been sold. The sisters then distributed 'as presents a few copies of what we cannot sell' to Wordsworth, Tennyson, Lockhart, and De Quincey, 'in acknowledgement of the pleasure and profit we have often and long derived from your work'. (One wonders why Charlotte did not include Thackeray.) Within a few months their novels were published, and in 1848 the sheets were taken over by Smith, Elder & Co., publishers of *Jane Eyre*.

There are successful examples of husband-and-wife authorship. ANDREW LANG's wife translated or told some of the tales in the later *Fairy Books*. STEVENSON's wife collaborated with him in *The Dynamiters*. J. L. and BARBARA HAMMOND wrote their trilogy on the Industrial Revolution.[2] Among subjects taken by the co-biographers LAWRENCE and ELISABETH HANSON are the Brontës, Jane Carlyle, George Eliot, General Gordon, Gauguin, Van Gogh.

Reference has already been made to MARJORIE and C. H. B. QUENNELL preparing their 1,049 drawings and 'reconstructions' in pen and colour for *A History of Everyday Things in England* and similar books.[3] Their eldest son Peter, who made a contribution while still at school, tells how having inked in the architectural background upon a sheet of Bristol-board, his father would leave a series of spaces in the foreground to hold his mother's figures, for he had never learned to draw the human body. Once she had completed her task, he –

brought up the background to join the outline of the figures, and added the artists' joint initials, M. & C.H.B.Q. cunningly laced together in a decorative monogram. He designed it, as a symbol of their happy partnership, with particularly loving care.[4]

PRIESTLEY collaborated with JACQUETTA HAWKES, his third wife, in *Dragon's Mouth* and *Journey Down a Rainbow*.

1 Quoted in Charlotte Brontë's letter to Aylott & Jones (publishers of their *Poems*), July 10, 1846. See *The Shakespeare Head Brontë: Their Lives, Friendships & Correspondence* (1932), ii, p. 102.
2 *The Village Labourer* (1911), *The Town Labourer* (1917), *The Skilled Labourer* (1919).
3 See page 223.
4 Peter Quennell: *The Marble Foot* (1976), p. 85.

Shortly after the death of his second wife Jane, WELLS wrote:

After the war (1914–18) we produced a book, *The Outline of History*. . . . We were not particularly equipped for the task and it meant huge toil for both of us. We would work at Easton long after midnight, making notes from piles of books or writing up and typing notes.[1]

She does not appear on the title page of the published work, but is acknowledged in the final paragraph of the Introduction: '. . . without her constant help and watchful criticism, its completion would have been impossible.'[2]

TENNYSON's wife became his literary adviser. He said he was 'proud of her intellect', and always discussed with her his work on hand. Their son declared: '. . . to her and to no one else he referred for a final criticism before publishing.'[3] Robert Graves, who rented a cottage from MASEFIELD at the bottom of his garden on Boar's Hill, said that Masefield 'used to read his day's work over to Mrs Masefield, and they corrected it together'.[4]

BYRON's last mistress interrupted *Don Juan* at the fifth Canto. Byron told Hobhouse:

I have agreed to a request of Madame Guiccioli not to continue the poem further. She had read the French translation, and thinks it a detestable production.[5]

The following year, he 'obtained a permission from my Dictatress to continue it,'

– provided always it was to be more guarded, and decorous, and sentimental in the continuation than in the commencement . . . but the embargo was only taken off upon these stipulations.[6]

MARIA EDGEWORTH collaborated with her father RICHARD in *Practical Education* (1798). Sir FREDERICK WEDMORE, with his daughter MILLICENT, edited *The Poems of the Love and Pride of England*.

STEVENSON collaborated with his stepson LLOYD OSBOURNE in *The Wrong Box*, *The Wrecker*, and *The Ebb-Tide*. Lloyd wrote:

---

1 Unpublished introduction by H. G. Wells to *The Book of Catherine Wells* (1928).
2 H. G. Wells: *The Outline of History: Being a Plain History of Life and Mankind* (1919–20), i, p. 3.
3 *Alfred Lord Tennyson* by his Son (1897), i, p. 331.
4 *Goodbye to All That* (1929), pp. 364–5.
5 Early July, 1821.
6 *Letters and Journals of Lord Byron* ed. R. E. Prothero (Lord Ernle) (1898–1901), vi, p. 95.

He liked the comradeship – my work coming in just as his energy flagged, or *vice versa*; and he liked my applause when he – as he always did – pulled us magnificently out of sloughs. In a way, I was well fitted to help him. I had a knack for dialogue – I mean, of the note-taking kind. I was a kodaker: he an artist and a man of genius. I managed the petty makeshifts and inventions which were constantly necessary; I was the practical man, so to speak, the one who paced the distances, and used the weights and measures. . . .[1]

But Stevenson's friends Henley and Colvin, also his own wife, regarded it as a serious mistake.

WELLS was assisted by his son Gip (as well as Julian Huxley) in *The Science of Life*, and by his younger son Frank in work on films. In the greyer area of oral editorship, for more than twenty years RATTIGAN'S mother was the first to hear almost every one of his plays.

II

Among examples of collaboration between friends are the plays of BEAUMONT and FLETCHER. According to Aubrey, during the seven years that the two collaborated they shared a bed, a wench, and their clothes.

STEELE and ADDISON'S *The Tatler*, thirty-six papers in all, paved the way for *The Spectator*. It seems remarkable that Sir Roger de Coverley is a composite creation. John Drinkwater described how

Steele first struck out the portrait in an admirable pastiche; Addison went on and elaborated the knight's adventures and London humours.[2]

In his early thirties, with his friend Deyverdun's help, GIBBON composed in French an introduction to the history of Switzerland. They then co-operated in publishing two volumes of *Memoires litteraires de la Grande Bretagne*, which were dedicated to Lord Chesterfield.

COLERIDGE'S first collection *Poems on Various Subjects* included four sonnets by LAMB, and Frederick Wedmore draws attention[3] to the generous way in which these men spoke of each other. Coleridge wrote in his introduction:

The effusions signed C.L. were written by Mr Charles Lamb, of the India

---

1 Quoted by Graham Balfour: *The Life of Robert Louis Stevenson* (1901), ii, pp. 33–34.
2 *The Outline of Literature* ed. John Drinkwater (1923–4), i, pp. 273–4.
3 See *On Books and Arts* (1899), p. 33.

House; independently of the signature, their superior merit would have sufficiently distinguished them.

Two years later, the anonymous publication of *Lyrical Ballads* (1798) opened with the seventy pages of Coleridge's *The Rime of the Ancient Mariner* and ended with WORDSWORTH's *Lines composed a few miles above Tintern Abbey*. In this major book of 210 pages, three other poems were by Coleridge and nineteen by Wordsworth. There were four pages of 'Advertisement' or preface by 'the author':

> It is the honourable characteristic of Poetry that its materials are to be found in every subject which can interest the human mind. . . . Readers of superior judgment may disapprove of the style . . . it is apprehended that the more conversant the reader is with our elder writers . . . the fewer complaints of this kind will he have to make.

Five hundred copies were printed, but their sale was so 'slow' and 'heavy' that Cottle parted, at a loss, with about three hundred to J. and A. Arch, a London bookseller. Wordsworth then recovered the copyright and offered it, through Coleridge, to Longman, who bought it for £80.

Twenty years afterwards, Coleridge wrote of their original plan:

> . . . it was agreed, that my endeavours should be directed to persons and characters supernatural, or at least romantic. . . . Mr Wordsworth, on the other hand, was to propose to himself as his object, to give the charm of novelty to things of every day. . . .[1]

He continued:

> With this view I wrote the 'Ancient Mariner,' and was preparing among other poems, the 'Dark Ladie,' and the 'Christobel,' (*sic*) in which I should have more nearly realized my ideal. . . . But Mr Wordsworth's industry had proved so much more successful, and the number of his poems so much greater, that my compositions, instead of forming a balance, appeared rather an interpolation of heterogeneous matter. Mr Wordsworth added two or three poems written in his own character, in the impassioned, lofty, and sustained diction, which is characteristic of his genius.[2]

The second and enlarged edition published in January 1801,[3] with the Preface containing 'our joint opinions on Poetry',[4] bore, on Cole-

---

1 *Biographia Literaria; or Biographical Sketches of My Literary Life and Opinions* (1817), ii, p. 2.
2 *Ibid.*, ii, p. 3.
3 Known as the 1800 edition.
4 Coleridge to Stuart: Sept. 30, 1800.

ridge's insistence, Wordsworth's name alone, although now five of the poems were by Coleridge. Coleridge also went along with *The Ancient Mariner* being moved from front position to back of the first volume. But a long footnote, by Wordsworth, – 'The Poem of my Friend has indeed great defects. . . .' – was not seen by Coleridge until it appeared in print.

While his friends Poole and the Wedgwoods had advised him not to abandon his success as a political journalist in London, Wordsworth had encouraged him to settle among the Lakes to edit this edition, and to finish 'the long and beautiful poem of CHRISTABEL'[1] for inclusion in it. On Saturday, October 4, 1800, Coleridge, 'very wet', came in while the Wordsworths were at dinner. Dorothy writes: 'Exceedingly delighted with the second part of "Christabel".' On Sunday:

Coleridge read a second time 'Christabel' – we had increasing pleasure.

On Monday, October 6:

A rainy day. Coleridge intending to go but did not get off. We walked after dinner to Rydale. After tea read 'The Pedlar'. Determined not to print 'Christabel' with the *Lyrical Ballads*.

Tuesday, 'Coleridge went off at eleven o'clock.'

His admiration for Wordsworth and his poetry was so great that he was prepared to trifle with his poetical reputation. His wife, Southey, Poole, Lamb, and the Wedgwoods, all in their several ways saw this. At Greta Hall, on Thursday night, October 9, he wrote to his friend Humphry Davy:[2]

The 'Christabel' was running up to 1,300 lines,[3] and was so much admired by Wordsworth that he thought it indelicate to print two volumes with his name, in which so much of another man's was included; and, which was of more consequence, the poem was in direct opposition to the very purpose for which the lyrical ballads were published. . . . I assure you I think very differently of 'Christabel.' I would rather have written 'Ruth,' and 'Nature's Lady,' than a million such poems.[4]

But Richard Holmes[5] sees in a Notebook entry the devastation that

---

1 Wordsworth's draft of the Preface, which he sent to Cottle as late as Sept. 20, 1800.
2 Cr. baronet, 1818; inventor of the miners' safety lamp.
3 Printed lines, including conclusion to Pt. II, number 677. If there was a discarded portion, it has never come to light.
4 *Letters of Samuel Taylor Coleridge* ed. Ernest Hartley Coleridge (1895), i, p. 337.
5 *Coleridge: Early Visions* (1989), p. 283.

Wordsworth's rejection of *Christabel* meant. In the magnificent situation of his study, with unparalleled views of landscape scenery, –

He knew not what to do – something he felt, must be done – he rose, drew his writing-desk suddenly before him – sate down, took the pen – & found that he knew not what to do.[1]

The space that *Christabel* would have occupied was filled with Wordsworth's *Michael*, and a few weeks after publication, in a letter to Poole, Coleridge referred to his friend's poem as 'divine'.[2]

III

DICKENS collaborated with WILKIE COLLINS in various stories which appeared in *Household Words* and *All the Year Round*. His amateur theatrical, *The Frozen Deep*, was written by Collins with a large input of suggestions and revisions by himself. A practice more prevalent than now, WALTER BESANT collaborated on many successful novels with JAMES RICE, and ISRAEL ZANGWILL worked with LOUIS COWEN on *The Premier and the Painter*.

When CONRAD was forty and staying with the Garnetts at Limpsfield, he met FORD HERMANN HUEFFER, a fledgling writer of twenty-four, living nearby. Jocelyn Baines calls their meeting 'the most important event in Conrad's literary life'.[3] The older man, with three published novels to his credit and a book of *Tales* shortly to come out, was depressed with one of his many writing blocks and even considering going again to sea. He proposed they should collaborate and this was facilitated by the Conrads at this time renting a farm from him near Aldington, and the Hueffers moving to a cottage in that town. *The Inheritors* was completed and accepted in a little over a year, followed by *Romance* two years after – worked from an early draft of Hueffer's called 'Seraphina'.

The happy collaboration of *Prunella* came about when GRANVILLE-BARKER asked LAURENCE HOUSMAN to write 'a grown-up fairy-tale play' for the Barker-Vedrenne Management about to start at the Court Theatre:

1 Oct. 30, 1800.
2 March 16, 1801: *Letters of Samuel Taylor Coleridge* (1895), i, p. 350.
3 *Joseph Conrad: A Critical Biography* (1960).

God gave me the grace to say that I could not do it alone; but only if he would do it with me.[1]

DOROTHY L. SAYERS shared the authorship of *The Documents in the Case* with ROBERT EUSTACE (Dr Eustace Barton), who suggested the plot and the form of the end. Team Work, 'that despised and – theatrically speaking – rather *démodé* thing', was used by Val Gielgud, the radio producer, to describe the success of *The Man Born to be King*:

And when Miss Sayers is kind enough to say that I never refused a fence, I think it is only fair to add that in her turn she never, or hardly ever, refused to alter the course![2]

PRIESTLEY'S first work for the theatre was a collaboration with EDWARD KNOBLOCK in making *The Good Companions* a play, with Richard Addinsell's music. Virtually his last was to collaborate with IRIS MURDOCH in dramatising her novel *A Severed Head*. R. C. SHERRIFF worked with VERNON BARTLETT on a version of *Journey's End* as a novel.

Sometimes results have been less successful. Richard D'Oyly Carte, at the time of the rift between Gilbert and Sullivan, called in BARRIE but even he had doubts about writing a comic opera, and when he came to the second act called on CONAN DOYLE to assist. On the first night of *Jane Annie, or The Good Conduct Prize* at the Savoy, they sat in a box but knew there would be no curtain call. The CONRAD-HUEFFER partnership petered out after ten and a half years, in the fragment *The Nature of a Crime*, just before their final quarrel. KIPLING, at twenty-seven, produced a romance *The Naulahka*, with his close friend WOLCOTT BALESTIER. BENNETT, in his late thirties, when EDEN PHILLPOTTS was considerably richer and more successful than himself, collaborated with him in two full-length plays, neither of which was produced or published. They also worked together on the equally lack-lustre thriller serials *The Sinews of War* and *The Statue* – Phillpotts always managing to evade most of the writing.

QUILLER-COUCH took up the intentions of an author who was dead. Sir Sidney Colvin, Stevenson's literary executor, wanted *St Ives* continued from Chapter Thirty-One and first approached Barrie who, chastened by *Jane Annie*, decided upon 'Q'. Barrie offered to tell him

1 Laurence Housman: *The Unexpected Years* (1937), p. 131.
2 Production Note by Val Gielgud: *The Man Born to be King: A Play-Cycle on the Life of our Lord and Saviour Jesus Christ* written for broadcasting by Dorothy L. Sayers (1943), p. 41.

anything about Scotland, and then worried him by sending lists of illegible Scots words.[1]

Contributions are again made which do not enjoy published acknowledgement. ELIOT allowed EZRA POUND to change *The Waste Land* radically and content himself with a handsome dedication. Peter Ackroyd describes Pound as locating 'in the typescripts . . . the underlying rhythm of the poem'.

Pound heard the music and cut away what was for him the extraneous material. . . .[2]

GERALD HAXTON told Robin Maugham that, when wandering about the world with his uncle, it was *he* who would stay up late in the club in some place like Penang and 'get pally' with planters and lawyers: 'I'd get them drunk and they would tell me stories, such as *The Letter*, which I got for Willie from a lawyer in Singapore.'[3] MAUGHAM, at seventy, confirmed to his nephew when Gerald Haxton died:

. . . in one way or another – however indirectly – all I've written during the last twenty years has something to do with him. . . .[4]

Leonard Woolf tells of a collaboration that never was. He relates that WELLS's original plan for *The Outline of History* was 'to take a room in the Central Hall and meet once a week with the following friends: Gilbert Murray, Lionel Curtis, J. A. Spender . . . John Hilton, William Archer, and myself'.

I think that he even got to the point of apportioning provisionally periods to some of us . . . but then Wells got tired of it and told me that he was in fact writing the book on his own.[5]

Yet the title page persists in bearing: 'Written with the advice and editorial help of . . . Professor Gilbert Murray' and a different set of names: 'Mr Ernest Barker, Sir H. H. Johnston, Sir E. Roy Lankester'. Wells, who was fifty-three, told Bennett that *The Outline of History* had taken 'more than a year of fanatical toil', upon which Bennett commented:

I cannot get over it. It's a life's work.

1 See Denis Mackail: *The Story of J.M.B.: a biography* (1941), p. 258.
2 Peter Ackroyd: *T. S. Eliot* (1984), p. 119.
3 Robin Maugham: *Conversations with Willie* (1978), pp. 29–30.
4 *Ibid.*, p. 81.
5 *Beginning Again* (1964), pp. 192–3. But see also page 274.

CHAPTER FIFTEEN

Collaboration with Illustrators

I

This has resulted in immortal work, but not always without friction and pain. Robert Seymour had felt his dignity threatened by the young DICKENS making the letter-press in *Pickwick* more important than the illustrations. His tragic suicide followed two days after a quarrel, the amenable and shy 'Phiz' (Hablot Browne) succeeding him. *Nicholas Nickleby*, all the great novels of Dickens's middle period, and *A Tale of Two Cities* were illustrated by him.

The strain of working with DODGSON was considerable. He would constantly send messages to Sir John Tenniel: 'Don't give Alice so much crinoline' – or 'The White Knight must not have whiskers; he must not be made to look old.' After *Through the Looking Glass* Tenniel commented: '. . . the faculty of making drawings for book illustration departed from me.'[1]

When THACKERAY, on the other hand, at the time of *Philip* was beginning to find it troublesome to draw on wood, George Smith brought the talented Frederick Walker, then twenty-one and excessively nervous, to his house to give him a trial. 'I am going to shave,' said Thackeray. 'Would you mind drawing my back?' Smith recorded:

Thackeray's idea of giving his back to Walker as a subject, was as ingenious as it was kind; for I believe, if Walker had been asked to draw Thackeray's face, instead of his back, he would hardly have been able to hold his pencil.[2]

WILLIAM MORRIS's relations with Burne-Jones were the easy ones of friends. After a day out, when the illustrations for *The Earthly Paradise* were still going forward, Morris and his friends returned to Lymington where Burne-Jones and Georgiana were on holiday. William Allingham put in his diary:

1 Stuart Dodgson Collingwood: *The Life & Letters of Lewis Carroll* (1898), p. 146.
2 Leonard Huxley: *The House of Smith, Elder* (1923), pp. 142–3.

Ned said, 'I'm very sorry, but I've been so lazy I've not done a single thing for the book'; to which Morris gave a slight grunt. Then Ned produced his eight or nine designs for the wood-blocks, whereupon Morris laughed right joyously and shook himself. . . .[1]

Mackail records that once at The Grange, the home of Burne-Jones in Fulham, Morris was 'perhaps for the hundredth time – pressing for more and yet more designs for woodcuts for the Kelmscott Press'.

'You would think,' Sir Edward said, turning to me with his wonderful smile, 'to listen to Top, that I was the only artist in the world.' 'Well,' said Morris quietly, 'perhaps you wouldn't be so far wrong.'[2]

When it became evident that Morris's health was seriously declining, Burne-Jones said: 'What I should do, or how I should get on without him, I don't in the least know. I should be like a man who has lost his back.'[3]

GRAHAME said to E. H. Shepard, who had agreed to illustrate a new edition of *The Wind in the Willows* and visited the author, now seventy-one, at Pangbourne: 'I love these little people, be kind to them.'[4] When he saw the proofs, he chuckled, 'I'm glad you've made them real.' But he did not live to see the finished work.

Tenniel and Lewis Carroll, Sidney Paget and Sherlock Holmes, Maxfield-Parrish and Kenneth Grahame, E. H. Shepard and A. A. Milne, Shepard and Grahame, text and picture are inseparable. A. A. Milne wrote of Shepard and himself:

. . . our names have been associated on so many title pages that I am beginning to wonder which of us is which.[5]

Sometimes the illustrator has taken the initiative. It was on Tenniel's advice that a sequence introducing a wasp in a wig was omitted, also that Alice in the railway carriage, instead of laying hold of the old lady's hair, was made to catch at the goat's beard which 'seemed to melt away as she touched it'.[6] CHRISTOPHER MILNE wrote that 'the

---

1 William Allingham: *A Diary* ed. H. Allingham & D. Radford (1907), p. 142.
2 J. W. Mackail: *The Life of William Morris* (1899), ii, p. 337.
3 *Ibid.*, ii, p. 349.
4 Quoted by Peter Green: *Kenneth Grahame: A Study of his Life, Work and Times* (1959), p. 346.
5 *Fun and Fantasy: A Book of Drawings* by Ernest H. Shepard (1927), with an Introduction by A. A. Milne.
6 Stuart Dodgson Collingwood: *The Life & Letters of Lewis Carroll* (1898), pp. 146–8. See *Through the Looking-Glass, and What Alice Found There* (1872), p. 54.

Pooh who had been developing under my father's pen began to develop under Shepard's pen as well'. In a comparison of the early Poohs in *Winnie the Pooh* with the later Poohs in *The House at Pooh Corner*, 'the eye that starts ... level with the top of Pooh's nose, gradually moves downwards and ends up as a mere dot' in which 'the whole of Pooh's character can be read'.[1]

II

WILDE alludes to a collaboration of author, illustrator, and designer. In a letter to *The Speaker*, he replied to a paragraph in that paper which had adversely criticized the designs and decorations of *A House of Pomegranates*:

Mr Shannon is the drawer of dreams, and Mr Ricketts is the subtle and fantastic decorator. ... The writer of the paragraph goes on to state that he does not 'like the cover'. This is, no doubt, to be regretted, though it is not a matter of much importance, as there are only two people in the world whom it is absolutely necessary that the cover should please. One is Mr Ricketts, who designed it, the other is myself, whose book it binds. We both admire it immensely![2]

Constable and Company Ltd., whose relations to SHAW were those of an agent, faithfully adopted his American spelling, used spaced letters instead of italics for emphasis, and omitted the apostrophe from common contractions. His books appeared when books were still a delight to handle: dumpy small octavo volumes with apple-green grained cloth, gilt tops and other edges uncut, followed by slim octavo hairy brick-red cloth, top edges gilt, and medium octavo bright green cloth of the Limited Collected Edition, t.e.g., o.e.uncut. Then there were those individual volumes: *The Intelligent Woman's Guide to Socialism and Capitalism* in medium octavo mild green cloth, with interlocking design picked out in gold on spine and front board, t.e.g., o.e.uncut; the slim crown octavo black papered boards of *The Adventures of the Black Girl in her Search for God*, with white design by John Farleigh and his woodcuts inside; the crown octavo blue cloth *Geneva*, t.e.g., and its companion volume *In Good King Charles's Golden Days* in red, t.e.g., both with illustrations by Felix Topolski – the days

1 *The Enchanted Places* (1974), pp. 77–78.
2 Nov. 28, 1891. Quoted by Stuart Mason: *Bibliography of Oscar Wilde* (1914), p. 366.

of richness, of cloth not clever fake, when titles appeared in an upright position on spines and each illustration faced the page it was illustrating, not to mention notes appearing on pages to which they belonged.

PART FIVE

THE MARK OF THE GIFT

The Brontë Sisters
from the painting by Branwell Brontë
in the National Portrait Gallery

Emery Walker Ltd. phsc.

CHAPTER ONE
The Case is Put

Looking back to his meeting with SWINBURNE, Max Beerbohm observed that he had known 'no man of genius who had not to pay, in some affliction or defect either physical or spiritual, for what the gods had given him'.

Here, in this fluttering of his tiny hands, was a part of the price that Swinburne had to pay.[1]

The view finds support in a letter COLERIDGE wrote to SOUTHEY who was unwell and suffering with his eyes at the time Coleridge's own health was 'very indifferent':

It is a theory of mine that virtue and genius are diseases of the hypochondriacal and scrofulous genera, and exist in a peculiar state of the nerves and diseased digestion, analogous to the beautiful diseases that colour and variegate certain trees.

He added 'by way of comfort' that he believed 'the virtue and genius produce the disease', not the other way round – 'Heaven knows, there are fellows who have more vices than scabs . . . with fewer ideas than plaisters.'[2]

In varying degrees, Pope, Lamb, Carlyle, Charles Kingsley, Meredith, A. E. Housman, Bennett, Lytton Strachey all suffered from stomach upsets and many from neuralgia – what Coleridge calls 'a peculiar state of the nerves and diseased digestion'. CARLYLE compared the dyspepsia which had tormented him from a child, with 'a rat gnawing at the pit of the stomach'. By nineteen, he was already a victim of dyspepsia neurasthenia. While Paganini's diaries were confined for a year to 'Purgativo. Vomitivo. Figlio purga. Vomi-purga . . .', Carlyle included such details all his life in conversation and correspondence with friends. He further ruined his digestion by daily doses of castor

1 *And Even Now* (1920), p. 66.
2 Dated Christmas Day, 1802: *Letters of Samuel Taylor Coleridge* ed. Ernest Hartley Coleridge (1895), i, p. 416.

oil. Yet the fact that he went out all weathers suggests his symptoms were nervous in origin more than physical, and after *Frederick*, his last major work, his health improved. In the case of BENNETT, he did not begin to complain of insomnia 'and other intellectual complaints' until he started to write in his mid-twenties.

H. E. BATES suggests 'the hard continuous slog to master my craft' brought on a physical condition he would 'increasingly . . . endure for another twenty years':

For weeks on end I would suffer acute abdominal pains which in turn induced bouts of depression accompanied by tensions both mental and nervous.[1]

Many more examples follow from the wider implications of Beerbohm's remark.

1 *The Blossoming World: An Autobiography ii* (1971), p. 64. See also p. 89.

CHAPTER TWO

General Affliction

Few great authors have been so physically afflicted as Pope and Johnson. Even POPE's friends could not help referring, however affectionately,[1] to his 'little, tender, and crazy carcase'.[2] Swift told him in a letter: 'You pay dearly for the great talents God hath given you.'[3] One of his enemies, the critic Dennis, spoke of his body as 'that of downright monkey'. Pope himself wrote of 'this long disease, my Life'.[4]

Both parents were forty-six when their puny child was born. The constant headaches which caused a permanent contraction above his eyebrows he inherited from his mother, and from his father a tendency to curvature of the spine. Sir Joshua Reynolds described him as 'very hump-backed' but mentioned, as did many others, 'a very large and very fine eye'. I remember a seminar conducted by Professor Tillotson, ostensibly on Hardy, which began by his taking from a drawer a recent photograph of one of Pope's portraits in the National Portrait Gallery and asking us to observe the eyes.

Johnson's description of him has considerable pathos. He tells of his voice, when young, 'so pleasing, that he was called in fondness the little Nightingale....'[5]

He is said to have been beautiful in his infancy; but ... as bodies of a tender frame are easily distorted, his deformity was probably in part the effect of his application. His stature was so low that, to bring him to a level with common tables, it was necessary to raise his seat....

After middle-age, he was 'so weak as to stand in perpetual need of female attendance; extremely sensible of cold so that he wore a kind of fur doublet, under a shirt....'

1 Geoffrey Tillotson: *Pope & Human Nature* (1958), pp. 150–1.
2 George Sherburn: *The Early Career of Pope* (1934), p. 44.
3 Oct. 30, 1727.
4 *Epistle to Dr Arbuthnot* (1735), l.128.
5 *The Lives of the English Poets* (Dublin ed. 1779–81), ii, p. 268.

When he rose, he was invested in boddice made of stiff canvas, being scarce able to hold himself erect till they were laced, and he then put on a flannel waistcoat. One side was contracted. His legs were so slender, that he enlarged their bulk with three pair of stockings, which were drawn on and off by the maid; for he was not able to dress or undress himself. . . . His weakness made it very difficult for him to be clean. His hair had fallen almost all away; and he used to dine sometimes with Lord Oxford privately, in a velvet cap. His dress of ceremony was black, with a tye-wig, and a little sword.[1]

The disease which arrested his development to that of a twelve-year-old boy is thought today to have been tuberculosis of the bone[2] – probably contracted like Johnson's scrofula from the milk of his wet-nurse.

From the TB infection in the glands of his neck, JOHNSON was left with scarred face, imperfect hearing and short sight. When he was four, his mother took him to be touched by Queen Anne and the gold amulet which she hung round his neck remained until death. He suffered also from St Vitus's Dance.

1 *Ibid.*, pp. 382–3.
2 Pott's disease.

CHAPTER THREE

Nervous Affliction

O ne day the painter Hogarth called on Samuel Richardson and, while they were talking, noticed a person standing by a window in the room, shaking his head and rolling himself about in a ridiculous manner. He assumed this person to be 'an ideot' put by relatives under the care of Richardson. When this character (who was JOHNSON) suddenly came forward and joined the discussion, bursting into an eloquent invective against George II, Hogarth looked at him with astonishment and thought that 'this ideot' had been for the moment inspired.[1]

Fanny Burney, after dinner with the Thrales at Streatham when Johnson had been present, noted in her *Diary* 'the cruel infirmities to which he is subject; for he has almost perpetual convulsive movements, either of his hands, lips, feet, or knees, and sometimes of all together'.[2] Boswell goes into considerable detail:

Talking to himself was, indeed, one of his singularities. . . . I was certain that he was frequently uttering pious ejaculations; for fragments of the Lord's Prayer have been distinctly overheard. . . . While talking, or even musing as he sat in his chair, he commonly held his head to one side towards his right shoulder, and shook it in a tremulous manner, moving his body backwards and forwards, and rubbing his left knee in the same direction, with the palm of his hand. In the intervals of articulating he made various sounds with his mouth, sometimes as if ruminating . . . sometimes giving a half-whistle, sometimes making his tongue play backwards from the roof of his mouth, as if clucking like a hen, and sometimes protruding it against his upper gums in front, as if pronouncing quickly under his breath, *too, too, too.* . . . Generally, when he had concluded a period, in the course of a dispute . . . he used to blow out his breath like a whale. This, I suppose, was a relief to his lungs; and seemed in him to be a contemptuous mode of expression, as if he had made the arguments of his opponent fly like chaff before the wind.[3]

1 James Boswell: *The Life of Samuel Johnson, LL.D.* (1791). Aetat. 30: 1739.
2 *Diary & letters of Madame D'Arblay* ed. by her Niece (1842–6), i, p. 38.
3 *Op. cit.*., Aetat.55: 1764.

Sir Joshua Reynolds declared that Johnson could sit still when told to do so, as well as any man:

> Those motions or tricks ... are improperly called convulsions.... My opinion is, that it proceeded from a habit which he had indulged himself in, of accompanying his thoughts with certain untoward actions, and those actions always appeared to me as if they were meant to reprobate some part of his past conduct.[1]

Johnson himself seems to confirm this, for a very young girl, a niece of his friend Christopher Smart, asked him outright:

> 'Pray, Dr Johnson, why do you make such strange gestures?'
> 'From bad habit,' he replied. 'Do you, my dear, take care to guard against bad habits.'[2]

Reynolds told how Johnson and he had visited Mr Banks in Dorsetshire, and 'the conversation turning upon pictures which Johnson could not well see, he retired to a corner of the room, stretching out his right leg as far as he could reach before him, then bringing up his left leg, and stretching his right still further on'.

The old gentleman observing him, went up to him, and in a very courteous manner assured him, though it was not a new house, the flooring was perfectly safe. The Doctor started from his reverie, like a person waked out of his sleep, but spoke not a word.[3]

My friend, Mrs Glyn White, suggests very plausibly that he was checking his footing because of poor sight.

Boswell thought that Johnson's behavioural pattern of compulsive movements had an element of superstition going back to childhood. One of these was to retrace his steps so that he could begin again by a certain number in order that either his right or left foot (Boswell was not sure which) should be first when he came close to the door or passage. Having done this, he would break from his abstraction, walk briskly on and join his companion.[4] In walking through Richmond Park, GEORGE BORROW 'would step out of his way constantly to touch a tree, and he was offended if the friend he was with seemed to observe it'. According to Watts-Dunton who made a comparison with Johnson, he touched 'objects along his path ... to save himself from the evil

1 *Ibid.*, Aetat. 30: 1739.
2 *Ibid.*, Aetat. 74: 1783, footnote.
3 *Ibid.*, Aetat. 30: 1739.
4 *Ibid.*, Aetat. 55: 1764.

chance', and never conquered the superstition.[1] When G. K. CHESTER-
TON lit a cigar or cigarette, he always made a sign in the air with the
match and Miss Denham, his sub-editor on *G.K.'s Weekly*, likened it
to Johnson's compulsive tapping of railings.

ROBERT GRAVES'S own 'compulsion-neuroses' made him notice
them in others. On a visit to Professor GILBERT MURRAY at Boar's
Hill, Graves sat talking to him in his study while he walked up and
down. Graves suddenly asked: 'Are you trying to avoid the flowers on
the rug or to keep to the squares?' Murray wheeled around sharply.

'You're the first person who has caught me out,' he said. 'No, it's not the
flowers or the squares; it's a habit that I have got into of doing things in
sevens. I take seven steps, you see, then I change direction and go another
seven steps, then I turn around.'[2]

A Professor of Psychology had assured him it wasn't dangerous – until
you found youself getting into multiples of seven.

CHESTERTON, like Johnson, used to pull faces and make noises when
reading. J. S. MILL, from the age of thirty, showed involuntary nervous
movements and had 'an almost ceaseless spasmodic twitching over one
eye' – clear evidence, according to Leslie Stephen, that he 'had suffered
from excessive intellectual strain'.[3] Carlyle, after a visit, wrote of Mill's
eyes 'twinkling and jerking with wild lights and twitches. . . .'[4] WIL-
LIAM MORRIS, at work or at meals, constantly shifted and fidgeted.
Canon Rawnsley, in *Reminiscences among the Peasantry of Westmorland*,[5]
quoted one old man who said that WORDSWORTH 'talked a deal to
hiseen. I often seead his lips a ganin.'

Watts-Dunton told Beerbohm that SWINBURNE'S infirmity of the
hands had begun before Eton days and the family, naturally alarmed,
had consulted a specialist, who said it resulted from 'an excess of
electric vitality' and any attempt to stop it would be harmful.[6] Stephen
Potter observed at Oxford how the attention of his fellow students was
'screwed up' by 'the trembling affection' of Professor RALEIGH'S hand,
'which made turning over the pages a distinct and difficult action'.[7]

1 Theodore Watts-Dunton: *Old Familiar Faces* (1916), pp. 61–62.
2 *Goodbye to All That* (1929), p. 364.
3 *D.N.B.*
4 To Jane Welsh Carlyle: July 24, 1836.
5 1898.
6 Max Beerbohm: *And Even Now* (1920), p. 66.
7 *The Muse in Chains: A Study in Education* (1938), p. 211.

LEONARD WOOLF spoke of a trembling of his own hands never entirely absent, but his was hereditary. He believed the tremor to be a symptom of a psychological flaw: he was afraid of making a fool of himself – 'of going out to dinner, or of a week-end at Garsington with the Morrells'.

What shall I say to Mr Jones, or to Lady Ottoline Morrell, or Aldous Huxley? My hand trembles at the thought of it, and so do my soul, heart, and stomach.

He had learnt to conceal everything 'except the trembling hand'. When, as a young man, he sat on the bench as Police Magistrate or District Judge in Ceylon – as it was then – the tremor did not normally affect his notes, but if he had to write '. . . and for these reasons I find the accused guilty of . . . and sentence him to . . .', his hand began to tremble so violently that it was sometimes impossible to write legibly.[1] Twice, on the strength of this tremor, he was given complete exemption from military service in World War I, one doctor erroneously supposing it to be chorea or St Vitus's Dance.[2] Sir William Hardman thought SWINBURNE's 'curious kind of nervous twitching' resembled or approached St Vitus's Dance when he had met him, then twenty-six, at Rossetti's.

Mrs Gaskell noticed that CHARLOTTE BRONTË had a nervous tremor when meeting strangers, for a little shiver would run over her from time to time. T. S. ELIOT even became unwell.

After World War I, SASSOON on a lecture tour in the United States, was befriended by Sam Behrman and wrote:

While with him, I became so voluble and engrossed in what I was saying that my limbs were liable to conduct themselves absent-mindedly. My movements were uncontrolled and precipitate. . . .

In a New York taxi he extended his legs and cracked the glass behind the driver. Sam explained that his companion wasn't used to travelling in midget cabs and that his legs were 'subject to spasms of reflex action'.[3] After demanding twenty dollars for the damage, the driver agreed to accept ten. There was another incident, this time at the Claridge. They were sitting on a narrow balcony above the restaurant, and 'were carrying on an animated discussion which was causing me to perform unconscious operations with my legs'.

1 *Sowing* (1960), pp. 98–99.
2 *Beginning Again* (1964), pp. 91, 179.
3 *Siegfried's Journey* (1945), pp. 206–7.

My legs were on the ledge of the balcony, thereby exercising pressure against a heavy box of floral decorations. When the box toppled off the ledge I had time to observe that it had just missed a large party of smoked salmon and lager beer consumers below.

This time Sam 'hurried me away', remarking outside 'that my legs would end by getting him arrested'.[1]

With the onset of Parkinson's disease, Sir JOHN BETJEMAN had a dread of falling over deep steps:

Failing eyesight (an allusion to cataracts) is not nearly as bad as failing limbs.

A. J. P. TAYLOR became a victim in his late seventies – 'most of the time I am shaking more or less'.

The most difficult problem is to go downstairs – upstairs not so bad.[2]

It was diagnosed in Sir OSBERT SITWELL at fifty-eight. Maggs, in one of their catalogues, described a 'bizarrely typed letter to Sassoon'[3] from MAURICE BARING, then fifty-nine – 'probably a sad symptom' of the same disease.

When GIBBON was at Westminster School, 'a strange nervous affection alternately contracted his legs' causing excruciating pain and making him frequently absent. At thirteen, it seemed he would remain for life an 'illiterate cripple', yet the following year his health improved rapidly.

1 *Ibid.*, pp. 209–10.
2 *An Old Man's Diary* (1984), pp. 143–4.
3 Dated Sept. 26, 1933.

CHAPTER FOUR

Strangeness of Appearance

There was not only the matter of SWINBURNE's hands. Lord Redesdale saw his cousin arrive at Eton, with his Bowdler's *Shakespeare* under his arm:

What a fragile little creature he seemed as he stood there between his father and mother. . . . He was strangely tiny. His limbs were small and delicate; and his sloping shoulders looked far too weak to carry his great head, the size of which was exaggerated by the touzled mass of red hair standing almost at right angles to it.[1]

LAMB's fine head, said by Hunt to be worthy of Aristotle, surmounted a slender petite frame perched on seemingly frail spindly legs. According to George Smith, CHARLOTTE BRONTË's head 'seemed too large for her body'.[2] WILKIE COLLINS had an overlarge head, with a protuberance on his forehead; his hands and feet were unusually small.

Lord Birkenhead described KIPLING's head as 'peculiar', with its forehead retreating sharply from the 'massive eyebrow ridges' while its 'massive' lower jaw had a deep central cleft. 'Owing to its width, his face appeared somewhat Mongolian.' His complexion was that of an Indian, and the small head close to his shoulders gave him his nickname 'The Beetle' at school.[3]

Edmund Gosse first met SWINBURNE, who was thirty-three, in the studio of Ford Madox Brown. He went so far as to say of his future friend:

He was not quite like a human being.

There was 'a low settee in the middle of the studio'.

Every now and then, without breaking off talking or bending his body, he hopped on to this sofa, and presently hopped down again, so that I was

---

1 Edmund Gosse: *The Life of Algernon Charles Swinburne* (1917), p. 319.
2 'Charlotte Brontë', *The Cornhill Magazine*, No. 54, Dec. 1900.
3 *Rudyard Kipling* (1978), p. 37.

reminded of some orange-crested bird – a hoopoe, perhaps – hopping from perch to perch in a cage.

Gosse, only in his early twenties, found it 'rather startling'.[1] Beerbohm, another young man, noticed that at sixty-two Swinburne had a peculiar deportment of straining his long neck 'so tightly back that he all receded from the waist upwards'. It 'made the back of his jacket hang quite far away from his legs; and so small and sloping were his shoulders that the jacket seemed ever so likely to slip right off'.[2] When BEERBOHM reached that age, Sir Harold Nicolson drove to his villa at Rapallo and received the same sort of shock:

He is quite round; his cheeks are chubby with a scarlet nose, like two melons with a peppercorn between them. And his head has sunk sideways a trifle.[3]

Yeats saw GEORGE MOORE sitting among art students in some café in Paris, 'a man carved out of a turnip . . . pop-eyed'. While he had Swinburne's long neck and sloping shoulders, his hair instead of bright red was pale yellow.

J. A. Steuart described STEVENSON in his university days as 'the queerest looking object you could conceive'.

To begin with he was badly put together, a slithering loose flail of a fellow, all joints, elbows, and exposed spindle-shanks. . . . He was so like a scarecrow that one almost expected him to creak in the wind.[4]

Lady (Shane) Leslie, daughter of the Chief Justice of Samoa, remembered Stevenson in his last years, for as a little American girl she and her elder sister had joined his 'celebrated French class' and lived day by day with the family.

Stevenson's build was the most fragile I have ever seen in a man. He had the slenderest feet and hands. . . .[5]

G. Lissant Cox recalled LYTTON STRACHEY as a boy at Abbotsholme:

He was a strange bird from my point of view.

Another remembered his greater sophistication, his 'taught know-

---

1 Edmund Gosse: *The Life of Algernon Charles Swinburne* (1917), pp. 200–1.
2 Max Beerbohm: *And Even Now* (1920), p. 65.
3 *Diaries & Letters 1930–1939* ed. Nigel Nicolson (1966), p. 166.
4 *Robert Louis Stevenson* (1927), p. 75.
5 'A Centenary Tribute', *The Daily Telegraph*, Nov. 11, 1950.

ledge', and how he talked about the play while he washed, turning round naked to go on talking, oblivious that he was circumcised while the other boys were not.[1] Leonard Woolf wrote of Lytton who was his friend:

By public school standards he did not look right, speak right, or even act right. . . .[2]

Malcolm Muggeridge came to acquire real affection for the WEBBS as human beings behind their 'fantastic façade', but admits that SIDNEY 'really was a ridiculous looking man, with tiny legs and feet, a protruding stomach, and a large head'.[3]

DRYDEN's nickname was 'Poet Squab':

. . . a sleepy eye he had and no sweet feature.

A large mole on the right cheek appears in all his portraits. When DEFOE was in hiding, the government advertised him as having 'a brown complexion . . . a hooked nose . . . and a large mole near his mouth'. GIBBON's shortness was accentuated by fat, and Leslie Stephen found the portrait at thirty-seven 'with features so overlaid . . . even at this time, as to be almost grotesque'.[4] Another biographer spoke of a dropsy long lurking in his condition.

With the relish of a young man just twenty-six, Henry James described his meeting with GEORGE ELIOT:

She is magnificently ugly – deliciously hideous. . . . Now in this vast ugliness resides a most powerful beauty which, in a very few minutes steals forth and charms the mind. . . .

He ended by 'falling in love':

Yes behold me literally in love with this great horse-faced blue-stocking. . . . Altogether she has a larger circumference than any woman I have ever seen.[5]

For one so appreciative of beauty, WALTER PATER had 'an impassive frog-like face' – 'a nose very low at the bridge', a prodigious chin, and 'a curious malformation of the mouth. . . .'[6] There was also 'the Pater

1 Michael Holroyd: *Lytton Strachey: A Critical Biography* (1967–8), i, pp. 63–64.
2 *Downhill All the Way* (1967), p. 251.
3 *Chronicles of Wasted Time* (1972–3), i, p. 147.
4 *D.N.B.*
5 To Henry James, snr., May 10, 1869.
6 Thomas Wright: *The Life of Walter Pater* (1907), i, pp. 86–87.

Poke', a slightly misformed back rather common in the family.[1] He
was once heard to say:

I would give ten years of my life to be handsome.[2]

A tactful suggestion by his very concerned friends led to the Bismarkian
moustache so conspicuous in his later portraits. It is assumed he never
really recovered from a 'dreadful' kick given him by a boy at school,
which left a peculiarity in his gait until his death at fifty-five.

The woman in DOROTHY L. SAYERS, so painfully evident in passion-
ate love affairs in her late twenties, was not served by her looks. Val
Gielgud, who produced her play-cycle on the life of Christ, *The Man
Born to be King*, said she resembled 'an amiable bull-terrier'.

Virginia Woolf compared KATHERINE MANSFIELD to 'a Japanese
doll with the fringe combed quite straight across her forehead',[3] while
Lytton Strachey and Dorothy Brett both spoke of her 'mask'. It was
BENNETT's quiff, combined with prominent teeth, fobwatch, and curious stiff walk that made him instantly recognizable.

We are told by J. R. Findlay, who knew DE QUINCEY in the last
seven years of his life, that no one meeting him in the street would be
likely to forget the experience:

He walked with considerable rapidity . . . and with an odd one-sided, and yet
straightforward, motion, moving his legs only, and neither his arms, head, nor
any other part of his body. . . . His hat, which had the antediluvian aspect
characteristic of the rest of his clothes, was generally stuck on the back of his
head. . . .[4]

To passers-by there was something in VIRGINIA WOOLF's appearance
which struck them as 'strange and laughable'. Her husband wrote that
'this laughter of the street distressed her':

I think this element was closely connected with the streak in her which I call
genius. For in conversation she might, at any moment, leave the ground, as I
used to call it . . . and give some . . . almost lyrical description . . . one felt it
to be a kind of inspiration.[5]

ALDOUS HUXLEY, at forty-one, went to the Zoo with his sixteen-year-
old son and Ivan Moffatt, Matthew's school-friend. According to

1 *Ibid.*, p. 12.
2 *Ibid.*, p. 192.
3 *Diary*: Dec. 7, 1925.
4 *Personal Recollections of Thomas De Quincey* (1886), p. 11.
5 Leonard Woolf: *Beginning Again* (1964), pp. 29–31.

Moffatt, Huxley wore a floppy overcoat like a character from Edward Lear. A string of mocking little boys followed as he recited to the animals and teased the baboons.

He must have had eyes in his back – just as he was about to feed some monkeys, he whipped round and proferred the carrot to the little boys. They fled with shrieks.[1]

Six foot tall, her nose described by Gertrude Stein as 'one of the wonders of creation', Dame EDITH SITWELL played the role of a great eccentric. Sargent, when he had painted the family portrait, counselled the sensitive thirteen-year-old not to be ashamed of her conspicuous looks, and the woman accentuated them wearing dresses ankle-length and accessories seen on nobody else. A few years before she died, she told John Freeman that she couldn't wear fashionable clothes – 'I really would look so extraordinary if I wore coats and skirts.'[2] Yet Alvaro Guevara and Wyndham Lewis painted a serenity: a garden enclosed behind the façade; and Cecil Beaton, who met her at thirty-nine, took many photographs of 'a young faun-like creature' whom he described as altogether beautiful. ERIC GILL's habitual use of knee socks and a belted workman's smock (often mistaken for a monk's habit) set him apart.

WORDSWORTH had a premature appearance of old age. He laughingly told De Quincey that a fellow-passenger had said to him, seated outside a stage-coach:

'Ay, ay, another dozen of years will show us strange sights; but you and I can hardly expect to see them.' – 'How so?' said Wordsworth. . . . 'How old do you take me to be?' 'Oh, I beg pardon,' said the other; 'I meant no offence – but . . .' looking at Wordsworth more attentively – 'you'll never see three-score, I'm of opinion'; (meaning to say that Wordsworth *had* seen it already) . . . he appealed to all the other passengers; and the motion passed (nem. con.), that Wordsworth was rather over than under sixty.[3]

Wordsworth then told them that he had not yet completed his thirty-ninth year. Watts-Dunton believed that BORROW when quite a young man had white hair.[4] This silvery whiteness of his thick crop seemed to add to the beauty of his face, but also 'gave a strangeness to it'.

1 Sybille Bedford: *Aldous Huxley: A Biography* (1973–4), i, p. 316.
2 May 1959: BBC TV series, 'Face to Face'.
3 *Selections Grave and Gay, from Writings Published and Unpublished* by Thomas De Quincey (1853–60), ii, pp. 251–2.
4 Theodore Watts-Dunton: *Old Familiar Faces* (1916), p. 43.

There was 'a certain incongruity' between his Roman-Greek features and the Scandinavian complexion, 'luminous and sometimes rosy as an English girl's'.

What struck the observer, therefore, was not the beauty but the strangeness of the man's appearance.[1]

EDMUND GOSSE prolonged a youthful appearance – his boyish looks in his mid-twenties did not please him; Austen Chamberlain described the Clark Lecturer of thirty-five as 'seeming a boy coming up to Cambridge at an unusually early age'.[2]

ORWELL's eyes, like those of D. H. Lawrence and T. E. Lawrence, were startlingly blue. Ruth Pitter remembers Orwell as a schoolboy of seventeen on holiday from Eton:

I knew at once he was an interesting person. He looked at me with his very keen look, his eyes were an exact pair.[3]

---

1 *Ibid.*, p. 54.
2 Ann Thwaite: *Edmund Gosse: a literary landscape* (1984), p. 251.
3 Bernard Crick: *George Orwell: A Life* (1980), p. 76.

CHAPTER FIVE
Small in Stature

A mong those extremely small were Pope (four feet six), Keats (five foot but broad shouldered), Charlotte Brontë ('tiny'), Hardy ('gnomic'), Barrie ('almost a dwarf'). The dalesmen knew Hartley Coleridge affectionately as 'Li'le Hartley', Masefield spoke with similar affection of 'little Binyon', Hugh Walpole for Henry James was 'belovedst little Hugh', and Sassoon called Wilfred Owen 'my little friend'. Elizabeth Gräfin von Arnim (Countess Russell) stood barely five foot at eighteen, and in her fifties apparently never looked older than fourteen. To Wells she was 'Little e'. He doubted if she weighed six stone. At a poets' reading in the Aeolian Hall,[1] attended by the Queen and the two Princesses, DE LA MARE was unable to reach the lectern.

Smallpox ravaged eight-year-old GOLDSMITH and left its mark for life. There is the story of the child dancing in his Irish kitchen and the old fiddler taunting him with 'Aesop' because of his looks. The boy's retort came swift in mental pain:

Heralds proclaim aloud this saying – see Aesop dancing and his monkey playing.

In better days as a man he assumed a comic dignity by adorning his little person in plum-colour, blue silk and velvet. GIBBON too, put on elaborate finery which made things worse. MARIA EDGEWORTH (like Edith Sitwell and Matthew Arnold) suffered considerably when young from mechanical gadgets – hers were intended to make her taller. At one stage she was even hanging by her neck, but with no change to her diminutive stature.

DE QUINCEY is described by J. R. Findlay as 'a very little man (about 5 feet 3 or 4 inches). . . . His features . . . aristocratically fine'.

His face . . . appeared, when closely examined, to be seamed with a million

1 April 8, 1943.

of wrinkles crossing each other in every direction possible, but as fine as if drawn by the point of a very fine needle.

Findlay believed the cause of his clothes looking so peculiar was 'that he had become much thinner in ... later years, whilst he wore, and did wear, I suppose till the end of his life, the clothes that had been made for him years before'.[1] Dorothy Wordsworth described his person as 'unfortunately diminutive', but added that there was 'a sweetness in his looks, especially about the eyes which soon overcomes the oddness of your first feeling at the sight of so very little a man'.[2]

Thackeray's eldest daughter recalled CHARLOTTE BRONTË visiting their old bow-windowed drawing-room in Young Street – 'a tiny, delicate, serious, little lady, pale, with fair straight hair, and steady eyes' being led in from the hall by her father and the publisher George Smith. The dinner coming as a relief to the solemnity, they all smile – 'as my father stoops to offer his arm; for, genius though she may be, Miss Brontë can barely reach his elbow'.[3]

George Smith arrived home when she was staying with his mother and himself. Thackeray had called and Smith found them alone in the drawing-room, Thackeray standing, looking anything but happy. She was taking him to task for announcing her identity in public after his lecture. Smith recalled 'the spectacle of this little woman, hardly reaching to Thackeray's elbow, but somehow, looking stronger and fiercer than himself. . . .'[4]

Mrs Gaskell wrote of her first meeting with Charlotte Brontë:

She is (as she calls herself) *undeveloped*; thin and more than half a head shorter than I. . . .[5]

Her hands and feet were the smallest she had ever seen. She ascribed Charlotte's 'nervous dread of encountering strangers' to an idea that she was ugly. 'I notice,' said Charlotte, 'that after a stranger has once looked at my face he is careful not to let his eyes wander to that part of the room again!' Mrs Gaskell protested that 'a more untrue idea never entered into any one's head',[6] but Charlotte's publisher and friend believed 'she would have given all her genius and her fame to

1 *Personal Recollections of Thomas De Quincey* (1886), p. 10.
2 Letter to Mrs Thomas Clarkson, Dec. 8, 1808.
3 Anne Thackeray Ritchie: *Chapters from Some Memoirs* (1894), pp. 60–61.
4 *A Memoir* (1902), p. 100.
5 *The Life of Charlotte Brontë* (1857), ii, p. 171.
6 *Ibid.*, ii, p. 290.

have been beautiful'.[1] Thackeray echoed the same sentiment to Lucy
Baxter at the time *Villette* appeared:

The poor little woman of genius! . . . rather than any earthly good or mayhap
heavenly one she wants some Tomkins or another to love her. . . . But you
see she is a little bit of a creature without a penny worth of good looks. . . .[2]

James Bryce heard J. R. GREEN preach at St Philip's, Stepney, and
never forgot the impression made on him 'by the impassioned sen-
tences . . . from the fiery little figure in the pulpit with its thin face
and bright black eyes'.[3]

R. C. Sherriff had long admired BARRIE's plays, and seen his portrait,
before the widow of Captain Scott arranged an invitation to tea. But
until the door opened on the Adelphi Terrace landing he hadn't
realised how small Barrie was.

His coat seemed too big for him. The sleeves came down over his hands, and
when he put them into his jacket pockets he had to straighten his short arms
to get them there. . . . He looked down at my feet and replied, 'Come in.' He
walked in front of me . . . a curious little rolling sort of walk, slow, as if he
wasn't very interested in where he was going.[4]

Rebecca West described BEERBOHM as 'extraordinarily like a little
Chinese dragon in white porcelain . . . perfectly round forehead and
blue eyes that press forward in their eagerness; and his small hands
and feet have the neat compactness of paws'. T. E. LAWRENCE had a
body long for his legs, a large jaw, and small hands and feet. He broke
a bone in his leg when he went to the rescue of a boy being bullied in
the school playground and, according to his mother, this fall halted
his growth.

Richard Burton described DYLAN THOMAS as 'short, bandy, prime,
obese. . . .' At twenty-one, when Caitlin first met him, he 'was slim,
tiny and light':

I suppose he couldn't have been much more than seven stone. He was always
self-conscious about his height. . . . He would tell people that he was an inch
or two taller than I was, but really he was the same sort of height, which was
5 ft 2 in.[5]

Others short in stature include Blake (not quite five feet six), Samuel

1 George Smith: 'Charlotte Brontë', *The Cornhill Magazine* No. 54, Dec. 1900.
2 Mar. 11, 1853.
3 *Letters of John Richard Green* ed. Leslie Stephen (1901), p. 58.
4 *No Leading Lady: An Autobiography* (1968), pp. 176–7.
5 Caitlin Thomas *with* George Tremlett: *Caitlin: A Warring Absence* (1986), p. 3.

Rogers, Swinburne (five feet four and a half), Kipling (five feet six). Byron achieved his romantic image in spite of his five feet eight; when Lady Blessington met Byron in Genoa, she had imagined him 'taller, with a more dignified and commanding air. . . .' Alfred Austin, who succeeded Tennyson as Poet Laureate, was barely five foot. Maugham was sensitive of his five feet seven, the same height as Evelyn Waugh and Wells.

CHAPTER SIX

Outsized

Shaw described WILDE in a letter to Frank Harris as 'an over-grown man, with something not quite normal about his bigness'. He recalled that Lady Wilde's hands were enormous: 'and the gigantic splaying of her palm was reproduced in her lumbar region'.

I have always maintained that Oscar was a giant in the pathological sense, and that this explains a good deal of his weakness.[1]

Ross had never met the odd 'elephantine' gait in anyone else. At Trinity, Dublin, sixteen-year-old Wilde was as tall as his tutor Mahaffy, six feet three.

CHESTERTON was gargantuan – six feet four and weighing twenty stone. Curiously he had little feet which, like his voice, did not seem to belong to the rest of him. His wife thought Wells was beneficial because he took him out walking, but when the two men were together Chesterton would plead: 'We won't go for a walk today, will we?'[2] When he was forty he had a serious illness. Dr Pocock found the bed partly broken under the weight, and his patient's hips higher than his head. He ordered a water-bed and heard, before the patient sank into a coma: 'I wonder if this bally ship will ever get to shore.'[3] On his second visit to America, he got stuck in the door of the car and Father O'Donnell tried to help. Chesterton said it reminded him of an old Irishwoman:

'Why don't you get out sideways?'
'I have no sideways.'[4]

Henry James thought it 'very tragic' that Chesterton's 'mind should be imprisoned in such a body'.[5] When DOROTHY L. SAYERS became

1 *The Works of Bernard Shaw* (1930–1), xxix, p. 304.
2 Maisie Ward: *Gilbert Keith Chesterton* (1944), p. 323.
3 *Ibid.*, p. 329.
4 *Ibid.*, p. 496.
5 Leon Edel: *Henry James: A Biography* (1953–72), v, p. 373.

President of the Detection Club, she found the robes, which had been made for Chesterton, a perfect fit. CONAN DOYLE was an accomplished athlete and games player. At twenty-one, he stood over six foot, with a 43-inch chest, and weighed over sixteen stone.

LYTTON STRACHEY had a tall, lanky frame and wore a long beard. ALDOUS HUXLEY at the Villa Huley had an extra-long bed, with extra-long sheets from England and an extra-long red quilt. Juliette Baillot, who first met him at Garsington, said:

His six foot four seemed even taller because of the slenderness of his body and his slight stoop.[1]

Again she recalled:

How very tall he was – even in that big room – with his legs wound round chairs.[2]

He told Stephen Spender they were the wrong height, and that the great creative geniuses were 'short and robust . . . with almost no neck to divide the nerves of the body from the centres of the brain'.[3] Stephen Potter called Professor RALEIGH 'the tallest man in Oxford, and seeming even taller because of his delicate structure and long sad face'.[4]

ORWELL, six feet three (the height of Thackeray and Osbert Sitwell), was always bothered about where to buy size twelve boots. He had an idée fixe they were more procurable in America. It was the only favour he asked of his friend David Astor, who wrote off to the Astor Estate in New York. Malcolm Muggeridge was sent on the quest when he was Washington correspondent, also Dwight Macdonald in New York – even the firm Harcourt Brace joined in. Susan Watson, in return for a brooch at Christmas, went on a shopping marathon to find him a pair of size twelve gloves. Geoffrey Gorer said:

He was too big for himself . . . if he'd been younger you would have said 'coltish'. He was liable to knock and trip over things. I mean, he was a gangling, physically badly co-ordinated young man. . . .[5]

1 Sybille Bedford: *Aldous Huxley: A Biography* (1973–4), i, p. 60. (He was 6 ft. 4½.)
2 *Ibid.*, i, p. 73.
3 Stephen Spender: *World Within World* (1951), p. 163. Cf. Coleridge quoting 'citizen Tourdes, the French translator of Spallanzani', on the relative distance between heart and head determining 'the sagacity or stupidity of all bipeds and quadrupeds'. (To Humphry Davy: Dec. 2, 1800. *Letters, cit.*, i, p. 342.)
4 *The Muse in Chains: A Study in Education* (1937), p. 210.
5 'The Road to the Left', BBC 1 *Omnibus* programme, 1970.

(PALEY was described by Leslie Stephen as 'curiously clumsy'.[1])

BORROW was 'the mighty figure' – 'this silvery-haired giant' – 'of almost gigantic proportions' – 'considerably above six feet (*sic*) in height' – 'certainly six feet three' – a man looking like a 'colossal clergyman'. But his affliction did not lie here:[2]

At seventy years of age, after breakfasting at eight o'clock in Hereford Square (South Kensington), he would walk to Putney, meet one or more of us at Roehampton, roam about Wimbledon and Richmond Park with us, bathe in the Fen Ponds with a north-east wind cutting across the icy water ... run about the grass afterwards like a boy to shake off some of the water-drops, stride about the park for hours, and then ... eat a dinner at Roehampton that would have done Sir Walter Scott's eyes good to see. Finally, he would walk back ... home late at night.[3]

If portions of *Piers Plowman* are autobiographical, then WILLIAM LANG-LAND was taunted by his nickname 'Long Will'.

1 *D.N.B.*
2 See pages 300–1 and 358–9.
3 Theodore Watts-Dunton: *Old Familiar Faces* (1916), p. 31.

CHAPTER SEVEN
Defective Eyesight

The initial cause of MILTON's blindness has been given that from the age of twelve he stayed with his books until midnight. Then, at forty, he was invited to become Cromwell's Latin Secretary, and during three years of further intensive application he lost the use of first one eye and then the other. It was candles and oil that weakened the sight of our forbears, for I am assured that use does not wear out the eyes – only using them in poor light.

SWIFT weakened his eyes further by obstinately refusing to wear spectacles. The prominence of BLAKE's eyes indicated his short-sightedness, although he wore glasses only occasionally. POPE, about twenty-five, had a serious desire to be painter as well as poet, but was near-sighted and, as Johnson said, 'not formed by nature for a painter'.[1]

Throughout their acquaintance Boswell had supposed JOHNSON to be merely near-sighted. Afterwards in *The Life*, he declared that the 'scrophula' had hurt his friend's visual nerves so much 'that he did not see at all with one of his eyes, though its appearance was little different from that of the other'. He found support for this in one of Johnson's prayers which had 'Almighty God, who hast restored light to my eye. . . .'[2] Yet Johnson's attention and 'perceptive quickness' (when unaffected by 'the hyp.'), made him distinguish all manner of objects 'with a nicety that is rarely to be found'. Boswell gave an example from their Highland tour:

When . . . I pointed out to him a mountain which I observed resembled a cone, he corrected my inaccuracy, by shewing me, that it was indeed pointed at the top, but that one side of it was larger than the other.[3]

As a child, MARIA EDGEWORTH suffered from eyes so inflamed as to

1 *The Lives of the English Poets* (Dublin ed. 1779–81), ii, p. 293.
2 *Prayers & Meditations Composed by Samuel Johnson* ed. George Strahan (1785), p. 27.
3 *The Life of Samuel Johnson, LL.D.* (1791), Aetat. 3–19: 1712–1728.

threaten her sight. When she stayed on holiday with Thomas Day, her father's friend at Anningsley, he dosed her with tar-water.

WORDSWORTH, who read assiduously from boyhood, had to abandon the practice in middle-age. At forty-two, there was fear he might go blind. His eye trouble persisted and sometimes he wore a green shade. When he was sixty-one, he took his daughter Dora to visit Scott at Abbotsford, and a little urchin in Carlisle exclaimed: 'There's a man wi' a veil, and a lass drivin'!'[1] Carlyle met him several times at London parties and said that Wordsworth 'carried in his pocket something like a skeleton brass candlestick in which, setting it on the dinner table, between the most afflictive or nearest of the chief lights, he touched a little spring and there flirted out, at the top of his brass implement, a small green circle which prettily enough threw his eyes into shade and screened him from that sorrow'.

DE QUINCEY was acutely short-sighted, and Thomas Medwin described SHELLEY at twenty-eight: '. . . somewhat bent, owing to near-sightedness, and his being forced to lean over his books, with his eyes almost touching them. . . .'[2]

TENNYSON, at twenty-one, thinking he was going blind, wrote:

. . . a sad thing to barter the universal light even for the power of 'Tiresias and Phineus, prophets old'.

His son tells that he took to a milk diet for some months, which apparently 'did good'. He used an eye-glass and spectacles, and held his hearing to be compensation for short-sight. He 'could hear the shriek of a bat', which he claimed was the test of a fine ear.[3] When he was fifty-two, he described his audience at Osborne:

Nor . . . do I very well recollect what Her Majesty said to me; but I loved the voice that spoke, for being very blind I am much led by the voice.[4]

Nearly seventy-six, he excused himself from attending the wedding of Princess Beatrice:

Your Majesty is most gracious, but I think that blind as I am, and, I fear, growing blinder, I am best away from the wedding. . . .[5]

THACKERAY, always very short-sighted, told his daughter that in his

1 Sept. 1831.
2 *The Life of Percy Bysshe Shelley* (1847), ii, p. 2.
3 *Alfred Lord Tennyson: A Memoir by his Son* (1897), i, pp. 79–80 & footnote.
4 *Ibid.*, i, p. 486.
5 *Ibid.*, ii, pp. 441–2.

school-days he could not 'even see the balls which he was set to stop at cricket'. DICKENS's eyes were giving trouble when he launched *The Daily News* at thirty-three.

CHARLOTTE BRONTË, according to Mary Taylor's earliest impression of her at Roe Head School, at fourteen, 'looked a little old woman: so short-sighted that she always appeared to be seeking something, and moving her head from side to side to catch a sight of it':

When a book was given her she dropped her head over it till her nose nearly touched it, and when she was told to hold her head up, up went the book after it, still close to her nose, so that it was not possible to help laughing.[1]

At twenty-eight, she wrote to M. Heger that 'à present j'ai la vue trop faible pour écrire – si j'écrivais beaucoup je deviendrais aveugle':

Cette faiblesse de vue est pour moi une terrible privation. . . .[2]

EDWARD LEAR had a constant dread of losing his already poor sight and then being unable to support himself by his art. At twenty-six, he wrote:

. . . my eyes are so sadly worse, that no bird under an ostrich shall I soon be able to see to do.[3]

Towards the end of his life, his right eye had become virtually useless. GEORGE DU MAURIER, after a year's training as a painter in Paris, lost the sight of one eye with the threat of losing the other. Still in his early twenties, he decided he must confine his ambition to drawing in black-and-white. His other eye remained unaffected, and at twenty-six he came to London where illustrators were in great demand. Within three more years he succeeded John Leech on the staff of *Punch*.

FRANCIS KILVERT wondered what Daisy Thomas thought of his 'poor disfigured eyes':

She must know. She must see. Yet it does not seem to make any difference against me with her.[4]

In a Cottage lecture at Crafta Webb, he spoke 'on the parable of the Good Shepherd and told the people of my own blindness and difficulty in knowing my own sheep by sight and calling them by name'.[5]

1 E. C. Gaskell: *The Life of Charlotte Brontë* (1857), i, p. 106.
2 *The Shakespeare Head Brontë: Their Lives, Friendships & Correspondence* (1932), ii, p. 11.
3 Vivien Noakes: *Edward Lear: The Life of a Wanderer* (1968), p. 48.
4 *Diary*: Sept. 18, 1871.
5 *Diary*: Feb. 20, 1878.

When STEVENSON was thirty-four and again critically ill, at Hyères, his weak eyes could not bear light. He lay in a darkened room, forbidden to use his right arm or speak above a whisper. He asked his wife to bring pieces of large card with paper affixed and, writing painfully with his left hand, amused himself with composing *A Child's Garden of Verse*. KIPLING's eyes, perhaps affected by his mother's six-day labour, were neglected when he was a foster-child at Lorn Lodge. His extreme short sight from the age of eleven caused him to wear thick glasses constantly – pebble lenses framed in blue steel. Without them his eyes were 'strange, vibrating and blind'.

GALSWORTHY was handicapped by short sight even at prep school. H. V. Marrot held it 'the legacy of . . . early excess . . . in the matter of reading'.[1] As with Thackeray, it handicapped him in cricket. Rudolf Sauter described his uncle when he was over fifty-nine, riding at Bury 'with that monocle or pince-nez which he never failed to supplant by spectacles when beyond the sight of prying eyes (and to replace it punctiliously as he again approached the village)'.[2]

JOYCE called himself an 'international eyesore'. His first acute attack of glaucoma came when he was thirty-five and walking down a street in Zurich. The sudden pain immobilized him for about twenty minutes until he was able 'to crawl into a tram. . . .'[3] Over thirteen years he had a series of twenty-five operations for iritis, glaucoma and cataracts. Sometimes for short intervals he was totally blind. To revise the fifth chapter of *Finnegans Wake* for publication in *The Criterion*, he needed three magnifying glasses and the help of his son. Sir Harold Nicolson visited him, then fifty-two, in his flat in the Rue Galileo and noted:

Huge concave spectacles which flicked reflections of the light as he moved his head like a bird, turning it with that definite insistence to the speaker as blind people do who turn to the sound of a voice.[4]

AUDEN's eyes were very weak and, like Wordsworth, he wore a shade; in his room he spoke with a lamp behind him. ERIC LINKLATER was handicapped by bad eyesight; it disqualified him for a life at sea.

1 *The Life & Letters of John Galsworthy* (1935), p. 35.
2 *Ibid.*, p. 586.
3 His letter to Ezra Pound, Aug. 20, 1917: Richard Ellmann: *James Joyce* (revised ed. 1982), p. 412.
4 *Diaries & Letters 1930–39* ed. Nigel Nicolson (1966), p. 164.

J. DOVER WILSON, at eighty-five, explained why his edition of Shake-speare's Sonnets had been delayed two years:

Like most old men I was suffering from cataract. . . .

An operation had only made things worse – 'by the time the first proofs were received the Editor could no longer see a line of print.' A. L. Rowse wrote to him, claiming to have solved in his new *William Shake-speare* all the problems of the Sonnets, but Dover Wilson did not reply.

. . . a blind man is virtually cut off from access to his authorities.[1]

CYRIL CONNOLLY, a relatively younger man of sixty-nine, had his cataracts tackled at Moorfields by Patrick Trevor-Roper. Connolly had always feared blindness – 'total eclipse without all hope of day'. But he was already fatally ill. JOHN GOWER became blind eight years before death; Sir EDWIN ARNOLD's sight failed him for the last nine or ten years.

Such divers people as Pepys, Maria Edgeworth, and Aldous Huxley enjoyed a happier sequel. The famous *Diary* closed with PEPYS only thirty-six, believing himself 'to undo my eyes almost every time that I take a pen in my hand' and asking God to prepare him for 'all the discomforts that will accompany my being blind'. His eyesight improved; four years after these words he became administrative head of the Navy. MARIA EDGEWORTH, almost entirely blind for two years when she was fifty-one, felt compelled to give up reading, writing and needlework – after which time her eyes completely recovered. Sixteen-year-old HUXLEY had to leave Eton owing to serious eye trouble. Almost blind for eighteen months, he taught himself Braille and Sir George Clark, then twenty-one, tutored him. When his sight began to improve, he wrote his first novel on the typewriter. Sir John Gielgud remembers him 'with his thick glasses and long stooping body' often coming to their house in South Kensington, for Huxley was a great friend of Lewis, Sir John's eldest brother.[2] Three times during World War I he was rejected by the Army as totally unfit. At thirty-seven, he had 'a queer pair' of glasses which he called 'my white-eyed poppies' and which had 'a sort of pebbly lens in the centre surrounded by a sort of silver shield'. But he told Robert Nichols: 'I daren't put

1 *The Sonnets*, New Cambridge Shakespeare (1966), Preface, pp. viii–ix.
2 *Early Stages* (1939), p. 44.

them on in public – they make everybody laugh.'[1] By the time he was forty-five, the task of reading had become increasingly difficult and fatiguing. Then, four years later, his little book *The Art of Seeing* repaid a debt of gratitude –

to the pioneer of visual education, the late Dr W. H. Bates, and to his disciple, Mrs Margaret D. Corbett, to whose skill as a teacher I owe the improvement in my own vision.

Within a couple of months of treatment, he claimed he was reading without spectacles 'and, what was better still, without strain and fatigue'.[2]

George Gould, the Philadelphia eye specialist, argued that CAR-LYLE's dyspeptic symptoms which plagued his life were eye-strain brought on by astigmatism.[3]

1 Sybille Bedford: *Aldous Huxley: A Biography* (1973–4), i, p. 249.
2 *The Art of Seeing* (1943), Preface, pp. vii, vi.
3 W. R. Bett: *The Infirmities of Genius* (1952), pp. 17–18.

CHAPTER EIGHT
Defective Hearing

When he was forty-five, SWINBURNE accepted Victor Hugo's invitation to meet him in Paris, regretting afterwards only that deafness had prevented him for hearing a word of the speech that his Master made in his honour. At The Pines Watts-Dunton had to 'roar' at him, and Beerbohm commented how Swinburne's 'frail, sweet voice rose and fell, lingered, quickened, in all manner of trills and roulades':

> That he himself could not hear it, seemed to me the greatest loss his deafness inflicted on him. One would have expected this disability to mar the music; but it didn't . . . the tones were under good control.[1]

HARRIET MARTINEAU suffered deafness from an early age, and a juvenile illness left JOHN G. LOCKHART partially deaf for life. The same social handicap made W. R. INGE feel isolated during his formative time as Fellow of Hertford College. At forty-two, he wrote of 'increasing ear trouble'.[2] It may partly explain why, during prolonged choral services at St Paul's, the Dean read a book in his stall.

> The noise gets on my nerves. . . .[3]

Asked about the ear-trumpet their father had brandished at guests, EVELYN WAUGH's grown-up daughters dismissed it as a quirk and insisted he could hear. But Waugh himself, on being asked why he had become a recluse at Combe Florey, said society now bored him because of his deafness.[4] Significantly, music (as with Inge) meant nothing in his life. He recorded in his autobiography that like his father he gradually lost the hearing of his left ear in middle life – 'I blame it on heredity'.[5]

1 *And Even Now* (1920), pp. 67–68.
2 Adam Fox: *Dean Inge* (1960), p. 62.
3 Diary: June 7, 1911. Quoted by Fox, *ibid.*, p. 115.
4 Interview with John Freeman, June 1960: BBC TV series 'Face to Face'.
5 *A Little Learning: The First Volume of an Autobiography* (1964), pp. 1–2.

A mastoid operation at fourteen left VYVYAN HOLLAND deaf in his left ear. It prevented him from satisfying his ambition at the time 'to become a civil engineer by way of Cooper's Hill'.[1] HENRY GREEN deflected his head to the side of his better ear; at forty-seven, he whose inspiration came from 'hearing older people talk' was severely deaf and wrote no more.

1 *Son of Oscar Wilde* (1954), p. 156.

CHAPTER NINE
Crippled

S COTT's lameness resulted from an attack of poliomyelitis when he was about eighteen months old. They discovered when they went to bathe him as usual that he had lost the power of his right leg. About his third year he was sent to stay in the country with his grandfather Dr Rutherford, and someone recommended 'that so often as a sheep was killed for the use of the family, I should be stripped, and swathed up in the skin warm as it was flayed from the carcass of the animal'.

In this Tartar-like habiliment I well remember lying upon the floor . . . while my grandfather . . . used every excitement to make me try to crawl.[1]

He remembered 'a cross child's maid upbraiding me with my infirmity as she lifted me coarsely and carelessly over the flinty steps . . . the *suppressed bitterness* of the moment, and conscious of my infirmity, the envy with which I regarded the easy movements and elastic steps of my more happily formed brothers'.[2] At the High School of Edinburgh, 'in the winter play hours, when hard exercise was impossible', he used to compensate for his lameness by telling his tales to an admiring audience.[3]

'Although the limb affected was much shrunk and contracted', as he grew older he became tall and muscular, and was 'rather disfigured than disabled by my lameness'.

This personal disadvantage did not prevent me from taking much exercise on horseback, and making long journies on foot, in the course of which I often walked from twenty to thirty miles a-day.[4]

An attack of polio at thirty-four, left RICHMAL CROMPTON LAMBURN

1 J. G. Lockhart: *Memoirs of the Life of Sir Walter Scott, Bart.* (1837–8), i, pp. 15 – 16.
2 *Ibid.*, i, p. 98.
3 *Ibid.*, i, p. 29.
4 *Ibid.*, i, p. 49.

with a stiff 'dead' leg which caused her to leave teaching for full-time writing.

BYRON was born with a club-foot and, at ten, a quack Lavender forcibly straightened it and screwed it in a wooden instrument. Mrs Byron sent her boy limping for treatment, and it amused Lavender to send the young lord to fetch his beer. At this time Byron read Latin with an American, Dummer Rogers, who was moved to exclaim: 'Such pain as I *know* you must be suffering, my Lord!' 'Never mind, Mr Rogers,' came the reply, 'you shall not see any signs of it in *me*.' The following year he was rescued by his mother's attorney, John Hanson, who took him to London where Dr Matthew Baillie prescribed a brace and later a special boot.

He swam the Hellespont at twenty-two – pluming himself over it 'more than I could possibly do on any kind of glory, political, poetical, or rhetorical'. He vied with Leander, but may also have seen it as a victory over his own physical humiliation. His companion Ekenhead beat him, on his second attempt, by five minutes. Neither of them was tired, only rather chilled after an hour and a half in the water. When he was thirty-five, he told Lady Blessington:

My poor mother, and after her my schoolfellows, by their taunts, led me to consider my lameness as the greatest misfortune, and I have never been able to conquer this feeling. . . .[1]

On running home in the rain from school, ANNA SEWELL at fifteen fell and injured her ankle. She was heavily bled but from that time, according to her mother, Anna's life as a semi-invalid began. Ten years later, she struggled against a more severe form of lameness when she could scarcely take more than a few steps at a time. Her biographer suggests the cause was not a sprain but a dislocation, which among undernourished children is slow to mend. As a child, Anna had been encouraged often to give her meat dinner to the poor and substitute a bowl of thick porridge for herself.

She was a sensitive child and may well have developed a sense of guilt about eating while others starved. . . .[2]

MATTHEW ARNOLD's doctors insisted that the curving of his legs,

---

1 Marguerite Gardiner, Countess of Blessington: *Conversations with Lord Byron* (1834), p. 129.
2 Susan Chitty: *The Woman Who Wrote 'Black Beauty': A Life of Anna Sewell* (1971), p. 110.

before he was two, could be cured only by putting him in irons. After wearing them fifteen months, he fell off a sofa in his father's study and cut his head – a wound which took long to heal. Next summer, his parents removed the leg irons in defiance of the doctors and for months afterwards he was clumsy and slow – which probably resulted in his nickname in the family: 'Crab' or 'Crabby'. Even when he was ten and had come home from Buckland's school, his legs were still worrying his parents for they engaged a sergeant to drill him. Park Honan points out that Arnold's jottings for his mother 'show plainly that he remembered the iron fetters ten years after he wore them'.[1] He also seems to suggest that Arnold's dandyism up at Balliol was an attempt to court popularity by becoming '*beautiful*', after thick straps and heavy braces had isolated the child and rendered it ugly.[2]

Twelve-year-old HENLEY contracted a tubercular disease which necessitated the amputation of his foot. When he was twenty-four, his doctors told him they wanted to take his other leg to save his life; he went to Joseph Lister at the Edinburgh Infirmary and was his patient there for twenty months, with the result that this leg was saved. While there, he offered his *In Hospital* series of poems to *The Cornhill* and the editor, Leslie Stephen, lecturing in Edinburgh, went to the infirmary to seek him out. A day or two later he took Stevenson along, who described in a letter:

It was very sad to see him . . . in a little room with two beds, and a couple of sick children in the other bed; a girl came in to visit the children, and played dominoes on the counterpane with them; the gas flared and crackled, the fire burned in a dull, economical way; Stephen and I sat on a couple of chairs, and the poor fellow sat up in his bed with his hair and beard all tangled, and talked as cheerfully as if he had been in a king's palace. . . .[3]

Stevenson soon brought him piles of Balzac, and on hearing the patient might sit in a chair, he carried an armchair from home on his head. He also took him for his first outing:

I had a business to carry him down the long stair and more of a business to get him up again, but while he was in the carriage it was splendid. . . . You can imagine what it was to a man who had been eighteen months in a hospital ward.

Barrie remembered Henley, perhaps at one of his Saturday night at-

1 *Matthew Arnold: A Life* (1981), p. 92.
2 *Ibid.*, p. 15.
3 Feb. 14, 1875. *Vailima Letters*, to Sidney Colvin (1895), i, p. 86.

homes, 'in dispute as to whether, say, Turgenieff or Tolstoi could hang the other on his watch-chain':

he sometimes clenched the argument by casting his crutch at you; Stevenson responded in the same gay spirit by giving that crutch to John Silver. . . .[1]

w. h. davies jumped a fast passenger train on his way to the Klondyke, and fell. He had let Three-Fingered Jack jump first, who was slow in leaving him room.

. . . I attempted to stand, but found that something had happened to prevent me from doing this. Sitting down in an upright position, I then began to examine myself, and now found that the right foot was severed from the ankle.[2]

He was taken to the waiting-room where he brought out his pipe until the doctor arrived. Afterwards he said he had done this to save himself fainting in front of an audience. But the local reporter noted it and, when in a second operation the leg was amputated at the knee, the 'kind-hearted race' of Canadians inquired every hour and sent him books and delicacies. He returned to London, living two years in Rowton House where he published his first volume of poems. St john ervine, at thirty-five, suffered the amputation of a leg as the result of shell wounds in World War I.

wells believed it was probably the breaking of his leg between the ages of seven and eight that led him to be writing his *Autobiography* – 'instead of being a worn-out, dismissed and already dead shop assistant'. It happened outside the scoring tent in the cricket field when the grown-up son from The Bell skylarked with him and he fell. 'Enthroned on the sofa in the parlour', after a basic and painful setting, a newly found interest in reading 'now got me securely'. His father fetched books from the Literary Institute in Market Square and the people at The Bell sent round luxuries, 'endless apologies', and more books.[3]

When shaw was forty-one, a tightly laced shoe produced an abscess on his instep and necrosis of the bone was discovered. During the two weeks before his illness, he had attended three first-nights as a dramatic critic, four Vestry committees and one Fabian committee – spoken at two County Council election meetings, written his weekly criticism,

1 *Courage*: Rectorial Address delivered at St Andrew's, May 3, 1922, pp. 39–40.
2 *Autobiography of a Super-tramp* (1908), p. 162.
3 *Experiment in Autobiography* (1934), i, pp. 76–77.

revised a Fabian pamphlet and dealt with correspondence. A letter to Ellen Terry begins:

If I make another stroke with a pen I shall go mad. Oh Ellen, I am the world's pack-horse. . . .

He married on crutches that same year.

MEREDITH, at fifty-seven, began to develop a spinal complaint. He had perhaps, over-indulged in his 'beetle exercise' – throwing up and catching a heavy iron weight at the end of a wooden shaft. Paraplegia, in his last sixteen years, confined him to his chair.

When I ceased to walk briskly part of my life was ended.[1]

A weakness in his ankles was the cause of BENNETT's peculiar walk; it also led him to wear boots instead of shoes.

1 *D.N.B.*

CHAPTER TEN
Peculiar Speech

Their voice has singularized certain writers. According to his friend Hogg, it was SHELLEY's 'one physical blemish . . . intolerably shrill, harsh, and discordant . . . it was perpetual, and without any remission, – it excoriated the ears'.[1] But Peacock qualified this statement to times of excitement:

Then his voice was not only dissonant like a jarring string, but he spoke in sharp fourths, the most unpleasing sequence of sound that can fall on the human ear: but it was scarcely so when he spoke calmly, and not at all when he read . . . he seemed then to have his voice under perfect command; it was good both in tune and in tone . . . low and soft. . . . I have heard him read almost all Shakespeare's tragedies, and some of his more poetical comedies, and it was a pleasure to hear him. . . .[2]

SAMUEL ROGERS, whose breakfasts were 'celebrated throughout Europe',[3] was so softly spoken that he claimed no one would have listened to him if he had not said unkind things. When Harriet Martineau (who as we have seen was deaf) dined with Mr and Mrs Buller, she regretted that J. S. MILL's 'singularly feeble voice cut us off from conversation in that direction'. DRYDEN's voice, according to Swift, sounded 'weak and remote'.[4] CHESTERTON's was tiny, rather high-pitched. He spoke of it as 'the mouse that came forth from the mountain'. LYTTON STRACHEY, when he was thirty-two, told Ottoline Morrell that 'his small voice would prevent his going into politics, which he would rather like to do, but how could he ever make speeches with his thin tiny voice?'[5] ERIC GILL's gentle, husky voice did not carry when he was lecturing in a large hall.

DICKENS had a way of talking, like others in his family, as if the

---

1 *Life of Percy Bysshe Shelley* (1858), i, p. 56.
2 *Memoirs of Shelley* (1858–62).
3 Charlotte Brontë to her father, June 26, 1851.
4 *The Battle of the Books* (1704: written in 1697).
5 Michael Holroyd: *Lytton Strachey: A Critical Biography* (1967–8), ii, p. 75.

tongue was too large for the mouth. It was another trait observed by Eleanor P. (Mrs Christian) on a visit to Broadstairs in his early years.[1]

BENJAMIN JOWETT had a piping treble. WELLS, world historian and popular educator, had ironically a squeaky voice not unlike C. E. M. Joad's. JOAD once described being at his home in Hampstead when, unknown to him, a recording of a Brains Trust programme was being broadcast. He heard from the next room this man with a ridiculously high pitch who seemed to be stealing some of *his* ideas, and was horrified to be told it was himself. Normally LYTTON STRACHEY's voice was low-pitched but, according to his friend Leonard Woolf, 'every now and again it went up into a falsetto, almost a squeak'. His devastating wit owed much 'to the perfect turn of the sentence and the delicate stiletto stab of the falsetto voice'.[2]

JOYCE's voice never broke. As a child, his singing voice was not a treble but a weak tenor. ORWELL had a gravelly voice. Hugh Kingsmill said that Orwell reminded him of a gate swinging on a rusty hinge, and Malcolm Muggeridge comments: 'I saw what he meant.'[3] After a sniper's bullet in Spain, Orwell had been told that his vocal cords were irretrievably damaged, but with a course of electrotherapy speech returned low and hoarse which eventually led to his permanent, rather even, toneless way of talking. W. W. SKEAT had to abandon a vocation in the Church due to an illness affecting his throat; he resigned from his second curacy at twenty-six. Lord DAVID CECIL explained in an interview the excessive speed of his own speech. Among his earliest memories were 'voices of aunts and uncles enthusiastically arguing'.

... the reason I speak as fast as I do is that I had to in order to get a word in when I was young.

At the rehearsal of David Jones's radio play *In Parenthesis*, in which Private Dai Evans is killed by the falling shell, Richard Burton said that DYLAN THOMAS 'screamed as I have never heard, but sometimes imagined a scream, and we were all appalled':

And there was a funny silence and Dylan said that he bet I couldn't do that scream like that with a cigarette in my mouth, and I noted that he had indeed monumentally screamed with a cigarette in his mouth, and went stunned back to my crossword.

---

1 Una Pope-Hennessy: *Charles Dickens 1812–1870* (1945), p. 70.
2 Leonard Woolf: *Sowing* (1960), pp. 120–1.
3 *Chronicles of Wasted Time* (1972–3), ii, p. 65.

CHAPTER ELEVEN
Affliction of Stammer

L AMB described his persona of Elia as 'a stammering buffoon',[1] but Hazlitt paid tribute to his friend:

> He always made the best pun, and the best remark in the course of the evening. . . . No one ever stammered out such fine, piquant, deep, eloquent things in half a dozen half sentences as he does.[2]

De Quincey wrote of DOROTHY WORDSWORTH:

At times, the self-counteraction and self-baffling of her feelings caused her even to stammer, and so determinately . . . that a stranger who should have seen her . . . in that state of feeling would have certainly set her down for one plagued with that infirmity of speech as distressingly as Charles Lamb himself.[3]

On account of some hesitation in his speech which he finally overcame, LEIGH HUNT was not sent to university.

CHARLES KINGSLEY, having been set long passages in Latin and Greek, would go into his father's study under the anxiety of a beating if he forgot, and this has been put forward as part-cause of his stammer. In later years he claimed that heavy doses of calomel given him as a child for biliousness had contracted his under jaw, and that his nerves had been 'ruined by croup and brain fever in childhood'. He always referred to his stammer as 'hesitation'. When about forty, he consulted the speech therapist Dr James Hunt who taught him not to speak while inhaling, which had the effect of making him speak very slowly. David Masson, as a young journalist, was unaware that Kingsley stammered, and at a Chartist meeting where Kingsley had intervened – to sympathize with the cause not the means – whispered to a friend: 'The man's drunk!' Kingsley never 'hesitated' when preaching from notes.

J. S. MILL used prolonged pauses because of a nervous delivery and

---

1 'New Year's Eve', *Elia* (1823), p. 64.
2 *The Plain Speaker* (1826), i, p. 79.
3 *The Collected Writings of Thomas De Quincey* ed. David Mason (1889–90), ii, p. 238.

speaking too quickly. DODGSON was another who had to speak slowly. He practised by reciting scenes from Shakespeare. Partly on account of his stammering he never proceeded to priest's orders after he had been ordained deacon. His diary of Sunday, August 31st, 1862, records that he read the service that afternoon in the church at Putney:

I got through it all with great success, till I came to read out the first verse of the hymn before the sermon, where the two words 'strife strengthened', coming together were too much for me. . . .

One of his child friends recorded:

Our headmistress had announced that Mr Dodgson would give an address in the High School Studio . . . my mother . . . sent me along to hear it with a friend. . . . Now Mr Dodgson suffered from some impediment . . . and on this occasion he opened his mouth wide enough for his tongue to be seen wagging up and down, and . . . carried away by the theme of his discourse, he became quite emotional . . . and I had difficulty in suppressing my giggles . . . on our return home . . . I was made to feel thoroughly ashamed of myself. . . .[1]

JOSEPH SHORTHOUSE had his studies interrupted at fifteen by a bad nervous stammer. The young Wells, sitting in Cust's office, noted that the tall and reserved LEWIS HIND spoke with an impediment.

Much of BENNETT's neurotic nature is thought to have stemmed from a domineering father who poked fun at his boy's stutter. When he was living at 9 Fulham Park Gardens, a speech specialist visited him for more than a year. Bennett even paid a 'mental healer' in Bloomsbury who claimed she could cure him by remote control. Maugham wrote:

It may be that except for the stammer which forced him to introspection Arnold would never have become a writer.

Robin Maugham wrote that without his stammer his uncle in turn 'would probably have become a lawyer – like his brothers. . . . Perhaps his impediment made his fame'.[2] MAUGHAM was humiliated at school through his affliction.

. . . I had read in the Bible that if you had faith you could move mountains. My uncle assured me that it was a literal fact. One night, when I was going back to school next day, I prayed to God with all my might that he would

---

1 Derek Hudson: *Lewis Carroll: An illustrated biography* (1976), p. 254.
2 *Conversations with Willie: Recollections of W. Somerset Maugham* (1978), pp. 25–26.

take away my impediment. . . . I woke full of exaltation and it was a real, a terrible shock, when I discovered that I stammered as badly as ever.[1]

In his autobiographical novel *Of Human Bondage*, Philip Carey prays with similar conviction that his club-foot may be cured before the beginning of next school term, and Maugham uses the subsequent disillusionment to explain his hero's loss of religious faith.

Sassoon recorded that WILFRED OWEN spoke with a slight stammer when he came to his room at Craiglockhart – but this 'was no unusual thing in that neurosis-pervaded hospital'.[2] Dover Wilson wrote of his friend ALFRED POLLARD catching a 'bad stammer . . . from an elder brother at the age of three and . . . never afterwards able to throw off'. It was this accident 'made him a librarian, and hence, for a man of his active mind, a bibliographer and scholar'.[3] PHILIP LARKIN, as a young man, was afflicted by a stammer.

1 *The Summing Up* (1938), pp. 252–3.
2 *Siegfried's Journey 1916–1920* (1945), p. 58.
3 *Milestones on the Dover Road* (1969), pp. 237–8.

CHAPTER TWELVE
The Incidence of TB

In past years pulmonary tuberculosis took a savage toll, ORWELL being perhaps the last of our writers to suffer this way. Less than two years before he died, he was injected with the new drug streptomycin as yet untested,[1] imported 'by some kind of wire-pulling' from the United States and paid for by David Astor.

STERNE's constitution was frail, common to all his family, and there was a tendency to asthma. In his last year at Cambridge he suffered a haemorrhage of the lungs. At forty-nine, a celebrity in Paris with more than half the volumes of *Tristram Shandy* published, he had another attack, which led to his wife and daughter accompanying him to Toulouse. He began a seven-months' tour of France and Italy, but five years later came back to die in Old Bond Street lodgings.

KEATS's walking tour with Charles Armitage Brown, in northern England and Scotland, aggravated the latent disease. After walking 642 miles, his health broke down and he arrived back at Wentworth Place – 'as brown and shabby as you can imagine', Mrs Dilke wrote. 'I cannot tell you what he looked like.' Not yet twenty-three, he came back to nurse his younger brother Tom, who a few months later died in his arms. His own fatal illness began just after a year: his *annus mirabilis*, when he wrote *The Eve of St Agnes*, *Lamia*, the *Odes*, and the two versions of *Hyperion*. He caught a chill returning to Hampstead on top of a coach, and Brown persuaded him to go to bed.

Before his head was on the pillow he slightly coughed, and I heard him say, 'That is blood from my mouth.' I went towards him; he was examining a single drop upon the sheet. 'Bring me a candle, Brown, and let me see this blood.' After regarding it ... he looked up in my face with a calmness of countenance I can never forget, and said, 'I know the colour of that blood –

---

1 1948.

it is arterial blood . . . that drop of blood is my death-warrant. . . .' I ran for a surgeon; my friend was bled; and at five in the morning I left him in a quiet sleep.[1]

A 'sopha-bed' was made up for him in Brown's sitting-room downstairs. He slowly recovered to the extent that within three months Brown went again to Scotland and Keats intended to accompany him. But he turned back at Gravesend. The following month he fell ill and Leigh Hunt, distressed at seeing him alone, insisted on moving him to his own house at Kentish Town where he remained about seven weeks. He occasionally visited Hampstead with Hunt. William Hone, the antiquary, saw him resting on a seat at the end of Well Walk – 'sitting and sobbing his dying breath into a handkerchief, gleaning parting looks towards the quiet landscape he had delighted in'. His doctors telling him that his only hope was to winter in Italy, he went to Rome, accompanied by the artist Joseph Severn, for the last few months of his life.

After the death of her brother Branwell, EMILY BRONTË began to sink rapidly. In a letter to Ellen Nussey, Charlotte explained that Emily refused to see a doctor even though her pulse 'the only time she allowed it to be felt, was found to beat 115 per minute'.

. . . she will not give an explanation of her feelings, she will scarcely allow her illness to be alluded to. . . . More than once I have been forced boldly to regard the terrible event of her loss as possible, and even probable.[2]

Mary Robinson – it is thought, writing down Ellen Nussey's memories – describes how Charlotte went over the moors searching for a sprig of heather, however pale and dry, to take to her sister.[3] But Emily looked with indifferent eyes on the flower laid on her pillow. On the morning of her death she persisted in rising and dressing herself. She sat on the hearth combing her long brown hair until the comb, now in the Brontë Museum, slipped from her fingers and started to smoulder in the cinders where it had to stay till the servant came in to pick it up. At noon she agreed to see a doctor. Towards two o'clock her sisters begged her to let them put her to bed. 'No, no,' she cried, and she made to die standing, like her brother, leaning with one hand upon

---

1 Charles Armitage Brown's MS sketch, slightly adapted by Richard Monckton Milnes in his *Life, Letters, & Literary Remains, of John Keats* (1848), ii, pp. 53–4.
2 Nov. 23, 1848. *The Shakespeare Head Brontë: Their Lives, Friendships & Correspondence* (1932), ii, p. 288.
3 See A. Mary F. Robinson: *Emily Brontë* (1883), pp. 228–9.

the sofa. Mrs Gaskell described Keeper, Emily's fierce bulldog, joining the mourners – following them into the church while the burial-service was read. She added that Anne 'drooped and sickened more rapidly from that time'.

ANNE BRONTË wanted to get to the seaside. She told Ellen Nussey, who accompanied Charlotte in taking her to Scarborough five months later:

I long to do some good in the world before I leave it. I have many schemes in my head. . . . I should not like them all to come to nothing, and myself to have lived to so little purpose.[1]

On the way, 'by her request', they went to York Minster. As she gazed at its structure she was quite overcome, and began: 'If finite power can do this, what is the . . . ?' Her weakness was great and she clasped her hands on reaching her room, but still prayed by her bed 'on bended knee'. On the second day of their arrival at Scarborough she drove on the sands, taking the reins lest the boy should tax the donkey too harshly. On the next she walked a little in the afternoon and sat near the beach. The following day before noon, a physician was sent for and she begged him to tell her the truth as she was not afraid to die. At two that afternoon, having counselled her sister, 'Take courage, Charlotte – take courage,' she died. To save the father further anguish, she was buried at Scarborough.

When Charlotte returned to Haworth, 'the dogs seemed in strange ecstasy' as though they thought others 'long absent were not far behind'.

I left Papa soon, and went into the dining-room: I shut the door – I tried to be glad that I was come home. I have always been glad before. . . . The great trial is when evening closes and night approaches. At that hour, we used to assemble in the dining-room – we used to talk.[2]

She confided in her publisher's reader, W. S. Williams:

Her quiet, Christian death did not rend my heart as Emily's stern, simple, undemonstrative end did. I let Anne go to God, and felt He had a right to her. I could hardly let Emily go. I wanted to hold her back then, and I want her

---

1 Apl. 5, 1849.
2 Letter to Ellen Nussey, June 23, 1849. Quoted by E. C. Gaskell: *The Life of Charlotte Brontë* (1957), ii, pp. 111–2.

back now. . . . Papa has now me only – the weakest, puniest, least promising of
his six children. Consumption has taken the whole five.[1]

And a little over a week later:

Anne had had enough of life such as it was – in her twenty-eighth year she
laid it down as a burden. I hardly know whether it is sadder to think of that
than of Emily turning her dying eyes reluctantly from the pleasant sun. . . .
Branwell – Emily – Anne are gone like dreams – gone as Maria and Elizabeth
went twenty years ago. One by one I have watched them fall asleep on my
arm – and closed their glazed eyes – I have seen them buried one by one –
and – thus far – God has upheld me.[2]

The last three all died within nine months, Branwell thirty-one and
Emily thirty. Charlotte lived six more years and died in childbirth,
almost thirty-nine.

II

J. R. GREEN was only twenty-six when his health gave way, working as
a dedicated priest in the derelict parish of Hoxton. A year's rest was
ordered, but this he could not afford. When he was nearly twenty-eight
he was appointed by Bishop Tait to St Philip's, Stepney, and during
an outbreak of cholera shortly after his appointment he was working,
like other clergy in the parishes, as 'officer of health, inspector of
nuisances, ambulance superintendent, as well as spiritual consoler and
burier of the dead'.[3] He was often seen going to infected houses
between two prostitutes who had volunteered to help him, such women
often being his best helpers. On one occasion he asked some burly
draymen to help him carry a dangerously ill man from an upper room.
On their refusal, the slight priest attempted the burden himself, falling
down a whole flight of stairs, his patient fortunately unharmed. An
attack of haemorrhage came a month after his marriage at thirty-nine,
when for some years he had been an historian full-time by reason of
his loss of faith. The deceptive nature of the disease was shown that
same year, for on a visit to Tennyson at Aldworth the poet told him:

1 June 4, 1849. *The Shakespeare Head Brontë: Their Lives, Friendships & Correspondence* (1932),
ii, pp. 337–8.
2 June 13, 1849: *ibid.*, ii, pp. 339–40.
3 *Letters of John Richard Green* ed. Leslie Stephen (1901), p. 55.

You're a jolly vivid man, and I'm glad to have known you; you're as vivid as lightning.[1]

When he was forty-three, his wife was told by Sir Andrew Clark that her husband could not live six weeks; he survived nearly two years. It is a story, writes Stephen, 'of a brave man's struggle to do his work to the last . . . and . . . he was cheered and supported throughout by a devotion worthy of its object'.[2] Mrs Green took down his rapid dictation until he could manage, for a short time, a table placed across his sofa. Once, because it was supposed to be harmful, he refused all drink for forty-eight hours. He was working two months before he died.

STEVENSON – 'thin-legged, thin-chested, slight unspeakably . . .'[3] – was sickly from a child. His cousin doubted if his weight had ever reached eight stone. From the age of thirty he began to suffer alarming lung haemorrhages. In a health resort at Royat, haemorrhage, sciatica and ophthalmia coincided and for a time he was both blind and speechless, for whenever there was a serious risk of haemorrhage his doctors forbad him to speak. His wife wrote to his mother from Nice:

The doctors says, 'Keep him alive till he is forty, and then although a winged bird, he may live to ninety.' But between now and forty he must live as though he were walking on eggs. . . .[4]

But Stevenson had no intention of behaving like a sick man. He told his stepson:

I do not ask for health, but I will go anywhere and live in any place where I can enjoy the ordinary existence of a human being.[5]

At Bournemouth, his wife found him in his bedroom with so much blood coming from his mouth that he could not speak. Even she seemed at a loss. He managed to pull towards him the bottle of ergotine and measuring out the dose, wrote on a pad always by: 'Don't be frightened; if this is death, it is an easy one.' During his last years in Samoa, he had but two to three slight haemorrhages that were cured within a very few days, and his favourite exercise was riding. One evening, after working on *Weir of Hermiston*, he was talking light-

1 *Ibid.*, p. 393.
2 *Ibid.*, pp. 392–3.
3 Henley's sonnet.
4 May 18, 1884.
5 Graham Balfour: *The Life of Robert Louis Stevenson* (1901), ii, p. 146.

heartedly to his wife on the verandah when he suddenly put both hands
to his head, crying 'What's that?' and then asking, 'Do I look strange?'
– he fell and died shortly after. He was forty-four.

FLECKER, at twenty-nine, corresponded with Basil Dean about
reducing the MS of *Hassan*, but they never met. Barrie was with Dean
throughout its long dress rehearsal at His Majesty's Theatre, and wrote
to him from his flat after midnight:

Tonight you will have such a night in the theatre as never again in your life.[1]

Flecker's masterpiece was played before one of the most distinguished
audiences ever assembled there, including most of the leading dramatists of the time, but Flecker had died eight years previously in a Swiss
sanatorium, thirty years of age.

When D. H. LAWRENCE, at twenty-eight, married Frieda Weekley,
already his lungs were affected. Some years later, when Secker had
refused *Lady Chatterley's Lover* and he decided to print it in Florence,
its sale was then forbidden and the pirating began; he wrote to Lady
Ottoline Morrell:

You ask me, do I feel very much? – and I do. . . . The hurts, and the bitterness
sink in, however much one may reject them with one's spirit. They sink in,
and there they lie, inside one, wasting one. . . . Then the microbes pounce.[2]

Long after Lawrence's death, Aldous Huxley told the Nolans that
Lawrence had died of chagrin, that TB was a disease of chagrin.[3]
Were Shelley and Byron nearer the truth after all? Keats too, rejected
'the hurts, and the bitterness . . . with . . . spirit' (as his closest circle
were quick to point out), but Lawrence and Huxley are saying *The
Quarterly* and *Blackwood's* still had power to hasten his death.

In the opinion of Robert Nichols, Frieda was 'worse than useless as
regards Lawrence's health'. In her absence, Huxley and his wife who
were close friends of Lawrence during his last three and a half years,
actually persuaded him to go to a doctor in Paris. Huxley wrote to his
own brother:

Then Frieda returned (from London). Lawrence felt himself reinforced. He
refused to go back to the doctor and set off with Frieda . . . to Majorca. . . .
He doesn't *want* to know how ill he is . . . and meanwhile just wanders about.[4]

1 Dean's *Introduction* to the Festival of Britain production (1951).
2 1928.
3 Sybille Bedford: *Aldous Huxley: A Biography* (1973–4), i, p. 215.
4 *Ibid.*, i, p. 213.

The Huxleys, present at the end, were staggered that Frieda did not even keep a cup for his exclusive use. Huxley told Nichols that on the Thursday or Friday before he died, Lawrence had said, 'Frieda, you have killed me.'[1] The dying man ordered Frieda's bed to be moved to across the foot of his own, so that he could see her. After great suffering he asked for the morphine. She was holding his ankle.

... it felt so full of life, all my days I shall hold his ankle in my hand.[2]

He was forty-four.

ORWELL's disease was called bronchiectasis and he also had 'a lesion in one lung which was never diagnosed when I was a boy'.[3] Cyril Connolly remembered him at St Wulfric's prep school:

Tall, pale, with ... flaccid cheeks ... one of those boys who seem born old.[4]

Refusing like Stevenson to think of himself as incurably ill, Orwell followed the pattern of Keats and Green by undergoing excessive physical strain. In his late twenties he lived in great poverty, for the purpose of copy. At thirty-six, he was classified as Class IV in World War II, and T. R. Fyvel on first meeting him then, noticed 'deep lines etched in grooves down his cheeks'.[5] At Canonbury Square, Susan Watson, his housekeeper and nurse for his adopted baby Richard, had not known he was a sick man until her shock of seeing him walk down the passage with blood running from his lips. When she asked if she should send for a doctor, he replied that doctors were no good – 'Ice and cold water in a cloth please, and put it on my head.'[6] He kept in bed for a fortnight, and reassured Susan that he would live until Richard reached thirteen.

He wrote most of *Nineteen Eighty-Four* at Barnhill, on the island of Jura. A year after his arrival, he sent to Mrs Miranda Christen (now Mrs Wood) who was renting his Canonbury flat, what she calls 'presumably the initial draft', for typing. The material came in instalments at fortnightly intervals, and was 'partly self-typed, partly handwritten'.[7] He then had to go into Hairmyres Hospital for seven months. His

1 *Ibid.*, i, p. 228.
2 Frieda Lawrence: *'Not I, But The Wind. . . .'* (1934), p. 295.
3 Letter to A. S. F. Gow, Apl. 13, 1946.
4 *Enemies of Promise* (1938), p. 211.
5 *George Orwell: a personal memoir* (1982), p. 99.
6 Bernard Crick: *George Orwell: A Life* (1980), p. 352.
7 *Nineteen Eighty-Four Facsmile of Extant MS* ed. Peter Davison (1984), Introduction, p. xi.

doctors removed his typewriter but were able to return it towards the end. On discharge, he had to spend half his day in bed, and got down to revising the first draft. He wrote to David Astor:

I have got so used to writing in bed that I think I prefer it, though of course it's awkward to type there.

He wrote to Anthony Powell:

It's awful to think I've been mucking about with this book since January of 1947 . . . but of course I was seriously ill for 7 or 8 months of the time. . . .[1]

Mrs Wood believes '. . . he destroyed the bulk of my typing when he was doing the final version'.[2] The task of typing out a clean draft within two or three weeks, hastened his death. Bill Dunn, who was labouring for neighbours but also helped in and out of Barnhill, said the room was thick with paraffin fumes from a leaky stove. Orwell had gone back to heavy smoking; four days before Christmas he told both Fred Warburg and David Astor: 'I am really very unwell indeed.'[3] After some months in Cotswold Sanatorium he died in University College Hospital, aged forty-seven.

Others who died from this same scourge are: George Herbert (nearly thirty-nine), Jane Austen (forty-one), Thomas Hood (almost forty-six), J.A. Symonds (fifty-two),[4] Llewelyn Powys (fifty-five). Katherine Mansfield, who may have contracted it from Lawrence,[5] died aged thirty-four. On his last Sunday, GEORGE HERBERT 'rose suddenly from his Bed or Couch' and, taking one of his instruments in his hand, sang his poem *The Sundayes of mans life.*[6]

1 Nov. 1948.
2 *Nineteen Eighty-Four Facsmile of Extant MS* ed. Peter Davison (1980), p. xii.
3 Bernard Crick: *George Orwell: A Life* (1980), pp. 382–3.
4 She is variously described as dying from Addison's Disease.
5 See Claire Tomalin: *Katherine Mansfield: A Secret Life* (1987), p. 163.
6 Izaak Walton: *The Life of George Herbert* (1670), p. 113.

CHAPTER THIRTEEN
Recovery From TB

SHELLEY, at twenty-two, was told by Dr Pemberton, Physician Extraordinary to the King and Fellow of the Royal Society, that abscesses had formed on his lungs and he should not expect to live very long. 'Suddenly,' says Mary, 'a complete change took place, and . . . every symptom of pulmonary disease vanished.'[1]

RUSKIN, as an undergraduate at Oxford, experienced 'one evening . . . about ten o'clock, a short tickling cough . . . preceded by a curious sensation in the throat, and followed by a curious taste in the mouth, which I presently perceived to be that of blood'. One of his doctors, Sir James Clarke, ordered him to winter in Italy and to postpone his Schools. He had another slight haemorrhage in Naples. Only his mother refused to recognize a mortal sign. Dr Joan Evans describes it as 'rather . . . the fundamental malaise of adolescence' than 'the phthisis' that the doctors feared. His affliction was to be of the mind and not the body. He lived to within a month of eighty-one.

WELLS spoke of his own case traversing 'all the accepted medical science of the eighties'. At twenty-one, he smashed his left kidney when one of the 'bigger louts' at Holt Academy fouled him at football.

. . . I . . . found myself staring at a chamber-pot half full of scarlet blood.

His lungs began 'imitating' his kidney and the handkerchief into which he coughed 'was streaked with blood'.[2] The Wrexham doctor pronounced him consumptive. On arrival at Up Park he was installed next to the room of his mother, who was housekeeper. There on his back, ice-bags clapped to his chest, he suffered his most serious haemorrhage. Nearly fifty years later, he could still remember 'the little tickle and trickle of blood in the lungs' that preceded another attack (just as

1 *The Poetical Works of Percy Bysshe Shelley* ed. Mrs Shelley (1839), i, p. 56.
2 *Experiment in Autobiography* (1934), i, pp. 296–9.

Ruskin describes), and the anxiety about coughing 'too soon' and 'too much'.[1]

After his first marriage he had a relapse 'hurrying down the slope of Villiers Street to Charing Cross Underground Station'. Once more his handkerchief was stained brightly scarlet after a fit of coughing. 'A grand attack' came on at three next morning. Again sponge-bags of ice had to be adjusted to his chest and there was a basin with 'blood and blood and more blood'.

I suppose I was extremely near death that night. ...[2]

When he was courting Jane at University Correspondence College, neither of them 'expected to live ten years'.[3] The 'degenerative process' at work in his lung covered a period of about five years and then ceased, leaving it scarred. But as late as 1900, at thirty-four, he was building his house at Sandgate 'specially facing . . . the sun, with bedrooms, living rooms, loggia and study all on one floor, because I believed I should presently have to live in a bath-chair. . . .' There were 'resistances that finally won'.

All the while an essential healthiness was doing its successful utmost to bring me back to physical normality.[4]

Although he became diabetic, he lived to a month short of his eightieth birthday, one year less than Ruskin.

At King's School, Canterbury, MAUGHAM's lungs were found to be affected (both mother and sister had died of TB), and he was placed for a term at a tutor's at Hyères. In World War I, he still remembered enough medicine to understand the haemorrhages he had been having.

An X-ray photograph showed clearly that I had tuberculosis of the lungs.[5]

He returned from his under-cover mission to Russia very ill indeed. The most eminent specialist he could find in London packed him off to a sanatorium in the North of Scotland, and for the next two years he lay in bed reading, reflecting, and studying the invalid life about him. The disease was diagnosed in ALAN SILLITOE after his Malaya

1 *Experiment in Autobiography* (1934), i, p. 301.
2 *Ibid.*, i, pp. 367–8.
3 *H. G. Wells in Love: Postscript to An Experiment in Autobiography* ed. G. P. Wells (1984), p. 27.
4 *Experiment in Autobiography*, i, pp. 299–300.
5 *The Summing Up* (1938), p. 204.

experience in World War II. During the eighteen months he spent in hospital he read widely and began to write. Wells similarly looked back to his four-month convalescence at Up Park as a time of 'mental opportunity'. Maugham on recovery went to China – and died a nonagenarian.

On coming back to England at nineteen, MASEFIELD was 'on the way to consumption' and an early death, but a kindly uncle, John Parker, 'screwed my guardians into advancing me a little of my father's money so that I could rest and get treated'.[1] Masefield was nearly eighty-nine when he died. MALCOLM MUGGERIDGE developed as a boy 'vague TB symptoms', and was boarded out for a while in the Cotswolds, at Sheepscombe.

I doubt if I was particularly ill, but I just remember coughing rather a lot and feeling inordinately tired. . . .[2]

Miss Lidiard, who had charge of him, took him with her when she used to visit the Colony, a Socialist commune, only a mile or so away. Eight-year-old A. J. P. TAYLOR, in his second year at The Downs School, was diagnosed as having a lung in danger of collapse.

My Buxton doctor . . . therefore recommended that I should spend all my life in the open air. . . . During school hours I sat outside the open classroom window, wrapped in rugs and with a foot muff.[3]

He also took his meals in the open with other boys taking turns to provide him with company. Both Muggeridge and Taylor lived to be octogenarians.

DE QUINCEY claimed that the regular use of opium had conquered all his 'pulmonary symptoms', which when he was between the ages of twenty-two and twenty-four had caused 'the physicians at Clifton and the Bristol Hotwells' virtually to regard him as 'a condemned subject'.[4]

1 Constance Babington Smith: *John Masefield: A Life* (1978), p. 52.
2 *Chronicles of Wasted Time* (1972–3), i, p. 39.
3 *A Personal History* (1983), p. 35.
4 *Confessions of an English Opium-Eater* (revised & enlarged ed., 1856), pp. 246–7. See also DYLAN THOMAS, next chapter.

CHAPTER FOURTEEN
Other Chest-Related Diseases

The following provide examples of what has been called the English condition on account of our climate. When CHARLES KINGSLEY was a seventeen-year-old student at King's College, London, it was discovered he had a seriously congested left lung. The application of some 'tartarised blistering stuff' left a large adhesion of the pleura, and a lung which was a liability in foggy weather.[1] In his forties at Cambridge, after a fit of coughing and expectoration, he was heard to exclaim that Satan had got into his lungs.

KENNETH GRAHAME, when nearly five, caught scarlet fever from his dying mother, which left a legacy of bronchial complaints. Stricken with pneumonia and empyema in the year of his marriage, he underwent surgery involving section of the ribs and nearly died. BARRIE, at thirty-four, arrived at Kirriemuir to tell his mother of his coming marriage, when he became gravely ill with pleurisy and pneumonia. His future wife and his sister's husband who was a doctor, came north and just managed to save him. This was the origin of the 'no ordinary cough' which Denis Mackail described as filling visitors to the Adelphi flat with 'sympathy and alarm'.[2] At the same age, KIPLING lay on the point of death with acute lobar pneumonia, only to be brought back by the exceptional skill of his doctors and his wife who nursed him with such devotion.

DOROTHY L. SAYERS at Godolphin caught measles in an acute form and developed pneumonia. Her mother and a specialist were called, but in his absence the school doctor administered a saline injection which saved her life. The illness 'left her looking like something thrown up by a famine, and almost completely bald':

---

1 Susan Chitty: *The Beast & the Monk: A Life of Charles Kingsley* (1974), p. 50.
2 *The Story of J.M.B.* (1941), p. 2.

For such a thing to happen to any eighteen-year-old girl could be traumatic. To one already sensitive about her height, her glasses and general clumsiness it was devastating.[1]

Throughout her life her hair would fall out at times of stress. She bought a wig, and after the trauma of giving birth to an illegitimate child she wore a silver one as seen in her portrait by John Gilroy.

ERIC GILL when he was fifty-four went down with bronchitis – making use of his time in bed writing lectures on Sculpture, Modern Building, and Art and Revolution. He never protected his nose when carving, and it was thought dust had affected his lungs. A few years later there was a recurrence from which he partially recovered to the extent of picking fruit at Pigotts. But he wrote to Austen Harrison: 'I wish I was well and strong as I used to be. I'm a crock at present.'[2] A few months later as he sat rolling a cigarette in his workshop he was told he had cancer of the lung, and a week after an operation he died aged fifty-eight. ELIOT in later years suffered from 'persistent bronchial trouble and emphysema exacerbated by his smoking'.[3] From middle life JOHNSON suffered from chronic bronchitis, together with emphysema.

By his sixties, asthma, and 'the little worries of life' had made inroads upon DESMOND MACCARTHY, but when Leonard Woolf sat with him and G. E. Moore at Rodmell he noticed that from time to time the years fell away and there was all the former 'charm of his character and conversation'.[4] Shortly before his death MacCarthy had attended a Memoir Club meeting and Woolf describes him in Gordon Square, suffering terribly, beaten by life.[5] A serious illness while at Eton, left a permanent abscess in RICHARD PORSON's lungs, causing him to be a frequent asthma sufferer. CHARLES LAMB was usually gasping for breath. Other asthma sufferers were JOHN LOCKE and J. M. SYNGE.

DYLAN THOMAS suffered serious lung haemorrhages as a little boy, which may have recurred in his late teens. They left him with weakened, scarred lungs and a tendency to bronchitis, in addition asthma, a condition aggravated by chain-smoking from the age of fifteen. Bad lungs caused his exemption from military service in World War II.

1 Janet Hitchman: *Such a Strange Lady: An introduction to Dorothy L. Sayers (1893–1957)* (1975), p. 29.
2 Aug. 20, 1940. Robert Speaight: *The Life of Eric Gill* (1966), p. 298.
3 Peter Ackroyd: *T. S. Eliot* (1984), p. 260.
4 *The Journey Not the Arrival Matters* (1969), p. 49.
5 *Beginning Again* (1964), p. 143.

CHAPTER FIFTEEN

Some Other Physical Conditions

A fter a severe attack of cramps and 'spasms' when he was forty-six,
THACKERAY was asked if he had taken the best medical advice.
He said that he had, 'but what is the use of advice if you don't
follow it?'

They tell me not to drink, and I *do* drink. . . . They tell me not to eat, and I
do eat.[1]

His lack of control was bound up with his loneliness following his
wife's mental deterioration. He had developed a weight of fifteen stone,
but prolonged illness rendered him thin at fifty.

HARDY, at forty, suffered from an internal bleeding. To save an
operation, since *A Laodicean* was unfinished and running in *Harper's*
Magazine, he lay on his back for nearly five months with his body
sloping down from feet to head. In this unnatural position – 'often in
pain and perturbation of spirit'[2] – he dictated to his wife most of the
last five books of his novel.

Throughout SHAW's long life he enjoyed exceptional vitality. His
friend, St John Ervine, remarked:

His appearance was impressive: long and lean – over six foot – slim and
well-knit. It was part of his pride to look well, and when he walked down a
street his strides were long. He looked fit even when he wasn't. . . .[3]

At twenty-five (and vaccinated), he had fallen victim to smallpox in the
epidemic of 1881, and this was the reason for his famous red beard.
He once developed a hydrocele, 'a very inconvenient sort of localized
dropsy'.[4] Ervine said:

---

1 *The Letters & Private Papers of William Makepeace Thackeray* ed. Gordon N. Ray (1945–
6), iv, p. 455.
2 F. E. Halliday: *Thomas Hardy: His Life & Work* (1972), pp. 90–91.
3 'An Appreciation of George Bernard Shaw': BBC broadcast, Nov. 2, 1950.
4 *The Works of Bernard Shaw* (1930–1), xxii, p. 30.

There was a time just before the war when he had pernicious anaemia, and that was the only time I saw him under the weather.[1]

Shaw, then eighty-one, had been treated by inoculations of liver extract; he claimed the illness 'would have killed anyone twenty years younger'. RUPERT BROOKE, at Cambridge, did not have enough antibodies to deal with any small cut or wound. He died of septicaemia at twenty-seven, on a French hospital ship in the Aegean, during the first year of World War I. ELIOT's blood was the thinnest a doctor had ever tested. Until he was fifty-nine when he had an operation, he wore a truss for a congenital double hernia. 'No one,' writes Peter Ackroyd, 'has speculated on the physiological origins of his need for order and control.'[2]

Eliot was also a victim of tachycardia. Alan Jenkins points out that when STEPHEN POTTER wrote Counter Crocked Ankle Play, he was in fact a sufferer from 'paroxysmal tachycardia'.[3]

NOVICE GAMESMAN: Something wrong?
FRITH-MORTEROY (*rubs his chest with his knuckles*): No. No. It's only the old pump.
N.G.: Pump?
F.-M.: Yes. The ancient ticker. . . . I'm supposed not to be using it full out at the moment. . . .
N.G.: Good Lord.[4]

C. S. LEWIS suffered urinary troubles from his thirties.

1 Radio broadcast, *cit.*
2 *T. S. Eliot* (1984), p. 260.
3 *Stephen Potter: Inventor of Gamesmanship* (N.D.), p. 155.
4 *The Theory & Practice of Gamesmanship or The Art of Winning Games Without Actually Cheating* (1947), pp. 38, 40.

CHAPTER SIXTEEN

The Sphynx and Circe of Medicine[1]

The rheumatic fever or endocarditis from which BURNS died at thirty-seven, had sown its seeds early. In his infancy the roof of the family cottage blew off, and mother and child had to be carried through an Atlantic gale to shelter with a neighbour. As a boy of thirteen, on his father's farm at Mount Oliphant, he was submitted to the exposure and strain of a man's work at the plough. Then, at twenty-eight, he sprained his ankle in Edinburgh, and 'with a bruised limb extended on a cushion' was 'under the care of a surgeon'. The following year he wrote: 'I fear my knee will never be entirely well.' W. R. Bett surmises that the sprain had localized the rheumatic infection in his knee, from which it spread to other parts of his body.

WILLIAM MORRIS was wholly crippled for some time, when he was thirty-one, from a severe attack of rheumatic fever brought on by a chill which he caught while travelling the daily ten miles between his works in Red Lion Square and his Red House at Upton. Another such sufferer was seventeen-year-old STEPHEN SPENDER, soon after his father's death; he lay almost completely paralysed in both legs for some weeks.

I used to lie in bed looking out of my window up the hill . . . and wondering how people walked, and still more why those who were able to do so were not everlastingly grateful simply that they could put one foot in front of the other.[2]

JOYCE, at twenty-five, had to go into a Trieste hospital for a month, suffering from the same complaint. Roaming the pampas in Argentina, W. H. HUDSON contracted typhus and rheumatic fever which left him weakened.

Johnson records a statement by MILTON at the time he was working

---

1 Metaphors used by W. R. Bett to describe the mysterious disease of rheumatic fever and the enigma of rheumatism itself: *The Infirmities of Genius* (1952), p. 146.
2 *World Within World* (1951), p. 20.

on *Paradise Lost* 'that if it were not for the gout, his blindness would be tolerable'.

In the intervals of his pain, being made unable to use the common exercises, he used to swing in a chair, and sometimes played upon an organ.[1]

GRAY, never robust, had inherited gout from his parents, but kept attacks under control by 'great temperance ... particularly in ... his drinking'.[2] One of the symptoms in middle life was lethargy. WILKIE COLLINS suffered most of his adult life from rheumatic gout. CONRAD contracted the same complaint after the voyage up the Congo in his thirties had nearly killed him. His wife, Jessie, observed that his gout was always brought on by stress. Later on in his life, he was often in pain at his desk, from rheumatism which had become chronic. SMOL-LETT was another victim of chronic rheumatism, but he also had pain from a neglected ulcer.

1 *The Lives of the English Poets* (Dublin ed. 1779–81), i, p. 177.
2 *The Poems of Mr. Gray, prefixed by Memoirs of his Life* by W. Mason (1775), p. 399.

CHAPTER SEVENTEEN
Calculi

PEPYS, when he was twenty-five, survived the then perilous operation of being 'cut of the stone at Mrs Turner's in Salisbury
Court, and did resolve while I live to keep it a festival'.[1] Every
anniversary he thanked God for deliverance from 'my old pain'.[2] He
celebrated with a dinner, and intended 'for ever to have Mrs. Turner
and her company with me . . . as I did the last year at my house'.[3]
DEFOE underwent the operation as an old man:

> . . . the very apparatus is enough to chill the blood, and sink a man's soul
> within him.[4]

SCOTT, from the age of fifty-four, suffered from violent fits of cramp
in the stomach caused by undiagnosed gall-stones. When he was dictating *The Bride of Lammermoor* his suffering made itself heard every time
he paused, so much so that his amanuensis, William Laidlaw, begged
him to put the work aside.

> Nay, Willie, only see that the doors are fast. I would fain keep all the cry as
> well as all the wool to ourselves; but as to giving over work, that can only be
> when I am in woollen.[5]

Claire Tomalin suggests that SHELLEY's acute spasmodic pain of the
Italian years may have been due to kidney stones.[6] At the time he
wrote *Stanzas, Written in Dejection, Near Naples*, Mary Shelley records
that 'constant and poignant suffering exhausted him'.[7] After an absence
of nearly seven years, Medwin at Pisa immediately recognised the
'emaciated, and somewhat bent' figure, but noticed that his hair 'was

1 *Diary*: March 26, 1660.
2 *Ibid.*, March 26, 1664.
3 *Ibid.*, March 26, 1660.
4 See William Lee: *Daniel Defoe: his life, & recently discovered writings* (1869), iii, p. 430.
5 J. G. Lockhart: *Memoirs of the Life of Sir Walter Scott, Bart.* (1837-8), iv, pp. 257-8.
6 *Shelley & his World* (1980), p. 82.
7 *The Poetical Works of Percy Bysshe Shelley* ed. Mrs. Shelley (1839), ii, p. 357.

partially interspersed with grey'[1] although Shelley was only twenty-eight. SHAW, another non-wine-bibbing vegetarian, recalled a racking stone in the kidney – 'probably inherited from a long line of alcoholic ancestors'. MEREDITH, at sixty-four, had his first of three operations for stone in the bladder.

DICKENS wore a wide flannel belt to protect a weak left kidney. From boyhood he was tormented by 'spasmodic attacks', which may have been caused by a stone in the kidney passage. His father died after an operation to remove stones in the bladder.

1 Thomas Medwin: *The Life of Percy Bysshe Shelley* (1847), ii, p. 2.

CHAPTER EIGHTEEN

Organic Stress

The autopsy on COLERIDGE showed traces of a progressive disease going back at least to just before he was twenty-three. A greatly enlarged heart and liver, also cysts on his lungs, may well have contributed to his procrastination even if he had not been addicted to opium. They may explain some of the neurotic and hypochondriac features in the letter which, at twenty-four, he wrote to his friend and benefactor, Thomas Poole:

. . . I am very unwell. On Wednesday night I was seized with an intolerable pain from my right eye, cheek, jaw, and that side of the throat. I was nearly frantic, and ran about the house naked, endeavouring by every means to excite sensations in different parts of my body, and so to weaken the enemy by creating diversion. It continued from one in the morning till half past five, and left me pale and fainting. It came on fitfully, but not so violently, several times on Thursday, and began severer threats towards night; but I took between sixty and seventy drops of laudanum. . . . But *this morning* (Saturday) he returned in full force. . . . Giant-fiend of a hundred hands, with a shower of arrowy death-pangs he transpierced me, and then he became a wolf, and lay a-gnawing at my bones! I am not mad . . . but in sober sadness I have suffered this day more bodily pain than I had before a conception of. . . . My medical attendant decides it to be altogether nervous. . . . I take twenty-five drops of laudanum every five hours. . . .[1]

By the time he was forty-two, he had long been in the habit of taking two quarts of laudanum a week, and had once taken a quart in twenty-four hours.[2] A truer estimate of his industry, taking into account sixty surviving Notebooks, is now being made.

After LYTTON STRACHEY had left Cambridge, he wrote that the family doctor 'says . . . there is not sufficient room in my torso for my lungs, liver and lights, so that they . . . press . . . upon the heart'.[3] At twenty-nine, he went to a health sanatorium near Stockholm, which

---

1 Dated Nov. 5, 1796.
2 Leslie Stephen: *D.N.B.*
3 Michael Holroyd: *Lytton Strachey: A Critical Biography* (1967–8), i, p. 288.

had a hall of semi-mechanised apparatuses looking 'exactly like a torture chamber'[1] – and the following year he went again, this time often being subjected to a stomach pump.

1 *Ibid.*, i, p. 446.

Headaches and Pains

WORDSWORTH during his early thirties suffered headaches so prostrating that, combined with the pain in his chest and side, and above all sleeplessness, he feared he would not be able to continue his poetic vocation. POPE thought he could cure his own headaches by drinking inordinate quantities of coffee. When he stayed from home, he was the bane of servants for he demanded coffee throughout the night.

THACKERAY's headaches at Charterhouse and Cambridge were so severe that leeches were applied – 'for the purpose of banishing that troublesome head ache which had there taken up its quarters (of course its "head" quarters)'.[1] He may have been a migraine sufferer like Dodgson and Kipling. About once a month until he was seventy, SHAW had 'a blinding and severe headache' which lasted the whole day. He told St John Ervine he could not get rid of it 'in the normal manner'. BARRIE's headaches had begun at university.

When H. V. MORTON was thirty, he believed he was dying of spinal meningitis. He climbed a hill overlooking Jerusalem and, turning as accurately as he could in the direction of England, 'gave way to such a wave of home-sickness that almost shames me now. . . .'

I took a vow that if my pain in the neck did not end for ever on the windy hills of Palestine I would go home in search of England. I would go through the lanes of England, and I would lean over English bridges and lie on English grass watching an English sky.[2]

This was the origin of his *Search* series. ERIC GILL feared his own life in some danger when, at forty-eight, he suffered two days' intense headache; a neurologist who examined him ascribed it to benign meningitis.

---

1 Letter to Mother, May 28, 1829.
2 *In Search of England* (1927), pp. 1–2.

CHAPTER TWENTY

'Whatever you do, Ronnie, avoid piles.'

aemorrhoids were one of the many more common ailments of POPE, exacerbated by his condition. When DICKENS was twenty-nine, a few months before his first American tour, he had to undergo a painful operation without relief of anaesthetics.

I laboured under the complaint called Fistula, the consequence of too much sitting at my desk.

FRANCIS KILVERT suffered 'a painful attack of emerods' in the last year of his short life.[1]

LYTTON STRACHEY, when he appeared before the Hampstead Tribunal as a Conscientious Objector in World War I, was also a sufferer. Philip Morrell solemnly passed the bearded man a light blue air cushion, which he inflated before sitting himself cautiously and spreading a rug about his knees. When they asked the favourite chestnut: 'What would you do if you saw a German soldier attempting to rape your sister?' – he looked at Elinor, at Marjorie, at Pernel, who were all lined up with his brothers behind, and replied with his characteristic squeak: 'I should try and interpose my own body.'[2]

At forty-three, EVELYN WAUGH had a painful operation for the same complaint, although he claimed to Christopher Sykes that it was done for 'perfectionism' and not from immediate necessity.[3] ELIOT was operated on, at sixty-two, at the London Clinic. He told Ronald Duncan: 'Whatever you do, Ronnie, avoid piles.'[4] PRIESTLEY underwent the operation at seventy-eight. He told his daughter it was not a major one, 'though I cannot pretend I am looking forward to it'.[5] A sufferer from eczema, diarrhoea, vomiting and sore eyes, GERARD MANLEY HOPKINS had an operation for piles.

1 *Diary*, Nov. 14, 1878.
2 Michael Holroyd: *Lytton Strachey: A Critical Biography* (1967–8), ii, pp. 178–9.
3 Christopher Sykes: *Evelyn Waugh: A Biography* (1975), pp. 303–4.
4 Peter Ackroyd: *T. S. Eliot* (1984), p. 304.
5 To Mary Priestley: Nov. 10, 1972. Quoted by Vincent Brome: *J. B. Priestley* (1988), p. 461.

349

CHAPTER TWENTY-ONE
Pursued by a Demon

F rom the age of five or six EDWARD LEAR had epileptic attacks,
sometimes several in twenty-four hours, and he feared one day
their severity might leave him paralysed or insane. He spoke of
himself as 'pursued by a Demon'. Still after the age of forty they came,
as many as twenty a month, which he marked with little crosses in his
diary. Yet all through his life nobody outside his family seems to have
known. At sixty-seven, he wrote:

... it is wonderful that these fits have never been discovered – except that
partly apprehending them beforehand, I go to my room.[1]

Byron and William Morris were epileptic.[2] R. D. BLACKMORE's epileptic fits caused him to give up the Law. SWINBURNE, at twenty-six,
had an epileptiform fit in Whistler's studio, and five years later had to
be carried out of the British Museum Reading Room – having 'fainted
right out' and cut his head. By then it may have been inebriation –
probably alcoholic epilepsy.

GRAHAM GREENE was diagnosed an epileptic on the strength of intermittent fainting attacks as a boy and a young man. He writes:

With the hindsight of forty years, free from any recurrence, I don't believe
it, but I believed it then.[3]

1 Vivien Noakes: *Edward Lear: The Life of a Wanderer* (1968), pp. 20, 134, 321 (note 21).
2 Shaw called Morris's attacks 'eclampsia'.
3 *A Sort of Life* (1971), p. 188.

CHAPTER TWENTY-TWO
The Adventure of Living[1]

Fifteen-year-old WINIFRED HOLTBY, a boarder at Queen Margaret's School, Scarborough, suffered an acute attack of scarlet fever with complications – a potential sowing of Bright's disease if after-effects go unchecked. When she was thirty-one, the strain and fatigue of two-years' travelling each weekend to Cottingham to help nurse her father, then coming back on Mondays to London to write the leader and notes for *Time and Tide*, contributed to the early onset of her illness. The following year, she was afflicted with her first severe headache due to high blood pressure, and the following spring she had her first attack.

Next year she consulted Dr Obermer, an Austrian biochemist[2] who, for a ludicrous fee ('because, he said, he learnt so much from her case'), kept her under observation for the rest of her short life. She was in a nursing home at Earl's Court for several weeks, until he could establish a routine of treatment that would enable her still to write. Unknown to her intimate friend Vera Brittain, who had taken her there, instead of going straight to bed she rang up H. G. Wells and told him her days were numbered and that she had always wanted to meet him. She went to his flat in the Outer Circle, Regent's Park, and they spoke tête-à-tête for two hours.

Then, at thirty-six, she caught mumps from the Brittains' small son John, and the children's doctor was perturbed by her blood pressure. That summer she walked over the Malvern Hills with the Shaws, but there was a growing inability of the drug padutin to support her. She crossed over to Wimereux to bring news in person to Vera of her father's death, and became very ill, but rallied on the return crossing

---

1 The title of Winifred Holtby's last article before going into a nursing home for the final time.
2 Variously described as a 'German-Austrian specialist in arterial diseases': *Chronicle of Friendship: Vera Brittain's Diary of the Thirties 1932–1939* ed. Alan Bishop (1986), p. 372: note to p. 34.

with her friend. She still looked after the Brittains' children as their second mother.

That September, Dr Obermer ordered her into a Devonshire Street nursing home. Vera Brittain repeated the now 'sadly familiar' process of packing her friend's case and helping her to dress. While Vera paid the driver of their taxi, Winifred 'walked erect up the steps'[1] and rang the bell. For the first few days she endeavoured to lead a normal life with a secretary, but then relapsed into coma. A course of injections restored her to consciousness, and she said to her friend: '. . . I was beginning to get frightened. . . . I wanted St John[2]. . . . He knows what it's like when pain frightens you. . . .'[3] At the end of the week a merciful injection sent her to sleep. Earlier in the day, she had twice begged Vera to come back at night, when it would be quiet, '. . . and straighten out the tangles in my mind'.[4] She never knew that her friend came as she had promised.

MARY WEBB while still young contracted Graves' disease. J. M. SYNGE was only twenty-six when he showed first signs of Hodgkin's disease; an enlarged gland was removed from the side of his neck. Similar swellings recurred and he died a month before his thirty-eighth birthday.

1 Vera Brittain: *Testament of Friendship: The Story of Winifred Holtby* (1940), p. 430.
2 St John Ervine.
3 *Testament of Friendship*, p. 433.
4 *Ibid.*, p. 436.

CHAPTER TWENTY-THREE

The Menace of Cancer

Some thirty years before the use of crude anaesthetics, MME. D'ARBLAY[1] underwent a mastectomy at fifty-nine in Paris. Her journal contents itself with the single epithet – 'a dreadful operation'.[2] Her niece, who edited the journals, tells us that so courageously did she bear this horrendous ordeal, and such was her concern for her husband and those about her, that her French friends united in calling her 'L'Ange'.[3]

She not only survived but that same year she brought her seventeen-year-old son back to England to escape conscription. Within two years she returned to Paris to be with her husband but, on Napoleon's escape from Elba, General D'Arblay was with the guard protecting the Bourbon king. The intrepid woman found herself in Brussels before and after Waterloo.

We were all at work more or less in making lint. For me, I was about amongst the wounded half the day, the *British*, *s'entend!*[4]

When she heard that her husband had received 'a furious kick from a wild horse',[5] she crossed parts of the Rhineland to Trèves. Back in England, writing up her journals and editing her father's *Memoirs*, she was given another name (was it by Sir Walter Scott who visited her?): 'she lived to be a classic'.[6] She survived 'the stiletto of a surgeon' twenty-eight years.

RONALD KNOX thought he was ailing from the effects of an operation when he went, in the care of Evelyn Waugh and his wife, to a hotel in Torquay. After a week, he spent another one with Evelyn in a hotel

---

1 Née Fanny Burney.
2 *Diary & Letters of Madame D'Arblay* ed. by her Niece (1842–6), vi, p. 355. 1812.
3 *Ibid.*, vi, p. 347.
4 *Ibid.*, vii, p. 178. 1815.
5 *Ibid.*, vii, p. 211. 1815.
6 *Ibid.*, vii, p. 384.

at Sidmouth, before staying a fortnight at Combe Florey. In Evelyn's library he prepared his Romanes lecture *On English Translation*.[1] He then learned he had cancer of the liver. The following month, in the Sheldonian, he managed by sitting down to read his swan-song. He had come to Oxford as scholar half a century ago, and had served as fellow and lecturer, Anglican chaplain to Trinity, and Roman Catholic chaplain to the university. Harold Macmillan, now hearing that his old friend was coming to London for a second opinion, invited him to Number Ten, and there Sir Horace Evans confirmed that nothing could be done. Knox died two months later. When LYTTON STRACHEY died after three final months of suffering, ulcerated colitis had been diagnosed but a post-mortem revealed cancer of the stomach. He was fifty-one.

RATTIGAN said of the leukaemia scare he was given: 'It started me thinking of dying and honestly I wasn't frightened.' He went out to Bermuda. Eighteen months before he died, cancer was diagnosed by a local doctor. He flew over to watch rehearsals of his *Cause Célèbre* and to attend the first night. When he was told his cancer must shortly be fatal, he moved himself out of a London hospital room into a gilded suite at Claridge's.

When this happens, you suddenly stop counting the cost of anything. So in the time that is left I shall work harder. . . . But I get tired, so very tired.[2]

Five days before ALDOUS HUXLEY died, malignancies in head and neck, he taught himself to compose using a tape-recorder, although he was very hoarse. At the end, on his request, he was inoculated with LSD.

ANGELA CARTER lost her fight at fifty-one, and Salman Rushdie paid tribute to a 'true wizard' who succeeded in 'cutting Death down to size'.

1 *Literary Distractions* (1958), pp. 36–58.
2 Harold Hobson: 'The playwright who always hid his pain': *The Sunday Times*, Dec. 4, 1977.

CHAPTER TWENTY-FOUR
Dogged by Suffering

S WIFT, at fifty-four, told Archbishop King:

I row after health like a waterman, and ride after it like a postboy, and find little success.[1]

STEVENSON wrote to Meredith from Samoa:

For fourteen years I have not had a day's real health. I have wakened sick and gone to bed weary....[2]

Lewis Hind remembered the way HENLEY 'manoeuvred his big maimed body, ever seeking a way to rest it, kneeling on a chair, with his hands clutching the rail, crouching this way and that way, and talking, always talking'.[3] From the age of fifty to the end of his life, KIPLING suffered with duodenal ulcers. His daughter said:

He suffered frightful and incessant pain over a very long period. . . . The most he ever said, when doubled up in agony, was: 'Just leave me alone; I'll be all right soon.'

Lord Birkenhead paid tribute 'to the creative vitality and courage of this man that . . . in the midst of this prolonged misery and constant dread of cancer', he continued to maintain his output.[4] H. E. BATES suffered abdominal pains from 'something known as a duodenal diverticulum'. Before a successful operation at forty-one, he speaks of his pain becoming 'a scourge' torturing him by day, and keeping him 'agonisingly awake at night'.[5]

BENNETT suffered not only from a terrible stammer but for all his writing life from hypochondria, headaches, neuralgia, insomnia, a sluggish liver, his kidneys, and indigestion. Leonard Woolf had the

1 1721.
2 1893.
3 *Authors and I* (1921), p. 134.
4 *Rudyard Kipling* (1978), p. 322.
5 *The World in Ripeness: An Autobiography* iii (1972), pp. 38, 60.

impression that his friend LYTTON STRACHEY 'was hardly ever completely well':

One felt that he always had to husband his bodily forces in the service of his mind. . . .[1]

EVELYN WAUGH was spoken of by a friend as 'seldom completely well'; he 'suffered permanently and terribly from insomnia'[2] which he first recorded at twenty-one, and the mental depression that accompanies it.

At the age of twenty-two, following her brief love affair with Floryan Sobieniowski, KATHERINE MANSFIELD endured a 'terrible operation' and for the rest of her short life was 'never quite well'. She suffered from gonorrhoeal arthritis, heart trouble, and later, repeated attacks of pleurisy so-called. When she was twenty-nine, she told Ida Baker:

You see I am never one single hour without pain. If it's not my lungs it is (far more painful) my back. And then my legs *ache*. . . .[3]

THACKERAY's 'old enemy' was a urethral stricture after an early venereal infection had been cured. Throughout his life he complained of his 'hydraulics' and needed periodic and painful instrumentation.

HENRY JAMES at eighteen injured his back while assisting volunteers to put out a stable fire on the outbreak of the American Civil War. When he was fifty-six, he wrote to his friend Howard Sturgis:

. . . if you have a Back, for heaven's sake take care of it. . . . I did bad damage . . . to mine. . . . I've been saddled with it for life, and . . . verily write *with* it.

A notebook entry recalls 'suffering tortures from my damnable state of health':

Some of my doses of pain were very heavy; very weary were some of my months and years.[4]

HARRIET MARTINEAU's early life was dogged by ill health (as well as by poverty). In addition to her deafness, she suffered from heart disease and other complaints. At thirty-seven, a serious illness lasted five years. CATHERINE COOKSON inherited a crippling vascular disorder remain-

1 *Sowing* (1960), p. 123.
2 Frances Donaldson: *Evelyn Waugh: Portrait of a Country Neighbour* (1967), pp. xiii, 55.
3 Ida Baker: *Katherine Mansfield: The Memories of L.M.* (1971), p. 122.
4 Leon Edel: *Henry James: A Biography* (1953–72), i, pp. 184–5.

ing with her all her life. In maturity she suffered a nervous breakdown lasting ten years and leaving its legacy. The prestigious Whitbread Book of the Year Prize for 1987 was won by twenty-two-year-old CHRISTOPHER NOLAN, who suffers from cerebral palsy. He communicates by eye language and a unicorn-pointer which, strapped to his forehead, strikes the typewriter keys when his chin is cradled by his mother.

CHAPTER TWENTY-FIVE
Spiritual Affliction or Defect

I

Perhaps by 'spiritual affliction or defect' Beerbohm meant Tennyson's 'black moods', or Barrie's 'long silences', or Arnold saying to Clough: 'I am past thirty, and three parts iced over,' and to his favourite sister: 'I am fragments.' Or Huxley who, according to his tutor, was *impaired* by three devastating blows – his mother's early death when he was fourteen, the threat of blindness two years later, then, when Aldous was twenty, his brother Trev hanging himself from a tree.

Hardy told Sidney Lee that he had 'always felt a tragic atmosphere encircled LESLIE STEPHEN's history and was suggested in some indefinable way by his presence'.[1] While RADCLYFFE HALL was writing *The Master of the House*, she led a life of austerity in keeping with a condition of her skin which caused both her and her companion to believe that, for a time, she was privileged to bear the stigmata.

TENNYSON was surrounded by people thinking of his happiness and doing their utmost to help him. Yet the overriding impression of his grandson was of a shy man very much living alone and turned in upon himself.[2] BORROW in his books conveys an image of one like Boswell consorting readily with any he might meet on his travels. But in his life this social ease was restricted, except for his wife and daughter, to gipsies and other outcasts and wanderers. Watts-Dunton, who himself had gone with the gipsies, was introduced by Dr Gordon Hake when Borrow was 'considerably advanced in years'. At first the reception was off-putting.

My own shyness had been long before fingered off by the rough handling of the world, but his retained all the bloom of youth, and a terrible barrier it was.[3]

1 Nov. 22, 1906.
2 'Tennyson: Portrait of a Poet', Study Record, BBC, RESR 12.
3 *Old Familiar Friends* (1916), p. 45.

Then, knowing that Borrow was very learned 'in the obscure English pamphlet literature of the last century', Watts-Dunton to the bewilderment of Dr Hake mentioned Ambrose Gwinett. Borrow said, 'You know that pamphlet about Ambrose Gwinett?'

'Know it?' said I, in a hurt tone as though he asked me if I knew 'Macbeth'; 'of course I know Ambrose Gwinett, Mr Borrow, don't you?'

After some further discussion, 'Hake!' he cried, 'your friend knows everything' – and to himself he murmured, 'Wonderful man! Knows Ambrose Gwinett!'[1] Watts-Dunton doubted whether any one got to understand Borrow better than he did, or realise 'more fully . . . how lovable was his nature, with all his singularities'.[2] GRAHAM GREENE confessed himself to be shy.

St John Ervine maintained that SHAW 'was a very shy man'.

People always laugh when I tell them that, but all those tricks and platform conceits were devices a shy man uses when he wishes to assert himself. . . . I mention this shyness because it explains what he sometimes said or did, which made him seem callous and even cruel when he was only clumsy from shyness.

Ervine spoke of Shaw as 'a solitary-minded man who had nearly all he wanted in his own mind, but who won and kept the affection of many dissimilar minds'. He said that Shaw 'would do more for his friends than his friends were prepared to do for themselves'.[3] Leonard Woolf, admitting Shaw 'was always extremely nice to Virginia and me', added that 'personally he was almost the most impersonal person I have ever known'.

If one met him anywhere, he would come up and greet one with what seemed to be warmth and pleasure, and he would start straight away with a fountain of words scintillating with wit and humour . . . but if you happened to look into that slightly fishy, ice-blue eye of his. . . . It was not looking at you . . . it was looking . . . into a distant world . . . inhabited entirely by G.B.S. . . .[4]

There was an occasion when Shaw met them on the way to the Flower Walk in Kensington Gardens, one fine Sunday afternoon. He had just come back from a voyage round the world[5] in a luxury liner, and stood for a quarter of an hour with arms folded – 'his beard wagging as he

1 *Ibid.*, pp. 47–48.
2 *Ibid.*, p. 26.
3 'An Appreciation of George Bernard Shaw': BBC broadcast, Nov. 2, 1950.
4 *Beginning Again* (1964), p. 120.
5 1933.

talked'. When the Woolfs turned to go, they found themselves the centre of a circle of fifteen or twenty people who had recognised Shaw and stopped to listen. It struck Woolf then, the 'oration' might just as well have been addressed to the strangers.[1] Woolf coined a phrase 'the Shavian pyrotechnical monologue'.[2]

MAUGHAM declared himself openly:

I do not think I have ever addressed someone I did not know in a railway carriage or spoken to a fellow passenger on board ship unless he first spoke to me.[3]

Again:

I do not much like being touched and I have always to make a slight effort over myself not to draw away when someone links his arm in mine.[4]

ELIOT described himself afflicted all his life by 'aboulie', an emotional condition defined by Ackroyd as 'a withdrawal into negative coldness'.[5] T. E. LAWRENCE was ashamed 'of my solitary unlikeness which made me no companion'.[6] He shared with Hardy and Maugham a Peter-Pan aversion to being touched.

In officers' messes ... I've lived about as merrily as the last-hooked fish choking out its life in a boat-load of trippers.[7]

After he had resigned from the Colonial Office where he worked with Churchill, and from his research fellowship on completing *Seven Pillars of Wisdom* at All Souls, he joined the ranks of the RAF as John Hume Ross. The complicated and tortured man tried to explain to Robert Graves:

It was a necessary step forced on me ... by a despairing hope that I'd find myself on common ground with men: by a little wish to make myself a little more human than I had become ... by an itch to make myself ordinary in a mob of likes. ... It's going to be a brain-sleep, and I'll come out of it less odd than I went in: or at least less odd in other men's eyes.[8]

Geoffrey Gorer said that ORWELL, whom he had known in his book-

1 *Beginning Again* (1964), p. 122.
2 *Ibid.*, p. 125.
3 *The Summing Up* (1938), p. 48.
4 *Ibid.*, p. 80.
5 *T. S. Eliot* (1984), p. 115.
6 *Seven Pillars of Wisdom* (Trade edition 1935), p. 562.
7 *The Mint: A day-book of the RAF Depot between August and December 1922 with later notes* by 352087 A/c Ross (1955), p. 150.
8 Letter: Nov. 12, 1922.

shop days, was a very lonely man until he met Eileen. Even inanimate objects conspired against him. His gas stove would always be going wrong, or his radio breaking down.

I would have said he was an unhappy man. . . . He was fairly well convinced that nobody would like him, which made him prickly.[1]

II

Some post-dated their age. BYRON told Lady Blessington: 'Though only thirty-six, I feel sixty in mind.'[2] SHELLEY, the day before he drowned, told Mrs Hunt: 'If I die to-morrow, I have lived to be older than my father; I am ninety years of age.' CHARLES KINGSLEY, at twenty-two, wrote to his mother: 'I shall be an old man before I am forty. . . .' ELIOT, in his early forties, wrote of himself in *Ash Wednesday*:

(Why should the agèd eagle stretch its wings?)

STEVENSON confided to Lloyd Osbourne that he had a 'tortured soul' and 'of moments when he had longed for death'.[3] The daughter of the Master of Trinity sometimes met A. E. HOUSMAN returning from one of his long afternoon walks at Cambridge.

How intensely he had suffered might be guessed by anyone who saw his face. . . . Perhaps he had recalled some of his own wretchedness as he walked alone and the sadness in his face was as poignant as on the face of a man experiencing the bitterness of sorrow for the first time.[4]

The price exacted of the genius of BEATRICE WEBB and that of VIRGINIA WOOLF was not physical, for both had Garbo's beauty of bone structure. Malcolm Muggeridge writes of his aunt by marriage:

The thing that struck me at once was her beauty. . . . She was also, as I sensed, tragic. . . .

He connected her affliction with restless walks along the Embankment and her prayers in a silent Westminster Abbey. When he spent a

1 'The Road to the Left': BBC TV *Omnibus* programme, 1970.
2 Marguerite Gardiner, Countess of Blessingham: *Conversations with Lord Byron* (1834), p. 70.
3 'An Intimate Portrait of R L S by His Stepson, Lloyd Osbourne': *Scribner's Magazine*, Feb. 1924, p. 168.
4 Richard Perceval Graves: *A. E. Housman: The Scholar-Poet* (1979), pp. 242–3.

weekend at Passfield Corner, he would see Beatrice Webb before breakfast roaming about the garden – 'in the style of a tigress pacing up and down its cage'.[1] A friend of WILLIAM MORRIS likened him, at thirty-seven, to 'a caged lion' pacing up and down the room.[2]

Susan Watson remembered ORWELL's nightmares in the Canonbury flat, and sometimes his screaming in sleep. He was 'not easy to live with at all'.[3]

1 *Chronicles of Wasted Time* (1972–3), i, pp. 147–8.
2 J. W. Mackail: *The Life of William Morris* (1899), i, p. 215.
3 Bernard Crick: *George Orwell: A Life* (1980), *op. cit.*, pp. 347–8.

CHAPTER TWENTY-SIX

Strangeness of Manner and Personality

I

Masefield, on meeting J. M. SYNGE, immediately noticed his 'strange personality', and Masefield's wife also, recording in her diary:

His personality was strange and I don't think anyone who hadn't known him could imagine him at all.[1]

Janet Hitchman, the first biographer of DOROTHY L. SAYERS, found that everyone she spoke to who had known Dorothy or worked for her, at some time in the conversation said 'she was – such a strange lady'.[2] Part of the strangeness may have been that the Christian apologist and translator of Dante had a masculine streak which liked dirty jokes and wearing the lapel badge of the beer-drinking Froth Blowers. A reporter who interviewed her among her cats and cacti was confronted with a backside of Lady Wilde proportions as she poked the fire. Then, still holding the poker, she had lectured him on the Trinity for more than an hour. She wrote to a BBC producer: 'I will kill them if they give my name as Dorothy Sayers.'[3] She insisted on the 'L' with the fanaticism of Betsy Trotwood for her patch of green.

Conrad Aiken described ELIOT as 'a strange creature, full of protestations of friendship . . . but makes no move to see me. . . .'[4] Eliot was at the bank and spending weekends with his nervously sick wife at Fishbourne. It was a time of considerable pressure, financially and emotionally. He established a secret retreat in Burleigh Mansions, Charing Cross Road. Mary Hutchinson was instructed to ask the porter for 'Captain Eliot' – the Sitwells for 'The Captain' – and to knock

1 Constance Babington Smith: *John Masefield: A Life* (1978), p. 78 note.
2 *Such a Strange Lady: An introduction to Dorothy L. Sayers 1893–1957* (1975), p. 12.
3 *Ibid.*, p. 192.
4 To R. N. Linscott: June 20, 1923. Quoted by Peter Ackroyd: *T. S. Eliot* (1984), p. 136.

three times. His artistic friends noticed that he wore pale-green face powder to make himself 'interesting' – or to communicate his suffering by visual means.

Coleridge described HAZLITT's manners as 'singularly repulsive – brow-hanging, shoe-contemplative, strange'. Hazlitt's father said that at puberty William had 'passed under a cloud, which unfitted him for social intercourse'. G. U. Yule was 'shocked' at the sight of A. E. HOUSMAN after a gap of thirteen years. The Professor of Latin at Cambridge, now fifty-three, 'seemed a different man, walking solitary and alone with unseeing eyes that recognised none and repelled advance'. Yule had been his assistant at University College, London, and was taking up a post at St John's. 'When we did speak', Housman was 'cordial but tongue-tied'.[1]

According to Leonard Woolf, the 'genius' of his Aunt ANNE RITCHIE, 'like most things about her and in her was a shade out of control':

Virginia noted that 'she said things that no human being could possibly mean; yet she meant them'.[2]

ALISON UTTLEY, in an interview a year before she died, told Sally Brompton that she talked to animals and they talked back to her. She regarded all inanimate objects as being alive – 'ever since I learned about atoms . . .' She believed that even her teapot was alive.[3] For that matter, ORWELL would suddenly declare over a Fleet Street lunch: 'All tobacconists are Fascists!' – as though, writes Muggeridge, 'this was something so obvious that no one could possibly question his statement'.[4]

II

Lady Ritchie wrote of 'a sort of second-sight my father used sometimes to speak of':

Occasionally when he described places, he said he could hardly believe he had not been there; and in one of the battles in *Esmond*, he told us that the very

---

1 Richard Perceval Graves: *A. E. Housman: The Scholar-Poet* (1979), p. 168.
2 *Beginning Again* (1964), p. 71.
3 *The Daily Mail*: Jan. 17, 1975.
4 'A Knight of the Woeful Countenance': *The World of George Orwell* ed. Miriam Gross (1971).

details of the foreground were visible to him as he wrote, even to some reeds growing by a streamlet, and the curve of the bank by which it flowed.[1]

Before its publication, THACKERAY had written to his daughters:

What I was pleased with was to find Blenheim was just exactly the place I had figured to myself except that the village is larger, but I fancy I had actually been there – so like the aspect of it was to what I looked for – and who knows perhaps one *does* go to places in the spirit – I saw the brook wh. H. Esmond crossed, and almost the spot where he fell wounded. . . .[2]

William Smith remembered how CHATTERTON would invite him for a walk in Redcliffe meadows, and at the place proposed read aloud one of his Rowley manuscripts.

He would frequently lay himself down, fix his eyes upon the church, and seem as if he were in a kind of trance. Then, on a sudden and abruptly, he would tell me, 'that steeple was burnt down by lightning: that was the place where they formerly acted plays.'[3]

Walmesley's nephew, who was a boy of fourteen when Chatterton had shared his room in the house at Shoreditch, said 'that C. to his knowledge never slept while they lay together; that he never came to bed till very late, sometimes three or four o'clock, and was always awake when he (the nephew) waked; and got up at the same time, about five or six – that almost every morning the floor was covered with pieces of paper not so big as sixpences, into which he had torn what he had been writing before he came to bed'. The niece added:

. . . that he used to sit up almost all night, reading and writing; and that her brother said he was afraid to lie with him; for, to be sure, he was a *spirit*, and never slept; for he never came to bed till it was morning, and then, for what he saw, never closed his eyes.[4]

FRANCIS THOMPSON was a difficult guest of the Meynells who for nineteen years, until he died, sheltered him. Lewis Hind wrote:

. . . no poet ever had such a home. . . . He would arrive for dinner thinking it was luncheon, and come prepared to dine at bedtime.

Often he would interject into the general conversation something 'about an overcoat that someone had stolen from him years before'.[5]

1 *Biographical Edition of Thackeray's Works, with Lady Ritchie's Introductions* (1898–9), vii.
2 June 18–20, 1852. See *The History of Henry Esmond, Esquire* (1852), ii, pp. 160, 162–3.
3 Jacob Bryant: *Observations upon the Poems of Thomas Rowley &c.* (1781), p. 530.
4 The Rev. Sir Herbert Croft: *Love and Madness. A Story Too True* (1780), p. 192.
5 *Authors and I* (1921), p. 277.

CHESTERTON's impracticability and absentmindedness were sublime. All trivia of daily routine, dressing or shaving, were done for him. He could not be trusted to go shopping and bring back the correct article or change. He left the management of his income and tax to his wife and to his secretary. Maisie Ward supplies the standard text of the telegram he sent his wife, and which has become a legend 'told as from a hundred different cities':

Am in Market Harborough. Where ought I to be?[1]

(Christopher Hollis gives Liverpool.)[2] When Chesterton came to St Michael's, Bedford Park, to attend the christening of the son of his former secretary, Canon T. P. Stevens asked him afterwards whether it were true that he had once agreed to speak in the Free Trade Hall in Leeds and was found standing outside St Andrew's Hall in Glasgow. He said he could not recall the incident but if Belloc had said so, it was true.[3] J. S. MILL was another who suffered 'great ineptness'[4] for his practical affairs, a result of his excessively intellectual education, and his wife also took complete charge.

When ALDOUS HUXLEY was forty-eight, his wife wrote to her sister Suzanne that he had become more and more absorbed by his books and ideas.

One has to plot to make him go to bed early or keep his siesta as one does for a child ... and the moment his work gets going he is so absorbed that he forgets ... Mère, and Noële and Matthew, and the house and our bank account, and to take his medicine and not to tire himself and to answer his letters.

Maria believed that he was outside life more than ever.

But he is touching, because he is trying so hard to help me, he wipes the plates for instance when I'm washing up. . . .[5]

ORWELL, instead of eating the shepherd's pie that his wife Eileen had left for him, absentmindedly ate the boiled eels put for the cat.[6]

BENNETT was so obsessively finicky that he once sent his wife a

1 *Gilbert Keith Chesterton* (1944), p. 222.
2 *Writers & Their Work: No. 3: G. K. Chesterton* (1950), pp. 23–24. Published for the British Council & the National Book League.
3 T. P. Stevens: *Cassock & Surplus: Incidents in Clerical Life mainly in London* (1947), p. 121.
4 Earlier draft of *Autobiography*.
5 Sybille Bedford: *Aldous Huxley: A Biography* (1973–4), ii, pp. 28–29.
6 See Bernard Crick: *George Orwell: A Life* (1980), p. 295.

closely written four-page letter complaining she had moved the piano a few inches. He had a mania for punctuality and precision. He recorded in his diary:

I passed sixty-eight seagulls sitting on the fence.

The entry for the last day of 1899 reads:

This year I have written 353,340 words, grand total.

DODGSON, over a period of twenty-seven years, numbered and catalogued not only every letter received but wrote a precis of it, entering into his various reference volumes 98,721 letters. There was something too, about ink. Until about the age of thirty-nine he used black, going over for twenty years to purple, and finally reverting to black. Derek Hudson states:

. . . it is a fact that the 'purple period' tended in Dodgson's life to depression and unhappiness.[1]

---

1 *Lewis Carroll: An illustrated biography* (1976), p. 236.

CHAPTER TWENTY-SEVEN

Plain Inconsideration?

The line between eccentricity and plain inconsideration may sometimes be fine. POPE, 'when he wanted to sleep ... *nodded in* company: and once slumbered at his own table, while the Prince of Wales was talking of poetry'.[1]

WORDSWORTH, sitting at De Quincey's tea-table in Dove Cottage, took from an adjacent shelf a volume of Burke's *Works* and used a butter knife on its uncut pages.

... he tore his way into the heart of the volume with this knife, that left its greasy honours behind it upon every page. . . . The book was to me an eyesore ... for many a year. . . .[2]

One evening in the Bay of Spezzia, SHELLEY invited Jane Williams with her two babies into his new cockleshell of a dinghy. She thought they would do no more than float near the shore, but when they were well out he shipped his sculls and fell into the deepest reverie. Their craft with its precious cargo was fragilely poised. Petrified, she watched the water lapping and sometimes spilling over the sides. All of a sudden and bending again to his sculls, he exclaimed joyously: 'Now let us together solve the great mystery!' With presence of mind she spoke of their dinner, her husband and Trelawny who would be waiting, the words of his Indian air, and so got him to shallow water – where she snatched up her babies so precipitously that, to the amusement of the others, he struggled out like a turtle, with the upturned skiff upon his back.[3] DICKENS, at twenty-five, used identical words. He whirled 'Eleanor P.' down the jetty at Broadstairs where waves soaked her best silk dress well above the knees. 'Dress,' he shouted in the wildest spirits, ' – talk not to me of dress when we already stand on the brink of the great mystery!'[4]

1 Samuel Johnson: *The Lives of the English Poets* (Dublin ed. 1779–81), ii, p. 384.
2 *The Collected Writings of Thomas De Quincey* ed. David Masson (1889–90), ii, p. 313.
3 See Edward Dowden: *The Life of Percy Bysshe Shelley* (1886), ii, pp. 502–3.
4 Una Pope-Hennessy: *Charles Dickens 1812–1870* (1945), pp. 71–72.

WILLIAM MORRIS had a superfluity of physical energy. At Marlborough his restless fingers sought relief in endless netting. With one
end fastened to his desk in the big schoolroom he would work at it for
hours, his fingers almost automatic. He acquired there a habit of tilting
back his chair, 'getting his legs twisted round it, and suddenly straight-
ening them out to the strain or collapse of the fabric'. Many of his
own Sussex chairs – besides chairs in other houses – bore the marks.[1]
At Oxford he had a habit of beating his head vigorously. In gusts of
temper he was known to drive his head against the wall making a deep
dent in the plaster, and to 'bite almost through the woodwork of a
window frame'. At Red Lion Square he hurled a beloved fifteenth-
century folio at the head of an offending workman, missed, and drove
a panel out of the workshop door.[2]

BARRIE's silences, terrible from his wife's point of view, could be
inflicted upon others. J. K. Jerome tells how once, dining out, Barrie
had been allotted a nervous companion and after a strained pause, he
asked, 'Have you ever been to Egypt?' (The story has variants like
Chesterton's telegram; Sherriff made it China.) 'No.' Then, after a
longer pause and to satisfy her curiosity, she inquired, 'Have you?'
'No.'[3] Sherriff's experience when he had tea at the Adelphi flat was
worse. Barrie lay so still on the settle, a little cushion behind his neck,
Sherriff began to worry whether his host were still alive and he should
not touch the top of the 'big pear-shaped head' to find if it had gone
cold.[4]

Frances Donaldson, whose knowledge of EVELYN WAUGH made her
'almost unique among people living' when she wrote her brief memoir,
knew him – together with her husband – 'at home, as part of a family'.
After the first time they had dined at Piers Court, Laura showed her
one morning her small farm, and told her 'it was an embarrassment
. . . not to be able to ask her neighbours to the house in the ordinary
way'.

The last time she had asked some people to tea, she said Evelyn had risen
about five o'clock in the afternoon and saying a formal good-bye had said he
must go and take a bath. He could never stand even short periods of active
boredom. . . .[5]

1 J. W. Mackail: *The Life of William Morris* (1899), i, p. 26.
2 *Ibid.*, i, pp. 215–16.
3 *My Life & Times* (1925), p. 122.
4 R. C. Sherriff: *No Leading Lady: An Autobiography* (1968), pp. 178–9.
5 *Evelyn Waugh: Portrait of a Country Neighbour* (1967), p. 13.

WILLIAM EMPSON wrote to Clifford Dyment if they couldn't arrange a meal together: 'Dear Mr Dyment, We met at that Ladies' Club dinner. I should be pleased if you would ring me up. . . .' Presumably Dyment did, and Empson was about to go on holiday. Empson wrote again: 'Dear Mr Dyment, I am back from ski-ing now. Let's have a Chinese meal in a few days – the Shanghai, Greek St . . . will Friday 7.30 do?' The day was confirmed, then Empson wrote a third time:

> Dear Dyment,
> I am sorry I was late to dinner; the waitress said you had been pacing up and down outside till just before I came. I was only ten minutes late by my watch; a man had turned up I hadn't seen for seven years or so; but it seems the watch was ten minutes late too. I wish you had sat down and ordered a drink. If you can suggest another day I hope we will have this meal after all.
>
> Yours sincerely
W Empson.

Did Dyment have the stamina to pursue his Chinese meal? The sequence of letters ends,[1] and now it is doubtful whether we shall ever know.

---

1 Unpublished. The 3 letters are undated.

CHAPTER TWENTY-EIGHT
Constitutional Melancholy

I

A characteristic of JOHNSON was his love of company, yet he was so ill when he was fifty-five with what Boswell calls 'the hypochondriack disorder' ever lurking about him, as to be entirely averse to society. Dr Adams as an old friend was admitted and found him 'in a deplorable state . . . groaning, talking to himself, and restlessly walking from room to room'.

He then used this emphatical expression . . . 'I would consent to have a limb amputated to recover my spirits.'[1]

Boswell himself, Kingsley and Ruskin suffered from the same neurosis, known as 'the hyp'.

GRAY too, 'in no small degree' owned 'her sway'. At twenty, he told Richard West:

If the default of your spiritual nerves be nothing but the effect of the hyp, I have no more to say. We all must submit to that wayward queen. . . .[2]

The following year, and still a student at Cambridge, he confided in the same friend:

Low spirits are my true and faithful companions; they get up with me, go to bed with me, make journeys and returns as I do; nay, and pay visits, and will even affect to be jocose, and force a feeble laugh with me; but most commonly we sit alone together. . . .[3]

Then, at twenty-six, after his Grand Tour and estrangement from Horace Walpole, he wrote to West of a more tolerable 'white melancholy', whose 'only fault . . . is insipidity; which is apt now and then to give a sort of ennui, which makes one form certain little wishes that signify nothing'.

1 James Boswell: *The Life of Samuel Johnson LL.D.* (1971), Aetat.55: 1764.
2 Dec., 1736.
3 Aug. 22, 1737.

But there is another sort, black indeed, which I have now and then felt.

From this, none but 'the Lord . . . and sunshiny weather' could bring deliverance.[1] Four days after those words had been written, his friend died of TB. The letter was returned unopened.

Three months later, out of his black despair, he wrote the *Ode on a Distant Prospect of Eton College* and *Ode to Adversity*. Mason, in his *Memoir*, was to caution the unfeeling reader against 'imputing to a splenetic melancholy what in fact sprung from the most benevolent of all sensations'. Mason, also, was 'inclined to believe that the *Elegy in a Country Church-yard* was begun, if not concluded' at this time.

His fugitive and elusive genius had not only flowered but saved him – coupled with his resolve to lead a life of private study. For 'some spirit', he wrote, 'something of genius (more than common) is required to teach a man how to employ himself: I say a man; for women, commonly speaking . . . have always something to do. . . .'

To find one's self business, I am persuaded, is the great art of life.[2]

BURNS described himself as prey to a 'constitutional melancholy of hypochondriacism that made me fly solitude'. His brother wrote of him as a ploughman on his father's farm:

I doubt not but the hard labour and sorrow of this period . . . was in a great measure the cause of that depression of spirits with which Robert was so often afflicted through his whole life afterwards.[3]

At twenty-two, when he had 'joined with a flax-dresser' in Irvine 'to learn his trade', he wrote to his father at Lochlea:

The weakness of my nerves has so debilitated my mind, that I dare neither review past wants, nor look forward . . . I am quite transported at the thought, that . . . perhaps very soon, I shall bid an eternal adieu to all the pains . . . and disquietudes of this weary life; for I assure you I am heartily sick of it . . . I foresee that poverty and obscurity probably await me. . . .[4]

At thirty-five, two years from death, he wrote to his friend, Alexander Cunningham:

My constitution and frame were *ab origine*, blasted with a deep incurable taint of hypochondria, which poisons my existence.[5]

1 May 27, 1742.
2 June 22, 1760.
3 'Gilbert's Narrative': letter of Gilbert Burns to Mrs Dunlop.
4 Dec. 27, 1781.
5 Feb. 25, 1794.

KINGSLEY, a manic-depressive, oscillated regularly between high moods and deep melancholy. Throughout his thirties, he suffered a nervous collapse almost every year. At forty, he wrote:

I can't think; I can't write; I can't ride – I have neither wit, nerve nor strength for anything, and if I try I get a hot head, and my arms and legs begin to ache. . . .[1]

ANNA SEWELL's mother described her daughter's life as one of 'constant frustration':

. . . how often did my heart yearn over those apparently wasted faculties. . . .[2]

Ironically, her disapproval of painting which Anna loved and therefore felt constrained to forgo, might have fed this psychological condition. At twenty-five, Anna's hypochondria took the form of pains in her chest and a weak back so that, like certain other Victorian spinsters who were 'gentlewomen', she retired to her bed. A 'weakness' in her head meant she could not concentrate, and Margaret Sewell wrote:

My aunt could never read or write for more than a short time at a sitting.[3]

Apart from four years which he described as 'the summer of my life' EDMUND GOSSE was visited by deep depression which made him at such times 'scarcely fit for human society'[4] while his body seemed 'a collapsed and abject thing'.[5] CHURCHILL's manic depression went back in his family to the first Duke of Marlborough. Another depressive was EDWARD THOMAS whose condition caused terrible suffering to him and his wife.

EVELYN WAUGH, wrote Frances Donaldson, a friend of the Waughs from the time Evelyn was mid-forty, 'suffered from a melancholia of Johnsonian proportions . . . he found life so terribly boring he could hardly endure from day to day'.[6] Douglas Woodruff remembered him

1 Letter to John Bullar, Nov. 19, 1859 Susan Chitty: *The Beast & the Monk: A Life of Charles Kingsley* (1974), p. 239.
2 Mary Sewell: *Reminiscences* (1880).
3 Susan Chitty: *The Woman who wrote 'Black Beauty': A Life of Anna Sewell* (1971), p. 111.
4 Ann Thwaite: *Edmund Gosse: a literary landscape* (1984), p. 196.
5 Letter to his future wife, Feb. 13, 1875: *ibid.*, p. 153.
6 *Evelyn Waugh: Portrait of a Country Neighbour* (1967), p. xiii.

in White's calling for champagne and then looking gloomily at the bottle. 'It sounded as though it was going to be jolly,' said Waugh sadly, 'and then somehow it isn't.'[1]

GRAHAM GREENE described himself as 'a manic-depressive' fighting a 'life-long war against boredom'.[2] When he was engaged to be married and tutoring an eight-year-old boy as well as writing his second novel, 'the oppression of boredom' was such that on his free day he went the length of fabricating to a dentist the symptoms of an abscess in order to have a perfectly good tooth removed – 'the boredom was for the time being dispersed'.[3] (This makes more credible what Johnson said of amputation.) Greene admitted at sixty-seven:

... indeed it descends on me too often today.[4]

Lord CLARK spoke of himself as a fellow sufferer. From the age of sixteen he was subject to *accidie, maladie des moines* when nothing seemed to be worth doing.

In my own case it developed into hypochondria. For some years I believed intermittently, but with absolute conviction, that I was dying of paralysis.

Like Johnson, he tried 'immensely long walks' – Clark also played squash racquets for Oxford. The hypochondria returned in his early thirties when he thought he had a heart disease, then about twenty years later it reappeared for the last time when he felt he had symptoms of paralysis, which then disappeared.[5]

SHELLEY, after sitting opposite in a coach to an old woman who had very fat legs, believed he was afflicted with elephantiasis. Peacock describes him drawing the skin of his hands, arms and neck very tight and, if he discovered any 'deviation', immediately doing the same to the person next to him – if this were a young woman, it was misunderstood. He exaggerated his other symptoms and described his life as 'a series of illness', but although his health was poor this was neurosis. Dean INGE revealed the 'hypochondriacal' miseries of his earlier life.

---

1 *Evelyn Waugh & his World* ed. David Pryce-Jones (1973), p. 132.
2 *A Sort of Life* (1971), p. 131.
3 *Ibid.*, pp. 154–5.
4 *Ibid.*, p. 127.
5 Kenneth Clark: *Another Part of the Wood: A Self-Portrait* (1974), pp. 91–92.

II

WORDSWORTH acknowledged his dual nature in *The Prelude*:

> ...from the first
> Having two natures in me, joy the one
> The other melancholy.... [1]

Something of the same dichotomy was in ANDREW LANG, who said: 'I have a gay mind, but a melancholy soul.' J. K. JEROME wrote of his own childhood: '... about the East End of London there is a menace, a haunting terror that is to be found nowhere else' – and adds:

> It was these surroundings ... that gave to me, I suppose, my melancholy, brooding disposition. I can see the humorous side of things and enjoy the fun when it comes, but look where I will, there seems to me always more sadness than joy in life. [2]

According to Leonard Woolf, melancholy mingled with gentleness and charm was an integral part of G. LOWES DICKINSON and his Cambridge generation which numbered ROGER FRY.

WORDSWORTH spoke of his melancholy at Cambridge:

> ...I must rank
> A melancholy from humours of the blood
> In part, and partly taken up.... [3]

It was always an element in BYRON's character, from the time he sat brooding as a schoolboy on 'his' tomb on Harrow Hill. He found material early to hand: the death of his cousin Margaret Parker at fifteen, 'one of the most beautiful of evanesant beings'. Scott wrote of him at twenty-seven in the year of his marriage:

> He was often melancholy – almost gloomy. When I observed him in this humour, I used either to wait until it went off of its own accord, or till some natural and easy mode occurred of leading him into conversation, when the shadows almost always left his countenance, like the mist rising from a landscape. [4]

G. M. HOPKINS, when he was forty-one, told Robert Bridges of fits of

1 1805–6 version: Bk. X, ll.868–70.
2 *My Life and Times* (1925), pp. 15–16.
3 *Op. cit.*, Bk. VI, ll.191–2.
4 J. G. Lockhart: *Memoirs of the life of Sir Walter Scott, Bart.* (1837–8), iii, pp. 337–8.

sadness that resembled madness though not affecting his judgment. BORROW 'was subject to fits of serious depression'.[1]

HARDY, extending his deep sympathy to Rider Haggard on the death of his nine-year-old son 'Jock', added:

Though to be candid, I think the death of a child is never really to be regretted, when one reflects on what he has escaped.

For years after his bereavement, RIDER HAGGARD 'suffered "acute mental depression", was constantly ill with psychosomatic disorders, and began to sink into a deepening melancholy'.[2] HARDY told Gosse:

You would be quite shocked if I were to tell you how many weeks and months in byegone years I have gone to bed never wishing to see daylight again.

Frances Donaldson said that EVELYN WAUGH was the only person she had ever known who seemed sincerely to long for death.

MAUGHAM did not usually seem morose in company. Ivor Brown acknowledged that when he met him in London he was sufficiently genial, but went on: '. . . there is no doubt . . . when alone, he had more than his fair share of "the dumps".' After Gerald Haxton died, Maugham, then sixty-nine, told his nephew: 'I think of Gerald every single minute that I'm awake. . . . You'll never know how great this grief has been to me.'[3] The night he moved back into the Villa Mauresque, he said to him: 'I shall never get over Gerald's death.'[4] When he was eighty-eight, he said of his villa, its valuable furniture and pictures, its wonderful garden on the edge of the Mediterranean with its exotically landscaped swimming-pool, his treasure of a cook, his butler serving dishes on silver plates, his footman and eight other servants: 'The place is no use to me anymore.'[5]

1 Theodore Watts-Dunton: *Old Familiar Faces* (1916), p. 30.
2 Peter B. Ellis: *H. Rider Haggard* (1978), pp. 141–2.
3 Robin Maugham: *Conversations with Willie* (1978), p. 81.
4 *Ibid.*, p. 89.
5 *Ibid.*, p. 141.

CHAPTER TWENTY-NINE
Insane from Unrequited Love

I

Alexander Cruden, Cowper, Lamb, Ruskin, were crossed in love and went mad. They may all, like Ruskin, have possessed an unstable genius but a broken love affair seems to have provided a trigger-point. Lamb recovered, in spite of being subjected to appalling pressures immediately afterwards, but even he never lost the fear of going mad. The others suffered intermittently for the rest of their lives.

CRUDEN's affection for a minister's daughter was not returned and his friends had to confine him, at twenty-two, privately. He went insane again at thirty-eight, on the death of Queen Caroline, seventeen days after he had sent her a dedicatory copy of his Biblical *Concordance* in the hope of patronage. At fifty-four, he quarrelled with his married sister who got him confined at Chelsea for seventeen days. Later, his paranoia reached the height of wanting his authority recognized by the King in Council, and to be nominated Corrector of the People by Act of Parliament. At sixty-three, the unfortunate man allowed himself to be knighted with mock ceremonies by the undergraduates at Cambridge.

COWPER's early melancholy as a child re-awoke when the young man began to be bored with his legal life in chambers. At this time he experienced a cumulative effect of disasters: his four-year courtship with his cousin Theodora was called off by her father, his own father died, and Russell – his closest friend from Westminster days – was accidentally drowned.

Another cousin offered him the prospect of applying for the post of Clerkship of the House of Lords, which was in his gift. But those jealous of the patronage introduced an oral examination to be given by the House, and this coming ordeal preyed on Cowper to the point of believing that his enemies would expose a genital abnormality. A series of suicide attempts convinced him he was damned. Before long he was raving and confined in The Home for Madmen at St Albans – at first, bound upon his bed for safety. The asylum was run by Dr Cotton, an Evangelical Christian, and one day in its garden Cowper picked up a Bible from a bench. Next day, his eyes filled with tears as he 'saw the sufficiency of the Atonement ... and ... believed ... overwhelmed with love and wonder'.

A year passed, and at thirty-three he looked for a 'calm retreat'. It was decided that with financial help from relatives he should take lodgings at Huntingdon to be near his brother, a Cambridge don. Within six months, he had the wonderful good fortune of being taken in as a lodger by an Evangelical family, the Unwins, and he experienced four years of 'the utmost enjoyment'. When the Rev. William Unwin died, they moved to Olney to be under the Rev. John Newton and here the pace quickened, Cowper being enrolled in parochial duties. 'I have heard many men preach,' reminisced a villager, 'but I have never heard anyone preach like Mr Cowper.' But his religion was no longer giving him 'the blessedness I knew'. He ministered to his dying brother. Then the Evangelical fervour, so successful in channelling his morbid fancies, petered out.

At forty-one (for two years) and at fifty-five (for six months), this man – so gentle and loving to all around him – became again a raving maniac. Both times were preceded by a dream in which he heard an irrevocable judgment pronounced by God. With the relentless logic of the insane, Cowper's was the unique soul predestined to fall from grace and nothing anybody could say, nothing he could do, could alter that. During sane stretches the conviction stayed but he led a dual life of normality – gardening, a little carpentry, tending his pet hares that the kindly villagers sent to help him, even cultivating friendships and, after forty-nine, pursuing creative work. When he was sixty-two, Mary Unwin – his beloved companion, 'My Mary' who had nursed and saved him in his longer illness – had a serious stroke. His unremitting care of her led to his final collapse. She had a third stroke, which turned her mind actively against him and, if in his twilight world he included her as a demon, 'for once,' comments his biographer, 'this delusion may have been less unbearable than the truth'.[1]

It is the story of an unlikely man with a genius not only for poetry

1 David Cecil: *The Stricken Deer or The Life of Cowper* (1929), p. 278.

but affection.[1] It becomes now, the remarkable story of his distant family and friends. His cousin Lady Harriet Hesketh, down-to-earth with her remedies, nicknames and gifts, left London at sixty to take sole charge of two insane people in the country. Two years afterwards when she could not go on, the Rev. John Johnson ('Johnny Johnson of Norfolk') gave up his curacy to have them for the rest of their lives. He had the idea of moving house around East Dereham to find an environment to suit Cowper most, and it seems that for him more than the others a shadow lingered of the man who had won such affection. If Johnny went away to take a service, Cowper – very frail – would be waiting at the gate. William Hayley had already secured for Cowper a £300 pension. He tried to hoist him with his own petard. He described a vision he had received, in which Cowper's mother kneeling at the throne of God told him her son would be restored – and, as a sign, eminent people would be writing to him of the good he had done through his poetry. He managed to solicit a few such as Wilberforce; Cowper dismissed it as a mocking hope. They were utterly at sea. David Cecil admits:

There is something comic about them. . . . But there is nothing comic about their love.[2]

In the penultimate year of his life, when Cowper was sixty-seven, his intellect momentarily cleared for the writing of *The Castaway*:

> . . .
> No voice divine the storm allay'd,
>   No light propitious shone;
> When, snatch'd from all effectual aid,
>   We perish'd, each alone:
> But I beneath a rougher sea,
> And whelm'd in deeper gulphs than he.

Every night he went into the abyss. By day he sometimes sat rigid, listening with bated breath, for the demons to steal up on him and take him alive. Shortly before he died, the doctor asked him how he felt. Cowper replied: 'I feel unutterable despair.' At the end, Johnny saw miraculous peace come upon the face. R. H. Mottram sketched a similar transformation (but that was two days after death) by the bedside of Galsworthy. It was noticed also on Jane Carlyle.

---

1 '. . . he had a genius for affection. . . .' (*Ibid.*, p. 18.)
2 *Ibid.*, pp. 278–9.

LAMB, at twenty, was confined a short time in a private madhouse. He wrote to Coleridge:

The six weeks that finished last year and begun this, your very humble servant spent very agreeably in a madhouse at Hoxton. I am got somewhat rational now, and don't bite any one.[1]

The cause probably lay in 'the fair hair, and fairer eyes, of Alice W(esto)n'. She seems to have ended at this time their 'passionate . . . love-adventure'[2] carried on from his boyhood.

RUSKIN'S reason became impaired around the age of forty, coincident with his falling in love with Rose La Touche who was still a child. On the point of breakdown he took a house at Mornex, on the Salève, near Geneva, and found temporary peace doing a good deal of writing in the summer-house at the end of a pretty garden. At fifty-two, he bought Brantwood on Coniston Water and by cruel irony, he who believed Nature the source of health and calm and moral law, began to be tormented by 'Storm-Cloud' and 'Plague-Wind'. Seven years later, during some months of acute mania, familiar objects in his room assumed the shape of demons. (Demons masqueraded to Cowper in the likeness of familiar friends.) Next year he resigned his Slade professorship and there was some improvement, but his resumption at Oxford the following year made a tragic anticlimax. Cowper translated Homer between his last two seizures; now Ruskin in *Praeterita* – 'speaking of what it gives me joy to remember'[3] – found similar serenity and escape. But after a sixth attack at seventy he could write only his signature, although he was to live eleven more years.

Some of EVELYN WAUGH's friends feared for his sanity when his first wife left him a year after marriage.

1 May 1796.
2 'New Year's Eve': *Elia* (1823), p. 63.
3 *Praeterita* (1886–8), i, p. v.

CHAPTER THIRTY

Other Instances of Insanity or Near Insanity

I

The 'Secret far dearer to him than his Life',[1] that JOHNSON confided to Mrs Thrale, may have been the delusion there were times he was mad. An entry in his own Pocket Diary, when he was sixty-one, runs: 'De pedicis et manicis insana cogitatio.'[2] In *Thraliana* she makes a marginal comment to an entry on him: '... the Fetters & Padlocks will tell Posterity the Truth.'[3] Raymond Mortimer believed that 'Johnson trusted her to keep him in confinement'.[4] The 'dreadful secret' mentioned in her diaries may have been not merely Johnson's terror of going mad but that she, at his request, innocently gave him floggings considered in their day a remedy. Her remark may then have been meant literally:

... and do not quarrel with your Governess for not using the Rod enough.[5]

But Johnson, a masochist like Swinburne and T. E. Lawrence, would have received a form of sexual gratification.

De Quincey and others commented upon DOROTHY WORDS-WORTH's wild, staring eyes. From about fifty-nine she was an invalid, and after Sara Hutchinson's death from flu' five years later, she contracted sclerosis. Her mind clouded, and the Child of the Open Air – who had criticised Coleridge at Allan Bank for never leaving his room – now sat before a huge fire giving out insufferable heat to others. Eventually she was confined to a wheelchair, and in summer William and Mary took a vociferous Dorothy round the garden of Rydal Mount. She remained a respected member of their household, still remem-

1 May 1, 1779: *Thraliana: The Diary of Mrs Hester Lynch Thrale (Later Mrs Piozzi) 1776–1784* ed. Katharine C. Balderston (2nd ed. 1951), i, p. 384.
2 Mar. 24, 1771: 'Insane thinking about fetters and handcuffs.'
3 *Op. cit.*, i, p. 415 note.
4 *Channel Packet* (1942), p. 43.
5 *Op. cit.*, i, p. 385 note.

bering poetry and reciting her brother's –'in so sweet a tone,' said Crabb Robinson, 'as to be quite pathetic'. The local people got some of it right:

> Miss Dorothy, she was ter'ble clever woman. She did as much of his poetry as he did and went completely off it at the latter end, wi' studying it, I suppose.[1]

About the time that Dorothy had been stricken, a friend who chanced to call at Greta Hall was taken by the hand and led by SOU-THEY into his study.

> ... at length ... he disclosed ... that within the last five minutes, Mrs Southey had, without previous indication or symptom, gone raving mad, and to that hopeless degree that within an hour he must take her to an asylum.[2]

Edith went for a few months to a Retreat for Lunatics at York, but when Southey brought her home again her condition got rapidly worse. He let his daughters shoulder the burden until Wordsworth urged upon Southey's brother the necessity for hiring a nurse. Edith died two years later. A year after Southey had remarried, he did not recognise Wordsworth who visited him, until he was told.

> Then his eyes flashed for a moment with their former brightness, but he sank into a state in which I had found him, patting with both hands his books affectionately, like a child.[3]

Southey's mind too, had gone, at sixty-five, although he lingered nearly three more years.

WILLIAM COLLINS suffered mental illness and an enfeebling disease for the last nine years of his short life. He was confined in a lunatic asylum and then his sister had care of him.

II

Only four months after the recovery of Charles Lamb from his derangement at twenty, *The Whitehall Evening Post*[4] reported:

On Friday afternoon the Coroner and a respectable Jury sat on the body of a

---

1 Rawnsley's *Reminiscences*, quoted by Hunter Davies: *William Wordsworth* (1980), p. 322.
2 *The Diaries of William Charles Macready* ed. Toynbee (1912), i, p. 185.
3 Wordsworth's visit, July 1840.
4 Monday, Sept. 26, 1796.

Lady in the neighbourhood of Holborn, who died in consequence of a wound from her daughter the preceding day. It appeared by the evidence adduced, that while the family were preparing for dinner, the young lady seized a case knife laying on the table, and in a menacing manner pursued a little girl, her apprentice, round the room; on the eager calls of her helpless, infirm mother to forbear, she renounced the first object, and with loud shrieks approached her parent. The child by her cries quickly brought up the landlord of the house, but too late – the dreadful scene presented to him the mother lifeless, pierced to the heart on a chair, her daughter yet wildly standing over her with the fatal knife, and the venerable old man, her father, weeping by her side, himself bleeding at the forehead from the effects of a severe blow he received from one of the forks she had been madly hurling about the room. . . . As her carriage towards her mother was ever affectionate in the extreme, it is believed that to the increased attentiveness, which her parents infirmities called for by day and night, is to be attributed the present insanity of this ill-fated young woman. . . . The jury of course brought in their verdict, Lunacy. The above unfortunate young person is a Miss LAMB, a mantua-maker in Little Queen Street. . . . She has been since removed to Islington madhouse.

Charles must have followed the landlord in, for it was he who somehow got the knife from his 'dear Dearest sister' and calmed or overcame her, while his favourite aunt, Hetty, crouched terror-stricken.

MARY was thirty-one. Already that week, in the family's cramped lodgings, had been signs she was near her breaking-point, and early the day before, Charles had tried to find Dr Pitcairn. The previous year, when she lay dangerously ill, Coleridge had observed that she and her brother doted on each other.[1] Now Charles undertook to himself that he would prevent her being incarcerated in the Bethlehem Hospital she had always feared. He achieved this, after some months, by entering into a solemn engagement that he would take her under his care for life. He stood out not only against friends, but his older brother John.

To bring her home in her father's lifetime was inadvisable so a room was taken for her at Hackney, where Charles spent as much time with her as he could get away from East India House and looking after his father, whose state was now worse. There was also Aunt Hetty, who had been coldly returned by a rich relative to be with her favourite nephew. He replied to an offer from Coleridge:

Your invitation went to my very heart; but you have a power of exciting interest, of leading all hearts captive, too forcible to admit of Mary's being

---

1 Letter to Southey, Dec. 1794.

with you. I consider her as perpetually on the brink of madness. I think you would almost make her dance within an inch of the precipice: she must be with duller fancies, and cooler intellects. I know a young man of this description who has suited her these twenty years, and may live to do so still, if we are one day restored to each other.[1]

Her intelligence had returned a few days after the tragedy. The reference here is to the fact that within less than a year of her release, Mary's reason had again lapsed. On his aunt's death, and two years later, his father's, Mary could be brought back home.

Seldom a year passed during the thirty-six they lived together, in which she was not 'from home' part of the time. They seldom could take a holiday and when they did, Mary, with her own hands, placed a strait-waistcoat among the things to be taken with them. One day a friend met brother and sister walking across the fields hand-in-hand, towards the old madhouse out Hoxton way, both weeping. Coleridge wrote to his wife, when Lamb was twenty-eight, that Mary had been taken to the private madhouse at Hugsden – 'Charles is cut to the heart.'

In later years attacks grew more frequent and lasted longer. He knew the first sign. If Mary became too excited in company, he would indicate to his guests to retire, and then by gentle talk try to compose her. If she entered a trance, he had been known to lift a boiling kettle from the hob and hold it facetiously above her head-dress. The move to Edmonton for her sake, after his superannuation at fifty, took him away from friends who were necessary to him. Her condition deteriorated, yet she outlived him thirteen years; Dorothy outlived Wordsworth by five.

De Quincey recalled CHARLES LLOYD, a fugitive from a madhouse, recounting to him beside Rydalmere the brutalities of his keepers and to which, when recaptured, he must return.[2] JOHN CLARE spent the last twenty-three years of his life in St Andrew's Asylum, Northampton, still writing poetry. Fear of madness was never far from Leslie Stephen. Bennett was another, for he expressed to Dorothy Cheston that after his father's mental degeneration he had always thought he would die the same way.

A. C. BRADLEY's powers of concentration began to fail with the outbreak of World War I, when he was sixty-three. The war preyed upon

1 Jan. 1798.
2 *The Collected Writings of Thomas De Quincey* ed. David Masson (1889–90), ii, p. 399.

his mind, and for twenty-one more years his life was 'a long gradual decay' in the care of his sister.

VIRGINIA WOOLF suffered from what doctors called neurasthenia. After a minor and then a major breakdown in childhood, she attempted her life at twenty-two by jumping out of a window. In the months before their marriage, Leonard became aware of 'the menace' under which she always lived,[1] but it took him some time to realize 'the razor edge of sanity upon which her mind was often balanced'. The emotional strain of their engagement caused her to go into a nursing home, and he was already 'troubled and apprehensive' when they returned from their honeymoon.[2] The second major breakdown in her life came within a year, when she heard the birds in the garden outside her window talking Greek. She swallowed a very large overdose of veronal which made Sir George Savage decide it would never be safe for her to have a child. Leonard consulted in turn five leading brain specialists:

... it seemed to me that what they knew amounted to practically nothing. They had not the slightest idea of the nature or the cause of Virginia's mental state. ...[3]

In the early acute stage of her depression she wanted Leonard to be with her continually, even though she sat silent for hours 'overwhelmed with hopeless melancholia ... making no response to anything said to her'. When food was put before her she took no notice at all.

I could usually induce her to eat a certain amount, but it was a terrible process. Every meal took an hour or two. ...[4]

In the second stage she was violently hostile to Leonard, and would not talk to him or allow him to come into her room.

EVELYN WAUGH, at fifty-two, experienced a brief time when, like his own Mr Pinfold,[5] he heard voices and suffered from other paranoid hallucinations. He had chosen for his travels that year to go to Ceylon, as it was then called. On the boat one of the passengers saw him talking to the toast-rack at breakfast. His letters to his wife mentioned a party of 'existentialists' who were using long-range telepathy to persecute

1 *Beginning Again* (1964), p. 75.
2 *Ibid.*, p. 148.
3 *Ibid.*, p. 160.
4 *Ibid.*, p. 163.
5 See *The Ordeal of Gilbert Pinfold: A Conversation Piece* (1967).

him. On his return a priest was called, who found him 'as mad as a coot'.[1] Waugh asked to be exorcised, but a doctor was fetched and the voices disappeared that night. According to Frances Donaldson, Waugh for six weeks before he left had been taking poisonously large quantities of bromide and chloral, and he recovered when the effects of the chloral left his body. He himself said:

I know that Laura has been putting it about that I've been ill. But it isn't true. I've been off my head.[2]

III

Because SWIFT said, 'I shall be like that tree, I shall die at the top,' and left a legacy to found St Patrick's Hospital for Imbeciles, his illness has been often misunderstood. He did not understand it himself. Turned forty, he told Archbishop King of 'a cruel distemper, a giddiness in my head, that would not suffer me to write or think of anything, and of which I am now recovering'.[3] Nearly twenty years later, he ascribed it to gorging a hundred golden pippins – this, he said, caused the giddiness – and to reading and sleeping in 'a fine seat' in Surrey – which produced the deafness:

These two friends have visited me, one or other, every year since, and being old acquaintance have now thought fit to come together.[4]

The best medical opinion is that both symptoms, together with vomiting, had their origin in his left ear, and that he suffered from Bilateral Ménière's disease or *labyrinthine vertigo*. Not until three years from the end did paralysis of the brain succeed senile decay for guardians to be appointed. The 4th EARL OF CHESTERFIELD, from his early sixties, may have been suffering from Ménière's disease.

Delany described Swift studying his image in a pier-glass and muttering over and over: 'Poor old man.' At another time he was heard talking to himself: 'I am what I am: I am what I am.' Annabella recorded that during their marriage BYRON talked to himself, like a small child: 'Byron's a fool – yes, he *is* a fool!' and 'Poor Byron . . . poor Byron!'

1 *Arena*, BBC 2: April 1987.
2 Frances Donaldson: *Evelyn Waugh: Portrait of a Country Neighbour* (1967), pp. 61–62.
3 Letter dated Jan. 6, 1708–9.
4 Letter to Mrs Howard: Aug. 19, 1727.

BEATRICE WEBB remembered 'as a small thing, sitting under the damp bushes, and brooding over the want of love around one':

. . . and turning in upon myself, and saying, 'Thou and I will live alone and if life be unbearable we will die'. . . . And then I said, 'I will teach thee what I feel, think and see, and we will grow wise together; then shall we be happy.'[1]

When KATHERINE MANSFIELD was twenty, at Beauchamp Lodge, Margaret Wishart often saw her talking to 'herself' in front of a mirror.[2]

In her notebooks Katherine was often uncertain as to whether she was 'I' or 'she'.[3]

C. DAY LEWIS confessed that from boyhood he was often staring into mirrors – 'not from vanity . . . but in a spirit of inquiry: "Are you real?" "Who are you?" and later, more teasingly still, "Which of you is *you?*"'[4] WILKIE COLLINS, in life as in his work, was obsessed with a second self.

Many times BLAKE appeared to his patron William Hayley 'on the verge of Insanity', but in Samuel Palmer's eyes he was 'the most practically sane'. DYLAN THOMAS's widow looks back on 'a genius with some kind of imbalance'.[5]

1 *My Apprenticeship* (1926), pp. 280–1.
2 Antony Alpers: *The Life of Katherine Mansfield* (1980), p. 73.
3 *Ibid.*, p. 58.
4 *The Buried Day* (1960), p. 21.
5 Caitlin Thomas *with* George Tremlett: *Caitlin: A Warring Absence* (1986), p. 95.

CHAPTER THIRTY-ONE

Genus Irritabile Vatum

I
t may be asked where does all this leave what Coleridge maintained:

The men of the greatest genius ... appear to have been of calm and tranquil temper, in all that related to themselves[1]

– or Lamb, that '... the greatest wits ... will ever be found to be the sanest writers'?[2]

They thought of SHAKESPEARE and SPENSER.

It is impossible for the mind to conceive of a mad Shakespear. (Lamb)
Shakespeare's evenness and sweetness of temper were almost proverbial in his own age. (Coleridge)
In Spencer ... no where do we find the least trace of irritability.... (Coleridge)

Coleridge included also, CHAUCER's 'manly hilarity', and MILTON's 'even greater self-possession ... as far as his poems, and poetic character are concerned'. He went on to consider the 'many and excellent models' that exist in 'advanced stages of literature', where 'a high degree of talent, combined with taste and judgment, and employed in works of imagination, will acquire for a man the *name* of a great genius'. It was here he discovered a dichotomy, but he still nailed Horace's sarcasm:

... even in instances of this kind, a close examination will often detect, that the irritability which has been attributed to the author's *genius* ... did really originate in an ill conformation of body, obtuse pain, or constitutional defect.... What is charged to the *author*, belongs to the *man*....[3]

CHESTERTON claimed that his 'absence of mind' was in fact presence of mind about his work. David Garnett wrote of VIRGINIA WOOLF as

---

1 *Biographia Literaria; or Biographical Sketches of My Literary Life & Opinions* (1817), i, p. 32.
2 'Sanity of True Genius': *The Last Essays of Elia* (1833).
3 *Op. cit.*, i, p. 35.

'a scholar whose critical works reveal the balanced orderly powers of a first-rate intelligence'.

At any moment she could write a biographical sketch, or an article in *The Times Literary Supplement* marshalling her facts and delivering her judgement with ease and wit.[1]

1 *Great Friends: Portraits of seventeen writers* (1979), p. 130.

Suicide

I

A s an attorney's apprentice in Bristol, CHATTERTON often spoke of suicide and once, before his companions, he pulled out a pistol putting it to his forehead. When Mr Bergum, his 'patron' for whom he had fabricated a pedigree, later refused him a loan at the last moment, he penned a suicide's farewell which even gave instructions for his epitaph:

TO THE MEMORY OF
THOMAS CHATTERTON

Reader, judge not. If thou art a Christian, believe that he shall be judged by a supreme power: to that power alone is he now answerable.

He also wrote to his employer's friend, Mr Clayfield, informing him of his intention, and this letter caused Mr Lambert to determine that he could no longer keep him.

For three months in London, the widow's son of Bristol established literary contacts and worked like a slave. In early July he sent his mother, sister and grandmother gifts he could ill afford.

Dear Mother, – I send you in the box – six cups and saucers, with two basins, for my sister. . . . A cargo of patterns for yourself, with a snuff-box. . . . Two fans: – The silver one is more grave than the other, which would suit my sister best. . . . Some British herb-snuff in the box. . . . Be assured, whenever I have the power, my will won't be wanting to testify that I remember you. . . .[1]

By the end of July, with practically all the magazines and periodicals closed for the summer, even the barest livelihood had failed him. David Masson describes him as having 'reached that extreme beyond which our fancies of human destitution cannot go'.[2]

On Friday evening, August 24th, 1770, the seventeen-year-old boy

1 July 8, 1770.
2 *Chatterton: A Story of the Year 1770* (1874), p. 246.

returned to the house of the sack-maker, Number 39[1] Brooke Street, Holborn, and climbed up to his room near the tiles. Mrs Wolfe, the barber's wife, said that earlier in the day his landlady, Mrs Angell, had told her that 'as she knew he had not eaten anything for two or three days, she begged he would take some dinner with her ... but he was offended at her expressions ... and assured her (though his looks showed him to be three parts starved) that he was not hungry'. His last meal may have been at the house of the apothecary Cross, when he had a supper of oysters and was observed 'to eat most voraciously'.[2]

The following day when he did not appear, his room was forced and his body discovered – as in the picture by Henry Wallis – lying in 'a prospect of roofs and chimneys round', with many small pieces of paper containing his writing over the floor. There were remains of arsenic between his teeth. On August 28th, the day after the coroner's inquest, the body in a parish shell was interred privately in the grave-yard of Shoe Lane Workhouse. A story persists that Mrs Chatterton arranged for the shell with her son's body to be taken to Bristol, where it was buried secretly (by reason of *Felo de se*) in the churchyard of St Mary Redcliffe, but that has never been fully authenticated.

II

VIRGINIA WOOLF, at fifty-eight, fell into what she called 'a trough of despair'.[3] Her husband consulted Octavia Wilberforce, Virginia's friend, who had 'to all intents and purposes' become her doctor. Octavia came to tea with them once a week, bringing Jersey milk and cream from her farm. Virginia thought they were 'just friendly visits, but from our point of view they were partly medical'.

Nearly two months afterwards, she took a walk in the water-meadows at Rodmell in pouring rain and Leonard went, as he often did, to meet her.

She came back ... soaking wet, looking ill and shaken. She said that she had slipped and fallen into one of the dykes.

He was not sure whether she had not tried to commit suicide. He told

1 Later numbered 4.
2 Thomas Warton: *Enquiry into authenticity of poems attributed to Thomas Rowley* (1782), p. 107.
3 *The Journey Not the Arrival Matters* (1969), p. 78.

Octavia that he thought Virginia was 'on the verge of danger'. He had to make 'the terrifying decision' of urging her to face her illness without at the same time driving her from depression into attempting her life, as had happened after a consultation with Dr Head. He suggested she should go and see Octavia at Brighton 'and consult her as a doctor as well as a friend', which she did, and Octavia was to come to Rodmell in a day or two.

We felt it was not safe to do anything more at the moment. . . . The decision was wrong and led to the disaster.[1]

Next day, Friday, March 28th, 1941, Leonard was in the garden, thinking she was in the house. But when he went in to lunch, a letter on the sitting-room mantelpiece made him run across the fields down to the river – only to find her walking-stick on the bank. Her body was found three weeks later floating in the Ouse.

The letter had begun 'Dearest', and expressed certainty she was going mad again. She felt it impossible to relive 'those terrible times'. She was unable to fight any longer. Her voices were beginning, and she could neither concentrate nor read – 'You see I can't even write this properly.' She knew she was spoiling his life and that without her he could work, as she was confident he would. It ended:

What I want to say is I owe all the happiness of my life to you. You have been entirely patient with me and incredibly good. I want to say that – everybody knows it. If anybody could have saved me it would have been you. Everything has gone from me but the certainty of your goodness. . . .[2]

Leonard believed she had written the letter, and one to her sister Vanessa, after eleven o'clock that morning.

SYLVIA PLATH, an outstanding student at college, wrote to her brother of a fear her mind would 'split open'. She made the first attempt on her life at twenty. Ten years later, abandoned with two babies in the freezing winter of 1962, she succeeded, although it may not have been her intent. In the knowledge that her nurse would shortly arrive she had taken pills and turned on the gas, but her nurse was delayed.

1 *Ibid.*, pp. 90–93.
2 *Ibid.*, pp. 93–4.

Attempted Suicide

I

On July 27th, 1603, awaiting trial and dining with the Lieutenant of the Tower, Sir WALTER RALEGH snatched a knife and tearing at his shirt stabbed himself 'under the right pap'. In spite of much blood, he had struck a rib a glancing blow. It was out of character – unless he intended to 'be cruel to himself'[1] to prevent his property being taken from his family, which would follow a conviction for treason.

The suicide attempts of COWPER (and Virginia Woolf) cannot be separated from a mental condition. Over two successive days in his shuttered chambers in the Temple, Cowper bungled his self-destruction four times: with a bowl of laudanum which he threw away; by leaning upon the blade of a penknife placed under his left breast, but the blade could not penetrate because its point was broken off; by hanging himself with a garter from his bedpost and then from the door, but both times it slipped away. In modern parlance they probably would be interpreted as cries for help. They heralded his first madness, and his further breakdowns followed the same pattern. He tried again to hang himself at forty-one; he tried once more to take his life at fifty-five.

After the publication of Browning's *Fifine at the Fair*, ROSSETTI seems to have read into it his guilt for the suicide of his wife ten years before. When his friend Dr Hake took him to his own home at Roehampton, he showed signs in the cab of persecution mania and these were repeated on the common next morning. Unknown to Dr Hake he had some laudanum, and tried to take his life by drinking it as Lizzie had done.

CONRAD, in his youth, had been gun-running for a Spanish Pre-

1 Letter to his wife: July 26 (?), 1603.

tender and got involved in a passionate love affair with a Basque beauty.[1] He fought a duel for her – and had a scar to prove it. But this may have been the result of shooting himself, narrowly missing his heart, after he had lost borrowed money at Monte Carlo. It all happened before he landed at Lowestoft, at twenty-one, resolved to learn English and obtain his master mariner's ticket.

II

One night in Lourenço Marques, MALCOLM MUGGERIDGE, at thirty-nine, was filled with 'the absurdity, futility, degradation' of his life as an MI6 officer in World War II. He drove some six miles along the coast road, undressed, and was soon swimming out of his depth.

Looking back I could scarcely see the shore.... Then suddenly, without thinking or deciding, I started swimming back.... They were the lights of ... my habitat, where I belonged.[2]

EVELYN WAUGH attempted to drown himself, having resigned from Arnold House to find Scott Moncrieff had decided not to employ him as secretary. It was not twinkling lights that caused him to head for shore – but stings of jellyfish.

The placid waters were full of the creatures.... I turned about, swam back through the track of the moon to the sands.... Then I climbed the sharp hill that led to all the years ahead.[3]

Fourteen-year-old VYVYAN HOLLAND lay down in the snow:

I decided that I would get away from all my troubles and not try to carry on the struggle.

During the Christmas holidays he had repeated 'a silly rhyme' (which he didn't understand), and on account of this was refused admittance to a house where he was supposed to be spending the day with distant relatives of his own age – 'if any of us had suspected that there had been anything wrong about the rhyme we certainly would not have repeated it to our elders'.

1 See *The Arrow of Gold* (1919): described by Conrad, and later his widow, as having an autobiographical basis.
2 *Chronicles of Wasted Time*, ii, pp. 183–4.
3 *A Little Learning: The First Volume of an Autobiography* (1964), p. 230.

... I left my bicycle against a tree and wandered into the wood. ... I thought of the Tite Street days, and of my wanderings. But most of all I thought of my parents and of the enigma of my father and pondered over the misery of being an unwanted orphan.[1]

After two hours, search parties found him. His ears had been slightly frost-bitten and he got a chill in the inner part of his left ear, which turned to a mastoid and meant a serious operation.

Before he reached sixteen, GRAHAM GREENE had attempted his life four times. He drank hypo under the false impression it was poisonous. He drained his 'blue glass bottle of hay-fever drops'.[2] He swallowed twenty aspirins before swimming in the school bath unattended. He ate a bunch of deadly nightshade. MASEFIELD ate laurel leaves when at nine or ten he tried to kill himself at school.

Then, at sixteen, GRAHAM GREENE spent 'perhaps the happiest six months of my life'[3] in the house of Kenneth Richmond, a psycho-analyst chosen by his father and elder brother. Three years later, just before going up to Oxford, he fell in love 'body and mind' with the governess of his younger brother and sister. She was twenty-nine or thirty, already engaged, and on discovering a small revolver belonging to his elder brother, who was away, he took it on Berkhamsted Common. What he now did he explains in terms of his 'boredom' – 'as deep as the love and more enduring' –

... I slipped a bullet into a chamber and, holding the revolver behind my back, spun the chambers round. ... I put the muzzle ... into my right ear and pulled the trigger. There was a minute click, and looking down at the chamber I could see that the charge had moved into the firing position. I was out by one.

Although he denies that this was suicide – rather 'a gamble with five chances to one against an inquest' – we are, I feel, justified in placing it here. At fairly long intervals he repeated the experience, whenever he felt a 'craving for the adrenalin drug'.[4] He took the gun to Oxford, but after the sixth time he lost the excitement and did not take it up again. EVELYN WAUGH recorded half-serious attempts at suicide in his youth.

When GRAHAM GREENE was twenty-two, about to marry and told

1 *Son of Oscar Wilde* (1954), p. 155.
2 *A Sort of Life* (1971), p. 86.
3 *Ibid.*, p. 96.
4 *Ibid.*, pp. 127–8.

he was epileptic, he stood on a platform in the Underground and tried to will himself to jump.

But suicide requires greater courage than Russian roulette.[1]

Later in life he practised another variation for he ascribes his motive for going to Kenya at the time of Mau Mau, or the French war in Vietnam and other hazardous situations, as 'the fear of boredom'[2] – very Evelyn Waugh. Lady CHITTY attempted suicide at Oxford; STEVIE SMITH attempted her own life at fifty-one.

1 *Ibid.*, p. 188.
2 *Ibid.*, p. 131.

CHAPTER THIRTY-FOUR
Contemplation of Suicide

W e have not finished with suicide, for it has sometimes occupied the mind without any action. KINGSLEY, on his second
long vacation from Cambridge, felt guilt at his 'year of
dissipation' – which included a visit to a prostitute – and Lady Chitty
believes that he may have contemplated suicide like his own hero in
Yeast.[1]

RUSKIN proposed to seventeen-year-old Rose La Touche, who
promised to give him an answer on her twentieth birthday. When she
failed to keep her word, he wrote to Mrs Cowper:

I went roaming about all Christmas Day, and the day after – so giddy and
wild that in looking back on it I can understand the worst thing that men can
do.[2]

The near fifty-year-old man did not know she was in a nursing home
– her last breakdown so violent she lay strapped to her bed. In an
airless and overcrowded immigrant train, on his 6,000-mile journey
to join Fanny Osbourne, STEVENSON was feverish and probably had
dysentery. He wrote to Sidney Colvin:

I had no idea how easy it was to commit suicide. . . . I died a while ago; I do
not know who it is that is travelling.[3]

In Wandsworth Prison, WILDE soon lost over two stone and came
near complete breakdown; but the doctor accused him of shamming.
'I was . . . so utterly miserable,' he told André Gide, 'that I wanted to
kill myself.' One morning dressing he fell bruising his ear, and fainted
in chapel. He found himself in the infirmary where for two months he
was given special food. After transfer to Reading, his health improved.

1 Susan Chitty: *The Beast & the Monk: A Life of Charles Kingsley* (1974), pp. 58–59.
2 Letter quoted by Joan Evans: *John Ruskin* (1954), p. 299.
3 Aug. 1879.

... I was filled with rage. I determined to commit suicide on the very day on which I left prison.[1]

For four years in her later twenties, BEATRICE WEBB suffered a crisis of 'personal unhappiness' during which the idea of suicide was never far away. When her father had a paralytic stroke, she spent some months with him, which meant giving up her new occupation of rent-collecting as well as her 'attempts at social investigation'. She wrote in her diary:

Life seems . . . a horrible fact. Sometimes I wonder how long I shall support it. . . . I am not strong enough to live without happiness. . . . I struggle through each new day waking with suicidal thoughts early in the morning. . . . Eight-and-twenty, and living without hope![2]

Nineteen-year-old MASEFIELD, after two years in America, arrived in Liverpool with six pounds and a revolver. He 'was going to try to get a job as a clerk'.

Failing that, I was going to shoot myself. I was desperately ill and sick. I hadn't the strength to face more hardships.[3]

As a boy at Lancing, EVELYN WAUGH thought 'a lot about suicide'. He recorded in his diary:

I really think that if I were without parents I should kill myself: as it is I owe them a certain obligation.[4]

---

1 *De Profundis* ('The complete text' 1949), p. 86.
2 Feb. 12, 1886: *My Apprenticeship* (1926), p. 282.
3 Constance Babington Smith: *John Masefield: A Life* (1978), p. 49.
4 July 18, 1921: Christopher Sykes: *Evelyn Waugh: A Biography* (1975), p. 33.

CHAPTER THIRTY-FIVE
The End of the Chapter

In developing Beerbohm's observation,[1] I have inevitably asked myself how much belongs in a special way to writers and does not merely describe the common human condition. We have to say that a profession which trains them to be particularly sensitive and articulate does not help. Certainly the study has shown that speech defects, loss of mobility, periods of convalescence (even deafness), have caused them to take up literature.

Recent knowledge on GALSWORTHY raises doubt even about writers who seem outside Beerbohm's observation, for here was a man (apart from short sight) whose whole façade – professional recognition and wider public esteem, happy marriage, gracious living, foreign travel – appeared everything desirable. A character in a Maugham story pinned a portrait of him on the partition in his bedraggled house in Haiphong, not that he knew he was a writer but because he 'liked his face'.[2] The frontispiece to H. V. Marrot's *The Life and Letters*, a photo taken at twenty-seven shows keen eyes under a high forehead; there is inner strength as well as physical charm.

It was known he was a sensitive man who had won important reforms of the prison system. These were acknowledged by Churchill as Home Secretary, both in the House and in private correspondence:

There can be no question that your admirable play[3] bore a most important part in creating that atmosphere of sympathy and interest which is so noticeable upon this subject at the present time. So far from feeling the slightest irritation at newspaper comments assigning to you the credit of prison reform, I have always felt uncomfortable at receiving the easily-won applauses which come to the heads of great departments whenever they have ploughed with borrowed oxen and reaped where they have not sown.[4]

1 See page 287.
2 Grosely in 'Mirage': *On a Chinese Screen* (1922).
3 *Justice: a tragedy in four acts* (1910).
4 Home Office. Private. July 30, 1910: H. V. Marrot: *The Life & Letters of John Galsworthy* (1935), p. 684. Gilbert Murray wrote to Galsworthy: 'How much greater it is to have saved

Wells once met Galsworthy on Hampstead Tube Station, looking very unhappy. He had been calculating the needless hours of suffering to be undergone that day by cattle denied the humane-killer.

But Galsworthy now takes his place beside Sheridan and Meredith – those tormented not at the beginning but at the end of their lives. We learn of his mysterious illness, diagnosed by his GP: 'My opinion ... was that something evil and final had got a firm grip and that the head symptoms were secondary and subsequent – that the trouble did not originate there.' From the mask of the dying man came one or two recognizable phrases:

Brigagen ... a ... abrigen ... brabrigen ... jump ... a spring ... goodbye, goodbye, goodbye.... Tax, two years, I've enjoyed too pleasant circumstances ... a year ... one draft ... children, how do it not here with our home.[1]

He was sixty-five when he died.

Just over two months previously, he had been awarded a Nobel Prize and, as with William Golding in our own time, it caused him to deprecate his creative powers. He locked himself in a darkened room to write his speech:

As I read to you these melancholy reminiscences, it seems to me as little true now that I shall ever be a writer worthy of the name.... Here is my pen – the ink in it is dry. Take it and give it to some other who will serve you better.

Virginia Woolf's epitaph 'Stuffed shirt!', which was always sadly uninformed, seems even more inappropriate.

a lot of men and women from two months of solitary confinement than to have sent any number of over-fed audiences into raptures!' (*Ibid.*, p. 267.)
1 Quoted by Dudley Barker: *The Man of Principle: A View of John Galsworthy* (1963), p. 233.

APPENDICES

Position in Family

The *only child* is in a distinct minority:

Kingsley Amis	Radclyffe Hall[3]	John Ruskin
John Betjeman	C. Day Lewis	Michael Sadleir
Lord Byron[1]	Desmond MacCarthy	Dorothy L. Sayers
Kenneth Clark	Denis Mackail	Peter Scott
Cyril Connolly	George Meredith	R. L. Stevenson
E. M. Forster[2]	Christopher Milne	A. J. P. Taylor
Edmund Gosse	Isaac Newton	W. M. Thackeray
	Alexander Pope[4]	&c.

Formidable names are found equally among eldest and younger child:

Eldest child	*Younger child*
Charles Dickens	Jane Austen
Edward Gibbon	Francis Bacon
Thomas Hardy	S. T. Coleridge[6]
Samuel Johnson	George Eliot
James Joyce[5]	T. S. Eliot
John Keats	Henry James
Lord Macaulay	D. H. Lawrence
John Milton	William Shakespeare
Sir Walter Scott	Bernard Shaw
P. B. Shelley	Alfred Tennyson
Edmund Spenser	Anthony Trollope
Jonathan Swift	H. G. Wells
W. B. Yeats	William Wordsworth

1 Augusta, his half-sister, was not brought up under the same roof.
2 A first baby died at birth.
3 Her mother lost the first child.
4 His half-sister Magdalen, perhaps nine years older, survived from their father's first marriage.
5 1st to survive/17.
6 10th/10.

APPENDIX B

Birthplaces

More English writers were born in London than in any other part of the United Kingdom. Perhaps less predictable is the number not born in England:

Eire

William Allingham
Samuel Beckett
Brendan Behan
George Berkeley
Elizabeth Bowen
Edmund Burke
Nevil Coghill
Edward Dowden
Maria Edgeworth
Philip Francis[1]
Oliver Goldsmith
Frank Harris
James Joyce
W. E. H. Lecky

J. S. Le Fanu
Charles Lever
C. Day Lewis
C. R. Maturin
George Moore
Thomas Moore
Iris Murdoch
Arthur Murphy
Sir William Napier
Kate O'Brien
Sean O'Casey
Liam O'Flaherty
Bernard Shaw
R. B. Sheridan

Thomas Southerne
H. de Vere Stacpoole
Richard Steele
James Stephens
Laurence Sterne
Bram Stoker
Swift
J. M. Synge
Nahum Tate
F. H. Trench
William Trevor
Rebecca West
Oscar Wilde
Charles Woolfe
W. B. Yeats

Australia
  Gilbert Murray
  Walter James Turner
  Elizabeth von Arnim
Canada
  Thomas Firbank
India
  Lawrence Durrell
  Rudyard Kipling
  George Orwell
  Eden Phillpotts
  Salman Rushdie

Argentina
  W. H. Hudson
Austria
  Norman Douglas
Bulgaria
  Michael Arlen
China
  Mervyn Peake
Czechoslovakia
  Tom Stoppard
France
  Hilaire Belloc

1 Reputed author of *Junius's Letters*.

Saki (H. H. Munro)
W. M. Thackeray
Jamaica
John Lucie-Smith
Malaya
Ivor Brown
New Zealand
Hugh Walpole
Katherine Mansfield
Singapore
Leslie Charteris
South Africa
William Plomer
Olive Schreiner
J. R. R. Tolkien
Laurens Van der Post
Angus Wilson
Trinidad
V. S. Naipaul

George du Maurier
W. S. Maugham
Robert Ross
Freya Stark
Germany
Sybille Bedford
Nikolaus Pevsner
Holland
Richard Lovelace (?)
Bernard de Mandeville
Hungary
Arthur Koestler
Baroness Orczy
Iran
Doris Lessing
Harold Nicolson[1]
Poland
Joseph Conrad
Sweden
J. R. Wise
USA
T. S. Eliot
Richard Ellman
Henry James
Wyndham Lewis[2]

Equally unexpected may then be the prominence of the north before
any of the Home Counties:

Scotland

William Archer
William Aytoun
J. M. Barrie
James Boswell
James Bridie
John Buchan
Robert Burns
Thomas Campbell
Thomas Carlyle
A. J. Cronin
Alexander Cruden

Arthur Conan Doyle
William Drummond of
    Hawthornden
James Frazer
John Galt
Kenneth Grahame
James Hogg
Wm. Douglas-Home
David Hume
Andrew Lang
Eric Linklater
David Livingstone

J. G. Lockhart
George Macdonald
J. W. Mackail
Ian Mackay
Henry Mackenzie
James Macpherson
David Masson
Hugh Miller
Edwin Muir
James Murray
A. S. Neill

1 Born in the British Embassy at Tehran.
2 Born at sea off the American coast.

Margaret Oliphant	Adam Smith	Thomas Urquhart
Thomas Pennant	Tobias Smollett	Robert Watt
Michael Scott[1]	Muriel Spark	G. J. Whyte-Melville
Sir Walter Scott	R. L. Stevenson	Andrew J. Young
Samuel Smiles	J. I. M. Stewart[2]	
	James Thomson	

Yorkshire	*Lancashire*	*Kent*
Roger Ascham	James Agate	Edwin Arnold
W. H. Auden	W. H. Ainsworth	Mrs Aphra Behn
Alfred Austin	Beryl Bainbridge	Robert Bridges
Alan Bennett	Laurence Binyon	William Caxton
Phyllis Bentley	Robert Bolt	Walter de la Mare
The Brontës	Anthony Burgess	James Elroy Flecker
William Congreve	F. H. Burnett	John Gower (?)
Miles Coverdale	Gilbert Cannan	George Grote
Margaret Drabble	Arthur H. Clough	William Hazlitt
William Empson	R. G. Collingwood	John Lyly
J. L. Hammond	Lettice Cooper	Christopher Marlowe
Winifred Holtby	Richmal Crompton	Nigel Nicolson
Ted Hughes	Thomas De Quincey	Peter Quennell
W. R. Inge	Walter Greenwood	Siegfried Sassoon
Storm Jameson	Felicia Hemans	Philip Sidney
Andrew Marvell	James Hilton	V. Sackville-West
J. B. Priestley	Holbrook Jackson	Charles Sedley
Arthur Ransome	R. Le Gallienne	Robert Speaight
Herbert Read	John Morley	H. G. Wells
Edith Sitwell	John Oxenham	A. N. Whitehead
Sacheverell Sitwell	Robert Service	Henry Wotton
Stevie Smith	A. J. P. Taylor	Thomas Wyatt
David Storey	Francis Thompson	
Geoffrey Tillotson	Gerrard Winstanley	
Keith Waterhouse		
John Wyclif		

Devon	*Surrey*	*Wales*[3]
Sir Richard Burton	William Cobbett	Roald Dahl

1 Author of *Tom Cringle's Log*.
2 'Michael Innes'.
3 However impressive these names, the literature of her language includes Twm O'r Nant ('the Welsh Shakespeare'), Gronwy Owen, and Dafydd ab Gwilym – 'the Welsh Ovid', whom George Borrow promoted to 'the Welsh Horace ... the Welsh Martial ... the greatest poetical genius that has appeared in Europe since the revival of literature' (*Wild Wales: Its People, Language, and Scenery*, 1862, ii, p. 298; p. 36; iii, p. 198; i, p. 9).

Agatha Christie
S. T. Coleridge
C. J. Cornish
H. A. Dobson
John Ford
J. A. Froude
John Gay
Richard Hooker
Charles Kingsley
Desmond MacCarthy
Beverley Nichols
Sir Walter Ralegh
Sir Joshua Reynolds
Robert Falcon Scott
J. H. Speke
J. C. Squire
L. A. G. Strong
P. C. Wren

John Evelyn
Ford Madox Ford
John Galsworthy
A. P. Herbert
Maurice Hewlett
Richard Hughes
Aldous Huxley
Thomas Malthus
Malcolm Muggeridge
R. C. Sherriff
Isaac Watts
Anna Wickham
J. Dover Wilson
P. G. Wodehouse
Edward Young

George Herbert
T. E. Lawrence
Richard Llewellyn
Arthur Machen
Bertrand Russell
Howard Spring
H. M. Stanley
Arthur Symons
Dylan Thomas
R. S. Thomas
Henry Vaughan
Thomas Vaughan
Brian Vesey-FitzGerald
Emlyn Williams

Warwickshire

Rupert Brooke
Cyril Connolly
Michael Drayton
George Eliot
Walter Landor
Philip Larkin
Rose Macaulay
H. V. Morton
C. T. Onions
Sax Rohmer
William Shakespeare
J. H. Shorthouse
G. M. Trevelyan
John Wyndham

Gloucestershire

A. C. Bradley
W. E. Henley
John Keble
Laurie Lee
Hannah More
Dennis Potter
Isaac Rosenberg
C. H. Sisson
Robert Southey
Frances Trollope
William Tyndale
Beatrice Webb

Hampshire

Richard Aldington
Jane Austen
Charles Dickens
F. L. Green
Radclyffe Hall
George Meredith
Mary Russell Mitford
Anne Moberly
George Saintsbury
Gilbert White
George Wither
Charlotte Yonge

Norfolk

George Borrow
Fanny Burney
Robert Greene
Rider Haggard
Harriet Martineau
R. H. Mottram
Thomas Paine
Francis T. Palgrave
Richard Porson

Leicestershire

Francis Beaumont
Robert Burton
George Fox
Ronald Knox
Hugh Latimer
Lord Macaulay
John Middleton Murry
C. P. Snow
George Otto Trevelyan

Staffordshire

Arnold Bennett
Vera Brittain
J. K. Jerome
Samuel Johnson
Henry Newbolt
Alfred Noyes
William Somerville
H. M. Tomlinson
John B. Wain

Anna Sewell
John Skelton (?)

Colin Wilson

Izaak Walton

Shropshire

Charles Burney
Charles Darwin
Herbert of Cherbury
William Langland (?)
Wilfred Owen
Herba Stretton
Mary Webb
Stanley Weyman
William Wycherley

Sussex

Wilfrid Blunt
William Collins
John Fletcher
Constance Garnett
Eric Gill
Thomas Otway
John Selden
P. B. Shelley
Angus Wilson

Oxfordshire

Maria Edgeworth
J. R. Green
Charles Reade
Dorothy Richardson
John Rocher
E. of Rochester[1]
Michael Sadleir
Dorothy L. Sayers

Somerset

Walter Bagehot
Thomas Chatterton
Henry Fielding (?)
Christopher Fry
John Locke
William Prynne
C. H. Sisson
J. A. Symonds

Suffolk

George Crabbe
Charles M. Doughty
Edward FitzGerald
M. R. James
John Lydgate
F. D. Maurice
Ouida (M. L. de la
    Ramée)
V. S. Pritchett

Wiltshire

Joseph Addison
John Aubrey
E. of Clarendon (E.
    Hyde)
Thomas Hobbes
Richard Jefferies
Francis Kilvert
Philip Massinger
Isaac Pitman

Worcestershire

'Hudibras' Butler
Philip Gosse
A. E. Housman
Laurence Housman
Hesketh Pearson
Fay Weldon
Mrs Henry Wood
J. H. Yoxall

Cambridgeshire

Frances Cornford
William Godwin
L. P. Hartley
G. A. Henty
Maynard Keynes
F. R. Leavis
Jeremy Taylor

N. Ireland

Joyce Cary
St John Ervine
George Farquhar
H. Montgomery Hyde
C. S. Lewis
Robert Lynd
Louis MacNeice

Middlesex

Matthew Arnold
Noel Coward
Leigh Hunt
Thomas Henry Huxley
Samuel Parr
Sylvia T. Warner

Northamptonshire

H. E. Bates
John Clare
John Dryden
Henry Kingsley
James Rice
Flora Thompson

Berkshire

Richard Adams
R. D. Blackmore
Thomas Hughes
Charles Knight
William of Malmesbury

1 2nd Earl. John Wilmot.

Cheshire	*Derbyshire*	*Dorset*
Lascelles Abercrombie	John Cowper Powys	William Barnes
Hall Caine	T. F. Powys	Thomas Hardy
C. L. Dodgson	Samuel Richardson	Llewelyn Powys
Christopher Isherwood	Herbert Spencer	Matthew Prior
Malcolm Lowry	Alison Uttley	Thomas Sprat

Hertfordshire	*Lincolnshire*	*Cornwall*
George Chapman	John Foxe	William Golding
William Cowper	Elizabeth Jennings	Arthur Quiller-Couch
Gordon Craig	Isaac Newton	A. L. Rouse
Graham Greene	Alfred Tennyson	D. M. Thomas
John Mandeville	Thomas Wilson (?)	

Essex	*Nottinghamshire*	*Durham*
John Drinkwater	'Erewhon' Butler	Catherine Cookson
G. M. Hopkins	D. H. Lawrence	Ralph Hodgson
William Morris	Arthur Mee	Compton Mackenzie
Ruth Pitter	Alan Sillitoe	

Herefordshire	*Bedfordshire*	*Cumberland*
William Langland (?)	John Bunyan	Dorothy Wordsworth
John Masefield	Wm. Hale White[1]	Wm. Wordsworth
Thomas Traherne		

Huntingdonshire	*Monmouthshire*	*Northumberland*
William Paley[2]	W. H. Davies	John Forster
Watts-Dunton	A. R. Wallace	R. S. Surtees

Buckinghamshire		*Westmorland*
Edmund Waller[3]		Frederick Wedmore

1 'Mark Rutherford'.
2 Born at Peterborough: in his time Northamptonshire.
3 Born at Coleshill: in his time Hertfordshire.

APPENDIX C

Orphans

The incidence of those who in childhood lost one parent, or both parents, is significantly high:

William Blackstone[1]
W. S. Blunt
Robert Bridges
The Brontës
Thomas Browne
John Bunyan
Anthony Burgess
F. H. Burnett
Fanny Burney
Lord Byron
Joyce Cary[2]
Thomas Chatterton[1]
S. T. Coleridge
Joseph Conrad
Abraham Cowley[1]
William Cowper
Richard Crashaw[3]
A. J. Cronin
Roald Dahl
Charles Darwin
Walter de la Mare
Thomas De Quincey
John Donne
John Drinkwater
George Eliot
Henry Fielding
Ford Madox Ford

E. M. Forster
J. A. Froude
Christopher Fry
E. C. Gaskell
Edward Gibbon
Oliver Goldsmith
Edmund Gosse
Kenneth Grahame
J. R. Green
Radclyffe Hall
Paul Harvey
George Herbert
Robert Herrick
Vyvyan Holland
Thomas Hood
A. E. Housman
Laurence Housman
Aldous Huxley
J. K. Jerome
Ben Jonson[1]
John Keats
'Evoe' Knox
Ronald Knox
C. Day Lewis
C. S. Lewis
Ian Mackay
John Masefield

---

1 Posthumous child.

2 Cary lost his mother at eight and his stepmother, of whom he was fond, when he was thirteen.

3 Crashaw lost both mother and stepmother before he was nine, and his father at thirteen or fourteen.

410

W. S. Maugham
George Meredith
William Morris
Isaac Newton[1]
Sean O'Casey
Samuel Parr
Walter Pater
J. B. Priestley
Matthew Prior
Samuel Rogers
Thomas Rohan
Bertrand Russell
Siegfried Sassoon
Mary Shelley
William Shenstone
R. B. Sheridan

Tobias Smollett
Howard Spring
Richard Steele
C. T. Stoneham
Jonathan Swift[1]
J. M. Synge
W. M. Thackeray
Leslie Thomas
James Thomson
Thomas Traherne
Izaak Walton
Rebecca West
Leonard Woolf
Virginia Woolf
Dorothy Wordsworth
William Wordsworth

1 Posthumous child.

APPENDIX D

Distribution of Public Schools

Eton	*Winchester*	*Westminster*
Maurice Baring	Matthew Arnold	Jeremy Bentham
Robert Bridges	William Bowles	John Cleland
David Cecil	Thomas Browne	George Colman[2]
Cyril Connolly	Kenneth Clark	George Colman[1]
Lord Dunsany	William Collins	Abraham Cowley
Henry Fielding	William Empson	William Cowper
Ian Fleming	S. R. Gardiner	John Dryden
Thomas Gray	A. P. Herbert	J. A. Froude
Julian Grenfell	Lionel Johnson	Edward Gibbon
Charles Greville	Julian Mitchell	Richard Hakluyt
Henry Hallam	Robert Nichols	G. A. Henty
Michael Holroyd	Thomas Otway	George Herbert
W. Douglas-Home	C. K. Scott Moncrieff	Ben Jonson
Aldous Huxley	William Somerville	M. G. Lewis
W. R. Inge	Arnold J. Toynbee	John Locke
Laurence Jones	Anthony Trollope	Henry Mayhew[3]
Alexander Kinglake	Nicholas Udall	A. A. Milne
Ronald Knox	Joseph Warton	Stephen Potter
John Lehmann	William Whitehead	Matthew Prior
Desmond MacCarthy	James Woodforde	Nicholas Rowe
F. W. Maitland	Henry Wotton	Robert Southey
Henry H. Milman	Edward Young	Angus Wilson
Nigel Nicholson		
George Orwell		
Eric Parker		
Richard Porson		
Anthony Powell		
P. B. Shelley		
Osbert Sitwell		
Sacheverell Sitwell		

1 The Elder.
2 The Younger.
3 Ran away.

Leslie Stephen[1]
A. C. Swinburne
Thomas Tyrwhitt
Edmund Waller
Horace Walpole
G. J. Whyte-Melville
Thomas Wilson

St Paul's	*Charterhouse*	*Rugby*
E. C. Bentley	Joseph Addison	Matthew Arnold
Laurence Binyon	F. W. Bateson	Rupert Brooke
William Camden	Max Beerbohm	Arthur H. Clough
G. K. Chesterton	William Blackstone	R. G. Collingwood
Walter de la Mare	C. J. Cornish	C. L. Dodgson
Philip Francis[2]	Richard Crashaw	Paul Harvey
Benjamin Jowett	G. Lowes Dickinson	Thomas Hughes
John Leland	Robert Graves	'Evoe' Knox
Denis Mackail	George Grote	Walter Landor[3]
Compton Mackenzie	Richard Hughes	Wyndham Lewis
John Milton	Richard Lovelace	Arthur Ransome
Samuel Pepys	Francis T. Palgrave	Salman Rushdie
E. V. Rieu	Richard Steele	Michael Sadleir
E. M. Shepard	W. M. Thackeray	Arthur P. Stanley
Edward Thomas	Ben Travers	A. N. Wilson
Leonard Woolf		

Harrow	*Christ's Hospital*	*Marlborough*
Lord Byron	Edmund Blunden	Clive Bell
Winston Churchill	William Camden	John Betjeman
Barry Cornwall[4]	S. T. Coleridge	Anthony Hope
John Galsworthy	C. Lewis Hind	Louis MacNeice
L. P. Hartley	Leigh Hunt	William Morris
John Mortimer	Charles Lamb	Beverley Nichols
Samuel Parr	Bernard Levin	Siegfried Sassoon
Terence Rattigan	John Middleton Murry	C. H. Sorley
R. B. Sheridan	David Ricardo (?)	
John Summerson	Samuel Richardson (?)	
J. A. Symonds		
G. M. Trevelyan		
George Otto Trevelyan		
Anthony Trollope		

1 Day-boy from 9½ until just 14.
2 Sir Philip Francis is thought to have written the letters of 'Junius'.
3 Left prematurely.
4 Pseudonym of B. W. Procter.

413

Merchant Taylors'

Lancelot Andrewes
Thomas Kyd
Thomas Lodge
Gilbert Murray
David Ricardo (?)
Samuel Richardson (?)
James Shirley
Edmund Spenser

Sherborne

John Le Carré
C. Day Lewis
John Cowper Powys
Llewelyn Powys
T. F. Powys
Alec Waugh
A. N. Whitehead

King's, Canterbury

John Lyly (?)
Christopher Marlowe
W. S. Maugham
Walter Pater
Hugh Walpole

Shrewsbury

Charles Burney
'Erewhon' Butler
Charles Darwin
Philip Sidney
Stanley Weyman

Cheltenham

A. C. Bradley
Ivor Brown
John Morley
F. W. H. Myers

Clifton

Joyce Cary
Roger Fry
Henry Newbolt
Arthur Quiller-Couch

King's College School

F. Anstey
Henry Kingsley
William Rossetti
Henry Sweet

Malvern

Lascelles Abercrombie
Michael Arlen
C. S. Lewis
H. de Vere Stacpoole

Manchester Grammar

James Agate
W. H. Ainsworth
Robert Bolt
Thomas De Quincey

Stonyhurst

Alfred Austin
Wilfrid Scawen Blunt[1]
Arthur Conan Doyle
Vyvyan Holland

Blundell's

R. D. Blackmore
C. E. M. Joad
J. C. Squire

Kilkenny

George Berkeley
William Congreve
Jonathan Swift

Berkhamsted

Graham Greene
Peter Quennell

Brighton College

C. T. Stoneham
L. A. G. Strong

Dauntsey's

Nigel Balchin
Desmond Morris

Dulwich

Ernest de Selincourt
P. G. Wodehouse

Edward VI School, Birmingham

C. T. Onions[2]
J. R. R. Tolkien

King Edward's Bromsgrove

A. E. Housman
Laurence Housman

1 Left after six months.
2 Camp Hill branch.

Lancing	*Repton*	*Uppingham*
Evelyn Waugh	Roald Dahl	Ronald Firbank[1]
J. Dover Wilson	Christopher Isherwood	James Elroy Flecker

Abbotsholme – Lytton Strachey
Badminton – Iris Murdoch
Bootham – A. J. P. Taylor
Cheltenham Ladies' College – Phyllis Bentley
Christ's College, Finchley – Eric Williams
City of London School – Kingsley Amis
Dover College – Richard Aldington
Eltham College – Mervyn Peake
Godolphin, Hammersmith – W. B. Yeats
Godolphin, Salisbury – Dorothy L. Sayers
Gresham's – W. H. Auden
Haileybury – Robert Speaight
Higham Hall – Benjamin Disraeli
King's, Rochester – Edwin Arnold
King's, Worcester – 'Hudibras' Butler
Leamington – Lytton Strachey
Leys – James Hilton
Oundle – Peter Scott
Oxford High[2] – John Drinkwater
Portora Royal, Enniskillen – Samuel Beckett
Queen Elizabeth College, Guernsey – Robert Sherard
Queen Margaret's, Scarborough – Winifred Holtby
Radley – Harold Monro[3]
St Edward's, Oxford – Kenneth Grahame
Tonbridge – E. M. Forster
United Services College, Westward Ho! – Kipling

Wellington

Jeffrey Archer
Harold Nicolson

1 Left after six months.
2 Changed name later to City of Oxford School.
3 Expelled for drinking.

Distribution of Colleges at Oxford and Cambridge

Balliol (Oxf.)	Trinity (Camb.)	Christ Church (Oxf.)
Matthew Arnold	Francis Bacon	W. H. Auden
Hilaire Belloc	Maurice Baring[1]	Robert Burton
A. C. Bradley	Clive Bell	William Camden
Ivor Brown	E. Bulwer-Lytton	H. F. Cary
Arthur H. Clough	Lord Byron	David Cecil[1]
Cyril Connolly[1]	Sydney Colvin	George Colman[2]
John Evelyn	Abraham Cowley	C. L. Dodgson
Graham Greene	G. Lowes Dickinson	S. R. Gardiner
Julian Grenfell[1]	John Dryden	Charles Greville[1]
L. P. Hartley	E. J. Furnivall	Richard Hakluyt
Anthony Hope	James Frazer	Henry Hallam
G. M. Hopkins	George Herbert	John Leland
Aldous Huxley[1]	Alexander Kinglake[1]	M. G. Lewis
C. E. M. Joad	John Lehmann[1]	John Locke
Benjamin Jowett	Lord Macaulay	Thomas More (?)
Ronald Knox[1]	Desmond MacCarthy[1]	Thomas Otway
Andrew Lang	F. W. Maitland[1]	Thomas Percy
Sidney Lee	Andrew Marvell	A. L. Rowse
J. G. Lockhart	F. D. Maurice	John Ruskin
Denis Mackail	A. A. Milne	Philip Sidney
J. W. Mackail	Christopher Milne	W. W. Skeat
C. E. Montague	R. Monckton Milnes	J. I. M. Stewart[3]
James Murray	F. W. H. Myers	Martin Tupper
Beverley Nichols	Isaac Newton	Stanley Weyman
Harold Nicolson	Richard Porson[1]	Emlyn Williams
Nigel Nicolson[1]	Michael Roberts	
Francis T. Palgrave	Bertrand Russell	

1 From Eton.
2 The Elder.
3 'Michael Innes'.

Anthony Powell[1]
Peter Quennell
E. V. Rieu
Michael Sadleir
Sacheverell Sitwell[1]
Adam Smith
Arthur P. Stanley
Henry Sweet
A. C. Swinburne[1]
J. A. Symonds
Geoffrey Tillotson
Arnold J. Toynbee
John Wyclif (?)

Peter Scott
Lytton Strachey
John Suckling
Alfred Tennyson
W. M. Thackeray
G. M. Trevelyan
George Otto Trevelyan
A. N. Whitehead
Leonard Woolf

Trinity (Oxf.)

John Aubrey
F. W. Bateson
Laurence Binyon
William Bowles
Sir Richard Burton[2]
George Chapman (?)
Kenneth Clark
James Elroy Flecker
Walter Landor[2]
Thomas Lodge
J. H. Newman
Arthur Quiller-Couch
Terence Rattigan
Thomas Warton

King's (Camb.)

Rupert Brooke
Gilbert Cannan
Leslie Charteris
G. Lowes Dickinson
E. M. Forster
Roger Fry
W. R. Inge
Prof. Walter Raleigh
Robert Ross
Salman Rushdie
Edmund Waller
Horace Walpole
Thomas Wilson

New (Oxf.)

John Galsworthy
Paul Harvey
A. P. Herbert
W. Douglas-Home
Lionel Johnson
Robert Sherard
R. C. Sherriff
William Somerville
D. M. Thomas
A. N. Wilson
James Woodforde
Henry Wotton
Edward Young

Magdalen (Oxf.)

Joseph Addison
John Betjeman
William Camden
William Collins
Edward Gibbon
John Lyly
Compton Mackenzie
Desmond Morris
Charles Reade
Kenneth Tynan

St John's (Camb.)

Roger Ascham
Richard Bentley
'Erewhon' Butler
Erasmus Darwin
Robert Greene
Robert Herrick
Thomas Nashe
Matthew Prior
Samuel Purchas
J. C. Squire

Merton (Oxf.)

Max Beerbohm
E. C. Bentley
Hartley Coleridge
T. S. Eliot
Louis MacNeice
Eric Parker
Stephen Potter
George Saintsbury
Richard Steele
Angus Wilson

1 From Eton.
2 Rusticated.

417

Oscar Wilde
George Wither

William Wordsworth
Thomas Wyatt

John Wyclif (?)

Queen's (Oxf.)

Joseph Addison
Jeremy Bentham
Edmund Blunden
William Collins
Thomas Middleton
Walter Pater
Thomas Pennant
Thomas Tyrwhitt
Henry Wotton
William Wycherley[1]
John Wyclif (?)

Trinity Hall (Camb.)

F. Anstey
E. Bulwer-Lytton
Lord Chesterfield
Ronald Firbank
Edward FitzGerald
Robert Herrick
Vyvyan Holland
F. D. Maurice
Samuel Pepys
J. B. Priestley
Leslie Stephen

Oriel (Oxf.)

J. A. Froude
Richard Hughes
Thomas Hughes
Mark Pattison
William Prynne
Sir Walter Ralegh
A. J. P. Taylor
Joseph Warton
Richard Whately
Gilbert White

Brasenose (Oxf.)

Jeffrey Archer
John Buchan
Robert Burton
William Golding
Henry H. Milman
John Mortimer
J. Middleton Murry
Henry Savile
Thomas Traherne

St John's (Oxf.)

Kingsley Amis
Robert Graves
J. L. Hammond
A. E. Housman
Philip Larkin
Gilbert Murray
A. W. Pollard
James Shirley
John B. Wain

Univ. Coll. (Oxf.)

Edwin Arnold
Walter Bagehot
R. G. Collingwood
Herbert of Cherbury
C. S. Lewis
V. S. Naipaul
Ernest de Selincourt
P. B. Shelley
Stephen Spender

Wadham (Oxf.)

Francis Kilvert
C. Day Lewis
Julian Mitchell
John Rocher
Earl of Rochester[3]
Charles Sedley
Thomas Sprat
L. A. G. Strong
Rex Warner

Somerville (Oxf.)

Vera Brittain
Winifred Holtby
Margaret Kennedy
Rose Macaulay
Mary Moorman
Iris Murdoch
Dorothy L. Sayers

Christ's (Camb.)

Walter Besant
Charles Darwin
James Hilton
John Milton[2]
William Paley
W. W. Skeat

1 Left without matriculating.
2 'The Lady of Christ's.'
3 2nd Earl. John Wilmot.

Corpus Christi (Camb.)

John Fletcher
Christopher Isherwood
Christopher Marlowe
Matthew Parker
John Cowper Powys
Llewelyn Powys

Corpus Christi (Oxf.)

Robert Bridges
Richard Hooker
John Keble
'Evoe' Knox
Henry Newbolt
Edward Young

Emmanuel (Camb.)

Michael Frayn
William Law
F. R. Leavis
Samuel Parr
Sir William Temple
Hugh Walpole

Pembroke (Oxf.)

Francis Beaumont[1]
William Blackstone
Thomas Browne[1]
William Camden[1]
Samuel Johnson
William Shenstone

Gonville & Caius (Camb.)

Charles M. Doughty
G. A. Henty
Harold Monro
Jeremy Taylor
J. Dover Wilson

Exeter (Oxf.)

Alan Bennett
R. D. Blackmore
William Morris
Alfred Noyes
J. R. R. Tolkien

Lincoln (Oxf.)

John Le Carré
John Morley
Robert Speaight
Edward Thomas
John R. Wise

Newnham (Camb.)

Margaret Drabble
Constance Garnett
Jacquetta Hawkes
Sylvia Plath
Claire Tomalin

Jesus (Camb.)

S. T. Coleridge
David Hartley
Thomas Malthus
Laurence Sterne

Jesus (Oxf.)

J. R. Green
T. E. Lawrence
Henry Vaughan (?)
Thomas Vaughan

Pembroke Hall (Camb.)

Lancelot Andrewes
Richard Crashaw
Thomas Gray
Edmund Spenser

Clare (Camb.)

Peter Ackroyd
Hugh Latimer
Siegfried Sassoon

Magdalen Hall (Oxf.)

Clarendon (E. Hyde)
Thomas Hobbes
William Tyndale

Hart Hall (Oxf.)

John Donne
John Selden
Jonathan Swift[2]

Magdalene (Camb.)

William Empson
Charles Kingsley
Samuel Pepys

Peterhouse (Camb.)

Nigel Balchin
Thomas Campion
Thomas Gray

Queens' (Camb.)

Thomas Fuller
James Rice
H. M. Tomlinson

Clare Hall (Camb.)

Robert Greene
William Whitehead

1 At that time, Broadgates Hall.
2 At 25, when he received MA.

419

Hertford (Oxf.)	*Worcester (Oxf.)*
C. J. Cornish	Thomas De Quincey
Evelyn Waugh	Henry Kingsley

Gloucester Hall (Oxf.) Richard Lovelace
Keble (Oxf.) F. H. Trench
Lady Margaret Hall (Oxf.) C. V. Wedgwood
Pembroke (Camb.) Ted Hughes
St Anne's (Oxf.) Elizabeth Jennings
St Catherine's Hall (Camb.) James Shirley
St Mary Hall (Oxf.) Thomas More[1] (?)
Selwyn (Camb.) Malcolm Muggeridge
Sidney Sussex (Camb.) Thomas Fuller

Fellows of All Souls, Oxford

Sir William Blackstone
T. E. Lawrence
John Leland
Thomas Linacre
Sir Charles Oman
A. L. Rowse
Jeremy Taylor
Edward Young

---

1 Local tradition. According to the family, he attended Canterbury Hall (which became Christ Church).

APPENDIX F

Other Universities

London

Richard Aldington[1]
Edwin Arnold *(King's)*
Walter Bagehot *(Univ. Coll.)*
Walter Besant *(King's)*
Anita Brookner *(King's)*
Robert Browning *(Univ. Coll.)*[2]
G. K. Chesterton *(Univ. Coll.)*[3]
William De Morgan *(Univ. Coll.)*
John Forster *(Univ. Coll.)*
F. J. Furnivall *(Univ. Coll.)*
W. S. Gilbert *(King's)*
Radclyffe Hall *(King's)*[4]
Thomas Hardy *(King's)*
Storm Jameson *(King's)*
Charles Kingsley *(King's)*[6]
Bernard Levin *(L.S.E.)*
David J. Lodge *(Univ. Coll.)*
James Murray
Prof. W. Raleigh *(Univ. Coll.)*
Michael Roberts *(King's)*
D. G. Rossetti *(King's)*
George Saintsbury *(King's)*
Stephen Spender *(Univ. Coll.)*
Freya Stark *(Bedford)*
Leslie Stephen *(King's)*[7]
John Summerson *(Univ. Coll.)*
H. G. Wells *(Royal Coll.)*[8]
Israel Zangwill

Edinburgh

Michael Arlen
William Aytoun
J. M. Barrie
James Boswell
Thomas Carlyle
Charles Darwin
Arthur Conan Doyle
W. Drummond of Hawthornden
Goldsmith
David Hume
Francis Jeffrey
J. W. Mackail
Henry Mackenzie
James Macpherson
David Masson
A. S. Neill
Mungo Park
Sir Walter Scott *(Old Coll.)*
C. K. Scott Moncrieff
Samuel Smiles
R. L. Stevenson
James Thomson (1700–48)
Robert Watt
Andrew J. Young

1 Left, after a year, without a degree.
2 At 17 or 18, attended Greek class for a very short time.
3 Attended lectures on English Literature.
4 Attended 1 yr.
5 Attended evening classes to improve French.
6 Before going to Magdalene (Camb.)
7 Attended between 15–17, and then went to Trinity Hall (Camb.).
8 In his time, the Normal School of Science.

Appendices

University of Dublin or Trinity College

Samuel Beckett
George Berkeley
Edmund Burke
William Congreve
Edward Dowden
Richard Ellmann
John Farquhar

Oliver Goldsmith
W. E. H. Lecky
J. S. Le Fanu
Charles Lever
Edward Malone
C. R. Maturin
Thomas Moore
Thomas Southerne

Jonathan Swift
J. M. Synge
Nahum Tate
William Trevor
James Ussher
Oscar Wilde
Charles Wolfe

Glasgow

James Boswell
James Bridie
John Buchan
Thomas Campbell
A. J. Cronin
James Frazer
Francis Jeffrey
Andrew Lang[2]
J. G. Lockhart
Michael Scott[3]
Adam Smith
Tobias Smollett
Robert Watt

Manchester

Lascelles Abercrombie
Robert Bolt
Anthony Burgess
George Gissing *(Owens)*[1]
John Oxenham
Francis Thompson *(Owens)*
Alison Uttley *(Ashburne House)*

Aberdeen

Alexander Cruden *(Marischal)*
Eric Linklater *(King's)*
George Macdonald
James Macpherson
David Masson *(Marischal)*
Thomas Urquhart *(King's)*

Birmingham

Desmond Morris
C. T. Onions *(Mason)*
Henry Reed
Francis Brett Young

National University of Ireland

Edward Dowden *(Univ. Coll., Cork)*[4]
James Joyce *(Univ. Coll., Dublin)*
Kate O'Brien *(Univ. Coll., Dublin)*

1 Expelled.
2 One session.
3 Author of *Tom Cringle's Log.*
4 In his time, Queen's College.

Other Universities

Harvard	Heidelberg	Leeds
T. S. Eliot	W. S. Maugham	Storm Jameson
Henry James	Henry Sweet	Herbert Read

Leiden	Paris	St Andrew's
Henry Fielding	T. S. Eliot *(Sorbonne)*[1]	Andrew Lang
Oliver Goldsmith[1]	Oliver Goldsmith (?)	Fay Weldon

Yale

Peter Ackroyd
Richard Ellmann

Bangor R. S. Thomas
Belfast (Queen's) Robert Lynd
Berlin Nikolaus Pevsner
Berne John Le Carré
Bonn Robert Sherard
Bristol C. H. Sisson
Exeter Robert Bolt
Frankfurt Nikolaus Pevsner
Leicester (Univ. Coll.) C. P. Snow
Leipzig Nikolaus Pevsner
Liverpool Lytton Strachey
Munich Nikolaus Pevsner
Nottingham (Univ. Coll.) D. H. Lawrence
Padua Oliver Goldsmith (?)
Reading (Univ. Coll.) Wilfred Owen
Strasbourg H. A. Dobson
Vienna Arthur Koestler

1 One year.

Index to Writers

Selected Topics

Interesting Links